The Idea of the
Public Sphere

The Idea of the Public Sphere

A Reader

Edited by Jostein Gripsrud, Hallvard Moe,
Anders Molander, Graham Murdock

In collaboration with Martin Eide, Karl Knapskog,
Leif Johan Larsen, Leif Ove Larsen, Peter Larsen

LEXINGTON BOOKS
A division of
ROWMAN & LITTLEFIELD PUBLISHERS, INC.
Lanham • Boulder • New York • Toronto • Plymouth, UK

Published by Lexington Books
A division of Rowman & Littlefield Publishers, Inc.
A wholly owned subsidiary of The Rowman & Littlefield Publishing Group, Inc.
4501 Forbes Boulevard, Suite 200, Lanham, Maryland 20706
www.lexingtonbooks.com

Estover Road, Plymouth PL6 7PY, United Kingdom

British Library Cataloguing in Publication Information Available

Library of Congress Cataloging-in-Publication Data

The idea of the public sphere : a reader / edited by Jostein Gripsrud . . . [et al.].
    p. cm.
  Includes bibliographical references and index.
  ISBN 978-0-7391-4197-7 (cloth : alk. paper) — ISBN 978-0-7391-4198-4 (pbk. : alk. paper) — ISBN 978-0-7391-4199-1 (electronic)
  1. Political science—Philosophy. I. Gripsrud, Jostein, 1952–
JA71.I33 2010
320.01--dc22

2010019745

∞™ The paper used in this publication meets the minimum requirements of American National Standard for Information Sciences—Permanence of Paper for Printed Library Materials, ANSI/NISO Z39.48-1992.

Printed in the United States of America

Contents

Preface

Jürgen Habermas' 1962 book *Strukturwandel der Öffentlichkeit* was published in Norwegian in 1971, eighteen years before it appeared in English. It was read in Norwegian all over Scandinavia and influenced work across a number of disciplines in both the arts and social sciences. This is part of the background for the present volume, which is one of the results of *con amore* work conducted by a mostly Norwegian group, most of whom work in media and communication studies. It started in 2004 when Jostein Gripsrud proposed a week-long autumn seminar in the south of France on theories of the public sphere to a group of colleagues and friends in the Department of Information Science and Media Studies at the University of Bergen: Martin Eide, Karl Knapskog, Leif Ove Larsen, Peter Larsen, and Hallvard Moe. He also invited the literary scholar Leif Johan Larsen (Bergen University College) and the social scientist Anders Molander (now based at the Center for the Study of Professions at Oslo University College). As a scholar with a particular interest in moral and political theory, Molander was asked to act as a guide and tutor. Finally Graham Murdock of the Department of Social Science at Loughborough University, UK (and previously a part time professor in the Department of Information Science and Media Studies at the University of Bergen) was also invited on board. Since its launch, the group has met for week-long seminars once or twice a year. This volume is one of the outcomes., one to which all members of the group have contributed.

The project was initially largely financed by the participants and their individual research allowances from the University of Bergen. We are very grateful for the further support received from the University of Bergen, partly through an allowance from Bergen University Fund and partly through the funding allocated to the Digi-Cult research program (*Democracy and the Digitization of Audiovisual Culture*, www.digicult.uib.no) of which the public sphere theory project became a part.

We sincerely hope the book will be useful for students and scholars in a variety of disciplines who share our interest in the public sphere.

Paris, Bergen, Oslo, Loughborough in March 2010,
Jostein Gripsrud, Hallvard Moe, Anders Molander, Graham Murdock

Acknowledgments

The editors thank the authors and publishers listed below for their permission to reprint.

Immanuel Kant
"An Answer to the Question: 'What is Enlightenment?'"
Translated from the German original ("Beantwortung der Frage: 'Was ist Aufklärung'" [1784]) by H. B. Nisbet. Published in H. S. Reiss, ed., *Kant: Political Writings*, 2nd edition. (© Cambridge University Press, 1970, 1991) 54–60. Reprinted by permission of Cambridge University Press.

G. W. F. Hegel
Excerpt from *Philosophy of Right*.
Translated from the German original (*Grundlinien der Philosophie des Rechts* [1821]) by T. M. Knox. G. W. F. Hegel, *Philosophy of Right* (© Oxford University Press, 1967) 204–208. Reprinted by permission of Oxford University Press, Inc.

Walter Lippmann
Excerpt from *The Phantom Public*.
Walter Lippmann, *The Phantom Public* (Harcourt, Brace and Co., New York, 1925. 6th reprint, Transaction Publishers, 2005. © 1993 Transaction Publishers) 3–67. Reprinted by permission of Transaction Publishers.

John Dewey
Excerpt from *The Public and its Problems*.
John Dewey, *The Public and its Problems* (H. Holt, New York 1927 © 1954 Mrs. John Dewey) 192–217. Reprinted by permission of Ohio University Press/Swallow Press, Athens, Ohio (www.ohioswallow.com).

Carl Schmitt
Excerpt from *The Crisis of Parliamentary Democracy.*
Translated from the German original (*Die geistesgeschichtliche Lage des heutigen Parlamentarismus* [1923]) by Ellen Kennedy. Carl Schmitt, *The Crisis of Parliamentary Democracy* (© 1986 Massachusetts Institute of Technology) 33–50. Reprinted by permission of the MIT Press.

Joseph Schumpeter
Excerpt from *Capitalism, Socialism and Democracy.*
Joseph Schumpeter, *Capitalism, Socialism and Democracy* (© 1942 Joseph Schumpeter) 250–273. Reprinted by permission of HarperCollins Publishers.

Hannah Arendt
Excerpt from *The Human Condition.*
Hannah Arendt, *The Human Condition*, 2nd edition (© 1958 The University of Chicago) 28–58. Reprinted by permission of University of Chicago Press.

Jürgen Habermas
"The Public Sphere: An Encyclopaedia Article"
Translated from the German original ("Öffentlichkeit" [1964]) by Sara Lennox and Frank Lennox. Published in *New German Critique* 3: 49–55. (© 1974 New German Critique). Reprinted by permission of New German Critique.

Oskar Negt and Alexander Kluge
Excerpt from *Public Sphere and Experience: Toward an Analysis of the Bourgeois and Proletarian Public Sphere.*
Translated from the German original (*Öffentlichkeit und Erfahrung. Zur Organisationsanalyse von bürgerlicher und proletarischer Öffentlichkeit,* © 1972 Suhrkamp Verlag, Frankfurt am Main). *Public Sphere and Experience: Toward an Analysis of the Bourgeois and Proletarian Public Sphere* (© 1993 by the Regents of the University of Minnesota) xliii–xlix. Reprinted by permission of Suhrkamp Verlag and University of Minnesota Press.

Nancy Fraser
"Rethinking the Public Sphere: A Contribution to the Critique of Actually Existing Democracy"
Published in C. Calhoun, ed., *Habermas and the Public Sphere* (© 1992 Massachusetts Institute of Technology) 109–143. Reprinted by permission of The MIT Press.

Jon Elster
"The Market and the Forum: Three Varieties of Political Theory"
Published in J. Elster and A. Hylland, eds., *Foundations of Social Choice Theory* (© 1986 Cambridge University Press/Universitetsforlaget) 103–132. Reprinted by permission of Cambridge University Press.

Niklas Luhmann
"Societal Complexity and Public Opinion"
Translated from the German original ("Gesellschaftliche Komplexität und öffentliche Meinung" [1981]) by John Bednarz Jr. Published in Niklas Luhmann, *Political Theory in the Welfare State* (© 1990 Walter de Gruyter) 203–219. Reprinted by permission of Walter de Gruyter.

Jürgen Habermas
Excerpt from *Between Facts and Norms: Contributions to a Discourse Theory of Law and Democracy.*
Translated from the German original (*Faktizität und Geltung: Beiträge zur Diskurstheorie des Rechts und des demokratischen Rechtsstaats* [1992]) by William Rehg. Jürgen Habermas, *Between Facts and Norms: Contributions to a Discourse Theory of Law and Democracy* (© 1996 Massachusetts Institute of Technology) 359–387. Reprinted by permission of The MIT Press.

John Rawls
"The Idea of Public Reason Revisited"
Published in *University of Chicago Law Review* 64(3): 765–807. (© 1997 The University of Chicago). Reprinted by permission.

Chantal Mouffe
"Deliberative Democracy or Agonistic Pluralism?"
Published in *Social Research* 66(3): 745–758. (© 1999 Chantal Mouffe). Reprinted by permission of the author.

Seyla Benhabib
Excerpt from *The Claims of Culture: Equality and Diversity in the Global Era.*
Seyla Benhabib, *The Claims of Culture: Equality and Diversity in the Global Era.* (© 2002 Princeton University Press) 133–146. Reprinted by permission of Princeton University Press.

Bernhard Peters
"National and Transnational Public Spheres"
Translated from the German original ("Nationale und transnationale Öffentlichkeiten. Eine Problemskiszze") by Keith Tribe. Published in Hartmut Wessler, ed., *Public Deliberation and Public Culture: The Writings of Bernhard Peters, 1993–2006* (© 2008 Bernhard Peters) 185–195. Reprinted by permission of Palgrave Macmillan.

James Bohman
"Expanding Dialogue: The Internet, Public Sphere, and Transnational Democracy"
Published in N. Crossley and J. M. Roberts, eds., *After Habermas: New Perspectives on the Public Sphere* (© 2004 Blackwell Publishing Ltd.) 131–155. Reproduced by permission of Blackwell Publishing Ltd.

Jürgen Habermas
"Religion in the Public Sphere"
Published in *European Journal of Philosophy* 14(1): 1–25. (© 2006 Blackwell Publishing Ltd.). Reproduced by permission of Blackwell Publishing Ltd.

Editors' Introduction

Louis XIV of France (1638–1715), the self-styled Sun King, insisted that he derived his right to rule from God and because his monarchical power was divinely ordained, so were all of his decisions, however arbitrary and contestable, from waging war to the mercantilist economic policies of his minister of finance for almost two decades, Jean-Baptiste Colbert. He also famously dressed and undressed in front of members of the court, the borderline between public and private being more fluid then than it later became.

These features of absolutist monarchy underline the radicalism of the changes that gathered momentum during the eighteenth century and the distinctiveness of the modern world they constructed. The birth of the idea of a sovereign people is at the heart of this rupture with the past.

According to this idea, people should no longer be the subjects of monarchs, emperors, and other unelected rulers, entitled to their protection but subjected to their arbitrary power. They should become citizens, with the right to participate in determining which laws and policies would govern them. This general right presupposes two concrete entitlements: the right to vote in elections for legislative bodies, and the right to freedom of expression. These twin rights, to vote and to voice, should make people into a "public" authorizing laws and policies.

The capitalist economy which expanded rapidly from the mid eighteenth century onwards saw the rise of a new class of factory owners and businessmen, a bourgeoisie, who pressed for their interests to be reflected in political decisions. The French revolution extended these demands to the general population and solidified the new identity of citizen. In the emerging democratic order, those charged with governing could no longer appeal to divine right to bolster their legitimacy, they were expected to fulfil the will of the people, as it was formed and expressed in the emerging political *public sphere*. This new space of action was made up of the myriad public sites where people came together to deliberate on common concerns, evaluate competing proposals for change, and eventually arrive at a *public opinion*.

The new emphasis on public discussion as the precondition of good government was underwritten by the intellectual movement known as the Enlightenment whose leading figures celebrated the exercise of our common human reason as the only viable foundation for the legitimate use of political power. Decisions were no longer to be taken on the basis of prejudice, faith, or entrenched ideas. Instead, they should be arrived at by subjecting competing positions to the tests of rational argument and empirical evidence.

The texts in this volume illustrate how the idea of the public sphere has developed over time, from its origins in the eighteenth century down to the present, and how from the outset it has been the focus of argument and disagreement. In selecting texts, we have singled out debates about fundamental questions regarding the public sphere's role in democratic societies and debates on issues of particular importance in today's socio-cultural and political situation. The book thus reflects both the continuities and innovations in this theoretical and political tradition.

This general introduction offers an overview of major themes and arguments in debates over the idea of the public sphere as a key concept in democratic theory. Further details are provided in the introductions to each section and to each extract.

THE IDEA OF THE PUBLIC AND THE PUBLIC SPHERE

The word "public" carries at least four different but interrelated meanings in contemporary language. First, we speak of physical spaces, such as city squares and parks, as being public when they are open to all and part of a shared "commons." Extending this metaphor, we think of information and cultural resources as public when they are freely accessible and communicable and therefore potentially "common." Second, we distinguish between public and private concerns. We identify the former with issues that are of common interest to all members of a polity and therefore the legitimate concern of governmental institutions and the latter with areas of life that should be left to people's private discretion and remain their personal secrets. This boundary is neither fixed nor self evident however. On the contrary, deciding on where the line between the public and private domains should be drawn has been a continuing focus of contention in democratic societies. Third, we employ the term public as a social category. We use it in both a relatively restricted sense, to describe everyone who participates in particular public events or forms of expression, as in the phrase "reading public," and in a more general sense to characterize the collective of citizens. Fourth, we describe the aggregate of individual views that emerge among a public of citizens on issues of the day as "public opinion." The contestations involved in the formation of public opinions are often called "public discourses." The reasons advanced in support of positions are thought of as public when they appeal to generally shared interests and principles.

These different uses of "public" are all present in the term "public sphere." Much Anglo-American discussion in this area however has been hampered by problems of translation. The original German title of Habermas's classic 1962 study, translated into English as *The Structural Transformation of the Public Sphere*, was *Strukturwandel der Öffentlichkeit*. The German word *Öffentlichkeit* was coined in the late eighteenth century, as an expression of the Enlightenment idea that legitimate political power presupposes openness and a free exchange of opinions about public matters. The neologism was formed by putting together the adjective "öffentlich" ("public") and the suffix "-keit" ("-ness") transforming "öffentlich" into a noun that signifies the quality or state manifest in the adjective. Translating it as "publicness" or "publicity" does not fully grasp Habermas' use of term however. For him, *Öffentlichkeit* designates a sphere of open (public) spaces and communication where a public discourse on matters of common concern can take place and lead to the formation of an opinion on part of the public of citizens that in turn may influence political decision making.

Öffentlichkeit then is not simply a description of the network of institutions that comprise the "public sphere." It also has a normative content and advances a principle of democratic legitimacy: that the exercise of governmental and state power should be both "public" (in contrast to "secret") and reflect the power of a deliberating public of free and equal citizens. As we will see later in this introduction, this, and other normative conceptions of the public sphere which emphasize its pivotal role in democratic rule, have been under concerted attack by "realistic" approaches that regard the public as a phantom.

Talking about *the* public sphere however, may seem somewhat misleading since there is clearly a plurality of publics connected to different collectivities (occupational, political, ethnic, religious, sexual) and geographic areas (local, national, regional, global), with different thematic foci (science, politics, economy, arts, sports, fashion) and modes and genres of communication. To what extent an overarching public composed of all the citizens of a particular state actually operates as a functioning whole will vary depending on political and socio-cultural factors as well as media technologies and structures. However, from a democratic point of view such a public is essential since without common attention, common issues and some kind of synthesizing of dispersed opinions there can be no well-functioning democratic rule.

In recent years, as we will return to below, at least two developments have raised new questions about the constitution of the public sphere. The first arises from the growth of transnational regional blocks and is illustrated by the much discussed prospects for a democratization of the European Union. One major obstacle is arguably the imbalance between the more and more state like characteristics of the Union on the one hand and the lack of a European-wide public sphere where *European* political issues can be discussed at the same time across all member states on the other. The second development is the Internet's increasing tendency to fragment, segment, and personalize popular participation. Instead of being exposed to a diversity of topics, views, and experiences and engaging in broadly based deliberations, pessimistic commentators follow Cass Sunstein in imagining the citizens of the future consuming only their "Daily Me."

Moreover, one should distinguish between publics within the legal-political system and publics in civil society. In a text included in the present book, Nancy Fraser uses the terms "strong" and "weak" publics, concepts later adopted by Jürgen Habermas. A parallel distinction is made by John Rawls between "the public political forum" and "the background culture." Democratic parliaments are strong publics where discussions are coupled with collectively binding decision making and structured by legal procedures. In contrast, weak publics in civil society have no regulated access to political power, opinion formation is uncoupled from decision making, and discourses can be free-floating without being restricted by institutionalized rules defining relevant competencies or valid arguments. However, such "weak" publics can have a profound moral and politic impact, changing the political agenda and putting strong deliberative bodies under pressure.

THE PUBLIC SPHERE CONTESTED

Popular political participation in democracies is based on citizens' right to vote in elections and on their right to express opinions freely and have free access to information and ideas. To what extent one can expect the formation of a reasoned public opinion based on vigorous, open, and principled deliberation on key issues and relevant proposals has been contested since the idea of the public sphere first appeared. Theorists have disagreed about how far it is possible to translate this ideal into workable practices. Optimistic commentators have seen the public sphere as essential to the full operation of a democratic system of governance and greeted successive innovations in communications, from the commercial press of the nineteenth century to the expansion of the Internet today, as opening new spaces for participation and engagement. Pessimists, on the other hand, have seen these emerging sites as platforms for populist deviations from Reason, ever more effective channels for distributing the propaganda of the powerful, or filled with trivia and sensations that deflect attention away from pressing political issues. For them, the ideal of the public sphere is too good to be true. They present themselves as "realistic" who are primarily preoccupied with the things as they are, rather than what they consider empty ideals. Optimists on the other hand, are either convinced that reality can approach the ideal or, at least, that the ideals offer yardsticks against which prevailing practices can be evaluated and possibly improved.

Our selection starts with a letter to the editor of *Berlinische Monatsschrift* that the German philosopher, Immanuel Kant, wrote in 1784 in response to a previous letter asking the question "What is Enlightenment?" Itself an intervention in a public debate, Kant's letter gives us a glimpse—a key example—of what was going on in the plethora of early journals and newspapers that were central to what Habermas would later call the classical public sphere. According to Kant, Enlightenment is man's emergence from a condition in which we fail to think and judge for ourselves. He thought it difficult, if not impossible, for each individual by themselves to escape from this "self-incurred immaturity" that has "become almost second nature," but argued that an entire public could enlighten itself provided they have the "most innocuous form" of freedom—the freedom to make "public use of one's reason in all matters." For Kant, the public use of reason was connected not only to personal autonomy but also to political legitimacy. To be legitimate, laws had to pass the test of public scrutiny so as to guarantee that the restrictions they placed on the freedom of citizens were justifiable to all. This principle of publicity, as Kant called it, is the starting point for all public justification theories of political legitimacy.

However, the idea of an enlightening and enlightened public was a normative vision soon to be confronted with more sceptical accounts of the public sphere. In our selection, the German philosopher Hegel is the first to voice an ambivalent attitude. To him, individual freedom was the basic "principle of the modern world" and one of its key manifestations was the right to criticism: "what is to be authoritative nowadays," he wrote, "derives its authority, not at all from force, only to a small extent from habit and custom, really from insight and argument." At the same time, he feared unorganized public opinion. His worries over how public opinion could represent the interference of particular private interests in government decisions and how ill informed and irrational the public could be, initiate a long and solid tradition of scepticism towards the public sphere.

Such liberals as John Stuart Mill, one of the most influential advocates of freedom of expression, also worried about public opinion. Mill was concerned that the increasing pressure on legislators to respond to public opinion, as presented in the emerging popular press, was replacing the old tyranny of inherited power with a new tyranny of the numerical majority that rode roughshod over unpopular views and endorsed received opinion without adequate scrutiny and debate.

In the 1920s, the American commentator, Walter Lippmann, raised another issue arguing that contemporary society had become too complex for ordinary people to fully understand and that accredited experts should take over the task of accomplishing a qualified understanding of public affairs. He dismissed the "ideal of the sovereign and omnicompetent citizen" as a phantom and confined the role of citizens to choosing among given alternatives. Lippmann's scepticism towards public opinion had some elements in common with the influential view of democracy later articulated by the Austrian-American economist Joseph Schumpeter. Against what he called the "classical doctrine of democracy"—the idea "that 'the people' hold a definite and rational opinion about every individual question and that they can give effect to this opinion by choosing 'representatives' who will see to it that that opinion is carried out"—Schumpeter argued for a realistic conception of democracy that reversed the roles of the people and the representatives: the selection of representatives is primary to the deciding of issues in the electorate. The role of the people is to produce a government, and democracy can thus be defined as a system of competition for votes between elites. To Schumpeter, the public sphere appeared as an arena for persuasion and "manufacturing of will" rather than discussion.

A prominent European public sphere sceptic was the German legal scholar Carl Schmitt who in the Weimar era set forth a critique of liberal democracy and its idea of "government by discussion." According to Schmitt, who later became member of the Nazi party and the "crown jurist" of The Third Reich, parliamentary business had become "an empty and trival formality." More and more decisions were taken by committees behind closed doors and parliamentary power was circumscribed by organized interest groups. Schmitt saw this as an unmasking of the rationalistic fiction that parliamentary debate was able to adequately synthesize the "particles of reason strewn unequally among human beings and bring public power under their control."

Those who have voiced a negative attitude towards the operations of the public sphere are then, a mixed bag. But so too are the many theorists who have held the public sphere as an essential element in a well functioning democracy.

In the first part of the twentieth century, John Dewey stands out as one of the most important defenders of an idea of democracy that emphasizes the role of public deliberation. According to Dewey a "public" was made up of all those affected by the consequences of human actions "to such a degree that it is deemed necessary to have those consequences systematically cared for." For a public to be democratic such consequences must be publicly debated. Essential to democracy is therefore "the improvement of the methods and conditions of debate." Hence democracy is not merely majority rule. It is primarily about the deliberative means by which majorities come into being. From this perspective Dewey opposed Walter Lippmann's scepticism and championed the public sphere as the pivotal arena where people learned to become more competent in their capacities as citizens and voters by pooling their knowledge and ideas and confronting opposing arguments. Dewey also formulated a broad conception of democracy as not simply a political decision making system but a distinctive form of society and a way of life.

Jürgen Habermas' 1962 book *The Structural Transformation of the Public Sphere* has been the major catalyst for the resurgence of debates over the public sphere. It was to some degree inspired by Hannah Arendt's study *The Human Condition* published four years earlier. While Arendt took the ancient Greek distinction between "oikos" and "polis" as her departure, Habermas reconstructed the liberal idea of a reasoning public and contrasted it with the actual public spheres in welfare state democracies where public dialogue was seen as replaced by public relations work. However, at the same time as he portrayed the development of the public sphere as a history of decline, a *Verfallsgeschichte*, Habermas maintained the public sphere as a critical concept. The book's blend of history, sociology and political philosophy remains unique and has inspired a continuous series of re-readings, re-interpretations and critiques which have introduced new issues into the debate and elicited responses from Habermas. In his magnum opus *Between Facts and Norms*, originally published in 1992, and based on his in between developed theory of communication, he takes the public sphere into reconsideration within the context of a discourse theory of law and democracy and tries to explain how deliberative processes in the public sphere can effectively influence political decision making. Habermas thereby attempts to bridge normative and empirical considerations and to answer the critique that the public is just phantom.

The debate on Habermas's first book is represented in our selection by two contributions. The first one is by Oscar Negt and Alexander Kluge who criticize Habermas for taking the bourgeois public sphere as an ideal type and excluding forms of subaltern publics. They question the distinctions between the public and the private that are fundamental to the bourgeois public sphere and sketches an alternative "proletarian public sphere" in which the close connections between work, personal life, culture and politics become visible and available for learning processes and as themes for debate. The second, by Nancy Fraser, is partly related. She oulines a conception of the public sphere beyond Habermas' ideal type. Fraser's version is more egalitarian, consists of a multiplicity of publics, questions the gendered distinction between what counts as private and public, and the sharp separation of state and civil society.

In today's debates on the public sphere, Habermas' discursive model of the public sphere is often criticized for being rationalistic and ignoring the role of passions in politics. This critique is in our selection represented by Chantal Mouffe, who defends a model of an agonistic public sphere. From the point of view of systems theory Niklas Luhmann puts forward a critique of the public sphere reminiscent of

Walter Lippmann's but with new means. More of a "family quarrel," in Habermas' own words, is his debate with John Rawls on the scope of public reason. To put it bluntly: while Rawls sees the supreme court in a constitutional democracy practicing judicial review as the exemplar of public reason, Habermas favours a much broader and less "juridified" conception. This disagreement is reflected in their dispute on the role of religion in the public sphere where Habermas is defending a less restrictive version of Rawls' requirement that citizens can introduce religious doctrines in public debates only if proper political reasons are presented in due course.

The range of discursive traditions covered in this collection contains useful prompts for further reflection. Arguably, developed democracies have gone some way towards putting the ideals of the public sphere into practice and where they fail, these ideals may still offer a basis for critiquing existing arrangements and formulating alternatives. On the other hand, the "realistic" diagnoses and views pinpoint real problems and offer important insights that are very much needed if we are to develop a feasible idea of a democratically functioning public sphere and develop better ways of realizing it in practice in contemporary conditions.

DEMOCRACY AND PUBLIC DELIBERATION

In the last two decades, democratic theory has taken a "deliberative turn" as a mixed group of theorists has challenged models of democracy focusing on voting and turned their attention to the role played by public reasoning in political decision making.

The arguments in play are rooted in three different models of collective decision making: voting, bargaining and deliberation.[1] Whereas voting is a procedure for aggregating individual preferences, and does not necessarily involve communication, both bargaining and deliberation depend on communication. Bargaining proceeds through the exchange of offers and counteroffers based on pre-existing positions. In contrast, deliberation is oriented towards mutual understanding and provisional consensus through open-ended argument.

According to voting centred theories, democratic politics can be conceived of as a market-like process. Information about individual political preferences is assembled through voting systems and governments (like companies) distribute goods and services in a way that as effectively as possibly satisfies the demands expressed by aggregated preferences. In this model, politics is assumed to be governed by private interests and the aim of voting procedures is to give every participant an equal opportunity to influence political decisions.

In contrast, deliberative theorists see democracy as a forum that participants enter with preferences that are potentially mutable rather than fixed. They take part in discussion and critique that may transform or at least clarify preferences. In this model, participants are supposed to subject themselves to the force of the better argument (i.e., be willing to change their opinions when faced with good reasons and provide generally acceptable reasons to others for what they propose). Consequently, in deliberative forums, even self-interested actors have to justify their proposals with reference to the public interest. According to its proponents deliberation promotes reciprocity and impartiality, and contributes to make outcomes more or less reasonable and thereby acceptable even to those who do not agree.

Jürgen Habermas' discourse theory, presented in his book *Between Facts and Norms*, has become a major point of reference for debates in this area. But it is also the most demanding version of deliberative democracy. Other writers have chosen to work with less idealizing presuppositions. Yet others have set out to investigate how deliberation actually works in both real-life political settings and experimental situations.[2]

Although the distinction between deliberation and voting is useful analytically, actually existing political situations are often much muddier. If deliberation fails to produce a working consensus, voting and majority decisions become necessary. At the same time, voting presupposes deliberation: the decision to decide by voting and decisions about the alternatives on offer can only be reached by arguing. Hence, just as no tenable model of democratic politics can entirely disregard the role of strategic action and bargaining it cannot ignore its deliberative dimension. The question, however, is how deliberation works, and to what extent there is an effective link between the public exchange of reasoning on common concerns and the actual decisions and actions taken by governments.

These are empirical questions, but deliberative democracy also present problems as a normative theory of political legitimacy. Let us mention four. First, even if voting has the drawback of taking preferences as given, it gives everyone a say independently of the capacity to make one's voice heard. It is thereby more inclusive and egalitarian than deliberation. Second, theorists of deliberative democracy derive the legitimizing force of public deliberation from both its democratic and deliberative qualities. However, there is no guarantee that decision making procedures based on democratic participation will also have deliberative qualities; that they will promote serious exchange of arguments, and vice versa. There may be a trade-off between participation and deliberation. This dilemma points to a third problem concerning the justification of deliberative democracy. Are there some intrinsic qualities of deliberative democracy that make it morally preferable? Is it, for example, better than other conceptions of democracy at embodying the fundamental principle that citizens should be treated as autonomous persons? Or is it that we expect something more just or more effective from deliberative decisions making? If we emphasize the epistemic qualities of deliberation (better justified outcomes), we may also be inclined to play them off against the participatory component of deliberative democracy. Fourth, whether we justify deliberative procedures in one way or the other, or by some combination, the concept of legitimacy being invoked is procedural. The outcomes of the decision making process are seen as legitimate because the conditions of deliberative procedure have been met. But can deliberative democracy do without a substantive account of legitimacy? This has been a particular point of contention between Habermas and John Rawls. While Habermas relies solely on discursive procedure as the touchstone of legitimacy, Rawls, in his influential theory of justice advances a set of substantive principles that can be used to assess any decision reached among citizens.

CULTURE AND POLITICS

In *The Structural Transformation of the Public Sphere* Habermas identified two public spheres: a political public sphere organized around discussion of issues of common concern, and a literary public sphere, or more accurately, a cultural public sphere, devoted to discussion of the problems and dilemmas encountered in everyday life as presented in cultural productions, particularly the newly emerging form of the novel.

The ultimate bestseller of the eighteenth century, Samuel Richardson's *Pamela* (1740) marked the beginning of a wave of literary fiction and established novel reading as a common element in the bourgeois lifestyle. Discussions of *Pamela* and the novels that followed, together with theatre plays and visual arts, were more open socially than the later political public sphere. Unlike the coffee houses that provided one of the important centers for political deliberation, and from which women were excluded, the salons where the latest cultural productions were discussed were in private homes and often convened by the woman of the house. Similarly, the popular literature that circulated "below stairs" was read and discussed by both male and female servants and workers.

As Habermas points out, this cultural public sphere emerged before the political sphere and despite the latter's relative initial closure around a male monopoly over business and public affairs, provided three essential resources for its development. First, it was within the cultural public sphere that the basic organizational forms and practices of rational-critical debate, such as rules for discussion, that were later transferred to the political sphere, were developed. Secondly, as Habermas notes, it was through cultural discussions that the subjectivity originating in the interiority of the conjugal family, by communicating with itself, attained clarity about itself and people came to understand themselves and their desires and motivations, more fully. Third, it was through their encounters with imagined strangers that they learned to identify with the destiny of others and tested their notions of right and wrong in the various walks of life. Without these key resources of empathy, self knowledge, as well as workable procedures, political deliberation is at best, severely impoverished and at worst, impossible.[3]

This centrality is pointed out by the German sociologist Bernhard Peters writing on "expressive communication":

Many symbolic acts connected in some way with political or public affairs make use of . . . aesthetic means of expression whose content is symbolic, rather than an argument or information. [They include] . . . visual forms of expression, music, film and, in general, important parts of art and popular culture. . . . Historical experience shows that such forms of public symbolisation can be introduced to rein in, or otherwise render ineffective, public discourse (war propaganda is the classic example here). On the other hand, as the experience of the 1960s shows, a revival of 'presentative' culture can also be accompanied by an extension of the public discursive sphere.[4]

Even if Peters did not pursue the theme further in his empirical work, his awareness of this lacuna in the theory of the public sphere does, however, at the same time separate him from the vast majority of contemporary contributors to the theory of the public sphere.

One reason for this situation is the concerted focus on deliberation in theories of the public sphere. From the beginnings of debate in this area, the political public sphere was seen to be organized around face-to-face talk, enhanced and extended by written commentary and debate in newspapers and magazines of opinion. By integrating the public sphere into a discourse theory of law and democracy, Habermas has further consolidated this emphasis. However, it is clear that the cultural forms developed within both "high" art and popular culture, together with the discourses that surround them, can play a central role in supporting people in their role as citizens, by shaping subjectivities, encouraging people to walk in other people's shoes, and providing models of rational deliberation. Investigating how the connections between the cultural and political public spheres operate and under what circumstances they might break down, should be a priority for future work on the public sphere.

MEDIA AND THE PUBLIC SPHERE

In the revised version of his model developed in *Between Facts and Norms*, Habermas argues that "the public sphere can best be described as a network for communicating ideas and points of view, which filters and synthesizes diverse 'streams of communication . . . in such a way that they coalesce into bundles of topically specified *public opinions.*"[5] From the outset, this network was organized around the interplay between face-to-face argument and mediated communication.

The discussions conducted in the proliferating public locations in the rapidly growing urban centres drew heavily on the resources offered by the expanding range of newspapers and magazines of opinion. The merchants, money men, and professionals who frequented the coffee houses of eighteenth century London arrived already armed with information and arguments they had gleaned from a vibrant and combative journalistic culture and from the moral stances they had rehearsed by reading fiction and attending the theatre. The lines between culture and politics, argument and activism were not always as clear cut as they later became. Henry Fielding, remembered now as the author of *Tom Jones* (1749), one of the key early novels, edited two controversial magazines of opinion, *The Champion* and *The Covent Garden Journal,* and played a major role in establishing London's first full-time police force, The Bow Street Runners.

At the same time, newspapers were subject to a raft of government controls and the struggle to liberate them from autocratic power becomes a central theme in the more general battle to establish a fully fledged democracy. In England, the last of the so called "taxes on knowledge," which had required newspapers to pay tax on each sheet of paper they used and each advertisement they accepted, was finally abolished in the 1850s. Many commentators welcomed the arrival of a market-based press as an essential precondition for a "free market in ideas" in which contending ideas and arguments would compete openly for attention and support. Competition was to be the guarantor of diversity.

Initially, most newspapers served particular cities or regions, but improved transport links with the arrival of the railways, saw the emergence of national press systems and as Benedict Anderson has argued persuasively, in his work on nations as imagined communities, national newspapers played a key role in creating a generalized space of shared information and common debate that transcended local interests and loyalties.[6]

As we noted earlier however, some observers, including John Stuart Mill, saw the new commercial dynamics of the newspaper business as a potential threat to the development of a mediated political public sphere. They feared that the drive to optimize readerships and advertising revenues would lead newspapers to organize debate around what Mill called "the deep slumber of decided opinion" and exclude dissenting and minority opinions. They felt that the press was coming to play a leading role in constructing public opinion rather than simply sifting and synthesizing it. They saw editors picking up on popular concerns, embellishing and amplifying them in carefully orchestrated coverage, and playing them back to their readers in a closed loop so that instead of being the outcome of sustained and open deliberation, the "public opinion" presented to legislators as the working consensus of the electorate, was manufactured in press offices.

The rapid growth of cheap mass-circulation newspapers at the end of the century, aimed at the growing number of literate white collar and skilled workers, raised other concerns, as commentators saw extended discussion of political issues and choices being squeezed out by coverage of crime, sports, scandal, and sensation. Far from extending the mediated political public sphere beyond the privileged ranks of the professional and business classes, the new titles seemed to be elevating entertainment over analysis, an accusation that continues to inform contemporary critiques of tabloidization. Added to which, the most active press proprietors were consolidating their control over the newspaper market by acquiring chains of titles and using them to promote their own particular views and prejudices. These challenges to the idea of the public sphere coincided with hard-won extensions of the right to vote, which led many critics to arrive at the same pessimistic conclusion as the American social commentator, Edward Ross, who lamented in 1910 that "the commercial news-medium does not adequately meet the needs of democratic citizenship."[7]

One response to this "democratic deficit" that gained widespread currency in Europe and elsewhere after World War I was the foundation of public service broadcasting institutions. Attracted by broadcasting's technical potential to achieve simultaneous national coverage the pioneers of public service broadcasting set out to construct a service, funded out of taxation and open to all, that addressed audiences as citizens. This ideal was pitched against the commercial broadcasting system established in the United States, which was seen to hail its listeners first and foremost as potential consumers for the products that advertiser paid to have promoted in and around its programmes.

From the outset, public service broadcasting was at heart an avowedly educational project. It set out to counter the ascendency of prevailing opinions by providing audiences with access to exposition and argument offered by designated experts. The problem was that this ambition left relatively few spaces for public participation. Hence, while they steadfastly refused to subscribe to Walter Lippmann's pessimistic conclusion that creating a genuine public was an impossible ideal, its supporters' efforts to foster the habits of principled deliberation through demonstration created exclusions that generated continual struggles over which ideas and arguments were granted a public platform, who was mandated to speak for them, and how deliberation should be conducted.

From the 1970s onward, faced with mounting pressure from social movements voicing the demands of women, ethic minorities, and other marginalized groups, public service broadcasters responded by developing new participatory program formats that opened broadcasting to an extended range of experiences, voices, and positions. How far this explosion of everyday talk brings us closer to realising the ideals of a political public sphere based on principled deliberation is open to argument however. Talk shows and phone in formats offer new arenas for name-calling and prejudice as well as new forums for open discussion based on tolerance and respect.

In the end however, broadcasting's potential for generalizing deliberation remains limited by its essential character as a vertical, top-down, system of distribution. The arrival of multi-channel systems has massively increased the number of programme slots available but has done nothing to change this. Which is one of the reasons why many commentators have greeted the expansion of the Internet with such enthusiasm. They see the Internet's promise of unlimited capacity and versatility finally overcoming the limits imposed on broadcasting and have greeted the proliferation of peer-to-peer networks as a solution to the formerly intractable problem of creating a genuinely inclusive mediated public sphere. Once again, whether the postings on Internet message boards, blogs, and networking sites constitute genuine instances of deliberation as against self display and promotion, is open to challenge. The possible impact of recent innovations in communications technology cannot be approached in isolation however. They are inextricably bound up with wider changes to the social bases of the public sphere, to which we now turn.

TRANSNATIONALISATION, MULTICULTURALISM, AND NEW TECHNOLOGIES

A decade into the twenty-first century, three interlinked phenomena have emerged as crucial to the future of the public sphere, as both an idea and an ideal: the transnationalization of the political, economic, and cultural domains; the growth of digital communication technologies; and the amplification of pluralism in multicultural societies.

Public spheres have never been confined solely to national borders. Transnational flows of information and cultural products were always a feature of mass media circuits, signaling broader social, political, and economic connections that we today would identify as signs of globalization. Nor did the rise of the nation-state as the modal unit of political organization confine either politics or culture solely to national containers. There were frequent tensions and slippages between states as administrative complexes and nations as imagined communities. Secessionist groups demanded their own autonomous states. Diasporic communities moved between shifting conceptions of belonging and exile.

Nevertheless, whether right or wrong, globalization processes are now perceived as more extensive, intense, and forceful. Whether it is large-scale migration movements, instabilities in the world's financial markets, the continuing global reach of American popular culture, or the perceived threats posed by climate change or terrorism, decisions and actions in particular places are seen to have global repercussions that ripple out over time.

This situation is supported by technological developments—not least by computer-mediated communication. The emerging global networks provide essential infrastructural supports for every kind and level of activity and intervention, from global trading and speculation, to the coordination of military action, to the distribution of vernacular creativity and the organization of personal relationships.

Potentially, at least, "virtual communication anywhere is communication every-where"[8]—unrestricted by national borders.

In a 1998 essay, Habermas described a new post-national constellation, which he saw as touching on "the most basic functions and legitimacy conditions of demo-cratic nation states."[9] He pointed to four levels where globalizing or transnational-izing processes impacted on the nation state's democratic processes. Three of these apply primarily to institutions and practices at the core of the political system, but the fourth deals with the periphery, including the public sphere: For Habermas, the idea of a nation of citizens, rendered possible through cultural integration, which can be politically mobilized, was threatened by fragmentation.

This threat had two faces. On one side, experiencing an influx of new immigrant cultures, national majority cultures were insisting more stridently on their unique-ness, their purity, and all too often, their superiority. In a worst-case scenario, this could end with coexisting cultures sealed off from each other. On the other side, global mass consumer culture, while partly leveling out national differences, has also fueled the construction of a new array of hybridized cultural forms. Taken to-gether, these two tendencies are pressing on the symbolic borders of the nation state by strengthening centrifugal forces within national societies. This argument sees three currents of change—transnationalization, new communication technologies and cultural pluralism—as interconnected and posing major new challenges to the idea of the public sphere and its theoretical foundations.

Commentators have been discomforted by these developments since, despite the long history of globalization, public spheres have always been conceptualized within the framework of the nation state. Merely multiplying the traditional concept is not enough. As Nancy Fraser has argued, the problem relates to both key terms, "public" and "sphere."[10] It is difficult to connect a notion of valid public opinion to social actors who do not represent a political citizenry or to ascribe the notion of communicative power to spheres that do not link with sovereign states.

The post-national constellation does not mean an absolute disempowering of the nation state. We need to be careful not to exaggerate the prospects of its suspen-sion. So far, nothing indicates the end of nation states as centers of democratic rule. Though their position is changing, they are still indisputably important as contain-ers of political action. Specific publics, arenas, and borders are changing, and chang-ing in importance, but this is more a process of complementing than replacing.

As James Bohman argues in his text in this reader, transnational public spheres should not be conceptualized as multiplications of national ones. Rather, they come into existence when a minimum of two culturally rooted public spheres start to overlap. Such spheres need not be national in scope. They might be defined by a thematic foci, such as the struggle for global justice, or a regional senses of belong-ing, as with Asian societies' increasing belief in their shared communalities. Defin-ing transnational public spheres in this way presupposes the continued existence of shared spaces where we can communicate based on common cultural assumptions. Because a number of these spheres remain linked to territorial entities, among them nation states, any idea of the public needs to conceptualize communication both within and across geographical borders.

Technological developments entail challenges to the idea of the public sphere on another level. The innovative potential in computer-mediated communication lies in the many-to-many mode of address: produced by the significantly lowering of the threshold for audience members to become speakers. As Slavko Splichal notes, "the internet brought about a new form of publicness—mediated and dialogical at the same time."[11] In the mass media age, the move from individual opinion to social opinion was still seen as primarily based on private conversation. With the Internet, a large portion of person-to-person conversation takes place in public. As a consequence, we need to rethink the boundaries between the private and public. We also need to conceptualize the ways in which both traditional mass media and novel online actors and arenas now provide effective channels to the centers of power.

These issues also raise empirical questions about the fragmentation of the public sphere. We need to understand to what extent and how subcultures are sealed off from each other, and with what consequences. Cass Sunstein addresses this question in his book *Republic.com 2.0*,[12] pointing to two key features of a well-functioning public sphere. First, people must be exposed to expressions, opinions, and perspectives they would not have chosen in advance; and, second, "many or most citizens should have a range of common experiences."[13]

Sunstein's argument rests on research evidence on group polarization showing that members of deliberating groups tend to end up at a more extreme position in the same general direction as their preferences before deliberation began. The inclusion of contending and dissenting voices in the same communicative space is crucial to countering this tendency that leads Sunstein to argue that, though it clearly has its merits, computer-mediated communication's newfound ease of filtering unwanted information often contributes to a segmentation of the public sphere, with dangerous balkanization, erosion of collective life, and extremism as the potential outcome. Other commentators have offered more optimistic accounts of contemporary developments[14] but they all recognize the urgency of this question. It is pressing because the potential offered by new media technologies has coincided with deep societal changes.

As a result of new migration movements, the multicultural composition of societies had become more prominent and evident. The result is both an array of hybridized cultural forms and a rise in radicalism. On the one hand, many western societies have seen a resurgence of extreme right politics. On the other hand, the world has also seen the rise of religious fundamentalism and its translation into acts of terrorism, which has been met by escalating state surveillance of private speech and public culture and increasing stigmatization.

The public sphere has always been segmented, but as societies become more socially and culturally diversified and divided it becomes harder to find the balance between positive and creative plurality and dangerous balkanization. Over the last decade, these developments have raised questions that go to the very heart of public sphere theory: How much difference is a well-functioning public sphere capable of handling? Is the idea of the public sphere fit for entrenched ethno cultural conflicts? Can we imagine the accommodation of religious convictions and expressions in the public sphere—and if so, how can they be translated into forms adapted to deliberation?

CONCLUDING REMARKS

Pressing questions are not new. As we have seen the idea of the public sphere has, from its inception, been formed and reformed in response to deep-seated shifts in wider patterns of social and cultural life, which have presented both new possibilities for its realization and new tensions.

Beginning as a sphere largely restricted to the men of the rising business, intellectual, and professional classes, it has gradually extended its social reach within western democracies as workers, women, and ethic minorities have fought for the right to make themselves heard on issues of common concern. This battle for inclusiveness is generally seen as a struggle within nation states, but as we saw in the previous section, the formation of regional groupings, like the EU, and the growing awareness that central issues, like climate change, require a globalized response, has posed the question of whether it is possible to create workable transnational public spheres.

Optimists see the rapid growth of the Internet, and its increasing migration from the highly unevenly distributed technology of personal computers to the much more accessible technology of mobile phones, as holding out the hope for a viable, borderless, space of encounter and deliberation. Pessimists point to the mounting evidence that the Internet is more likely to foster personal display rather than genuine social communication. Their anxieties chime with widespread concerns that contemporary market-driven culture places a premium on self expression and that personal preoccupations have rode roughshod over concern for the common good. Private interests have trumped the public interest. The citizens of mature democracies might have won the right to speak but have they lost the art of listening attentively and respectfully, without which true deliberation is impossible.

Other observers see the public sphere becoming increasingly organized around mediated communication, and the media, both old and new, becoming increasingly commercialized, accentuated the problems that commentators first saw arising with the growth of the popular commercial press in the second half of the nineteenth century. Media owners, whose properties now stretch across continents and multiple media sectors, can and do use them to promote views they favor and silence or ridicule ideas and arguments they oppose. Rupert Murdoch's newspapers on three continents spoke with one voice on the second invasion of Iraq. His Fox news channel in the United States militantly champions Republican positions. Silvio Berlusconi in Italy has successively deployed his media holdings to propel himself to the highest political office in the land, and then used his political power to pass laws that favor his business and personal interests. Tabloid news and commentary pursues its core goal of maximizing audiences by celebrating "common sense" and denigrating expert knowledge. John Stuart Mill's warning of the triumph of prevailing opinion and the maginalization of dissent is more pertinent now than ever.

Added to which, contemporary tabloid news and comment is more preoccupied than ever with the culture of celebrity, with the private lives and life styles of fashion models, film stars, sports stars, and television personalities. This has important consequences for the idea of the public sphere. Recent research in the UK suggests that the more people are immersed in these narratives the less interested they are in political affairs, leading the study's authors to conclude that "those who particularly follow celebrity culture are . . . the least likely to involve themselves in discussion about public-type issues."[15] Nor is the contemporary political domain entirely separated from the culture of celebrity. As a consequence, mediated public debate now is as likely, and often more likely, to focus on the personalities of politicians rather than the substance of the issues at stake and their ethical underpinnings.

As we have argued, the career of the public sphere as an idea is intimately tied to the wider struggle for realizing the visions of democratic polity and culture announced by the revolutions in North America and France and worked on by successive generations of intellectuals and activists. It is tempting to present this history as a narrative of progress. However, history shows that democracy can never be taken for granted either intellectually or practically. Democracy must be understood as a self-reflexive project continuously testing its normative principles against changing conditions. By clarifying concepts and raising awkward questions about the public sphere as a fundamental condition of democratic rule, the selections that follow provide intellectual resources for this task.

NOTES

1. Jon Elster, "Introduction," in *Deliberative Democracy*, ed. J. Elster (Cambridge: Cambridge University Press, 1998) and Jon Elster, *Explaining Social Behaviour* (Cambridge: Cambridge University Press, 2007), chapter 25.

2. Simone Chambers, "Deliberative Democratic Theory." *Annual Review of Political Science* 6 (2003): 307–326.

3. Jürgen Habermas, *The Structural Transformation of the Public Sphere: An Inquiry into a Category of Bourgeois Society* (Cambridge, Mass.: Polity Press, [1962] 1989), 51.

4. Bernhard Peters, "The Meaning of the Public Sphere," in *Public Deliberation and Public Culture. The Writings of Bernhard Peters, 1993–2005*, ed. H. Wessler (Basingstoke: Palgrave Macmillan, [1994] 2008), 58.

5. Jürgen Habermas, *Between Facts and Norms* (Cambridge, Mass.: MIT Press, [1992] 1996), 360.

6. Benedict Anderson, *Imagined Communities: Reflections on the Origins and Spread of Nationalism* (London: Verso, 1993).

7. Edward Ross, "The Suppression of Important News." *Atlantic Monthly*, 105 (1910): 310.

8. Hans-Jörg Trenz, "Uniting and Dividing. The European Public Sphere as an Unfinished Project," in *Manufacturing Europe: Spaces of Democracy, Diversity and Communication*, ed. I. Salovaara-Moring (Göteborg: Nordicom, 2009), 37.

9. Jürgen Habermas, *The Postnational Constellation—Political Essays* (Cambridge: Polity Press, [1998] 2001), 61.

10. Nancy Fraser, "Transnationalizing the Public Sphere. On the Legitimacy and Efficacy of Public Opinion in a Post-Westphalian World." *Theory, Culture & Society* 24, no. 4 (2007): 7–30.

11. Slavko Splichal, "In Search of a Strong European Public Sphere: Some Critical Observations on Conceptualizations of Publicness and the (European) Public Sphere." *Media, Culture & Society* 28, no. 5 (2006): 695–714, 702.

12. Cass R. Sunstein, *Republic.com 2.0.* (Princeton and Oxford: Princeton University Press, 2007).

13. Sunstein, *Republic.com 2.0.*, 5–6.

14. See; Yochai Benkler, *The Wealth of Networks. How Social Production Transforms Markets and Freedom.* (New Haven and London: Yale University Press, 2006); Matthew Hindman, *The Myth of Digital Democracy* (Princeton and Oxford: Princeton University Press, 2009).

15. Nick Couldry and Tim Markham "Celebrity Culture and Public Connection: Bridge or Chasm." *International Journal of Cultural Studies* 10, no. 4 (2007): 403–421.

Section I

Enlightenment and the Liberal Idea of the Public Sphere

INTRODUCTION

For the philosophers of the Enlightenment, the idea of reason was inextricably tied to publicity and public argument. Reason is public in the sense that it does not recognise any authority other than the better argument, and its public use must be free to bring about a process of enlightenment—"man's emergence from his self-incurred immaturity" and subservience to authority as the German philosopher Immanuel Kant put it in his famous dictum. The "public sphere" was understood as a sphere for critical discourse, placing all established powers and truths before the tribunal of reason.

However, for some time participation in public reasoning was restricted to the rising business and professional classes. It took the slow growth of literacy and the long struggle for a universal franchise to provide the basis for more inclusive participation. As this process gathered momentum more sceptical accounts of the public sphere emerged.

More than any other philosopher of his age, Kant emphasized the internal connection between reason and "publicity." In his *Critique of Pure Reason*, he described freedom of criticism as a necessary precondition for the exercise of reason, arguing that "the voice of reason is not that of a dictatorial and despotic power, it is rather like the vote of the citizens of a free state, every member of which must have the privilege of giving free expression to his doubts, and possess even the right of veto." This connection between reason and "publicity" is at the core of Kant's conception of justice: To be just, laws that limit freedom by specifying what is not permitted have to be justified with reasons showing that these restrictions can be willed by all. A just legal order is one which guarantees the greatest freedom possible to everyone that is compatible with the same freedom for all under general laws. "Publicity" is the test that laws must pass to be in accordance with this principle of justice.

For the German "romantic" philosopher G. W. F. Hegel the liberal conceptions of freedom was an "abstract" freedom, separating individuals from their historically evolved communities though he recognized the "principle of subjectivity" as one of

1

the modern world's great achievements. In contrast, "concrete freedom" not only allows individuals to pursue their particular interests and have their rights recognized, it also requires them to live "a universal life" as members of the state. For Hegel, it is the state that "allows the principle of subjectivity to progress to its culmination in the extreme of self-subsistent personal particularity, and yet at the same time brings it back to the substantive unity and so maintains this unity in the principle of subjectivity itself."

This "principle of subjectivity" entails the freedom of individuals to have and express "their own private judgements, opinions, and recommendations on affairs of state." The collective manifestation of this freedom is "public opinion." For Hegel, however, public opinion was a problematic force, as much to be "despised" as "respected" because it combined the true with the false, "the substantive" with "the purely particular and private opinions of the Many." He feared that individuals might form "a mass with an unorganised opinion and volition" and crystallize "into a powerful bloc in opposition to the state." He addressed this problem by assigning a central position to legislative assemblies arguing that they could act as the crucial mediating force between states and citizens.

England's leading liberal thinker, John Stuart Mill also had reservations about the growing political role of public opinion. He was adamant that the free development of individuality, the use of one's faculties in choosing and pursuing one's own good in one's own way, is basic to human well-being and that cultivating and defending this autonomy is the principal aim of a liberal society. One liberty to which Mill devoted special attention was freedom of expression. He justified this freedom with reference to the value of truth. No matter whether p is true or false, its suppression is wrong. If p is true we are "deprived of the opportunity of exchanging error for truth"; if false we "lose, what is almost as great a benefit, the clearer perception and livelier impression of truth, produced by its collision with error."

According to Mill, the only purpose for which power can rightfully be used against an individual is to prevent "harm to others." However, with regard to "compulsion and control" he was not only concerned with the use of legal penalties but also with the "moral coercion of public opinion." He saw public opinion as a growing and powerful constraint on the expression of minority opinions and feared that a new "tyranny of the majority" was replacing the old tyranny of the ruler.

IMMANUEL KANT

AN ANSWER TO THE QUESTION: "WHAT IS ENLIGHTENMENT?" (1784)[1]

The German philosopher Immanuel Kant (1724–1804) was born in Königsberg, Prussia, where he lived all his life. He studied philosophy and from 1755 worked as a professor. His works on epistemology, morality and law, religion, and aesthetics have had an influence on modern philosophy that can hardly be overestimated.

"An Answer to the Question: What is Enlightenment?" was published in the periodical Berlinische Monatsschrift in 1784. In an earlier issue, the clergyman and official Johann Friedrich Zöllner had claimed that before one starts to enlighten the people, one should answer the important question "What is enlightenment?" The newly coined metaphor "Aufklärung" (enlightenment) was at the time a fuzzy buzzword meaning almost anything. Kant gives his answer in the first sentences of his article: "Enlightenment is man's emergence from his self-incurred immaturity. Immaturity is the inability to use one's own understanding without the guidance of another." In his subsequent explanation, Kant claims that laziness and cowardice are the reasons why most people gladly remain immature. It is convenient not to think, and external authorities, such as books, doctors, and spiritual advisors, convince us that we do not have to think. The progress of enlightenment depends for Kant, on the freedom "to make public use of one's reason in all matters." The private use of reason, on the other hand, may be restricted without being an obstacle on the road to enlightenment. Kant uses the word "private" here to refer to the actions of a civil servant— an officer, a tax official or a clergyman—in contrast to the "public use of reason," where men of learning address "the entire reading public."

It is important to bear in mind the context of Kant's answer. In the article, he praises the absolutist king Frederic the Great. The degree of freedom and enlightenment in Prussia under Frederic is disputable. In his article, Kant maintained that he did not live in an enlightened age, but in "the age of enlightenment, the century of Frederic," but two years after its publication, Frederic died and heavy censorship was introduced on Kant's writings.

Enlightenment is man's emergence from his self-incurred immaturity. *Immaturity* is the inability to use one's own understanding without the guidance of another. This immaturity is *self-incurred* if its cause is not lack of understanding, but lack of resolution and courage to use it without the guidance of another. The motto of enlightenment is therefore: *Sapere aude!*[2] Have courage to use your own understanding!

Laziness and cowardice are the reasons why such a large proportion of men, even when nature has long emancipated them from alien guidance (*naturaliter maiorennes*),[3] nevertheless gladly remain immature for life. For the same reasons, it is all too easy for others to set themselves up as their guardians. It is so convenient to be immature! If I have a book to have understanding in place of me, a spiritual adviser to have a conscience for me, a doctor to judge my diet for me, and so on, I need not make any efforts at all. I need not think, so long as I can pay; others will soon enough take the tiresome job over for me. The guardians who have kindly taken upon themselves the work of supervision will soon see to it that by far the largest part of mankind (including the entire fair sex) should consider the step forward to maturity not only as difficult but also as highly dangerous. Having first infatuated their domestic animals, and carefully prevented the docile creatures from daring to take a single step without the leading-strings to which they are tied, they next show them the danger which threatens them if they try to walk unaided. Now this danger is not in fact so very great, for they would certainly learn to walk eventually after a few falls. But an example of this kind is intimidating, and usually frightens them off from further attempts.

Thus it is difficult for each separate individual to work his way out of the immaturity which has become almost second nature to him. He has even grown fond of it and is really incapable for the time being of using his own understanding, because he was never allowed to make the attempt. Dogmas and formulas, those mechanical instruments for rational use (or rather misuse) of his natural endowments, are the ball and chain of his permanent immaturity. And if anyone did throw them off, he would still be uncertain about jumping over even the narrowest of trenches, for he would be unaccustomed to free movement of this kind. Thus only a few, by cultivating their own minds, have succeeded in freeing themselves from immaturity and in continuing boldly on their way.

There is more chance of an entire public enlightening itself. This is indeed almost inevitable, if only the public concerned is left in freedom. For there will always be a few who think for themselves, even among those appointed as guardians of the common mass. Such guardians, once they have themselves thrown off the yoke of immaturity, will disseminate the spirit of rational respect for personal value and for the duty of all men to think for themselves. The remarkable thing about this is that if the public, which was previously put under this yoke by the guardians, is suitably stirred up by some of the latter who are incapable of enlightenment, it may subsequently compel the guardians themselves to remain under the yoke. For it is very harmful to propagate prejudices, because they finally avenge themselves on the very people who first encouraged them (or whose predecessors did so). Thus a public can only achieve enlightenment slowly. A revolution may well put an end to autocratic despotism and to rapacious or power-seeking oppression, but it will never produce a true reform in ways of thinking. Instead, new prejudices, like the ones they replaced, will serve as a leash to control the great unthinking mass.

For enlightenment of this kind, all that is needed is *freedom*. And the freedom in question is the most innocuous form of all—freedom to make *public use* of one's reason in all matters. But I hear on all sides the cry: *Don't argue!* The officer says: Don't argue, get on parade! The tax-official: Don't argue, pay! The clergyman: Don't argue, believe! (Only one ruler in the world says: *Argue* as much as you like and about whatever you like, *but obey*!)[4] All this means restrictions on freedom everywhere. But which sort of restriction prevents enlightenment, and which, instead of hindering it, can actually promote it? I reply: The *public* use of man's reason must always be free, and it alone can bring about enlightenment among men; the *private use* of reason may quite often be very narrowly restricted, however, without undue hindrance to the progress of enlightenment. But by the public use of one's own reason I mean that use which anyone may make of it as *a man of learning* addressing the entire *reading public*. What I term the private use of reason is that which a person may make of it in a particular *civil* post or office with which he is entrusted.

Now in some affairs which affect the interests of the commonwealth, we require a certain mechanism whereby some members of the commonwealth must behave purely passively, so that they may, by an artificial common agreement, be employed by the government for public ends (or at least deterred from vitiating them). It is, of course, impermissible to argue in such cases; obedience is imperative. But in so far as this or that individual who acts as part of the machine also considers himself as a member of a complete commonwealth or even of cosmopolitan society, and thence as a man of learning who may through his writings address a public in the truest sense of the word, he may indeed argue without harming the affairs in which he is employed for some of the time in a passive capacity. Thus it would be very harmful if an officer receiving an order from his superiors were to quibble openly, while on duty, about the appropriateness or usefulness of the order in question. He must simply obey. But he cannot reasonably be banned from making observations as a man of learning on the errors in the military service, and from submitting these to his public for judgement. The citizen cannot refuse to pay the taxes imposed upon him; presumptuous criticisms of such taxes, where someone is called upon to pay them, may be punished as an outrage which could lead to general insubordination. Nonetheless, the same citizen does not contravene his civil obligations if, as a learned individual, he publicly voices his thoughts on the impropriety or even injustice of such fiscal measures. In the same way, a clergyman is bound to instruct his pupils and his congregation in accordance with the doctrines of the church he serves, for he was employed by it on that condition. But as a scholar, he is completely free as well as obliged to impart to the public all his carefully considered, well-intentioned thoughts on the mistaken aspects of those doctrines, and to offer suggestions for a better arrangement of religious and ecclesiastical affairs. And there is nothing in this which need trouble the conscience. For what he teaches in pursuit of his duties as an active servant of the church is presented by him as something which he is not empowered to teach at his own discretion, but which he is employed to expound in a prescribed manner and in someone else's name. He will say: Our church teaches this or that, and these are the arguments it uses. He then extracts as much practical value as possible for his congregation from precepts to which he would not himself subscribe with full conviction, but which he can nevertheless undertake to expound, since it is not in fact wholly impossible that they may contain truth. At all events, nothing opposed to the essence of religion is present in such doctrines. For if the clergyman thought he could find anything of this sort in them, he would not be able to carry out his official duties in good conscience, and would have to resign. Thus the use which someone employed as a teacher makes of his reason in the presence of his congregation is purely *private*, since a congregation, however large it is, is never any more than a domestic gathering. In view of this, he is not and cannot be free as a priest, since he is acting on a commission imposed from outside. Conversely, as a scholar addressing the real public (i.e. the world at large) through his writings, the clergyman making *public use* of his reason enjoys unlimited freedom to use his own reason and to speak in his own person. For to maintain that the guardians of the people in spiritual matters should themselves be immature, is an absurdity which amounts to making absurdities permanent.

But should not a society of clergymen, for example an ecclesiastical synod or a venerable presbytery (as the Dutch call it), be entitled to commit itself by oath to a

certain unalterable set of doctrines, in order to secure for all time a constant guardian-
ship over each of its members, and through them over the people? I reply that this
is quite impossible. A contract of this kind, concluded with a view to preventing all
further enlightenment of mankind for ever, is absolutely null and void, even if it is
ratified by the supreme power, by Imperial Diets and the most solemn peace treaties.
One age cannot enter into an alliance on oath to put the next age in a position where
it would be impossible for it to extend and correct its knowledge, particularly on such
important matters, or to make any progress whatsoever in enlightenment. This would
be a crime against human nature, whose original destiny lies precisely in such progress. Later generations are thus perfectly entitled to dismiss these agreements as unau-
thorised and criminal. To test whether any particular measure can be agreed upon as
a law for a people, we need only ask whether a people could well impose such a law
upon itself. This might well be possible for a specified short period as a means of introducing a certain order, pending, as it were, a better solution. This would also mean
that each citizen, particularly the clergyman, would be given a free hand as a scholar
to comment publicly, i.e. in his writings, on the inadequacies of current institutions.
Meanwhile, the newly established order would continue to exist, until public insight
into the nature of such matters had progressed and proved itself to the point where,
by general consent (if not unanimously), a proposal could be submitted to the crown.
This would seek to protect the congregations who had, for instance, agreed to alter
their religious establishment in accordance with their own notions of what higher
insight is, but it would not try to obstruct those who wanted to let things remain as
before. But it is absolutely impermissible to agree, even for a single lifetime, to a permanent religious constitution which no-one might publicly question. For this would
virtually nullify a phase in man's upward progress, thus making it fruitless and even
detrimental to subsequent generations. A man may for his own person, and even then
only for a limited period, postpone enlightening himself in matters he ought to know
about. But to renounce such enlightenment completely, whether for his own person
or even more so for later generations, means violating and trampling underfoot the
sacred rights of mankind. But something which a people may not even impose upon
itself can still less be imposed on it by a monarch; for his legislative authority depends
precisely upon his uniting the collective will of the people in his own. So long as he
sees to it that all true or imagined improvements are compatible with the civil order,
he can otherwise leave his subjects to do whatever they find necessary for their salvation, which is none of his business. But it is his business to stop anyone forcibly hindering others from working as best they can to define and promote their salvation. It
indeed detracts from his majesty if he interferes in these affairs by subjecting the writings in which his subjects attempt to clarify their religious ideas to governmental supervision. This applies if he does so acting upon his own exalted opinions—in which
case he exposes himself to the reproach: *Caesar non est supra Crammaticos*[5]—but much
more so if he demeans his high authority so far as to support the spiritual despotism
of a few tyrants within his state against the rest of his subjects.

If it is now asked whether we at present live in an *enlightened* age, the answer is:
No, but we do live in an age of *enlightenment*. As things are at present, we still have
a long way to go before men as a whole can be in a position (or can even be put
into a position) of using their own understanding confidently and well in religious
matters, without outside guidance. But we do have distinct indications that the way

is now being cleared for them to work freely in this direction, and that the obstacles to universal enlightenment, to man's emergence from his self-incurred immaturity, are gradually becoming fewer. In this respect our age is the age of enlightenment, the century of *Frederick*.[6]

A prince who does not regard it as beneath him to say that he considers it his duty, in religious matters, not to prescribe anything to his people, but to allow them complete freedom, a prince who thus even declines to accept the presumptuous title of *tolerant*, is himself enlightened. He deserves to be praised by a grateful present and posterity as the man who first liberated mankind from immaturity (as far as government is concerned), and who left all men free to use their own reason in all matters of conscience. Under his rule, ecclesiastical dignitaries, notwithstanding their official duties, may in their capacity as scholars freely and publicly submit to the judgement of the world their verdicts and opinions, even if these deviate here and there from orthodox doctrine. This applies even more to all others who are not restricted by any official duties. This spirit of freedom is also spreading abroad, even where it has to struggle with outward obstacles imposed by governments which misunderstand their own function. For such governments can now witness a shining example of how freedom may exist without in the least jeopardising public concord and the unity of the commonwealth. Men will of their own accord gradually work their way out of barbarism so long as artificial measures are not deliberately adopted to keep them in it.

I have portrayed *matters of religion* as the focal point of enlightenment, i.e. of man's emergence from his self-incurred immaturity. This is firstly because our rulers have no interest in assuming the role of guardians over their subjects so far as the arts and sciences are concerned, and secondly, because religious immaturity is the most pernicious and dishonourable variety of all. But the attitude of mind of a head of state who favours freedom in the arts and sciences extends even further, for he realises that there is no danger even to his *legislation* if he allows his subjects to make *public* use of their own reason and to put before the public their thoughts on better ways of drawing up laws, even if this entails forthright criticism of the current legislation. We have before us a brilliant example of this kind, in which no monarch has yet surpassed the one to whom we now pay tribute.

But only a ruler who is himself enlightened and has no fear of phantoms, yet who likewise has at hand a well-disciplined and numerous army to guarantee public security, may say what no republic would dare to say: *Argue as much as you like and about whatever you like, but obey!* This reveals to us a strange and unexpected pattern in human affairs (such as we shall always find if we consider them in the widest sense, in which nearly everything is paradoxical). A high degree of civil freedom seems advantageous to a people's *intellectual* freedom, yet it also sets up insuperable barriers to it. Conversely, a lesser degree of civil freedom gives intellectual freedom enough room to expand to its fullest extent. Thus once the germ on which nature has lavished most care—man's inclination and vocation to *think freely*—has developed within this hard shell, it gradually reacts upon the mentality of the people, who thus gradually become increasingly able to *act freely*. Eventually, it even influences the principles of governments, which find that they can themselves profit by treating man, who is *more than a machine*,[7] in a manner appropriate to his dignity.*
Königsberg in Prussia, 30th September, 1784.

*I read today on the 30th September in Büsching's[8] *Wöchentliche Nachrichten* of 13th September a notice considering this month's *Berlinische Monatsschrift*. The notice mentions Mendelssohn's[9] answer to the same question as that which I have answered. I have not yet seen this journal, otherwise I should have held back the above reflections. I let them stand only as a means of finding out by comparison how far the thoughts of two individuals may coincide by chance.

NOTES

1. *Beantwortung der Frage: Was ist Aufklärung?*, AA VIII, 33–42. First published in *Berlinische Monatsschrift*, IV (12 December 1784): 481–94. There is a reference in the original edition of the *Berlinische Monatsschrift* to p. 516 of the number of that journal published on 5 December 1783. This reference is to an essay by the Rev. Zöllner, "Is it advisable to sanction marriage through religion?" The relevant passage reads (in translation): "*What is Enlightenment?* The question, which is almost as important as the question *What is truth?* should be answered before one begins to enlighten others. And yet I have never found it answered anywhere."

2. Literal translation: "Dare to be wise." Horace, *Epodes* I, 2, 40. Cf. Elizabeth M.Wilkinson and L.A. Willoughby (eds. and trans.). Friedrich Schiller, *On the Aesthetic Education of Man* (Oxford, 1967?), LXXIV ff.; cf. also Franco Venturi, "Was ist Aufklärung? Sapere Aude!" *Rivista Storica Italiana* LXXI (1959): 119 ff. Venturi traces the use made of this quotation from Horace throughout the centuries. Cf. also p. 5.

3. Those who have come of age by virtue of nature.

4. The allusion is to Frederick II (the Great), King of Prussia (1740–86).

5. "Caesar is not above the grammatians."

6. Kant here refers, of course, to Frederick the Great.

7. This allusion amounts to a repudiation of Julien Offray de La Mettrie's (1709–51) materialism as expressed in *L'Homme Machine* (1748).

8. Anton Friedrich Büshing (1724–93), professor in the University of Göttingen, theologian and leading geographer of the day, editor of the *Wöchentliche Nachrichten von neuen Landkarten, geographischen, statistischen und historischen Büchern*. Kant's reference is to XII, 1784 (Berlin, 1785), 291.

9. Moses Mendelssohn (1729–86), a leading philosopher of the German Enlightenment. The reference is to Mendelssohn's essay "Über die Frage: was heist Aufklärung?" ("On the question: what is Enlightenment?"), *Berlinische Monatsschrift* IV (9 September 1784): 193–200.

G. W. F. HEGEL

EXCERPT FROM *PHILOSOPHY OF RIGHT* (1821)

In his Philosophy of Right *(1821), the German philosopher Georg Wilhelm Friedrich Hegel (1770–1831) developed an idealistic theory of the state as a sphere of true universality beyond the separate needs and interests which dominate "civil society" (bürgerliche Gesellschaft), the latter being differentiated from the family, seen as the sphere of emotional ties. Hegel was the first in the history of political thought to make a clear distinction between the domains of the family, civil society, and state, and the resulting triad sets the stage for his understanding of the public sphere. 130 years later, Jürgen Habermas brought this triad to the fore in his theorising of the early public sphere in* Strukturwandel der Öffentlichkeit *([1962] 1989).*

In Hegel's system, the public sphere is located between civil society and the state. According to Hegel, "the principle of the modern world" was that "what every man is bound to recognize must seem to him justified." He saw the assembly of estates, representing the members of civil society, and its public transactions as an institutionalization of this principle, educating citizens, and making them conscious of their "true" interests. Its organized deliberations were then contrasted with public opinion presented as the unorganized way in which a people's opinions and wishes are made known. Hegel appreciated individuals' freedom to have and express their own judgements on public affairs but argued that public opinion must rise above the purely particular and private opinions of the many and merge with what is universal and true. In pursuit of this goal, the assembly of estates acts as a crucial "mediating organ" preventing the isolated individuals in civil society from "appearing as a mass or an aggregate and so from acquiring an unorganised opinion and volition and from crystallising into a powerful bloc in opposition to the organised state."

The following excerpt is from the third part of Philosophy of Right *on "ethical life" (Sittlichkeit). Ethical life entails the ensemble of institutions that ties individuals together in a modern society: the family, the institutions of civil society (market economy, law, and corporations) and the state. Hegel treats public opinion in the section on the state where he writes about the assembly of estates. This reflects his statist view on societal integration and his scepticism toward unorganized public opinion.*

§316. The formal subjective freedom of individuals consists in their having and expressing their own private judgments, opinions, and recommendations on affairs of state. This freedom is collectively manifested as what is called "public opinion," in which what is absolutely universal, the substantive and the true, is linked with its opposite, the purely particular and private opinions[1] of the Many. Public opinion as it exists is thus a standing self-contradiction, knowledge as appearance, the essential just as directly present as the inessential.

Addition: Public opinion is the unorganized way in which a people's opinions and wishes are made known. What is actually made authoritative in the state must operate in an organized manner as the parts of the constitution do. But at all times public opinion has been a great power and it is particularly so in our day when the principle of subjective freedom has such importance and significance. What is to be authoritative nowadays derives its authority, not at all from force, only to a small extent from habit and custom, really from insight and argument.

§317. Public opinion, therefore, is a repository not only of the genuine needs and correct tendencies of common life, but also, in the form of common sense (i.e., all-pervasive fundamental ethical principles disguised as prejudices), of the eternal, substantive principles of justice, the true content and result of legislation, the whole constitution, and the general position of the state.

At the same time, when this inner truth emerges into consciousness and, embodied in general maxims, enters representative thinking— whether it be there on its own account or in support of concrete arguments about felt wants, public affairs, the organization of the state, and relations of parties within it—it becomes infected by all the accidents of opinion, by its ignorance and perversity, by its mistakes and falsity of judgment. Since in considering such opinion we have to do with the consciousness of an insight and conviction peculiarly one's own, the more peculiarly one's own an opinion may be the worse its content is, because the bad is that which is wholly private and personal in its content; the rational, on the other hand, is the absolutely universal, while it is on peculiarity that opining prides itself.

> Hence it is not simply due to a subjective difference of view that we find it said that

> *Vox populi, vox Dei,*

> and on the other hand, as Ariosto has it,

> *Che '1 volgare ignorante ogn' un riprenda*
> *E parli più di quel che meno intenda*

or, as Goethe puts it, "the masses are respectable hands at fighting, but miserable hands at judging."[2] Both types of assertion are true at one and the same time of public opinion, and since it is such a hodgepodge of truth and endless error, it cannot be genuinely serious about both of these. But about which *is* it serious? The question may seem hard to answer, and it will actually be hard if we cling simply to the words in which public opinion is directly expressed. The substantial, however, is the heart of public opinion, and therefore it is with that alone that it is truly serious. What the substantial is, though, is not discoverable from public opinion, because its very substantiality implies that it is known in and from itself alone. The passion with which an opinion is urged or the seriousness with which it is maintained or attacked and disputed is no criterion of its real content; and yet the last thing which opinion could be made to see is that its seriousness is nothing serious.

A great genius[3] propounded as a problem for a public essay competition the question "whether it be permissible to deceive a people." The answer must have been that a people does not allow itself to be deceived about its substantive basis, the essence and specific character of its mind. On the other hand, it is self-deceived about the manner of its knowledge of these things and about its corresponding judgement of its actions, experiences, &c.

Addition: The principle of the modern world requires that what anyone is to recognize shall reveal itself to him as something entitled to recognition. Apart from that, however, everyone wishes to have some share in discussion and deliberation. Once he has had his say and so his share of responsibility, his subjectivity has been satisfied and he puts up with a lot. In France freedom of speech has turned out far less dangerous than enforced silence, because with the latter the fear is that men bottle up their objections to a thing, whereas argument gives them an outlet and a measure of satisfaction, and this is in addition a means whereby the thing can be pushed ahead more easily.

§318. Public opinion therefore deserves to be as much respected as despised—despised for its concrete expression and for the concrete consciousness it expresses, respected for its essential basis, a basis which only glimmers more or less dimly in that concrete expression. But in itself it has no criterion of discrimination, nor has it the ability to extract the substantive element it contains and raise it to precise knowledge. Thus to be independent of public opinion is the first formal condition of achieving anything great or rational whether in life or in science. Great achievement is assured, however, of subsequent recognition and grateful acceptance by public opinion, which in due course will make it one of its own prejudices.

Addition: Public opinion contains all kinds of falsity and truth, but it takes a great man to find the truth in it. The great man of the age is the one who can put into words the will of his age, tell his age what its will is, and accomplish it. What he does is the heart and the essence of his age, he actualizes his age. The man who lacks sense enough to despise public opinion expressed in gossip will never do anything great.

§319. Freedom of public communication—of the two modes of communication, the press and the spoken word, the first exceeds the second in range of contact but lags behind it in vivacity—satisfaction of the goading desire to say one's say and to have said it, is directly assured by the laws and by-laws which control or punish its excesses. But it is assured indirectly by the innocuous character which it acquires as a result principally of the rationality of the constitution, the stability of government, and secondly of the publicity of Estates Assemblies. The reason why the latter makes free speech harmless is that what is voiced in these Assemblies is a sound and mature insight into the concerns of the state, with the result that members of the general public are left with nothing of much importance to say, and above all are deprived of the opinion that what they say is of peculiar importance and efficacy. A further safeguard of free speech is the indifference and contempt speedily and necessarily visited on shallow and cantankerous talking.

To define freedom of the press as freedom to say and write whatever we please is parallel to the assertion that freedom as such means freedom to do as we please. Talk of this kind is due to wholly uneducated, crude, and superficial ideas. Moreover, it is in the very nature of the thing that abstract thinking should nowhere be so stubborn, so unintelligent, as in this matter of free speech, because what it is considering is the most fleeting, the most contingent, and the most personal side of opinion in its infinite diversity of content and tergiversation. Beyond the direct incitation to theft, murder, rebellion, &c., there lies its artfully constructed expression—an expression which seems in itself quite general and vague, while all the time it conceals a meaning anything but vague or else is compatible with inferences which are not actually expressed, and it is impossible to determine whether they rightly follow from it, or whether they were meant to be inferred from it. This vagueness of matter and form precludes laws on these topics from attaining the requisite determinacy of law, and since the trespass, wrong, and injury here are so extremely personal and subjective in form, judgment on them is reduced equally to a wholly subjective verdict. Such an injury is directed against the thoughts, opinions, and wills of others, but apart from that, these form the element in which alone it is actually anything. But this element is the sphere of the freedom of others, and it therefore depends on them whether the injurious expression of opinion is or is not actually an effective act.

Laws then [against libel, &c.] may be criticized by exhibiting their indeterminacy as well as by arguing that they leave it open to the speaker or writer to devise turns of phrase or tricks of expression, and so evade the laws or claim that judicial decisions are mere subjective verdicts. Further, however, against the view that the expression of opinion is an act with injurious effects, it may be maintained that it is not an act at all, but only opining and thinking, or only talking. And so we have before us a claim that mere opining and talking is to go unpunished because it is of a purely subjective character both in form and content, because it does not mean anything and is of no importance. And yet in the same breath we have the claim that this same opining and talking should be held in high esteem and respect—the opining because it is personal property and in fact pre-eminently the property of mind; the talking because it is only this same property being expressed and used.

But the substance of the matter is and remains that traducing the honour of anyone, slander, abuse, the contemptuous caricature of government, its ministers, officials, and in particular the person of the monarch, defiance of the laws, incitement to rebellion, &c., &c., are all crimes or misdemeanours in one or other of their numerous gradations. The rather high degree of indeterminability which such actions acquire on account of the element in which they are expressed does not annul this fundamental character of theirs. Its only effect is that the subjective field in which they are committed also determines the nature and form of the reaction to the offence. It is the field in which the offence was committed which itself necessitates subjectivity of view, contingency, &c., in the reaction to the offence, whether the reaction takes the form of punishment proper or of police action to prevent crimes. Here, as always, abstract thinking sets itself to explain away the fundamental and concrete nature of the thing by concentrating on isolated aspects of its external appearance and on abstractions drawn therefrom.

The sciences, however, are not to be found anywhere in the field of opinion and subjective views, provided of course that they be sciences in other respects. Their exposition is not a matter of clever turns of phrase, allusiveness, half-utterances, and semi-reticences, but consists in the unambiguous, determinate, and open expression of their meaning and purport. It follows that they do not fall under the category of public opinion (see Paragraph 316). Apart from this, however, as I said just now, the element in which views and their expression become actions in the full sense and exist effectively, consists of the intelligence, principles, and opinions of others. Hence this aspect of these actions, i.e. their effectiveness proper and their danger to individuals, society, and the state (compare Paragraph 218), depends on the character of the ground on which they fall, just as a spark falling on a heap of gunpowder is more dangerous than if it falls on hard ground where it vanishes without trace. Thus, just as the right of science to express itself depends on and is safeguarded by its subject-matter and content, so an illegitimate expression may also acquire a measure of security, or at least sufferance, in the scorn which it has brought upon itself. An offence of this sort is punishable on its own account too, but part of it may be accounted that kind of nemesis which inner impotence, feeling itself oppressed by the preponderating abilities and virtues of others, is impelled to vent in order to come to itself again in face of such superiority, and to restore some self-consciousness to its own nullity. It was a nemesis of a more harmless type which Roman soldiers vented against their generals when they sang scurrilous songs about them in triumphal processions in order in a way to get even with them for all the hard service and discipline they had undergone, and especially for the omission of their names from the triumphal honours. The former type of nemesis, the bad and hateful type, is deprived of its effect by being treated with scorn, and hence, like the public, which perhaps forms a circle of spectators of scurrility, it is restricted to futile malice and to the self-condemnation which it implicitly contains.

§320. Subjectivity is manifested in its most external form as the undermining of the established life of the state by opinion and ratiocination when they endeavour to assert the authority of their own fortuitous character and so bring about their own destruction. But its true actuality is attained in the opposite of this, i.e. in the subjectivity identical with the substantial will of the state, the subjectivity which constitutes the concept of the power of the crown and which, as the ideality of the whole state, has not up to this point attained its right or its existence.

Addition: Subjectivity has been treated once already [Paragraphs 279 ff.] as the apex of the state, as the crown. Its other aspect is its arbitrary manifestation in public opinion, its most external mode of appearance. The subjectivity of the monarch is inherently abstract, but it should be something concrete and so be the ideality which diffuses itself over the whole state. The state at peace is that in which all branches of civil life subsist, but they possess their subsistence outside and alongside one another as something which issues from the idea of the whole. The fact that it so issues must also come into appearance as the ideality.

NOTES

1. Hegel always regards "opinion" (*Meinung*) as something peculiarly "mine" (*mein*), and this accounts for his general attitude to it. None the less, there is no more etymological affinity between *Meinung* and *mein* than there is between "mind" and "mine."
2. Aristo's lines ("the ignorant vulgar reproves everyone and talks most of what int understands least") are from Orlando Furiose, Canto xxviii, Stanza i. Goethes lines are:

> *Zuschlagen muss die Masse,*
> *Dann ist sie respektabel;*
> *Urteilen gelingt ihr miserable.*

(Sprichwörtlich, ll. 398–400). Hegel substitutes *kann* for *muss* and *da* for *dann*. The translation given here of both quotations is taken from *Bosanquet: Philosophical Theory of the State* (London, 1930), p. 266.

    3. Frederick the Great, who sets as a question for the Berlin academy prize in 1778: *S'il peut être utile de tromper un peuple?*

JOHN STUART MILL

EXCERPT FROM *ON LIBERTY* (1859)

John Stuart Mill (1806–1873) was one of Victorian England's most prominent thinkers. He made important contributions to the development of political economy and to the philosophy of utilitarianism advanced by his sometime tutor, Jeremy Bentham. His best known book, On Liberty, *which appeared in 1859, continues to be read and discussed today as a major statement of liberalism's defense of the rights of the individual, including the right to freedom of speech.*

As he noted in his Autobiography, *he was concerned with how best "to unite the greatest individual liberty of action, with equal participation of all in the benefits of combined labour." He saw representative government as the form of rule best fitted to achieving this aim and called for women to be enfranchised and for minorities to be given a greater voice through proportional representation, though he also argued that the better educated should be given two votes. He feared that obliging government to follow general public opinion was creating a new tyranny of the majority, in which "the opinion of masses of merely average men are everywhere become, or becoming the dominant power."*

In 1855, the last of the state-imposed taxes on newspapers was abolished in England holding out the prospect of a "free market" in ideas. Mill welcomed this shift but recognized that in their efforts to maximize readership the commercial press tended to play to prevailing opinion, fostering a spirit of "social intolerance" that pressured "inquiring minds" with minority viewpoints "to keep the general principles and grounds of their convictions within their own breasts," an argument that would later be revisited in post World War II Germany in Elisabeth Noelle-Neumann's idea of a "spiral of silence."

Against this closure, he argued for continually testing all ideas and recommendations for action in open and principled deliberation. He advocated grounding this process in a "morality of public discussion" that required participants to throw "themselves into the mental position of those who think differently from them," to accord them equal respect and not "to stigmatise them," to "honestly state what their opinions are" without distorting or exaggerating them, and to keep "nothing back which tells in their favour." Jürgen Habermas was to return to versions of these same conditions when formulating the ethical underpinning for his conception of the political public sphere.

Chapter 2
Of the Liberty of Thought and Discussion.

The time, it is to be hoped, is gone by, when any defence would be necessary of the "liberty of the press" as one of the securities against corrupt or tyrannical government. No argument, we may suppose, can now be needed, against permitting a legislature or an executive, not identified in interest with the people, to prescribe opinions to them, and determine what doctrines or what arguments they shall be allowed to hear. This aspect of the question, besides, has been so often and so triumphantly enforced by preceding writers, that it needs not be specially insisted on in this place. [. . .] Let us suppose, therefore, that the government is entirely at one with the people, and never thinks of exerting any power of coercion unless in agreement with what it conceives to be their voice. But I deny the right of the people to exercise such coercion, either by themselves or by their government. The power itself is illegitimate. The best government has no more title to it than the worst. It is as noxious, or more noxious, when exerted in accordance with public opinion, than when in opposition to it. If all mankind minus one, were of one opinion, and only one person were of the contrary opinion, mankind would be no more justified in silencing that one person, than he, if he had the power, would be justified in silencing mankind. Were an opinion a personal possession of no value except to the owner; if to be obstructed in the enjoyment of it were simply a private injury, it would make some difference whether the injury was inflicted only on a few persons or on many. But the peculiar evil of silencing the expression of an opinion is, that it is robbing the human race; posterity as well as the existing generation; those who dissent from the opinion, still more than those who hold it. If the opinion is right, they are deprived of the opportunity of exchanging error for truth: if wrong, they lose, what is almost as great a benefit, the clearer perception and livelier impression of truth, produced by its collision with error.

It is necessary to consider separately these two hypotheses, each of which has a distinct branch of the argument corresponding to it. We can never be sure that the opinion we are endeavouring to stifle is a false opinion; and if we were sure, stifling it would be an evil still.

First: the opinion which it is attempted to suppress by authority may possibly be true. Those who desire to suppress it, of course deny its truth; but they are not infallible. They have no authority to decide the question for all mankind, and exclude every other person from the means of judging. To refuse a hearing to an opinion, because they are sure that it is false, is to assume that their certainty is the same thing as absolute certainty. All silencing of discussion is an assumption of infallibility. Its condemnation may be allowed to rest on this common argument, not the worse for being common.

Unfortunately for the good sense of mankind, the fact of their fallibility is far from carrying the weight in their practical judgment, which is always allowed to it in theory; for while every one well knows himself to be fallible, few think it necessary to take any precautions against their own fallibility, or admit the supposition that any opinion of which they feel very certain, may be one of the examples of the error to which they acknowledge themselves to be liable. Absolute princes, or others who are accustomed to unlimited deference, usually feel this complete confidence in their own opinions on nearly all subjects. People more happily situated, who sometimes hear their opinions disputed, and are not wholly unused to be set right when they are wrong, place the same unbounded reliance only on such of their opinions as are shared by all who surround them, or to whom they habitually defer: for in proportion to a man's want of confidence in his own solitary judgment, does he usually repose, with implicit trust, on the infallibility of "the world" in general. And the world, to each individual, means the part of it with which he comes in contact; his party, his sect, his church, his class of society: the man may be called, by comparison, almost liberal and large-minded to whom it means anything so comprehensive as his own country or his own age. Nor is his faith in this collective authority at all shaken by his being aware that other ages, countries, sects, churches, classes, and parties have thought, and even now think, the exact reverse.

He devolves upon his own world the responsibility of being in the right against the dissentient worlds of other people; and it never troubles him that mere accident has decided which of these numerous worlds is the object of his reliance, and that the same causes which make him a Churchman in London, would have made him a Buddhist or a Confucian in Pekin. Yet it is as evident in itself, as any amount of argument can make it, that ages are no more infallible than individuals; every age having held many opinions which subsequent ages have deemed not only false but absurd; and it is as certain that many opinions now general will be rejected by future ages, as it is that many, once general, are rejected by the present. [. . .]

In the present age—which has been described as "destitute of faith, but terrified at scepticism,"—in which people feel sure, not so much that their opinions are true, as that they should not know what to do without them—the claims of an opinion to be protected from public attack are rested not so much on its truth, as on its importance to society. There are, it is alleged, certain beliefs, so useful, not to say indispensable to well-being, that it is as much the duty of governments to uphold those beliefs, as to protect any other of the interests of society. In a case of such necessity, and so directly in the line of their duty, something less than infallibility may, it is maintained, warrant, and even bind, governments, to act on their own opinion, confirmed by the general opinion of mankind. It is also often argued, and still oftener thought, that none but bad men would desire to weaken these salutary beliefs; and there can be nothing wrong, it is thought, in restraining bad men, and prohibiting what only such men would wish to practise. This mode of thinking makes the justification of restraints on discussion not a question of the truth of doctrines, but of their usefulness; and flatters itself by that means to escape the responsibility of claiming to be an infallible judge of opinions. But those who thus satisfy themselves, do not perceive that the assumption of infallibility is merely shifted from one point to another. The usefulness of an opinion is itself matter of opinion: as disputable, as open to discussion and requiring discussion as much, as the opinion itself. There is the same need of an infallible judge of opinions to decide an opinion to be noxious, as to decide it to be false, unless the opinion condemned has full opportunity of defending itself. And it will not do to say that the heretic may be allowed to maintain the utility or harmlessness of his opinion, though forbidden to maintain its truth. The truth of an opinion is part of its utility. If we would know whether or not it is desirable that a proposition should be believed, is it possible to exclude the consideration of whether or not it is true? In the opinion, not of bad men, but of the best men, no belief which is contrary to truth can be really useful: and can you prevent such men from urging that plea, when they are charged with culpability for denying some doctrine which they are told is useful, but which they believe to be false? Those who are on the side of received opinions, never fail to take all possible advantage of this plea; you do not find *them* handling the question of utility as if it could be completely abstracted from that of truth: on the contrary, it is, above all, because their doctrine is "the truth," that the knowledge or the belief of it is held to be so indispensable. There can be no fair discussion of the question of usefulness, when an argument so vital may be employed on one side, but not on the other. And in point of fact, when law or public feeling do not permit the truth of an opinion to be disputed, they are just as little tolerant of a denial of its usefulness. The utmost they allow is an extenuation of its absolute necessity, or of the positive guilt of rejecting it. [. . .]

Let us now pass to the second division of the argument, and dismissing the supposition that any of the received opinions may be false, let us assume them to be
true, and examine into the worth of the manner in which they are likely to be held,
when their truth is not freely and openly canvassed. However unwillingly a person
who has a strong opinion may admit the possibility that his opinion may be false,
he ought to be moved by the consideration that however true it may be, if it is not
fully, frequently, and fearlessly discussed, it will be held as a dead dogma, not a
living truth.

There is a class of persons (happily not quite so numerous as formerly) who think
it enough if a person assents undoubtingly to what they think true, though he has
no knowledge whatever of the grounds of the opinion, and could not make a tenable defence of it against the most superficial objections. Such persons, if they can
once get their creed taught from authority, naturally think that no good, and some
harm, comes of its being allowed to be questioned. Where their influence prevails,
they make it nearly impossible for the received opinion to be rejected wisely and
considerately, though it may still be rejected rashly and ignorantly; for to shut
out discussion entirely is seldom possible, and when it once gets in, beliefs not
grounded on conviction are apt to give way before the slightest semblance of an argument. Waiving, however, this possibility—assuming that the true opinion abides
in the mind, but abides as a prejudice, a belief independent of, and proof against,
argument—this is not the way in which truth ought to be held by a rational being.
This is not knowing the truth. Truth, thus held, is but one superstition the more,
accidentally clinging to the words which enunciate a truth.

If the intellect and judgment of mankind ought to be cultivated, a thing which
Protestants at least do not deny, on what can these faculties be more appropriately
exercised by any one, than on the things which concern him so much that it is
considered necessary for him to hold opinions on them? If the cultivation of the
understanding consists in one thing more than in another, it is surely in learning the
grounds of one's own opinions. Whatever people believe, on subjects on which it
is of the first importance to believe rightly, they ought to be able to defend against
at least the common objections. But, some one may say, "Let them be taught the
grounds of their opinions. It does not follow that opinions must be merely par-
roted because they are never heard controverted. Persons who learn geometry do
not simply commit the theorems to memory, but understand and learn likewise
the demonstrations; and it would be absurd to say that they remain ignorant of the
grounds of geometrical truths, because they never hear any one deny, and attempt
to disprove them." Undoubtedly: and such teaching suffices on a subject like mathematics, where there is nothing at all to be said on the wrong side of the question.
The peculiarity of the evidence of mathematical truths is, that all the argument is on
one side. There are no objections, and no answers to objections. But on every subject on which difference of opinion is possible, the truth depends on a balance to
be struck between two sets of conflicting reasons. Even in natural philosophy, there
is always some other explanation possible of the same facts; some geocentric theory
instead of heliocentric, some phlogiston instead of oxygen; and it has to be shown
why that other theory cannot be the true one: and until this is shown and until we
know how it is shown, we do not understand the grounds of our opinion. But when
we turn to subjects infinitely more complicated, to morals, religion, politics, social

relations, and the business of life, three-fourths of the arguments for every disputed opinion consist in dispelling the appearances which favour some opinion different from it. The greatest orator, save one, of antiquity, has left it on record that he always studied his adversary's case with as great, if not still greater, intensity than even his own. What Cicero practised as the means of forensic success requires to be imitated by all who study any subject in order to arrive at the truth. He who knows only his own side of the case, knows little of that. His reasons may be good, and no one may have been able to refute them. But if he is equally unable to refute the reasons on the opposite side; if he does not so much as know what they are, he has no ground for preferring either opinion. [. . .]

To abate the force of these considerations, an enemy of free discussion may be supposed to say, that there is no necessity for mankind in general to know and understand all that can be said against or for their opinions by philosophers and theologians. That it is not needful for common men to be able to expose all the misstatements or fallacies of an ingenious opponent. That it is enough if there is always somebody capable of answering them, so that nothing likely to mislead uninstructed persons remains unrefuted. That simple minds, having been taught the obvious grounds of the truths inculcated on them, may trust to authority for the rest, and being aware that they have neither knowledge nor talent to resolve every difficulty which can be raised, may repose in the assurance that all those which have been raised have been or can be answered, by those who are specially trained to the task.

Conceding to this view of the subject the utmost that can be claimed for it by those most easily satisfied with the amount of understanding of truth which ought to accompany the belief of it; even so, the argument for free discussion is no way weakened. For even this doctrine acknowledges that mankind ought to have a rational assurance that all objections have been satisfactorily answered; and how are they to be answered if that which requires to be answered is not spoken? or how can the answer be known to be satisfactory, if the objectors have no opportunity of showing that it is unsatisfactory? If not the public, at least the philosophers and theologians who are to resolve the difficulties, must make themselves familiar with those difficulties in their most puzzling form; and this cannot be accomplished unless they are freely stated, and placed in the most advantageous light which they admit of . [. . .]

If, however, the mischievous operation of the absence of free discussion, when the received opinions are true, were confined to leaving men ignorant of the grounds of those opinions, it might be thought that this, if an intellectual, is no moral evil, and does not affect the worth of the opinions, regarded in their influence on the character. The fact, however, is, that not only the grounds of the opinion are forgotten in the absence of discussion, but too often the meaning of the opinion itself. The words which convey it, cease to suggest ideas, or suggest only a small portion of those they were originally employed to communicate. Instead of a vivid conception and a living belief, there remain only a few phrases retained by rote; or, if any part, the shell and husk only of the meaning is retained, the finer essence being lost. The great chapter in human history which this fact occupies and fills, cannot be too earnestly studied and meditated on. [. . .]

It still remains to speak of one of the principal causes which make diversity of opinion advantageous, and will continue to do so until mankind shall have entered a stage of intellectual advancement which at present seems at an incalculable distance. We have hitherto considered only two possibilities: that the received opinion may be false, and some other opinion, consequently, true; or that, the received opinion being true, a conflict with the opposite error is essential to a clear apprehension and deep feeling of its truth. But there is a commoner case than either of these; when the conflicting doctrines, instead of being one true and the other false, share the truth between them; and the nonconforming opinion is needed to supply the remainder of the truth, of which the received doctrine embodies only a part. Popular opinions, on subjects not palpable to sense, are often true, but seldom or never the whole truth. They are a part of the truth; sometimes a greater, sometimes a smaller part, but exaggerated, distorted, and disjoined from the truths by which they ought to be accompanied and limited. [. . .] Such being the partial character of prevailing opinions, even when resting on a true foundation; every opinion which embodies somewhat of the portion of truth which the common opinion omits, ought to be considered precious, with whatever amount of error and confusion that truth may be blended. No sober judge of human affairs will feel bound to be indignant because those who force on our notice truths which we should otherwise have overlooked, overlook some of those which we see. Rather, he will think that so long as popular truth is one-sided, it is more desirable than otherwise that unpopular truth should have one-sided asserters too; such being usually the most energetic, and the most likely to compel reluctant attention to the fragment of wisdom which they proclaim as if it were the whole. [. . .]

In politics, again, it is almost a commonplace, that a party of order or stability, and a party of progress or reform, are both necessary elements of a healthy state of political life; until the one or the other shall have so enlarged its mental grasp as to be a party equally of order and of progress, knowing and distinguishing what is fit to be preserved from what ought to be swept away. Each of these modes of thinking derives its utility from the deficiencies of the other; but it is in a great measure the opposition of the other that keeps each within the limits of reason and sanity. Unless opinions favourable to democracy and to aristocracy, to property and to equality, to cooperation and to competition, to luxury and to abstinence, to sociality and individuality, to liberty and discipline, and all the other standing antagonisms of practical life, are expressed with equal freedom, and enforced and defended with equal talent and energy, there is no chance of both elements obtaining their due; one scale is sure to go up, and the other down. Truth, in the great practical concerns of life, is so much a question of the reconciling and combining of opposites, that very few have minds sufficiently capacious and impartial to make the adjustment with an approach to correctness, and it has to be made by the rough process of a struggle between combatants fighting under hostile banners. On any of the great open questions just enumerated, if either of the two opinions has a better claim than the other, not merely to be tolerated, but to be encouraged and countenanced, it is the one which happens at the particular time and place to be in a minority. That is the opinion which, for the time being, represents the neglected interests, the side of human well-being which is in danger of obtaining less than its share. [. . .]

We have now recognized the necessity to the mental well-being of mankind (on which all their other well-being depends) of freedom of opinion, and freedom of the expression of opinion, on four distinct grounds; which we will now briefly recapitulate.

First, if any opinion is compelled to silence, that opinion may, for aught we can certainly know, be true. To deny this is to assume our own infallibility.

Secondly, though the silenced opinion be an error, it may, and very commonly does, contain a portion of truth; and since the general or prevailing opinion on any object is rarely or never the whole truth, it is only by the collision of adverse opinions that the remainder of the truth has any chance of being supplied.

Thirdly, even if the received opinion be not only true, but the whole truth; unless it is suffered to be, and actually is, vigorously and earnestly contested, it will, by most of those who receive it, be held in the manner of a prejudice, with little comprehension or feeling of its rational grounds. And not only this, but, fourthly, the meaning of the doctrine itself will be in danger of being lost, or enfeebled, and deprived of its vital effect on the character and conduct: the dogma becoming a mere formal profession, inefficacious for good, but cumbering the ground, and preventing the growth of any real and heartfelt conviction, from reason or personal experience.

Before quitting the subject of freedom of opinion, it is fit to take notice of those who say, that the free expression of all opinions should be permitted, on condition that the manner be temperate, and do not pass the bounds of fair discussion. Much might be said on the impossibility of fixing where these supposed bounds are to be placed; for if the test be offence to those whose opinion is attacked, I think experience testifies that this offence is given whenever the attack is telling and powerful, and that every opponent who pushes them hard, and whom they find it difficult to answer, appears to them, if he shows any strong feeling on the subject, an intemperate opponent. But this, though an important consideration in a practical point of view, merges in a more fundamental objection. Undoubtedly the manner of asserting an opinion, even though it be a true one, may be very objectionable, and may justly incur severe censure. But the principal offences of the kind are such as it is mostly impossible, unless by accidental self-betrayal, to bring home to conviction. The gravest of them is, to argue sophistically, to suppress facts or arguments, to misstate the elements of the case, or misrepresent the opposite opinion. But all this, even to the most aggravated degree, is so continually done in perfect good faith, by persons who are not considered, and in many other respects may not deserve to be considered, ignorant or incompetent, that it is rarely possible on adequate grounds conscientiously to stamp the misrepresentation as morally culpable; and still less could law presume to interfere with this kind of controversial misconduct. With regard to what is commonly meant by intemperate discussion, namely, invective, sarcasm, personality, and the like, the denunciation of these weapons would deserve more sympathy if it were ever proposed to interdict them equally to both sides; but it is only desired to restrain the employment of them against the prevailing opinion: against the unprevailing they may not only be used without general disapproval, but will be likely to obtain for him who uses them the praise of honest zeal and righteous indignation. Yet whatever mischief arises from their use, is greatest when they are employed against the comparatively defenceless; and whatever unfair advantage can be derived by any opinion from this mode of asserting it, accrues almost exclusively to received opinions. The worst offence of this kind which can be committed by a polemic, is to stigmatize those who hold the contrary opinion as bad and immoral men. To calumny of this sort, those who hold any unpopular opinion are peculiarly exposed, because they are in general few and uninfluential, and nobody but themselves feels much interest in seeing justice done them; but this weapon is, from the nature of the case, denied to those who attack a prevailing opinion: they can neither use it with safety to themselves, nor if they could, would it do anything but recoil on their own cause. In general, opinions contrary to those commonly received can only obtain a hearing by studied moderation of language, and the most cautious avoidance of unnecessary offence, from which they hardly ever deviate even in a slight degree without losing ground: while unmeasured vituperation employed on the side of the prevailing opinion, really does deter people from professing contrary opinions, and from listening to those who profess them. For the interest, therefore, of truth and justice, it is far more important to restrain this employment of vituperative language than the other; and, for example, if it were necessary to choose, there would be much more need to discourage offensive attacks on infidelity, than on religion. It is, however, obvious that law and authority have no business with restraining either, while opinion ought, in every instance, to determine its verdict by the circumstances of the individual case; condemning every one, on whichever side of the argument he places himself, in whose mode of advocacy either want of candour, or malignity, bigotry or intolerance of feeling manifest themselves, but not inferring these vices from the side which a person takes, though it be the contrary side of the question to our own: and giving merited honour to every one, whatever opinion he may hold, who has calmness to see and honesty to state what his opponents and their opinions really are, exaggerating nothing to their discredit, keeping nothing back which tells, or can be supposed to tell, in their favour. This is the real morality of public discussion: and if often violated, I am happy to think that there are many controversialists who to a great extent observeit, and a still greater number who conscientiously strive towards it.

Section II

"Mass Society," Democracy, and Public Opinion

INTRODUCTION

During the first decades of the twentieth century, universal suffrage was introduced in most European countries. An important prerequisite for this was the establishment of compulsory elementary school attendance. Most people were now able to read. The abolishing of illiteracy not only laid the foundation for economic growth and the development of a rational, well-informed public, it also offered new opportunities for manipulating the masses through the successful advertisement-financed popular press and the propaganda of various political groups.

Well into the interwar period, the political left and the conservative elite shared a sceptical view of democracy. While the communist movement considered parliamentary democracy a bourgeois regime, the traditionalist conservatives feared the masses and saw democracy as "mob rule." On the other side, neither the Fascists nor the Nazis feared the "masses" and mobilized them to assume power and liquidate democracy—Mussolini in 1922, Hitler in 1933, and Franco in 1936.

In the USA, the growing tensions between the idea of a public sphere and actual operation of democracy were dramatized in the 1920s in the famous debate between Walter Lippmann and John Dewey in which they advanced distinctively different approaches to democracy and the role of the public. In two influential books, *Public Opinion* (1922) and *The Phantom Public* (1925), Walter Lippmann had developed what he regarded as a "realistic" approach to democracy and the public sphere. During World War I, he had been active in propaganda efforts enthusiastically promoting a war that should "make the world safe for democracy." As a political writer, he was concerned with "the human factor" and the lack of correspondence between "the world outside and the picture in our heads." He soon came to dismiss the conception of the well-informed citizen as an illusion in a mass society. The idea that the mission of informing the citizen could be accomplished by the press was even more of a fiction in Lippmann's view. He therefore reached the conclusion that the task of accomplishing a qualified understanding of public affairs should be left to the experts, to those who were trained it, and a new machinery of knowledge

23

be established in the form of intelligence bureaus staffed by rational and unbiased experts. These intellectual mandarins would provide the basis for rationality among decision makers—who eventually could present their decisions to the voters. The idea of a public sphere and enlightened public discourse as a guide for decision makers, Lippmann regarded as illusion or as a "phantom."

John Dewey's book *The Public and its Problems* (1927) is an implicit response to Lippmann's elitism and pessimism. For him public deliberation has an important role to play in political decision-making and democracy should not be confined to experts and insiders. It is important to note though, that the two are unanimous in their description and critique of the conditions of contemporary democracy. Their deep disagreement on what was to be done was based on their contrasting views on human nature and on what democracy should be. Although Lippmann considered ordinary people as passive, irrational, and selfish, Dewey saw them as creative, rational, and responsible. Lippmann saw democracy as a merely technical form of government whose end was to secure a stable social, political, and economic order, Dewey insisted that democracy was not just a means to and end, but "a way of life," a never-ending, ever-changing process, and argued that the school system should take on the crucial democratic mission of qualifying people to become active participants, not by making them into experts, but by disseminating common knowledge and cultivating their abilities to discuss and judge.

The image of an emerging mass society and the growth of new instruments for "manufacturing of consent" is also a prominent thread in the writings of the Austro-Hungarian economist and political theorist Joseph Schumpeter. During the rise of Nazism, Schumpeter left Germany for the USA, and his theories on "competitive elitism" and "leadership democracy" echo Lippmann's views on human nature and democracy. Schumpeter dismisses what he labels "the classical doctrine of democracy" and its idea of the "common good." The public sphere in Schumpeter's approach is reduced to a market and a competitive arena for elite groups.

In Germany, the legal scholar and political thinker Carl Schmitt criticized parliamentary democracy for being too ineffective, and argued that the faith in rational discussion was unrealistic. Instead, he re-evaluated and legitimized dictatorship: In a modern state, there should be an effective dictatorial element with the right to declare a state of exception, set the laws aside, and use violence in the public interest. In 1933, Schmitt defended Hitler's suspension of the German constitutional order and became a member of the Nazi Party, holding several important offices.

WALTER LIPPMANN

EXCERPT FROM *THE PHANTOM PUBLIC* (1925)

Walter Lippmann (1889–1974) was an influential American editor, political commenta-
tor and public figure. He was a student at Harvard, where his contemporaries included John
Reed, who later produced an eyewitness account of the Bolshevik Revolution. A member of
the Harvard Socialist Club in his youth, Lippmann became more conservative while acting
as a political advisor and journalist. He was active in war-time propaganda and he wrote
Wilson's famous 14 points declaration, which marked the end of World War I. For thirty-
six years, from 1931, he wrote a column, "Today and Tomorrow," which was syndicated
in a wide range of newspapers.

The following excerpt from The Phantom Public *(1925) marks the logical conclu-*
sion of the analysis begun in Public Opinion *(1922) examining the role of "the human*
factor" and perception in politics and decision making. Here, the idea of the sovereign or
"omnicompetent" citizen is replaced by a portrait of the disenchanted man, who "lives in a
world which he cannot see, does not understand and is unable to direct." The citizen in a
modern mass democracy is, according to Lippmann, rather like a deaf spectator in the back
row. She knows very well that the idea of her sovereignty is a fiction, and realizes "in the
cold light of experience" that she will never be able to find time to fulfill the expectations
democratic theory has of her.

Lippmann represents a pessimistic—or in his own phrase "realistic"—approach to de-
mocracy and the public sphere. First, he rejects the conception of the well-informed and
well-experienced citizen as a fiction in a mass society. He then dismisses the idea of a public
sphere and an enlightened discourse as a "phantom." In his view, the task of accomplish-
ing a qualified understanding of public affairs should be left to specialists, and the role of
the public confined to choosing among alternatives. What the public does, according to
Lippmann, is not to express its opinions but to align itself for or against a proposal.

Lippmann has been seen as an elitist, skeptic, and cynic, representing a typical disil-
lusioned inter-war mentality. According to John Dewey, Lippmann gave up on citizens'
participation because of a lack of political imagination and faith in the progressive role of
education. Nevertheless, Lippmann's blunt approach in The Phantom Public *poses impor-*
tant challenges for our understanding of the public sphere.

Chapter I: The Disenchanted Man

1. The private citizen today has come to feel rather like a deaf spectator in the
back row, who ought to keep his mind on the mystery off there, but cannot quite
manage to keep awake. He knows he is somehow affected by what is going on. Rules
and regulations continually, taxes annually and wars occasionally remind him that
he is being swept along by great drifts of circumstance.

Yet these public affairs are in no convincing way his affairs. They are for the most
part invisible. They are managed, if they are managed at all, at distant centers, from
behind the scenes, by unnamed powers. As a private person he does not know for
certain what is going on, or who is doing it, or where he is being carried. No newspaper reports his environment so that he can grasp it; no school has taught him
how to imagine it; his ideals, often, do not fit with it; listening to speeches, uttering

opinions and voting do not, he finds, enable him to govern it. He lives in a world which he cannot see, does not understand and is unable to direct.

In the cold light of experience he knows that his sovereignty is a fiction. He reigns in theory, but in fact he does not govern. Contemplating himself and his actual accomplishments in public affairs, contrasting the influence he exerts with the influence he is supposed according to democratic theory to exert, he must say of his sovereignty what Bismarck said of Napoleon III.: "At a distance it is something, but close to it is nothing at all."[1] When, during an agitation of some sort, say a political campaign, he hears himself and some thirty million others described as the source of all wisdom and power and righteousness, the prime mover and the ultimate goal, the remnants of sanity in him protest. He cannot all the time play Chanticleer who was so dazzled and delighted because he himself had caused the sun to rise.

For when the private man has lived through the romantic age in politics and is no longer moved by the stale echoes of its hot cries, when he is sober and unimpressed, his own part in public affairs appears to him a pretentious thing, a second rate, an inconsequential. You cannot move him then with a good straight talk about service and civic duty, nor by waving a flag in his face, nor by sending a boy scout after him to make him vote. He is a man back home from a crusade to make the world something or other it did not become; he has been tantalized too often by the foam of events, has seen the gas go out of it, and, with sour derision for the stuff, he is saying with the author of *Trivia*:[2]

"'Self-determination,' one of them insisted.

"'Arbitration,' cried another.

"'Cooperation,' suggested the mildest of the party.

"'Confiscation,' answered an uncompromising female.

"I, too, became intoxicated with the sound of these vocables. And were they not the cure for all our ills?

"'Inoculation!' I chimed in. 'Transubstantiation, alliteration, inundation, flagellation, and afforestation!'"

2. It is well known that nothing like the whole people takes part in public affairs. Of the eligible voters in the United States less than half go to the polls even in a presidential year.[3] During the campaign of 1924 a special effort was made to bring out more voters. They did not come out. The Constitution, the nation, the party system, the presidential succession, private property, all were supposed to be in danger. One party prophesied red ruin, another black corruption, a third tyranny and imperialism if the voters did not go to the polls in greater numbers. Half the citizenship was unmoved.

The students used to write books about voting. They are now beginning to write books about nonvoting. At the University of Chicago Professor Merriam and Mr. Gosnell have made an elaborate inquiry[4] into the reason why, at the typical Chicago mayoral election of 1923, there were, out of 1,400,000 eligible electors, only 900,000 who registered, and out of those who registered there were only 723,000 who finally managed to vote. Thousands of persons were interviewed. About 30 per cent of the abstainers had, or at least claimed to have had, an insuperable difficulty about going to the polls. They were ill, they were absent from the city, they were women detained at home by a child or an invalid, they had had insufficient legal residence. The other 70 per cent, representing about half a million free and sovereign citizens of this Republic, did not even pretend to have a reason for not voting, which, in effect, was not an admission that they did not care about voting. They were needed at their work, the polls were crowded, the polls were inconveniently located, they were afraid to tell their age, they did not believe in woman suffrage, the husband objected, politics is rotten, elections are rotten, they were afraid to vote, they did not know there was an election. About a quarter of those who were interviewed had the honesty to say they were wholly uninterested.

Yet Bryce is authority for the statement that "the will of the sovereign people is expressed . . . in the United States . . . by as large a proportion of the registered voters as in any other country."[5] And certainly Mr. Lowell's tables on the use of the initiative and referendum in Switzerland in the main support the view that the indifference of the American voter is not unique.[6] In fact, realistic political thinkers in Europe long ago abandoned the notion that the collective mass of the people direct the course of public affairs. Robert Michels, himself a Socialist, says flatly that "the majority is permanently incapable of self-government,"[7] and quotes approvingly the remark of a Swedish Socialist Deputy, Gustaf F. Steffen, that "even after the victory there will always remain in political life the leaders and the led." Michels, who is a political thinker of great penetration, unburdens himself finally on the subject by printing a remark of Hertzen's that the victory of an opposition party amounts to "passing from the sphere of envy to the sphere of avarice."

There is then nothing particularly new in the disenchantment which the private citizen expresses by not voting at all, by voting only for the head of the ticket, by staying away from the primaries, by not reading speeches and documents, by the whole list of sins of omission for which he is denounced. I shall not denounce him further. My sympathies are with him, for I believe that he has been saddled with an impossible task and that he is asked to practice an unattainable ideal. I find it so myself for, although public business is my main interest and I give most of my time to watching it, I cannot find time to do what is expected of me in the theory of democracy; that is, to know what is going on and to have an opinion worth expressing on every question which confronts a self-governing community. And I have not happened to meet anybody, from a President of the United States to a professor of political science, who came anywhere near to embodying the accepted ideal of the sovereign and omnicompetent citizen.

Chapter II: The Unattainable Ideal

I have tried to imagine how the perfect citizen could be produced. Some say he will have to be born of the conjunction of the right germ plasms, and, in the pages of books written by Madison Grant, Lothrop Stoddard and other revivalists, I have seen prescriptions as to just who ought to marry whom to produce a great citizenry. Not being a biologist I keep an open but hopeful mind on this point, tempered, however, with the knowledge that certainty about how to breed ability in human beings is on the whole in inverse proportion to the writer's scientific reputation.

It is then to education that logically one turns next, for education has furnished the thesis of the last chapter of every optimistic book on democracy written for one hundred and fifty years. Even Robert Michels, stern and unbending antisentimentalist that he is, says in his "final considerations" that "it is the great task of social education to raise the intellectual level of the masses, so that they may be enabled, within the limits of what is possible, to counteract the oligarchical tendencies" of all collective action.

So I have been reading some of the new standard textbooks used to teach citizenship in schools and colleges. After reading them I do not see how any one can escape the conclusion that man must have the appetite of an encyclopædist and infinite time ahead of him. To be sure he no longer is expected to remember the exact salary of the county clerk and the length of the coroner's term. In the new civics he studies the problems of government, and not the structural detail. He is told, in one textbook of five hundred concise, contentious pages, which I have been reading, about city problems, state problems, national problems, international problems, trust problems, labor problems, transportation problems, banking problems, rural problems, agricultural problems, and so on *ad infinitum*. In the eleven pages devoted to problems of the city there are described twelve sub-problems.

But nowhere in this well-meant book is the sovereign citizen of the future given a hint as to how, while he is earning a living, rearing children and enjoying his life, he is to keep himself informed about the progress of this swarming confusion of problems. He is exhorted to conserve the natural resources of the country because they are limited in quantity. He is advised to watch public expenditures because the taxpayers cannot pay out indefinitely increasing amounts. But he, the voter, the citizen, the sovereign, is apparently expected to yield an unlimited quantity of public spirit, interest, curiosity and effort. The author of the textbook, touching on everything, as he thinks, from city sewers to Indian opium, misses a decisive fact: the citizen gives but a little of his time to public affairs, has but a casual interest in facts and but a poor appetite for theory.

It never occurs to this preceptor of civic duty to provide the student with a rule by which he can know whether on Thursday it is his duty to consider subways in Brooklyn or the Manchurian Railway, nor how, if he determines on Thursday to express his sovereign will on the subway question, he is to repair those gaps in his knowledge of that question which are due to his having been preoccupied the day before in expressing his sovereign will about rural credits in Montana and the rights of Britain in the Sudan. Yet he cannot know all about everything all the time, and while he is watching one thing a thousand others undergo great changes. Unless he can discover some rational ground for fixing his attention where it will do the most good, and in a way that suits his inherently amateurish equipment, he will be as bewildered as a puppy trying to lick three bones at once.

I do not wish to say that it does the student no good to be taken on a sightseeing tour of the problems of the world. It may teach him that the world is complicated, even if he comes out of the adventure "laden with germs, breathing creeds and convictions on you whenever he opens his mouth."[8] He may learn humility, but most certainly his acquaintance with what a high-minded author thought were American problems in 1925 will not equip him to master American problems ten years later. Unless out of the study of transient issues he acquires an intellectual attitude no education has occurred.

That is why the usual appeal to education as the remedy for the incompetence of democracy is so barren. It is, in effect, a proposal that school teachers shall by some magic of their own fit men to govern after the makers of laws and the preachers of civic ideals have had a free hand in writing the specifications. The reformers do not ask what men can be taught. They say they should be taught whatever may be necessary to fit them to govern the modern world.

The usual appeal to education can bring only disappointment. For the problems of the modern world appear and change faster than any set of teachers can grasp them, much faster than they can convey their substance to a population of children. If the schools attempt to teach children how to solve the problems of the day, they are bound always to be in arrears. The most they can conceivably attempt is the teaching of a pattern of thought and feeling which will enable the citizen to approach a new problem in some useful fashion. But that pattern cannot be invented by the pedagogue. It is the political theorist's business to trace out that pattern. In that task he must not assume that the mass has political genius, but that men, even if they had genius, would give only a little time and attention to public affairs.

The moralist, I am afraid, will agree all too readily with the idea that social education must deal primarily not with the elements and solutions of particular phases of transient problems but with the principles that constitute an attitude toward all problems. I warn him off. It will require more than a good conscience to govern modern society, for conscience is no guide in situations where the essence of the difficulty is to find a guide for the conscience.

When I am tempted to think that men can be fitted out to deal with the modern world simply by teaching morals, manners and patriotism, I try to remember the fable of the pensive professor walking in the woods at twilight. He stumbled into a tree. This experience compelled him to act. Being a man of honor and breeding, he raised his hat, bowed deeply to the tree, and exclaimed with sincere regret: "Excuse me, sir, I thought you were a tree."

Is it fair, I ask, as a matter of morality, to chide him for his conduct? If he had encountered a tree, can any one deny his right to collide with it? If he had stumbled into a man, was his apology not sufficient? Here was a moral code in perfect working order, and the only questionable aspect of his conduct turned not on the goodness of his heart or the firmness of his principles but on a point of fact. You may retort that he had a moral obligation to know the difference between a man and a tree. Perhaps so. But suppose that instead of walking in the woods he had been casting a ballot; suppose that instead of a tree he had encountered the Fordney-McCumber tariff. How much more obligation to know the truth would you have imposed on him then? After all, this walker in the woods at twilight with his mind on other things was facing, as all of us think we are, the facts he imagined were there, and was doing his duty as he had learned it.

In some degree the whole animate world seems to share the inexpertness of the thoughtful professor. Pawlow showed by his experiments on dogs that an animal with a false stomach can experience all the pleasures of eating, and the number of mice and monkeys known to have been deceived in laboratories is surpassed only by the hopeful citizens of a democracy. Man's reflexes are, as the psychologists say, conditioned. And, therefore, he responds quite readily to a glass egg, a decoy duck, a stuffed shirt or a political platform. No moral code, as such, will enable him to know whether he is exercising his moral faculties on a real and an important event. For effective virtue, as Socrates pointed out long ago, is knowledge; and a code of the right and the wrong must wait upon a perception of the true and the false.

But even the successful practice of a moral code would not emancipate democracy. There are too many moral codes. In our immediate lives, within the boundaries of our own society, there may be commonly accepted standards. But a political theorist who asks that a local standard be universally applied is merely begging one of the questions he ought to be trying to solve. For, while possibly it may be an aim of political organization to arrive at a common standard of judgment, one of the conditions which engenders politics and makes political organization necessary is the conflict of standards.

Darwin's story of the cats and clover[9] may be recommended to any one who finds it difficult to free his mind of the assumption that his notions of good and bad are universal. The purple clover is cross-fertilized by the bumblebee, and, therefore, the more bumblebees the better next year's crop of clover. But the nests of bumblebees are rifled by field mice which are fond of the white grubs. Therefore, the more field mice the fewer bumblebees and the poorer the crop. But in the neighborhood of villages the cats hunt down the field mice. And so the more cats the fewer mice, the more bumblebees the better the crop. And the more kindly old ladies there are in the village the more cats there will be.

If you happen not to be a Hindu or a vegetarian and are a beef-eating Occidental you will commend the old ladies who keep the cats who hunt the mice who destroy the bumblebees who make the pasture of clover for the cattle. If you are a cat you also will be in favor of the old ladies. But if you are a field mouse, how different the rights and wrongs of that section of the universe! The old ladies who keep cats will seem about as kindly as witches with pet tigers, and the Old Lady Peril will be debated hysterically by the Field Mouse Security League. For what could a patriotic mouse think of a world in which bumblebees did not exist for the sole purpose of producing white grubs for field mice? There would seem to be no law and order in such a world; and only a highly philosophical mouse would admit with Bergson that "the idea of disorder objectifies for the convenience of language, the disappointment of a mind that finds before it an order different from what it wants."[10] For the order which we recognize as good is an order suited to our needs and hopes and habits.

There is nothing universal or eternal or unchangeable about our expectations. For rhetorical effect we often say there is. But in concrete cases it is not easy to explain why the thing we desire is so righteous. If the farmers are able to buy less than their accustomed amount of manufactured foods there is disorder and a problem. But what absolute standard is there which determines whether a bushel of wheat in 1925 should, as compared with 1913, exchange for more, as many, or less manufactures? Can any one define a principle which shall say whether the standard of living of the farmers or of any other class should rise or fall, and how fast and how much? There may be more jobs than workingmen at the wage offered: the employers will complain and will call it a problem, but who knows any rule which tells how large a surplus of labor there ought to be and at what price? There may be more workingmen than jobs of the kind and at the places and for the wages they will or can take. But, although the problem will be acute, there is no principle which determines how many machinists, clerks, coal miners, bankers, or salesmen it is the duty of society to provide work for.

It requires intense partisanship and much self-deception to argue that some sort of peculiar righteousness adheres to the farmers' claims as against the manufacturers', the employers' against the wage-earners', the creditors' against the debtors', or the other way around. These conflicts of interest are problems. They require solution. But there is no moral pattern available from which the precise nature of the solution can be deduced.

If then eugenics cannot produce the ideal democratic citizen, omnicompetent and sovereign, because biology knows neither how to breed political excellence nor what that excellence is; if education cannot equip the citizen, because the school teacher cannot anticipate the issues of the future; if morality cannot direct him, first, because right or wrong in specific cases depends upon the perception of true or false, and, second, on the assumption that there is a universal moral code, which, in fact, does not exist, where else shall we look for the method of making the competent citizen? Democratic theorists in the nineteenth century had several other prescriptions which still influence the thinking of many hopeful persons.

One school based their reforms on the aphorism that the cure for the evils of democracy is more democracy. It was assumed that the popular will was wise and good if only you could get at it. They proposed extensions of the suffrage, and as much voting as possible by means of the initiative, referendum and recall, direct election of Senators, direct primaries, an elected judiciary, and the like. They begged the question, for it has never been proved that there exists the kind of public opinion which they presupposed. Since the Bryan campaign of 1896 this school of thought has made great conquests in most of the states, and has profoundly influenced the federal government. The eligible vote has trebled since 1896; the direct action of the voter has been enormously extended. Yet that same period has seen a decline in the percentage of the popular vote cast at presidential elections from 80.75 per cent in 1896 to 52.36 per cent in 1920. Apparently there is a fallacy in the first assumption of this school that "the whole people" desires to participate actively in government. Nor is there any evidence to show that the persons who do participate are in any real sense directing the course of affairs. The party machines have survived every attack. And why should they not? If the voter cannot grasp the details of the problems of the day because he has not the time, the interest or the knowledge, he will not have a better public opinion because he is asked to express his opinion more often. He will simply be more bewildered, more bored and more ready to follow along.

Another school, calling themselves revolutionary, have ascribed the disenchantment of democracy to the capitalistic system. They have argued that property is power, and that until there is as wide a distribution of economic power as there is of the right to vote the suffrage cannot be more effective. No serious student, I think, would dispute that socialist premise which asserts that the weight of influence on society exercised by an individual is more nearly related to the character of his property than to his abstract legal citizenship. But the socialist conclusion that economic power can be distributed by concentrating the ownership of great utilities in the state, the conclusion that the pervasion of industrial life by voting and referenda will yield competent popular decisions, seems to me again to beg the question. For what reason is there to think that subjecting so many more affairs to the method of the vote will reveal hitherto undiscovered wisdom and technical competence and reservoirs of public interest in men? The socialist scheme has at its root the mystical fallacy of democracy, that the people, all of them, are competent; at its top it suffers from the homeopathic fallacy that adding new tasks to a burden the people will not and cannot carry now will make the burden of citizenship easily borne. The socialist theory presupposes an unceasing, untiring round of civic duties, an enormous complication of the political interests that are already much too complicated.

These various remedies, eugenic, educational, ethical, populist and socialist, all assume that either the voters are inherently competent to direct the course of affairs or that they are making progress toward such a ideal. I think it is a false ideal. I do not mean an undesirable ideal. I mean an unattainable ideal, bad only in the sense that it is bad for a fat man to try to be a ballet dancer. An ideal should express the true possibilities of its subject. When it does not it perverts the true possibilities. The ideal of the omnicompetent, sovereign citizen is, in my opinion, such a false ideal. It is unattainable. The pursuit of it is misleading. The failure to achieve it has produced the current disenchantment.

The individual man does not have opinions on all public affairs. He does not know how to direct public affairs. He does not know what is happening, why it is happening, what ought to happen. I cannot imagine how he could know, and there is not the least reason for thinking, as mystical democrats have thought, that the compounding of individual ignorances in masses of people can produce a continuous directing force in public affairs.

Chapter III: Agents and Bystanders

1. When a citizen has qualified as a voter he finds himself one of the theoretical rulers of a great going concern. He has not made the complicated machine with its five hundred thousand federal officers and its uncounted local offices. He has not seen much of it. He is bound by contracts, by debts, by treaties, by laws, made before he was aware of them. He does not from day to day decide who shall do what in the business of government. Only some small fraction of it comes intermittently to his notice. And in those episodic moments when he stands in the polling booth he is a highly intelligent and public-spirited voter indeed who can discover two real alternatives and enlist his influence for a party which promises something he can understand.

The actual governing is made up of a multitude of arrangements on specific questions by particular individuals. These rarely become visible to the private citizen. Government, in the long intervals between elections, is carried on by politicians, officeholders and influential men who make settlements with other politicians, officeholders and influential men. The mass of people see these settlements, judge them, and affect them only now and then. They are altogether too numerous, too complicated, too obscure in their effects to become the subject of any continuing exercise of public opinion.

Nor in any exact and literal sense are those who conduct the daily business of government accountable after the fact to the great mass of the voters. They are accountable only, except in spectacular cases, to the other politicians, officeholders and influential men directly interested in the particular act.

Modern society is not visible to anybody, nor intelligible continuously and as a whole. One section is visible to another section, one series of acts is intelligible to this group and another to that.

Even this degree of responsible understanding is attainable only by the development of fact-finding agencies of great scope and complexity.[11] These agencies give only a remote and incidental assistance to the general public. Their findings are too intricate for the casual reader. They are also almost always much too uninteresting. Indeed the popular boredom and contempt for the expert and for statistical measurement are such that the organization of intelligence to administer modern affairs would probably be entirely neglected were it not that departments of government, corporations, trade unions and trade associations are being compelled by their own internal necessities of administration, and by compulsion of other corporate groups, to record their own acts, measure them, publish them and stand accountable for them.

The need in the Great Society not only for publicity but for uninterrupted publicity is indisputable. But we shall misunderstand the need seriously if we imagine that the purpose of the publication can possibly be the informing of every voter. We live at the mere beginnings of public accounting. Yet the facts far exceed our curiosity. The railroads, for example, make an accounting. Do we read the results? Hardly. A few executives here and there, some bankers, some regulating officials, some representatives of shippers and the like read them. The rest of us ignore them for the good and sufficient reason that we have other things to do.

For the man does not live who can read all the reports that drift across his doorstep or all the dispatches in his newspaper. And if by some development of the radio every man could see and hear all that was happening everywhere, if publicity, in other words, became absolute, how much time could or would he spend watching the Sinking Fund Commission and the Geological Survey? He would probably tune in on the Prince of Wales, or, in desperation, throw off the switch and seek peace in ignorance. It is bad enough today—with morning newspapers published in the evening and evening newspapers in the morning, with October magazines in September, with the movies and the radio—to be condemned to live under a barrage of eclectic information, to have one's mind made the receptacle for a hullabaloo of speeches, arguments and unrelated episodes. General information for the informing of public opinion is altogether too general for intellectual decency. And life is too short for the pursuit of omniscience by the counting in a state of nervous excitement of all the leaves on all the trees.

2. If all men had to conceive the whole process of government all the time the world's work would obviously never be carried on. Men make no attempt to consider society as a whole. The farmer decides whether to plant wheat or corn, the mechanic whether to take the job offered at the Pennsylvania or the Erie shops, whether to buy a Ford or a piano, and, if a Ford, whether to buy it from the garage on Elm Street or from the dealer who sent him a circular. These decisions are among fairly narrow choices offered to him; he can no more choose among all the jobs in the world than he can consider marrying any woman in the world. These choices in detail are in their cumulative mass the government of society. They may rest on ignorant or enlightened opinions, but, whether he comes to them by accident or scientific instruction, they are specific and particular among at best a few concrete alternatives and they lead to a definite, visible result.

But men are supposed also to hold public opinions about the general conduct of society. The mechanic is supposed not only to choose between working for the

Pennsylvania or the Erie but to decide how in the interests of the nation all the railroads of the country shall be regulated. The two kinds of opinion merge insensibly one into the other; men have general notions which influence their individual decisions and their direct experiences unconsciously govern their general notions. Yet it is useful to distinguish between the two kinds of opinion, the specific and direct, the general and the indirect.

Specific opinions give rise to immediate executive acts; to take a job, to do a particular piece of work, to hire or fire, to buy or sell, to stay here or go there, to accept or refuse, to command or obey. General opinions give rise to delegated, indirect, symbolic, intangible results: to a vote, to a resolution, to applause, to criticism, to praise or dispraise, to audiences, circulations, followings, contentment or discontent. The specific opinion may lead to a decision to act within the area where a man has personal jurisdiction that is, within the limits set by law and custom, his personal power and his personal desire. But general opinions lead only to some sort of expression, such as voting, and do not result in executive acts except in cooperation with the general opinions of large numbers of other persons.

Since the general opinions of large numbers of persons are almost certain to be a vague and confusing medley, action cannot be taken until these opinions have been factored down, canalized, compressed and made uniform. The making of one general will out of a multitude of general wishes is not an Hegelian mystery, as so many social philosophers have imagined, but an art well known to leaders, politicians and steering committees[12] It consists essentially in the use of symbols which assemble emotions after they have been detached from their ideas. Because feelings are much less specific than ideas, and yet more poignant, the leader is able to make a homogeneous will out of a heterogeneous mass of desires. The process, therefore, by which general opinions are brought to cooperation consists of an intensification of feeling and a degradation of significance. Before a mass of general opinions can eventuate in executive action, the choice is narrowed down to a few alternatives. The victorious alternative is executed not by the mass but by individuals in control of its energy.

A private opinion may be quite complicated, and may issue in quite complicated actions, in a whole train of subsidiary opinions, as when a man decides to build a house and then makes a hundred judgments as to how it shall be built. But a public opinion has no such immediate responsibility or continuous result. It leads in politics to the making of a pencil mark on a piece of paper, and then to a period of waiting and watching as to whether one or two years hence the mark shall be made in the same column or in the adjoining one. The decision to make the mark may be for reasons $a^1, a^2, a^3 \ldots a^n$: the result, whether an idiot or genius has voted, is A.

For great masses of people, though each of them may have more or less distinct views, must when they act converge to an identical result. And the more complex the collection of men the more ambiguous must be the unity and the simpler the common ideas.

3. In English-speaking countries during the last century the contrast between the action of men individually and in the mass has been much emphasized, and yet greatly misunderstood. Macaulay, for example, speaking on the Reform Bill of 1832, drew the conventional distinction between private enterprise and public action:

"In all those things which depend on the intelligence, the knowledge, the industry, the energy of individuals, this country stands preeminent among all countries of the world ancient and modern. But in those things which it belongs to the state to direct we have no such claim to superiority . . . can there be a stronger contrast than that which exists between the beauty, the completeness, the speed, the precision with which every process is performed in our factories, and the awkwardness, the crudeness, the slowness, the uncertainty of the apparatus by which offenses are punished and rights vindicated? . . . Surely we see the barbarism of the Thirteenth Century and the highest civilization of the Nineteenth Century side by side, and we see that the barbarism belongs to the government, and the civilization to the people."[13]

Macaulay was, of course, thinking of the contrast between factory production and government as it existed in England under Queen Victoria's uncles and the hard-drinking, hard-riding squirearchy. But the Prussian bureaucracy amply demonstrated that there is no such necessary contrast between governmental and private action. There is a contrast between action by and through great masses of people and action that moves without them.

The fundamental contrast is not between public and private enterprises, between "crowd" psychology and individual, but between men doing specific things and men attempting to command general results. The work of the world is carried on by men in their executive capacity, by an infinite number of concrete acts, plowing and planting and reaping, building and destroying, fitting this to that, going from here to there, transforming A into B and moving B from X to Y. The relationships between the individuals doing these specific things are balanced by a most intricate mechanism of exchange, of contract, of custom and of implied promises. Where men are performing their work they must learn to understand the process and the substance of these obligations if they are to it at all. But in governing the work of other men by votes or by the expression of opinion they can only reward or punish a result, accept or reject alternatives presented to them. They can say yes or no to something which has been done, yes or no to a proposal, but they cannot create, administer and actually perform the act they have in mind. Persons uttering public opinions may now and then be able to define the acts of men, but their opinions do not execute these acts.

4. To the realm of executive acts, each of us, as a member of the public, remains always external. Our public opinions are always and forever, by their very nature, an attempt to control the actions of others from the outside. If we can grasp the full significance of that conclusion we shall, I think, have found a way of fixing the rôle of public opinion in its true perspective; we shall know how to account for the disenchantment of democracy, and we shall begin to see the outline of an ideal of public opinion which, unlike that accepted in the dogma of democracy, may be really attainable.

Chapter IV: What the Public Does

1. I do not mean to say that there is no other attainable ideal of public opinion but that severely practical one which this essay is meant to disclose. One might aim to enrich the minds of men with charming fantasies, animate nature and society with spirits, set up an Olympus in the skies and an Atlantis at the end of the world. And one might then assert that, so the quality of ideas be fine or give peace, it does not matter how or whether they eventuate in the government of affairs.

Utopia and Nirvana are by definition their own sufficient reason, and it may be that to contemplate them is well worth the abandonment of feeble attempts to control the action of events. Renunciation, however, is a luxury in which all men cannot indulge. They will somehow seek to control the behavior of others, if not by positive law then at least by persuasion. When men are in that posture toward events they are a public, as I am here defining the term; their opinions as to how others ought to behave are public opinions. The more clearly it is understood what the public can do and what it cannot, the more effectively it will do what lies within its power to do well and the less it will interfere with the liberties of men.

The rôle of public opinion is determined by the fact that its relation to a problem is external. The opinion affects an opinion, but does not itself control the executive act. A public opinion is expressed by a vote, a demonstration of praise or blame, a following or a boycotting. But these manifestations are in themselves nothing. They count only if they influence the course of affairs. They influence it, however, only if they influence an actor in the affair. And it is, I believe, precisely in this secondary, indirect relationship between public opinion and public affairs that we have the clue to the limits and the possibilities of public opinion.

2. It may be objected at once that an election which turns one set of men out of office and installs another is an expression of public opinion which is neither secondary nor indirect. But what in fact is an election? We call it an expression of the popular will. But is it? We go into a polling booth and mark a cross on a piece of paper for one of two, or perhaps three or four names. Have we expressed our thoughts on the public policy of the United States? Presumably we have a number of thoughts on this and that with many buts and ifs and ors. Surely the cross on a piece of paper does not express them. It would take us hours to express our thoughts, and calling a vote the expression of our mind is an empty fiction.

A vote is a promise of support. It is away of saying: I am lined up with these men, on this side. I enlist with them. I will follow. I will buy. I will boycott. I will strike. I applaud. I jeer. The force I can exert is placed here, not there.

The public does not select the candidate, write the platform, outline the policy any more than it builds the automobile or acts the play. It aligns itself for or against somebody who has offered himself, has made a promise, has produced a play, is selling an automobile. The action of a group as a group is the mobilization of the force it possesses.

The attempt has been made to ascribe some intrinsic moral and intellectual virtue to majority rule. It was said often in the nineteenth century that there was a deep wisdom in majorities which was the voice of God. Sometimes this flattery was a sincere mysticism, sometimes it was the self-deception which always accompanies the idealization of power. In substance it was nothing but a transfer to the new sovereign of the divine attributes of kings. Yet the inherent absurdity of making virtue and wisdom dependent on 51 per cent of any collection of men has always been apparent. The practical realization that the claim was absurd has resulted in a whole code of civil rights to protect minorities and in all sorts of elaborate methods of subsidizing the arts and sciences and other human interests so they might be independent of the operation of majority rule.

The justification of majority rule in politics is not to be found in its ethical superiority. It is to be found in the sheer necessity of finding a place in civilized society for the force which resides in the weight of numbers. I have called voting an act of enlistment, an alignment for or against, a mobilization. These are military metaphors, and rightly so, I think, for an election based on the principle of majority rule is historically and practically a sublimated and denatured civil war, a paper mobilization without physical violence.

Constitutional democrats, in the intervals when they were not idealizing the majority, have acknowledged that a ballot was a civilized substitute for a bullet. "The French Revolution," says Bernard Shaw, "overthrew one set of rulers and substituted another with different interests and different views. That is what a general election enables the people to do in England every seven years if they choose. Revolution is therefore a national institution in England; and its advocacy by an Englishman needs no apology."[14] It makes an enormous difference, of course, whether the people fight or vote, but we shall understand the nature of voting better if we recognize it to be a substitute for fighting. "There grew up in the 17th and 18th Centuries in England," says Dwight Morrow in his introduction to Professor Morse's book, "and there has been carried from England to almost every civilized government in the world, a procedure through which party government becomes in large measure a substitute for revolution."[15] Hans Delbrück puts the matter simply when he says that the principle of majority rule is "a purely practical principle. If one wants to avoid a civil war, one lets those rule who in any case would obtain the upper hand if there should be a struggle; and they are the superior numbers."[16]

But, while an election is in essence sublimated warfare, we must take care not to miss the importance of the sublimation. There have been pedantic theorists who wished to disqualify all who could not bear arms, and woman suffrage has been deplored as a falsification of the value of an election in uncovering the alignment of martial force in the community. One can safely ignore such theorizing. For, while the institution of an election is in its historical origins an alignment of the physical force, it has come to be an aligns of force. It remains an alignment, though in advanced democracies it has lost most of its primitive association with military combat. It has not lost it in the South where the Negro population is disfranchised by force, and not permitted to make its weight felt in an election. It has not lost it in the unstable Latin American republics where every election is in some measure still an armed revolution. In fact, the United States has officially recognized this truth by proclaiming that the substitution of election for revolution in Central America is the test of political progress.

I do not wish to labor the argument any further than may be necessary to establish the theory that what the public does is not to express its opinions but to align itself for or against a proposal. If that theory is accepted, we must abandon the notion that democratic government can be the direct expression of the will of the people. We must abandon the notion that the people govern. Instead we must adopt the theory that, by their occasional mobilizations as a majority, people support or oppose the individuals who actually govern. We must say that the popular will does not direct continuously but that it intervenes occasionally.

Chapter V: The Neutralization of Arbitrary Force

1. If this is the nature of public action, what ideal can be formulated which shall conform to it?

We are bound, I think, to express the ideal in its lowest terms, to state it not as an ideal which might conceivably be realized by exceptional groups now and then or in some distant future but as an ideal which normally might be taught and attained. In estimating the burden which a public can carry, a sound political theory must insist upon the largest factor of safety. It must understate the possibilities of public action.

The action of a public, we had concluded, is principally confined to an occasional intervention in affairs by means of an alignment of the force which a dominant section of that public can wield. We must assume, then, that the members of a public will not possess an insider's knowledge of events or share his point of view. They cannot, therefore, construe intent, or appraise the exact circumstances, enter intimately into the minds of the actors or into the details of the argument. They can watch only for coarse signs indicating where their sympathies ought to turn.

We must assume that the members of a public will not anticipate a problem much before its crisis has become obvious, nor stay with the problem long after its crisis is past. They will not know the antecedent events, will not have seen the issue as it developed, will not have thought out or willed a program, and will not be able to predict the consequences of acting on that program. We must assume as a theoretically fixed premise of popular government that normally men as members of a public will not be well informed, continuously interested, nonpartisan, creative or executive. We must assume that a public is inexpert in its curiosity, intermittent, that it discerns only gross distinctions, is slow to be aroused and quickly diverted; that, since it acts by aligning itself, it personalizes whatever it considers, and is interested only when events have been melodramatized as a conflict.

The public will arrive in the middle of the third act and will leave before the last curtain, having stayed just long enough perhaps to decide who is the hero and who the villain of the piece. Yet usually that judgment will necessarily be made apart from the intrinsic merits, on the basis of a sample of behavior, an aspect of a situation, by very rough external evidence.

We cannot, then, think of public opinion as a conserving or creating force directing society to clearly conceived ends, making deliberately toward socialism or away from it, toward nationalism, an empire, a league of nations or any other doctrinal goal. For men do not agree as to their aims, and it is precisely the lack of agreement which creates the problems that excite public attention. It is idle, then, to argue that though men evidently have conflicting purposes, mankind has some all-embracing purpose of which you or I happen to be the authorized spokesman. We merely should have moved in a circle were we to conclude that the public is in some deep way a messianic force.

2. The work of the world goes on continually without conscious direction from public opinion. At certain junctures problems arise. It is only with the crises of some of these problems that public opinion is concerned. And its object in dealing with a crisis is to help allay that crisis.

I think this conclusion is unescapable. For though we may prefer to believe that the aim of popular action should be to do justice or promote the true, the beautiful and the good, the belief will not maintain itself in the face of plain experience. The public does not know in most crises what specifically is the truth or the justice of the case, and men are not agreed on what is beautiful and good. Nor does the public rouse itself normally at the existence of evil. It is aroused at evil made manifest by the interruption of a habitual process of life. And finally, a problem ceases to occupy attention not when justice, as we happen to define it, has been done but when a workable adjustment that overcomes the crisis has been made. If all this were not the necessary manner of public opinion, if it had seriously to crusade for justice in every issue it touches, the public would have to be dealing with all situations all the time. That is impossible. It is also undesirable. For did justice, truth, goodness and beauty depend on the spasmodic and crude interventions of public opinion there would be little hope for them in this world.

Thus we strip public opinion of any implied duty to deal with the substance of a problem, to make technical decisions, to attempt justice or impose a moral precept. And instead we say that the ideal of public opinion is to align men during the crisis of a problem in such a way as to favor the action of those individuals who may be able to compose the crisis. The power to discern those individuals is the end of the effort to educate public opinion. The aim of research designed to facilitate public action is the discovery of clear signs by which these individuals may be discerned.

The signs are relevant when they reveal by coarse, simple and objective tests which side in a controversy upholds a workable social rule, or which is attacking an unworkable rule, or which proposes a promising new rule. By following such signs the public might know where to align itself. In such an alignment it does not, let us remember, pass judgment on the intrinsic merits. It merely places its force at the disposal of the side which, according to objective signs, seems to be standing for human adjustments according to a clear rule of behavior and against the side which appears to stand for settlement in accordance with its own unaccountable will.

Public opinion, in this theory, is a reserve of force brought into action during a crisis in public affairs. Though it is itself an irrational force, under favorable institutions, sound leadership and decent training the power of public opinion might be placed at the disposal of those who stood for workable law as against brute assertion. In this theory, public opinion does not make the law. But by canceling lawless power it may establish the condition under which law can be made. It does not reason, investigate, invent, persuade, bargain or settle. But, by holding the aggressive party in check, it may liberate intelligence. Public opinion in its highest ideal will defend those who are prepared to act on their reason against the interrupting force of those who merely assert their will.

The action of public opinion at its best would not, let it be noted, be a continual crusade on behalf of reason. When power, however absolute and unaccountable, reigns without provoking a crisis, public opinion does not challenge it. Somebody must challenge arbitrary power first. The public can only come to his assistance.

3. That, I think, is the utmost that public opinion can effectively do. With the substance of the problem it can do nothing usually but meddle ignorantly or tyrannically. It has no need to meddle with it. Men in their active relation to affairs have to deal with the substance, but in that indirect relationship when they can act only through uttering praise or blame, making black crosses on white paper, they have done enough, they have done all they can do if they help to make it possible for the reason of other men to assert itself.

For when public opinion attempts to govern directly it is either a failure or a tyranny. It is not able to master the problem intellectually, nor to deal with it except by wholesale impact. The theory of democracy has not recognized this truth because it has identified the functioning of government with the will of the people. This is a fiction. The intricate business of framing laws and of administering them through several hundred thousand public officials is in no sense the act of the voters nor a translation of their will.

But although the acts of government are not a translation of public opinion, the principal function of government is to do specifically, in greater detail, and more continually what public opinion does crudely, by wholesale, and spasmodically. It enforces some of the working rules of society. It interprets them. It detects and punishes certain kinds of aggression. It presides over the framing of new rules. It has organized force which is used to counteract irregular force.

It is also subject to the same corruption as public opinion. For when government attempts to impose the will of its officials, instead of intervening so as to steady adjustments by consent among the parties directly interested, it becomes heavy-handed, stupid, imperious, even predatory. For the public official, though he is better placed to understand the problem than a reader of newspapers, and though he is much better able to act, is still fundamentally external to the real problems in which he intervenes. Being external, his point of view is indirect, and so his action is most appropriate when it is confined to rendering indirect assistance to those who are directly responsible.

Therefore, instead of describing government as an expression of the people's will, it would seem better to say that government consists of a body of officials, some elected, some appointed, who handle professionally, and in the first instance, problems which come to public opinion spasmodically and on appeal. Where the parties directly responsible do not work out an adjustment, public officials intervene. When the officials fail, public opinion is brought to bear on the issue.

4. This, then, is the ideal of public action which our inquiry suggests. Those who happen in any question to constitute the public should attempt only to create an equilibrium in which settlements can be reached directly and by consent. The burden of carrying on the work of the world, of inventing, creating, executing, of attempting justice, formulating laws and moral codes, of dealing with the technic and the substance, lies not upon public opinion and not upon government but on those who are responsibly concerned as agents in the affair. Where problems arise, the ideal is a settlement by the particular interests involved. They alone know what the trouble really is. No decision by public officials or by commuters reading headlines in the train can usually and in the long run be so good as settlement by consent among the parties at interest. No moral code, no political theory can usually and in the long run be imposed from the heights of public opinion, which will fit a case so well as direct agreement reached where arbitrary power has been disarmed.

It is the function of public opinion to check the use of force in a crisis, so that men, driven to make terms, may live and let live.

Chapter VI: The Question Aristotle Asked

These conclusions are sharply at variance with the accepted theory of popular government. That theory rests upon the belief that there is a public which directs the course of events. I hold that this public is a mere phantom. It is an abstraction. The public in respect to a railroad strike may be the farmers whom the railroad serves;

the public in respect to an agricultural tariff may include the very railroad men who were on strike. The public is not, as I see it, a fixed body of individuals. It is merely those persons who are interested in an affair and can affect it only by supporting or opposing the actors.

Since these random publics cannot be expected to deal with the merits of a controversy, they can give their support with reasonable assurance that it will do good only if there are easily recognizable and yet pertinent signs which they can follow. Are there such signs? Can they be discovered? Can they be formulated so they might be learned and used? The chapters of this second part are an attempt to answer these questions.

The signs must be of such a character that they can be recognized without any substantial insight into the substance of a problem. Yet they must be relevant to the solution of the problem. They must be signs which will tell the members of a public where they can best align themselves so as to promote the solution. In short, they must be guides to reasonable action for the use of uninformed people.

The environment is complex. Man's political capacity is simple. Can a bridge be built between them? The question has haunted political science ever since Aristotle first formulated it in the great seventh book of his *Politics.* He answered it by saying that the community must be kept simple and small enough to suit the faculties of its citizens. We who live in the Great Society are unable to follow his advice. The orthodox democrats answered Aristotle's question by assuming that a limitless political capacity resides in public opinion. A century of experience compels us to deny this assumption. For us, then, the old question is unanswered; we can neither reject the Great Society as Aristotle did, nor exaggerate the political capacity of the citizen as the democrats did. We are forced to ask whether it is possible for men to find a way of acting effectively upon highly complex affairs by very simple means.

I venture to think that this problem may be soluble, that principles can be elucidated which might effect a successful junction between the intricacies of the environment and the simplicities of human faculty. It goes without saying that what I shall present here is no final statement of these principles. At most and at best it may be a clue, with some illustrations, that can be developed by research. But even that much assurance seems to me rash in the light of the difficulties which the problem has always presented, and so, following Descartes, I add that "after all, it is possible I may be mistaken; and it is but a little copper and glass I take for gold and diamonds."[17]

NOTES

1. Cited Philip Guedalla, *The Second Empire.*
2. Logan Pearsall Smith, *More Trivia*, p. 41.
3. *Cf.* Simon Michelet, *Stay-at-Home Vote and Absentee Voters,* pamphlet of the National Get Out the Vote Club; also A. M. Schlesinger and E. M. Erickson, "The Vanishing Voter," *New Republic,* Oct. 15, 1924. The percentage of the popular to the eligible vote from 1865 to 1920 declined from 83.51 per cent to 52.36 per cent.
4. Charles Edward Merriam and Harvey Foote Gosnell, *Non-Voting: Causes and Methods of Control.*
5. James Bryce, *Modern Democracies,* Vol. II, p. 52.

6. A. Lawrence Lowell, *Public Opinion and Popular Government.* Cf. Appendices

7. Robert Michels, *Political Parties,* p. 390.

8. Logan Pearsall Smith.

9. As told by J. Arthur Thomson, *The Outline of Science,* Vol. III, p. 646.

10. *Creative Evolution,* Ch. III.

11. Cf. my *Public Opinion,* Chapters XXV and XXVI.

12. Cf. my *Public Opinion,* Chapters XIII and XIV.

13. Speech on the Reform Bill of 1832, quoted in the *Times* (London), July 12, 1923.

14. Preface to *The Revolutionist's Handbook,* p.179.

15. *Parties and Party Leaders,* p. xvi.

16. H. Delbrück, *Government and the Will of the People,* p. 15. Translated by Roy S. Mac-Elwee.

17. *Discourse on Method,* Part I.

JOHN DEWEY

EXCERPT FROM *THE PUBLIC AND ITS PROBLEMS* (1927)

In 1884, John Dewey (1859–1952) received his doctorate in psychology for a dissertation titled The Psychology of Kant. *From 1904 until his death in 1952, he was a professor of philosophy at Columbia University, NY. Together with Charles Sanders Peirce, William James and George Herbert Mead, he was one of the founders of American philosophical pragmatism. Although he dealt with a great variety of subjects in his writings, there is a remarkable coherence in his oeuvre, with democracy and education as intertwining themes. His name is intimately connected to "progressive education," and his thoughts and ideas have had an enormous impact on pedagogical thinking and practice around the world.*

After World War II, Dewey's writings on democracy were forgotten, but since the 1980s his ideas have been revived and his work has influenced a number of contemporary American "neo-pragmatists," such as Richard Rorty. Jürgen Habermas, who has maintained that ever since he read Dewey, Peirce, and Mead as a student, he has relied on this American version of the philosophy of praxis to compensate for the Marxism's weaknesses with respect to democratic theory.

Dewey's book The Public and Its Problems *(1927) was a reply to Walter Lippmann, and his conclusions are diametrically opposite to his. Dewey objects to the idea that democracy is a mere technical form of government and insists that should be seen as distinctive a way of life constituted by all the ways people live, work, and learn together. For Dewey, what people in a modern democracy need is common knowledge, including the abilities to discuss and judge. In the excerpt from the book presented here, he argues that democracy is not just majority rule, the important thing is the means by which a majority becomes a majority through antecedent debates and modifications of views to meet the opinions of minorities that next time may become a majority. Therefore for him, "the problem of the public" is how best to improve "the methods and conditions of debate, discussion and persuasion."*

Chapter VI: The Problem of Method

[. . .] One reason for the comparative sterility of discussion of social matters is because so much intellectual energy has gone into the supposititious problem of the relations of individualism and collectivism at large, wholesale, and because the image of the antithesis infects so many specific questions. Thereby thought is diverted from the only fruitful questions, those of investigation into factual subject-matter, and becomes a discussion of concepts. The "problem" of the relation of the concept of authority to that of freedom, of personal rights to social obligations, with only a subsumptive illustrative reference to empirical facts, has been substituted for inquiry into the *consequences* of some particular distribution, under given conditions, of specific freedoms and authorities, and for inquiry into what altered distribution would yield more desirable consequences.

As we saw in our early consideration of the theme of the public, the question of what transactions should be left as far as possible to voluntary initiative and agreement and what should come under the regulation of the public is a question of time, place and concrete conditions that can be known only by careful observation and reflective investigation. For it concerns consequences; and the nature of consequences and the ability to perceive and act upon them varies with the industrial and intellectual agencies which operate. A solution, or distributive adjustment, needed at one time is totally unfitted to another situation. That social "evolution" has been either from collectivism to individualism or the reverse is sheer superstition. It has consisted in a continuous re-distribution of social integrations on the one hand and of capacities and energies of individuals on the other. Individuals find themselves cramped and depressed by absorption of their potentialities in some mode of association which has been institutionalized and become dominant. They may think they are clamoring for a purely personal liberty, but what they are doing is to bring into being a greater liberty to share in other associations, so that more of their individual potentialities will be released and their personal experience enriched. Life has been impoverished, not by a predominance of "society" in general over individuality, but by a domination of one form of association, the family, clan, church, economic institutions, over other actual and possible forms. On the other hand, the problem of exercising "social control" over individuals is in its reality that of regulating the doings and results of some individuals in order that a larger number of individuals may have a fuller and deeper experience. Since both ends can be intelligently attained only by knowledge of actual conditions in their modes of operation and their consequences, it may be confidently asserted that the chief enemy of a social thinking which would count in public affairs is the sterile and impotent, because totally irrelevant, channels in which so much intellectual energy has been expended.

The second point with respect to method is closely related. Political theories have shared in the absolutistic character of philosophy generally. By this is meant something much more than philosophies of the Absolute. Even professedly empirical philosophies have assumed a certain finality and foreverness in their theories which may be expressed by saying that they have been non-historical in character. They have isolated their subject-matter from its connections, and any isolated subject-matter becomes unqualified in the degree of its disconnection. In social theory dealing with human nature, a certain fixed and standardized "individual" has been postulated, from whose assumed traits social phenomena could be deduced. Thus Mill says in his discussion of the logic of the moral and social sciences: "The laws of the phenomena of society are, and can be, nothing but the laws of the actions and passions of human beings united together in the social state. Men, however, in a state of society are still men; their actions and passions are obedient to the laws of *individual* human nature."[1] Obviously what is ignored in such a statement is that "the actions and passions" of individual men are in the concrete what they are, their beliefs and purposes included, because of the social medium in which they live; that they are influenced throughout by contemporary and transmitted culture, whether in conformity or protest. What is generic and the same everywhere is at best the organic structure of man, his biological make-up. While it is evidently important to take this into account, it is also evident that none of the *distinctive* features of *human* association can be deduced from it. Thus, in spite of Mill's horror of the metaphysical absolute, his leading social conceptions were, logically, absolutistic. Certain social laws, normative and regulative, at all periods and under all circumstances of proper social life were assumed to exist.

The doctrine of evolution modified this idea of method only superficially. For "evolution" was itself often understood non-historically. That is, it was assumed that there is a predestined course of fixed stages through which social development must proceed. Under the influence of concepts borrowed from the physical science of the time, it was taken for granted that the very possibility of a social science stood or fell with the determination of fixed uniformities. Now every such logic is fatal to free experimental social inquiry. Investigation into empirical facts was undertaken, of course, but its results had to fit into certain ready-made and second-hand rubrics. When even *physical* facts and laws are perceived and used, social change takes place. The phenomena and laws are not altered, but invention based upon them modifies the human situation. For there is at once an effort to regulate their impact in life. The discovery of malaria does not alter its existential causation, intellectually viewed, but it does finally alter the facts from which the production of malaria arises, through draining and oiling swamps, etc., and by taking other measures of precaution. If the laws of economic cycles of expansion and depression were understood, means would at once be searched for to mitigate if not to do away with the swing. When men have an idea of how social agencies work and their consequences are wrought, they at once strive to secure consequences as far as desirable and to avert them if undesirable. These are facts of the most ordinary observation. But it is not often noted how fatal they are to the identification of social with physical uniformities. "Laws" of social life, when it is genuinely human, are like laws of engineering. If you want certain results, certain means must be found and employed. The key to the situation is a clear conception of consequences wanted, and of the technique for reaching them, together with, of course, the state of desires and aversions which causes some consequences to be wanted rather than others. All of these things are functions of the prevalent culture of the period.

While the backwardness of social knowledge and art is of course connected with retarded knowledge of human nature, or psychology, it is also absurd to suppose that an adequate psychological science would flower in a control of human activities similar to the control which physical science has procured of physical energies. For increased knowledge of human nature would directly and in unpredictable ways modify the workings of human nature, and lead to the need of new methods of regulation, and so on without end. It is a matter of analysis rather than of prophecy to say that the primary and chief effect of a better psychology would be found in education. The growth and diseases of grains and hogs are now recognized as proper subjects of governmental subsidy and attention. Instrumental agencies for a similar investigation of the conditions which make for the physical and moral hygiene of the young are in a state of infancy. We spend large sums of money for school buildings and their physical equipment. But systematic expenditure of public funds for scientific inquiry into the conditions which affect the mental and moral development of children is just beginning, and demands for a large increase in this direction are looked upon askance.

Again, it is reported that there are more beds in hospitals and asylums for cases of mental disturbance and retardation than for all diseases combined. The public pays generously to take care of the results of bad conditions. But there is no comparable attention and willingness to expend funds to investigate the causes of these troubles. The reason for these anomalies is evident enough. There is no conviction that the sciences of human nature are far enough advanced to make public support of such activities worth while. A marked development of psychology and kindred subjects would change this situation. And we have been speaking only of antecedent conditions of education. To complete the picture we have to realize the difference which would be made in the methods of parents and teachers were there an adequate and generally shared knowledge of human nature.

But such an educational development, though intrinsically precious to the last degree, would not entail a control of human energies comparable to that which already obtains of physical energies. To imagine that it would is simply to reduce human beings to the plane of inanimate things mechanically manipulated from without; it makes human education something like the training of fleas, dogs and horses. What stands in the way is not anything called "free-will," but the fact that such a change in educational methods would release new potentialities, capable of all kinds of permutations and combinations, which would then modify social phenomena, while this modification would in its turn affect human nature and its educative transformation in a continuous and endless procession.

The assimilation of human science to physical science represents, in other words, only another form of absolutistic logic, a kind of physical absolutism. We are doubtless but at the beginning of the possibilities of control of the physical conditions of mental and moral life. Physiological chemistry, increased knowledge of the nervous system, of the processes and functions of glandular secretions, may in time enable us to deal with phenomena of emotional and intellectual disturbance before which mankind has been helpless. But control of these conditions will not determine the uses to which human beings will put their normalized potentialities. If any one supposes that it will, let him consider the applications of such remedial or preventive measures to a man in a state of savage culture and one in a modern community. Each, as long as the conditions of the social medium remained substantially unaltered, will still have his experience and the direction of his restored energies affected by the objects and instrumentalities of the human environment, and by what men at the time currently prize and hold dear. The warrior and merchant would be better warriors and merchants, more efficient, but warriors and merchants still.

These considerations suggest a brief discussion of the effect of the present absolutistic logic upon the method and aims of education, not just in the sense of schooling but with respect to all the ways in which communities attempt to shape the disposition and beliefs of their members. Even when the processes of education do not aim at the unchanged perpetuation of existing institutions, it is assumed that there must be a mental picture of some desired end, personal and social, which is to be attained, and that this conception of a fixed determinate end ought to control educative processes. Reformers share this conviction with conservatives. The disciples of Lenin and Mussolini vie with the captains of capitalistic society in endeavoring to bring about a formation of dispositions and ideas which will conduce to a preconceived goal. If there is a difference, it is that the former proceed more consciously. An experimental social method would probably manifest itself first of all in surrender of this notion. Every care would be taken to surround the young with the physical and social conditions which best conduce, as far as freed knowledge extends, to release of personal potentialities. The habits thus formed would have entrusted to them the meeting of future social requirements and the development of the future state of society. Then and then only would all social agencies that are available operate as resources in behalf of a bettered community life.

What we have termed the absolutistic logic ends, as far as method in social matters is concerned, in a substitution of discussion of concepts and their logical relations to one another for inquiry. Whatever form it assumes, it results in strengthening the reign of dogma. Their contents may vary, but dogma persists. At the outset we noted in discussion of the state the influence of methods which look for causal forces. Long ago, physical science abandoned this method and took up that of detection of correlation of events. Our language and our thinking is still saturated with the idea of laws which phenomena "obey." But in his actual procedures, the scientific inquirer into physical events treats a law simply as a stable correlation of changes in what happens, a statement of the way in which one phenomenon, or some aspect or phase of it, varies when some other specified phenomenon varies. "Causation" is an affair of historical sequence, of the order in which a series of changes takes place. To know cause and effect is to know, in the abstract, the formula of correlation in change, and, in the concrete, a certain historical career of sequential events. The appeal to causal forces at large not only misleads inquiry into social facts, but it affects equally seriously the formation of purposes and policies. The person who holds the doctrine of "individualism" or "collectivism" has his program determined for him in advance. It is not with him a matter of finding out the particular thing which needs to be done and the best way, under the circumstances, of doing it. It is an affair of applying a hard and fast doctrine which follows logically from his preconception of the nature of ultimate causes. He is exempt from the responsibility of discovering the concrete correlation of changes, from the need of tracing particular sequences or histories of events through their complicated careers. He knows in advance the sort of thing which must be done, just as in ancient physical philosophy the thinker knew in advance what must happen, so that all he had to do was to supply a logical framework of definitions and classifications.

When we say that thinking and beliefs should be experimental, not absolutistic, we have then in mind a certain logic of method, not, primarily, the carrying on of experimentation like that of laboratories. Such a logic involves the following factors: First, that those concepts, general principles, theories and dialectical developments which are indispensable to any systematic knowledge be shaped and tested as tools of inquiry. Secondly, that policies and proposals for social action be treated as working hypotheses, not as programs to be rigidly adhered to and executed. They will be experimental in the sense that they will be entertained subject to constant and well-equipped observation of the consequences they entail when acted upon, and subject to ready and flexible revision in the light of observed consequences. The social sciences, if these two stipulations are fulfilled, will then be an apparatus for conducting investigation, and for recording and interpreting (organizing) its results. The apparatus will no longer be taken to be itself knowledge, but will be seen to be intellectual means of making discoveries of phenomena having social import and understanding their meaning. Differences of opinion in the sense of differences of judgment as to the course which it is best to follow, the policy which it is best to try out, will still exist. But opinion in the sense of beliefs formed and held in the absence of evidence will be reduced in quantity and importance. No longer will views generated in view of special situations be frozen into absolute standards and masquerade as eternal truths.

This phase of the discussion may be concluded by consideration of the relation of experts to a democratic public. A negative phase of the earlier argument for political democracy has largely lost its force. For it was based upon hostility to dynastic and oligarchic aristocracies, and these have largely been reft of power. The oligarchy which now dominates is that of an economic class. It claims to rule, not in virtue of birth and hereditary status, but in virtue of ability in management and of the burden of social responsibilities which it carries, in virtue of the position which superior abilities have conferred upon it. At all events, it is a shifting, unstable oligarchy, rapidly changing its constituents, who are more or less at the mercy of accidents they cannot control and of technological inventions. Consequently, the shoe is now on the other foot. It is argued that the check upon the oppressive power of this particular oligarchy lies in an intellectual aristocracy, not in appeal to an ignorant, fickle mass whose interests are superficial and trivial, and whose judgments are saved from incredible levity only when weighted down by heavy prejudice.

It may be argued that the democratic movement was essentially transitional. It marked the passage from feudal institutions to industrialism, and was coincident with the transfer of power from landed proprietors, allied to churchly authorities, to captains of industry, under conditions which involved an emancipation of the masses from legal limitations which had previously hemmed them in. But, so it is contended in effect, it is absurd to convert this legal liberation into a dogma which alleges that release from old oppressions confers upon those emancipated the intellectual and moral qualities which fit them for sharing in regulation of affairs of state. The essential fallacy of the democratic creed, it is urged, is the notion that a historic movement which effected an important and desirable release from restrictions is either a source or a proof of capacity in those thus emancipated to rule, when in fact there is no factor common in the two things. The obvious alternative is rule by those intellectually qualified, by expert intellectuals.

This revival of the Platonic notion that philosophers should be kings is the more taking because the idea of experts is substituted for that of philosophers, since philosophy has become something of a joke, while the image of the specialist, the expert in operation, is rendered familiar and congenial by the rise of the physical sciences and by the conduct of industry. A cynic might indeed say that the notion is a pipe-dream, a revery entertained by the intellectual class in compensation for an impotence consequent upon the divorce of theory and practice, upon the remoteness of specialized science from the affairs of life: the gulf being bridged not by the intellectuals but by inventors and engineers hired by captains of industry. One approaches the truth more nearly when one says that the argument proves too much for its own cause. If the masses are as intellectually irredeemable as its premise implies, they at all events have both too many desires and too much power to permit rule by experts to obtain. The very ignorance, bias, frivolity, jealousy, instability, which are alleged to incapacitate them from share in political affairs, unfit them still more for passive submission to rule by intellectuals. Rule by an economic class may be disguised from the masses; rule by experts could not be covered up. It could be made to work only if the intellectuals became the willing tools of big economic interests. Otherwise they would have to ally themselves with the masses, and that implies, once more, a share in government by the latter.

A more serious objection is that expertness is most readily attained in specialized technical matters, matters of administration and execution which postulate that general policies are already satisfactorily framed. It is assumed that the policies of the experts are in the main both wise and benevolent, that is, framed to conserve the genuine interests of society. The final obstacle in the way of any aristocratic rule is that in the absence of an articulate voice on the part of the masses, the best do not and cannot remain the best, the wise cease to be wise. It is impossible for high-brows to secure a monopoly of such knowledge as must be used for the regulation of common affairs. In the degree in which they become a specialized class, they are shut off from knowledge of the needs which they are supposed to serve.

The strongest point to be made in behalf of even such rudimentary political forms as democracy has already attained, popular voting, majority rule and so on, is that to some extent they involve a consultation and discussion which uncover social needs and troubles. This fact is the great asset on the side of the political ledger. De Tocqueville wrote it down almost a century ago in his survey of the prospects of democracy in the United States. Accusing a democracy of a tendency to prefer mediocrity in its elected rulers, and admitting its exposure to gusts of passion and its openness to folly, he pointed out in effect that popular government is educative as other modes of political regulation are not. It forces a recognition that there are common interests, even though the recognition of *what* they are is confused; and the need it enforces of discussion and publicity brings about some clarification of what they are. The man who wears the shoe knows best that it pinches and where it pinches, even if the expert shoemaker is the best judge of how the trouble is to be remedied. Popular government has at least created public spirit even if its success in informing that spirit has not been great.

A class of experts is inevitably so removed from common interests as to become a class with private interests and private knowledge, which in social matters is not knowledge at all. The ballot is, as often said, a substitute for bullets. But what is more significant is that counting of heads compels prior recourse to methods of discussion, consultation and persuasion, while the essence of appeal to force is to cut short resort to such methods. Majority rule, just as majority rule, is as foolish as its critics charge it with being. But it never is *merely* majority rule. As a practical politician, Samuel J. Tilden, said a long time ago: "The means by which a majority comes to be a majority is the more important thing": antecedent debates, modification of views to meet the opinions of minorities, the relative satisfaction given the latter by the fact that it has had a chance and that next time it may be successful in becoming a majority. Think of the meaning of the "problem of minorities" in certain European states, and compare it with the status of minorities in countries having popular government. It is true that all valuable as well as new ideas begin with minorities, perhaps a minority of one. The important consideration is that opportunity be given that idea to spread and to become the possession of the multitude. No government by experts in which the masses do not have the chance to inform the experts as to their needs can be anything but an oligarchy managed in the interests of the few. And the enlightenment must proceed in ways which force the administrative specialists to take account of the needs. The world has suffered more from leaders and authorities than from the masses.

The essential need, in other words, is the improvement of the methods and conditions of debate, discussion and persuasion. That is *the* problem of the public. We have asserted that this improvement depends essentially upon freeing and perfecting the processes of inquiry and of dissemination of their conclusions. Inquiry, indeed, is a work which devolves upon experts. But their expertness is not shown in framing and executing policies, but in discovering and making known the facts upon which the former depend. They are technical experts in the sense that scientific investigators and artists manifest *expertise*. It is not necessary that the many should have the knowledge and skill to carry on the needed investigations; what is required is that they have the ability to judge of the bearing of the knowledge supplied by others upon common concerns.

It is easy to exaggerate the amount of intelligence and ability demanded to render such judgments fitted for their purpose. In the first place, we are likely to form our estimate on the basis of present conditions. But indubitably one great trouble at present is that the data for good judgment are lacking; and no innate faculty of mind can make up for the absence of facts. Until secrecy, prejudice, bias, misrepresentation, and propaganda as well as sheer ignorance are replaced by inquiry and publicity, we have no way of telling how apt for judgment of social policies the existing intelligence of the masses may be. It would certainly go much further than at present. In the second place, *effective* intelligence is not an original, innate endowment. No matter what are the differences in native intelligence (allowing for the moment that intelligence can be native), the actuality of mind is dependent upon the education which social conditions effect. Just as the specialized mind and knowledge of the past is embodied in implements, utensils, devices and technologies which those of a grade of intelligence which could not produce them can now intelligently use, so it will be when currents of public knowledge blow through social affairs.

The level of action fixed by *embodied* intelligence is always the important thing. In savage culture a superior man will be superior to his fellows, but his knowledge and judgment will lag in many matters far behind that of an inferiorly endowed person in an advanced civilization. Capacities are limited by the objects and tools at hand. They are still more dependent upon the prevailing habits of attention and interest which are set by tradition and institutional customs. Meanings run in the channels formed by instrumentalities of which, in the end, language, the vehicle of thought as well as of communication, is the most important. A mechanic can discourse of ohms and amperes as Sir Isaac Newton could not in his day. Many a man who has tinkered with radios can judge of things which Faraday did not dream of. It is aside from the point to say that if Newton and Faraday were now here, the amateur and mechanic would be infants beside them. The retort only brings out the point: the difference made by different objects to think of and by different meanings in circulation. A more intelligent state of social affairs, one more informed with knowledge, more directed by intelligence, would not improve original endowments one whit, but it would raise the level upon which the intelligence of all operates. The height of this level is much more important for judgment of public concerns than are differences in intelligence quotients. As Santayana has said: "Could a better system prevail in our lives a better order would establish itself in our thinking. It has not been for want of keen senses, or personal genius, or a constant order in the outer world, that mankind has fallen back repeatedly into barbarism and superstition. It has been for want of good character, good example, and good government." The notion that intelligence is a personal endowment or personal attainment is the great conceit of the intellectual class, as that of the commercial class is that wealth is something which they personally have wrought and possess.

A point which concerns us in conclusion passes beyond the field of intellectual method, and trenches upon the question of practical re-formation of social conditions. In its deepest and richest sense a community must always remain a matter of face-to-face intercourse. This is why the family and neighborhood, with all their deficiencies, have always been the chief agencies of nurture, the means by which dispositions are stably formed and ideas acquired which laid hold on the roots of character. The Great Community, in the sense of free and full intercommunication, is conceivable. But it can never possess all the qualities which mark a local community. It will do its final work in ordering the relations and enriching the experience of local associations. The invasion and partial destruction of the life of the latter by outside uncontrolled agencies is the immediate source of the instability, disintegration and restlessness which characterize the present epoch. Evils which are uncritically and indiscriminately laid at the door of industrialism and democracy might, with greater intelligence, be referred to the dislocation and unsettlement of local communities. Vital and thorough attachments are bred only in the intimacy of an intercourse which is of necessity restricted in range.

Is it possible for local communities to be stable without being static, progressive without being merely mobile? Can the vast, innumerable and intricate currents of trans-local associations be so banked and conducted that they will pour the generous and abundant meanings of which they are potential bearers into the smaller intimate unions of human beings living in immediate contact with one another? Is it possible to restore the reality of the lesser communal organizations and to penetrate and saturate their members with a sense of local community life? There is at present, at least in theory, a movement away from the principle of territorial organization to that of "functional," that is to say, occupational, organization. It is true enough that older forms of territorial association do not satisfy present needs. It is true that ties formed by sharing in common work, whether in what is called industry or what are called professions, have now a force which formerly they did not possess. But these ties can be counted upon for an enduring and stable organization, which at the same time is flexible and moving, only as they grow out of immediate intercourse and attachment. The theory, as far as it relies upon associations which are remote and indirect, would if carried into effect soon be confronted by all the troubles and evils of the present situation in a transposed form. There is no substitute for the vitality and depth of close and direct intercourse and attachment.

It is said, and said truly, that for the world's peace it is necessary that we understand the peoples of foreign lands. How well do we understand, I wonder, our next door neighbors? It has also been said that if a man love not his fellow man whom he has seen, he cannot love the God whom he has not seen. The chances of regard for distant peoples being effective as long as there is no close neighborhood experience to bring with it insight and understanding of neighbors do not seem better. A man who has not been seen in the daily relations of life may inspire admiration, emulation, servile subjection, fanatical partisanship, hero worship; but not love and understanding, save as they radiate from the attachments of a near-by union. Democracy must begin at home, and its home is the neighborly community.

It is outside the scope of our discussion to look into the prospects of the reconstruction of face-to-face communities. But there is something deep within human nature itself which pulls toward settled relationships. Inertia and the tendency toward stability belong to emotions and desires as well as to masses and molecules. That happiness which is full of content and peace is found only in enduring ties with others, which reach to such depths that they go below the surface of conscious experience to form its undisturbed foundation. No one knows how much of the frothy excitement of life, of mania for motion, of fretful discontent, of need for artificial stimulation, is the expression of frantic search for something to fill the void caused by the loosening of the bonds which hold persons together in immediate community of experience. If there is anything in human psychology to be counted upon, it may be urged that when man is satiated with restless seeking for the remote which yields no enduring satisfaction, the human spirit will return to seek calm and order within itself. This, we repeat, can be found only in the vital, steady, and deep relationships which are present only in an immediate community.

The psychological tendency can, however, manifest itself only when it is in harmonious conjunction with the objective course of events. Analysis finds itself in troubled waters if it attempts to discover whether the tide of events is turning away from dispersion of energies and acceleration of motion. Physically and externally, conditions have made, of course, for concentration; the development of urban, at the expense of rural, populations; the corporate organization of aggregated wealth, the growth of all sorts of organizations, are evidence enough. But enormous organization is compatible with demolition of the ties that form local communities and with substitution of impersonal bonds for personal unions, with a flux which is hostile to stability. The character of our cities, of organized business and the nature of the comprehensive associations in which individuality is lost, testify also to this fact. Yet there are contrary signs. "Community" and community activities are becoming words to conjure with. The local is the ultimate universal, and as near an absolute as exists. It is easy to point to many signs which indicate that unconscious agencies as well as deliberate planning are making for such an enrichment of the experience of local communities as will conduce to render them genuine centers of the attention, interest and devotion for their constituent members.

The unanswered question is how far these tendencies will reestablish the void left by the disintegration of the family, church and neighborhood. We cannot predict the outcome. But we can assert with confidence that there is nothing intrinsic in the forces which have effected uniform standardization, mobility and remote invisible relationships that is fatally obstructive to the return movement of their consequences into the local homes of mankind. Uniformity and standardization may provide an underlying basis for differentiation and liberation of individual potentialities. They may sink to the plane of unconscious habituations, taken for granted in the mechanical phases of life, and deposit a soil from which personal susceptibilities and endowments may richly and stably flower. Mobility may in the end supply the means by which the spoils of remote and indirect interaction and interdependence flow back into local life, keeping it flexible, preventing the stagnancy which has attended stability in the past, and furnishing it with the elements of a variegated and many-hued experience. Organization may cease to be taken as an end in itself. Then it will no longer be mechanical and external, hampering the free play of artistic gifts, fettering men and women with chains of conformity, conducing to abdication of all which does not fit into the automatic movement of organization as a self-sufficing thing. Organization as a means to an end would reënforce individuality and enable it to be securely itself by enduing it with resources beyond its unaided reach.

Whatever the future may have in store, one thing is certain. Unless local communal life can be restored, the public cannot adequately resolve its most urgent problem: to find and identify itself. But if it be reestablished, it will manifest a fullness, variety and freedom of possession and enjoyment of meanings and goods unknown in the contiguous associations of the past. For it will be alive and flexible as well as stable, responsive to the complex and world-wide scene in which it is enmeshed. While local, it will not be isolated. Its larger relationships will provide an inexhaustible and flowing fund of meanings upon which to draw, with assurance that its drafts will be honored. Territorial states and political boundaries will persist; but they will not be barriers which impoverish experience by cutting man off from his fellows; they will not be hard and fast divisions whereby external separation is converted into inner jealousy, fear, suspicion and hostility. Competition will continue, but it will be less rivalry for acquisition of material goods, and more an emulation of local groups to enrich direct experience with appreciatively enjoyed intellectual and artistic wealth. If the technological age can provide mankind with a firm and general basis of material security, it will be absorbed in a humane age. It will take its place as an instrumentality of shared and communicated experience. But without passage through a machine age, mankind's hold upon what is needful as the precondition of *a* free, flexible and many-colored life is so precarious and inequitable that competitive scramble for acquisition and frenzied use of the results of acquisition for purposes of excitation and display will be perpetuated. [. . .]

NOTE

1. J. S. Mill, *Logic*, Book VI, ch. 7, sec. 1. Italics mine.

JOSEPH A. SCHUMPETER

EXCERPT FROM *CAPITALISM, SOCIALISM AND DEMOCRACY* (1942)

Joseph Schumpeter (1883–1950) was an economist and political scientist born in Austria-Hungary. In 1911, he published his famous Theory of Economic Development *and the same year he became professor in economics at the University of Graz. Schumpeter served as Austrian Minister of Finance in 1919, presiding over the hyperinflation of the period, which soon ended his term of office. In 1932, he took up a position at Harvard University and in 1939 he published his monumental* Business Cycles.

Schumpeter's Capitalism, Socialism and Democracy *(1942) had a major impact after the war, within sociology and political science as well as economics. Here, Schumpeter argues that capitalism will destroy itself, but in a different way than Marx predicted. According to him, the disappearance of the dynamic entrepreneur in a more and more bureaucratized industrial life would pave the way for socialism.*

In the following excerpt, Schumpeter attacks what he regards as the classical doctrine of democracy, denying the existence of a Common Good and a Will of the People. He then develops his own theory of democracy, in which the only role of the people is to produce a government through elections, and where competition among elites for political leadership is the driving force.

Schumpeter's project was to establish a "realistic" and empirically based model of democracy. Like Lippmann, he took an elitist position on public life and attributed only a minor role to public participation and a correspondingly major role to political leadership. Democracy is seen as a struggle between competing elites, not as an instrument for advancing equality and human development through participation.

Schumpeter's interest in mass society and crowd psychology, which he shared with a number of other writers of the time, led him to underline influence of advertising and other methods of persuasion. He regarded it as evident that "the will of the people" could be fabricated or manufactured by the rulers and that a genuine public participation in politics therefore was an illusion. The public sphere in Schumpeter's approach is reduced to a market and a competitive arena for elite groups.

Chapter XXI: The Classical Doctrine of Democracy

I: The Common Good and the Will of the People

The eighteenth-century philosophy of democracy may be couched in the following definition: the democratic method is that institutional arrangement for arriving at political decisions which realizes the common good by making the people itself decide issues through the election of individuals who are to assemble in order to carry out its will. Let us develop the implications of this.

It is held, then, that there exists a Common Good, the obvious beacon light of policy, which is always simple to define and which every normal person can be made to see by means of rational argument. There is hence no excuse for not seeing it and in fact no explanation for the presence of people who do not see it except ignorance—which can be removed—stupidity and anti-social interest. Moreover, this common good implies definite answers to all questions so that every social fact and every measure taken or to be taken can unequivocally be classed as "good" or "bad." All people having therefore to agree, in principle at least, there is also a Common Will of the people (= will of all reasonable individuals) that is exactly coterminous with the common good or interest or welfare or happiness. The only thing, barring stupidity and sinister interests, that can possibly bring in disagreement and account for the presence of an opposition is a difference of opinion as to the speed with which the goal, itself common to nearly all, is to be approached. Thus every member of the community, conscious of that goal, knowing his or her mind, discerning what is good and what is bad, takes part, actively and responsibly, in furthering the former and fighting the latter and all the members taken together control their public affairs.

It is true that the management of some of these affairs requires special aptitudes and techniques and will therefore have to be entrusted to specialists who have them. This does not affect the principle, however, because these specialists simply act in order to carry out the will of the people exactly as a doctor acts in order to carry out the will of the patient to get well. It is also true that in a community of any size, especially if it displays the phenomenon of division of labor, it would be highly inconvenient for every individual citizen to have to get into contact with all the other citizens on every issue in order to do his part in ruling or governing. It will be more convenient to reserve only the most important decisions for the individual citizens to pronounce upon—say by referendum—and to deal with the rest through a committee appointed by them—an assembly or parliament whose members will be elected by popular vote. This committee or body of delegates, as we have seen, will not represent the people in a legal sense but it will do so in a less technical one—it will voice, reflect or represent the will of the electorate. Again as a matter of convenience, this committee, being large, may resolve itself into smaller ones for the various departments of public affairs. Finally, among these smaller committees there will be a general-purpose committee, mainly for dealing with current administration, called cabinet or government, possibly with a general secretary or scapegoat at its head, a so-called prime minister.[1]

As soon as we accept all the assumptions that are being made by this theory of the polity—or implied by it—democracy indeed acquires a perfectly unambiguous meaning and there is no problem in connection with it except how to bring it about. Moreover we need only forget a few logical qualms in order to be able to add that in this case the democratic arrangement would not only be the best of all conceivable ones, but that few people would care to consider any other. It is no less obvious however that these assumptions are so many statements of fact every one of which would have to be proved if we are to arrive at that conclusion. And it is much easier to disprove them.

There is, first, no such thing as a uniquely determined common good that all people could agree on or be made to agree on by the force of rational argument. This is due not primarily to the fact that some people may want things other than the common good but to the much more fundamental fact that to different individuals and groups the common good is bound to mean different things. This fact, hidden from the utilitarian by the narrowness of his outlook on the world of human valuations, will introduce rifts on questions of principle which cannot be reconciled by rational argument because ultimate values—our conceptions of what life and what society should be—are beyond the range of mere logic. They may be bridged by compromise in some cases but not in others. Americans who say, "We want this country to arm to its teeth and then to fight for what we conceive to be right all over the globe" and Americans who say, "We want this country to work out its own problems which is the only way it can serve humanity" are facing irreducible differences of ultimate values which compromise could only maim and degrade.

Secondly, even if a sufficiently definite common good-such as for instance the utilitarian's maximum of economic satisfaction[2] proved acceptable to all, this would not imply equally definite answers to individual issues. Opinions on these might differ to an extent important enough to produce most of the effects of "fundamental" dissension about ends themselves. The problems centering in the evaluation of present versus future satisfactions, even the case of socialism versus capitalism, would be left still open, for instance, after the conversion of every individual citizen to utilitarianism. "Health" might be desired by all, yet people would still disagree on vaccination and vasectomy. And so on.

The utilitarian fathers of democratic doctrine failed to see the full importance of this simply because none of them seriously considered any substantial change in the economic framework and the habits of bourgeois society. They saw little beyond the world of an eighteenth-century ironmonger.

But, third, as a consequence of both preceding propositions, the particular concept of the will of the people or the *volonté generalé* that the utilitarians made their own vanishes into thin air. For that concept presupposes the existence of a uniquely determined common good discernible to all. Unlike the romanticists the utilitarians had no notion of that semi-mystic entity endowed with a will of its own—that "soul of the people" which the historical school of jurisprudence made so much of. They frankly derived their will of the people from the wills of individuals. And unless there is a center, the common good, toward which, in the long run at least, *all* individual wills gravitate, we shall not get that particular type of "natural" *volonté generalé*. The utilitarian center of gravity, on the one hand, unifies individual wills, tends to weld them by means of rational discussion into the will of the people and, on the other hand, confers upon the latter the exclusive ethical dignity claimed by the classic democratic creed. *This creed does not consist simply in worshiping the will of the people as such* but rests on certain assumptions about the "natural" object of that will which object is sanctioned by utilitarian reason. Both the existence and the dignity of this kind of *volonté generalé* are gone as soon as the idea of the common good fails us. And both the pillars of the classical doctrine inevitably crumble into dust.

II: The Will of the People and Individual Volition

Of course, however conclusively those arguments may tell against, this particular conception of the will of the people, they do not debar us from trying to build up another and more realistic one. I do not intend to question either the reality or the importance of the sociopsychological facts we think of when speaking of the will of a nation. Their analysis is certainly the prerequisite for making headway with the problems of democracy. It would however be better not to retain the term because this tends to obscure the fact that as soon as we have severed the will of the people from its utilitarian connotation we are building not merely a different theory of the same thing, but a theory of a completely different thing. We have every reason to be on our guard against the pitfalls that lie on the path of those defenders of democracy who while accepting, under pressure of accumulating evidence, more and more of the facts of the democratic process, yet try to anoint the results that process turns out with oil taken from eighteenth-century jars.

But though a common will or public opinion of some sort may still be said to emerge from the infinitely complex jumble of individual and group-wise situations, volitions, influences, actions and reactions of the "democratic process," the result lacks not only rational unity but also rational sanction. The former means that, though from the standpoint of analysis, the democratic process is not simply chaotic for the analyst nothing is chaotic that can be brought within the reach of explanatory principles—yet the results would not, except by chance, be meaningful in themselves—as for instance the realization of any definite end or ideal would be. The latter means, since *that* will is no longer congruent with any "good," that in order to claim ethical dignity for the result it will now be necessary to fall back upon an unqualified confidence in democratic forms of government as such—a belief that in principle would have to be independent of the desirability of results. As we have seen, it is not easy to place oneself on that standpoint. But even if we do so, the dropping of the utilitarian common good still leaves us with plenty of difficulties on our hands.

In particular, we still remain under the practical necessity of attributing to the will of the *individual* an independence and a rational quality that are altogether unrealistic. If we are to argue that the will of the citizens *per se* is a political factor entitled to respect, it must first exist. That is to say, it must be something more than an indeterminate bundle of vague impulses loosely playing about given slogans and mistaken impressions. Everyone would have to know definitely what he wants to stand for. This definite will would have to be implemented by the ability to observe and interpret correctly the facts that are directly accessible to everyone and to sift critically the information about the facts that are not. Finally, from that definite will and from these ascertained facts a clear *and prompt* conclusion as to particular issues would have to be derived according to the rules of logical inference—with so high a degree of general efficiency moreover that one man's opinion could be held, without glaring absurdity, to be roughly as good as every other man's.[3] And all this the modal citizen would have to perform for himself and independently of pressure groups and propaganda,[4] for volitions and inferences that are imposed upon the electorate obviously do not qualify for ultimate data of the democratic process. The question whether these conditions are fulfilled to the extent required in order to make democracy work should not be answered by reckless assertion or equally reckless denial. It can be answered only by a laborious appraisal of a maze of conflicting evidence.

Before embarking upon this, however, I want to make quite sure that the reader fully appreciates another point that has been made already. I will therefore repeat that even if the opinions and desires of individual citizens were perfectly definite and independent data for the democratic process to work with, and if everyone acted on them with ideal rationality and promptitude, it would not necessarily follow that the political decisions produced by that process from the raw material of those individual volitions would represent anything that could in any convincing sense be called the will of the people. It is not only conceivable but, whenever individual wills are much divided, very likely that the political decisions produced will not conform to "what, people really want." Nor can it be replied that, if not exactly what they want, they will get a "fair compromise." This may be so. The chances for this to happen are greatest with those issues which are quantitative in nature or admit of gradation, such as the question how much is to be spent on unemployment relief provided everybody favors some expenditure for that purpose. But with qualitative issues, such as the question whether to persecute heretics or to enter upon a war, the result attained may well, though for different reasons, be equally distasteful to all the people whereas the decision imposed by a non-democratic agency might prove much more acceptable to them.

An example will illustrate. I may, I take it, describe the rule of Napoleon, when First Consul, as a military dictatorship. One of the most pressing political needs of the moment was a religious settlement that would clear the chaos left by the revolution and the directorate and bring peace to millions of hearts. This he achieved by a number of master strokes, culminating in a concordat with the pope (1801) and the "organic articles" (1802) that, reconciling the irreconcilable, gave just the right amount of freedom to religious worship while strongly upholding the authority of the state. He also reorganized and refinanced the French Catholic church, solved the delicate question of the "constitutional" clergy, and most successfully launched the new establishment with a minimum of friction. If ever there was any justification at all for holding that the people actually want something definite, this arrangement affords one of the best instances in history. This must be obvious to anyone who looks at the French class structure of that time and it is amply borne out by the fact that this ecclesiastical policy greatly contributed to the almost universal popularity which the consular regime enjoyed. But it is difficult to see how this result could have been achieved in a democratic way. Anti-church sentiment had not died out and was by no means confined to the vanquished Jacobins. People of that persuasion, or their leaders, could not possibly have compromised to that extent.[5] On the other end of the scale, a strong wave of wrathful Catholic sentiment was steadily gaining momentum. People who shared that sentiment, or leaders dependent on their good will, could not possibly have stopped at the Napoleonic limit; in particular, they could not have dealt so firmly with the Holy See for which moreover there would have been no motive to give in, seeing which way things were moving. And the will of the peasants who more than anything else wanted their priests, their churches and processions would have been paralyzed by the very natural fear that the revolutionary settlement of the land question might be endangered once the clergy—the bishops especially—were in the saddle again. Deadlock or interminable struggle, engendering increasing irritation, would have been the most probable outcome of any attempt to settle the question democratically. But Napoleon was able to settle it reasonably, precisely because all those groups which could not yield their points of their own accord were at the same time able and willing to accept the arrangement if imposed.

This instance of course is not an isolated one.[6] If results that prove in the long run satisfactory to the people at large are made the test of government for the people, then government by the people, as conceived by the classical doctrine of democracy, would often fail to meet it.

III: Human Nature in Politics

It remains to answer our question about the definiteness and independence of the voter's will, his powers of observation and interpretation of facts, and his ability to draw, clearly and promptly, rational inferences from both. This subject belongs to a chapter of social psychology that might be entitled Human Nature in Politics?[7] During the second half of the last century, the idea of the human personality that is a homogeneous unit and the idea of a definite will that is the prime mover of action have been steadily fading—even before the times of Theodule Ribot and of Sigmund Freud. In particular, these ideas have been increasingly discounted in the field of social sciences where the importance of the extra-rational and irrational element in our behavior has been receiving more and more attention, witness Pareto's *Mind and Society*. Of the many sources of the evidence that accumulated against the hypothesis of rationality, I shall mention only two.

The one—in spite of much more careful later work—may still be associated with the name of Gustave Le Bon, the founder or, at any rate, the first effective exponent of the psychology of crowds (*psychologie des foules*).[8] By showing up, though overstressing, the realities of human behavior when under the influence of agglomeration—in particular the sudden disappearance, in a state of excitement, of moral restraints and civilized modes of thinking and feeling, the sudden eruption of primitive impulses, infantilisms and criminal propensities—he made us face gruesome facts that everybody knew but nobody wished to see and he thereby dealt a serious blow to the picture of man's nature which underlies the classical doctrine of democracy and democratic folklore about revolutions. No doubt there is much to be said about the narrowness of the factual basis of Le Bon's inferences which, for instance, do not fit at all well the normal behavior of an English or Anglo-American crowd. Critics, especially those to whom the implications of this branch of social psychology were uncongenial, did not fail to make the most of its vulnerable points. But on the other hand it must not be forgotten that the phenomena of crowd psychology are by no means confined to mobs rioting in the narrow streets of a Latin town. Every parliament, every committee, every council of war composed of a dozen generals in their sixties, displays, in however mild a form, some of those features that stand out so glaringly in the case of the rabble, in particular a reduced sense of responsibility, a lower level of energy of thought and greater sensitiveness to non-logical influences. Moreover, those phenomena are not confined to a crowd in the sense of a physical agglomeration of many people. Newspaper readers, radio audiences, members of a party even if not physically gathered together are terribly easy to work up into a psychological crowd and into a state of frenzy in which attempt at rational argument only spurs the animal spirits.

The other source of disillusioning evidence that I am going to mention is a much humbler one—no blood flows from it, only nonsense. Economists, learning to observe their facts more closely, have begun to discover that, even in the most ordinary currents of daily life, their consumers do not quite live up to the idea that the economic textbook used to convey. On the one hand their wants are nothing like as definite and their actions upon those wants nothing like as rational and prompt. On the other hand they are so amenable to the influence of advertising and other methods of persuasion that producers often seem to dictate to them instead of being directed by them. The technique of successful advertising is particularly instructive. There is indeed nearly always some appeal to reason. But mere assertion, often repeated, counts more than rational argument and so does the direct attack upon the subconscious which takes the form of attempts to evoke and crystallize pleasant associations of an entirely extra-rational, very frequently of a sexual nature.

The conclusion, while obvious, must be drawn with care. In the ordinary run of often repeated decisions the individual is subject to the salutary and rationalizing influence of favorable and unfavorable experience. He is also under the influence of relatively simple and unproblematical motives and interests which are but occasionally interfered with by excitement. Historically, the consumers' desire for shoes may, at least in part, have been shaped by the action of producers offering attractive footgear and campaigning for it; yet at any given time it is a genuine want, the definiteness of which extends beyond "shoes in general" and which prolonged experimenting clears of much of the irrationalities that may originally have surrounded it.[9] Moreover, under the stimulus of those simple motives consumers learn to act upon unbiased expert advice about some things (houses, motorcars) and themselves become experts in others. It is simply not true that housewives are easily fooled in the matter of foods, *familiar* household articles, wearing apparel. And, as every salesman knows to his cost, most of them have a way of insisting on the exact article they want.

This of course holds true still more obviously on the producers' side of the picture. No doubt, a manufacturer may be indolent, a bad judge of opportunities or otherwise incompetent; but there is an effective mechanism that will reform or eliminate him. Again Taylorism rests on the fact that man may perform simple handicraft operations for thousands of years and yet perform them inefficiently. But neither the intention to act as rationally as possible nor a steady pressure toward rationality can seriously be called into question at whatever level of industrial or commercial activity we choose to look.[10]

And so it is with most of the decisions of daily life that lie within the little field which the individual citizen's mind encompasses with a full sense of its reality. Roughly, it consists of the things that directly concern himself, his family, his business dealings, his hobbies, his friends and enemies, his township or ward, his class, church, trade union or any other social group of which he is an active member—things under his personal observation, the things which are familiar to him independently of what his newspaper tells him, which he can directly influence or manage and for which he develops the kind of responsibility that is induced by a direct relation to the favorable or unfavorable effects of a course of action.

Once more: definiteness and rationality in thought and action[11] are not guaranteed by this familiarity with men and things or by that sense of reality or responsibility. Quite a few other conditions which often fail to be fulfilled would be necessary for that. For instance, generation after generation may suffer from irrational behavior in matters of hygiene and yet fail to link their sufferings with their noxious habits. As long as this is not done, objective consequences, however regular, of course do not produce subjective experience. Thus it proved unbelievably hard for humanity to realize the relation between infection and epidemics: the facts pointed to it with what to us seems unmistakable clearness; yet to the end of the eighteenth century doctors did next to nothing to keep people afflicted with infectious disease, such as measles or smallpox, from mixing with other people. And things must be expected to be still worse whenever there is not only inability but reluctance to recognize causal relations or when some interest fights against recognizing them.

Nevertheless and in spite of all the qualifications that impose themselves, there is for everyone, within a much wider horizon, a narrower field—widely differing in extent as between different groups and individuals and bounded by a broad zone rather than a sharp line—which is distinguished by a sense of reality or familiarity or responsibility. And this field harbors relatively definite individual volitions. These may often strike us as unintelligent, narrow, egotistical; and it may not be obvious to everyone why, when it comes to political decisions, we should worship at their shrine, still less why we should feel bound to count each of them for one and none of them for more than one. If, however, we do choose to worship we shall at least not find the shrine empty.[12]

Now this comparative definiteness of volition and rationality of behavior does not suddenly vanish as we move away from those concerns of daily life in the home and in business which educate and discipline as. In the realm of public affairs there are sectors that are more within the reach of the citizen's mind than others. This is true, first, of local affairs. Even there we find a reduced power of discerning facts, a reduced preparedness to act upon them, a reduced sense of responsibility. We all know the man—and a very good specimen he frequently is—who says that the local administration is not his business and callously shrugs his shoulders at practices which he would rather die than suffer in his own office. High-minded citizens in a hortatory mood who preach the responsibility of the individual voter or taxpayer invariably discover the fact that this voter does not feel responsible for what the local politicians do. Still, especially in communities not too big for personal contacts, local patriotism may be a very important factor in "making democracy work." Also, the problems of a town are in many respects akin to the problems of a manufacturing concern. The man who understands the latter also understands, to some extent, the former. The manufacturer, grocer or workman need not step out of his world to have a rationally defensible view (that may of course be right or wrong) on street cleaning or town halls. Second, there are many national issues that concern individuals and groups so directly and unmistakably as to evoke volitions that are genuine and definite enough. The most important instance is afforded by issues involving immediate and personal pecuniary profit to individual voters and groups of voters, such as direct payments, protective duties, silver policies and so on. Experience that goes back to antiquity shows that by and large voters react promptly and rationally to any such chance. But the classical doctrine of democracy evidently stands to gain little from displays of rationality of this kind. Voters thereby prove themselves bad and indeed corrupt judges of such issues,[13] and often they even prove themselves bad judges of their own long-run interests, for it is only the short-run promise that tells politically and only short-run rationality that asserts itself effectively.

However, when we move still farther away from the private concerns of the family and the business office into those regions of national and international affairs that lack a direct and unmistakable link with those private concerns, individual volition, command of facts and method of inference soon cease to fulfill the requirements of the classical doctrine. What strikes me most of all and seems to me to be the core of the trouble is the fact that the sense of reality[14] is so completely lost. Normally, the great political questions take their place in the psychic economy of the typical citizen with those leisure-hour interests that have not attained the rank of hobbies, and with the subjects of irresponsible conversation. These things seem so far off; they are not at all like a business proposition; dangers may not materialize at all and if they should they may not prove so very serious; one feels oneself to be moving in a fictitious world.

This reduced sense of reality accounts not only for a reduced sense of responsibility but also for the absence of effective volition. One has one's phrases, of course, and one's wishes and daydreams and grumbles; especially, one has one's likes and dislikes. But ordinarily they do not amount to what we call a will—the psychic counterpart of purposeful responsible action. In fact, for the private citizen musing over national affairs there is no scope for such a will and no task at which it could develop. He is a member of an unworkable committee, the committee of the whole nation, and this is why he expends less disciplined effort on mastering a political problem than he expends on a game of bridge.[15]

The reduced sense of responsibility and the absence of effective volition in turn explain the ordinary citizen's ignorance and lack of judgment in matters of domestic and foreign policy which are if anything more shocking in the case of educated people and of people who are successfully active in non-political walks of life than it is with uneducated people in humble stations. Information is plentiful and readily available. But this does not seem to make any difference. Nor should we wonder at it. We need only compare a lawyer's attitude to his brief and the same lawyer's attitude to the statements of political fact presented in his newspaper in order to see what is the matter. In the one case the lawyer has qualified for appreciating the relevance of his facts by years of purposeful labor done under the definite stimulus of interest in his professional competence; and under a stimulus that is no less powerful he then bends his acquirements, his intellect, his will to the contents of the brief. In the other case, he has not taken the trouble to qualify; he does not care to absorb the information or to apply to it the canons of criticism he knows so well how to handle; and he is impatient of long or complicated argument. All of this goes to show that without the initiative that comes from immediate responsibility, ignorance will persist in the face of masses of information however complete and correct. It persists even in the face of the meritorious efforts that are being made to go beyond presenting information and to teach the use of it by means of lectures, classes, discussion groups. Results are not zero. But they are small. People cannot be carried up the ladder.

Thus the typical citizen drops down to a lower level of mental performance as soon as he enters the political field. He argues and analyzes in a way which he would readily recognize as infantile within the sphere of his real interests. He becomes a primitive again. His thinking becomes associative and affective.[16] And this entails two further consequences of ominous significance.

First, even if there were no political groups trying to influence him, the typical citizen would in political matters tend to yield to extrarational or irrational prejudice
and impulse. The weakness of the rational processes he applies to politics and the
absence of effective logical control over the results he arrives at would in themselves
suffice to account for that. Moreover, simply because he is not "all there," he will
relax his usual moral standards as well and occasionally give in to dark urges which
the conditions of private life help him to repress. But as to the wisdom or rationality
of his inferences and conclusions, it may be just as bad if he gives in to a burst of
generous indignation. This will make it still more difficult for him to see things in
their correct proportions or even to see more than one aspect of one thing at a time.
Hence, if for once he does emerge from his usual vagueness and does display the
definite will postulated by the classical doctrine of democracy, he is as likely as not
to become still more unintelligent and irresponsible than he usually is. At certain
junctures, this may prove fatal to his nation.[17]

Second, however, the weaker the logical element in the processes of the public
mind and the more complete the absence of rational criticism and of the rationalizing influence of personal experience and responsibility, the greater are the opportunities for groups with an ax to grind. These groups may consist of professional
politicians or of exponents of an economic interest or of idealists of one kind or
another or of people simply interested in staging and managing political shows.
The sociology of such groups is immaterial to the argument in hand. The only point
that matters here is that, Human Nature in Politics being what it is, they are able to
fashion and, within very wide limits, even to create the will of the people. What we
are confronted with in the analysis of political processes is largely not a genuine but
a manufactured will. And often this artefact is all that in reality corresponds to the
volonté generaée of the classical doctrine. So far as this is so, the will of the people is
the product and not the motive power of the political process.

The ways in which issues and the popular will on any issue are being manufactured is exactly analogous to the ways of commercial advertising. We find the same
attempts to contact the subconscious. We find the same technique of creating favorable and unfavorable associations which are the more effective the less rational they
are. We find the same evasions and reticences and the same trick of producing opinion by reiterated assertion that is successful precisely to the extent to which it avoids
rational argument and the danger of awakening the critical faculties of the people.
And so on. Only, all these arts have infinitely more scope in the sphere of public
affairs than they have in the sphere of private and professional life. The picture of
the prettiest girl that ever lived will in the long run prove powerless to maintain the
sales of a bad cigarette. There is no equally effective safeguard in the case of political
decisions. Many decisions of fateful importance are of a nature that makes it impossible for the public to experiment with them at its leisure and at moderate cost. Even
if that is possible, however, judgment is as a rule not so easy to arrive at as it is in
the case of the cigarette, because effects are less easy to interpret.

But such arts also vitiate, to an extent quite unknown in the field of commercial
advertising, those forms of political advertising that profess to address themselves
to reason. To the observer, the antirational or, at all events, the extra-rational appeal and the defenselessness of the victim stand out more and not less clearly when
cloaked in facts and arguments. We have seen above why it is so difficult to impart

to the public unbiased information about political problems and logically correct inferences from it and why it is that information and arguments in political matters will "register" only if they link up with the citizen's preconceived ideas. As a rule, however, these ideas are not definite enough to determine particular conclusions. Since they can themselves be manufactured, effective political argument almost inevitably implies the attempt to twist existing volitional premises into a particular shape and not merely the attempt to implement them or to help the citizen to make up his mind.

Thus information and arguments that are really driven home are likely to be the servants of political intent. Since the first thing man will do for his ideal or interest is to lie, we shall expect, and as a matter of fact we find, that effective information is almost always adulterated or selective[18] and that effective reasoning in politics consists mainly in trying to exalt certain propositions into axioms and to put others out of court; it thus reduces to the psycho-technics mentioned before. The reader who thinks me unduly pessimistic need only ask himself whether he has never heard—or said himself—that this or that awkward fact must not be told publicly, or that a certain line of reasoning, though valid, is undesirable. If men who according to any current standard are perfectly honorable or even high-minded reconcile themselves to the implications of this, do they not thereby show what they think about the merits or even the existence of the will of the people?

There are of course limits to all this.[19] And there is truth in Jefferson's dictum that in the end the people are wiser than any single individual can be, or in Lincoln's about the impossibility of "fooling all the people all the time." But both dicta stress the long-run aspect in a highly significant way. It is no doubt possible to argue that given time the collective psyche will evolve opinions that not infrequently strike us as highly reasonable and even shrewd. History however consists of a succession of short-run situations that may alter the course of events for good. If all the people can in the short run be "fooled" step by step into something they do not really want, and if this is not an exceptional case which we could afford to neglect, then no amount of retrospective common sense will alter the fact that in reality they neither raise nor decide issues but that the issues that shape their fate are normally raised and decided for them. More than anyone else the lover of democracy has every reason to accept this fact and to clear his creed from the aspersion that it rests upon make-believe.

IV: Reasons for the Survival of the Classical Doctrine

But how is it possible that a doctrine so patently contrary to fact should have survived to this day and continued to hold its place the hearts of the people and in the official language of governments? The refuting facts are known to all; everybody admits them with perfect, frequently with cynical, frankness. The theoretical basis, utilitarian rationalism, is dead; nobody accepts it as a correct theory of the body politic. Nevertheless that question is not difficult to answer.

First of all, though the classical doctrine of collective action may not be supported by the results of empirical analysis, it is powerfully supported by that association with religious belief to which I have adverted already. This may not be obvious at first sight. The utilitarian leaders were anything but religious in the ordinary sense of the term. In fact they believed themselves to be anti-religious and they were so considered almost universally. They took pride in what they thought was precisely an unmetaphysical attitude and they were quite out of sympathy with the religious institutions and the religious movements of their time. But we need only cast another glance at the picture they drew of the social process in order to discover that it embodied essential features of the faith of protestant Christianity and was in fact derived from that faith. For the intellectual who had cast off his religion the utilitarian creed provided a substitute for it. For many of those who had retained their religious belief the classical doctrine became the political complement of it.[20]

Thus transposed into the categories of religion, this doctrine—and in consequence the kind of democratic persuasion which is based upon it—changes its very nature. There is no longer any need for logical scruples about the Common Good and Ultimate Values. All this is settled for us by the plan of the Creator whose purpose defines and sanctions everything. What seemed indefinite or unmotivated before is suddenly quite definite and convincing. The voice of the people that is the voice of God for instance. Or take Equality. Its very meaning is in doubt, and there is hardly any rational warrant for exalting it into a postulate, so long as we move in the sphere of empirical analysis. But Christianity harbors a strong equalitarian element. The Redeemer died for all: He did not differentiate between individuals of different social status. In doing so, he testified to the intrinsic value of the individual soul, a value that admits of no gradations. Is not this a sanction-and, as it seems to me, the only possible sanction[21]—of "everyone to count for one, no one to count for more than one"—a sanction that pours super-mundane meaning into articles of the democratic creed for which it is not easy to find any other? To be sure this interpretation does not cover the whole ground. However, so far as it goes, it seems to explain many things that otherwise would be unexplainable and in fact meaningless. In particular, it explains the believer's attitude toward criticism: again, as in the case of socialism, fundamental dissent is looked upon not merely as error but as sin; it elicits not merely logical counterargument but also moral indignation.

We may put our problem differently and say that democracy, when motivated in this way, ceases to be a mere method that can be discussed rationally like a steam engine or a disinfectant. It actually becomes what from another standpoint I have held it incapable of becoming, viz., an ideal or rather a part of an ideal schema of things. The very word may become a flag, a symbol of all a man holds dear, of everything that he loves about his nation whether rationally contingent to it or not. On the one hand, the question how the various propositions implied in the democratic belief are related to the facts of politics will then become as irrelevant to him as is, to the believing Catholic, the question how the doings of Alexander VI tally with the supernatural halo surrounding the papal office. On the other hand, the democrat of this type, while accepting postulates carrying large implications about equality and brotherliness, will be in a position also to accept, in all sincerity, almost any amount of deviations from them that his own behavior or position may involve. That is not even illogical. Mere distance from fact is no argument against an ethical maxim or a mystical hope. Second, there is the fact that the forms and phrases of classical democracy are for many nations associated with events and developments in their history which are enthusiastically approved by large majorities. Any opposition to an established regime is likely to use these forms and phrases whatever its meaning and social roots may be.[22] If it prevails and if subsequent developments prove satisfactory, then these forms will take root in the national ideology.

The United States is the outstanding example. Its very existence as a sovereign state is associated with a struggle against a monarchial and aristocratic England. A minority of loyalists excepted, Americans had, at the time of the Grenville administration, probably ceased to look upon the English monarch as *their* king and the English aristocracy as *their* aristocracy. In the War of Independence they fought what in fact as well as in their feeling had become a foreign monarch and a foreign aristocracy who interfered with their political and economic interests. Yet from an early stage of the troubles they presented their case, which really was a national one, as a case of the "people" versus its "rulers," in terms of inalienable Rights of Man and in the light of the general principles of classical democracy. The wording of the Declaration of Independence and of the Constitution adopted these principles. A prodigious development followed that absorbed and satisfied most people and thereby seemed to verify the doctrine embalmed in the sacred documents of the nation.

Oppositions rarely conquer when the groups in possession are in the prime of their power and success. In the first half of the nineteenth century, the oppositions that professed the classical creed of democracy rose and eventually prevailed against governments some of which—especially in Italy—were obviously in a state of decay and had become bywords of incompetence, brutality and corruption. Naturally though not quite logically, this redounded to the credit of that creed which moreover showed up to advantage when compared with the benighted superstitions sponsored by those governments. Under these circumstances, democratic revolution meant the advent of freedom and decency, and the democratic creed meant a gospel of reason and betterment. To be sure, this advantage was bound to be lost and the gulf between the doctrine and the practice of democracy was bound to be discovered. But the glamour of the dawn was slow to fade.

Third, it must not be forgotten that there are social patterns in which the classical doctrine will actually fit facts with a sufficient degree of approximation. As has been pointed out, this is the case with many small and primitive societies which as a matter of fact served as a prototype to the authors of that doctrine. It may be the case also with societies that are not primitive provided they are not too differentiated and do not harbor any serious problems. Switzerland is the best example. There is so little to quarrel about in a world of peasants which, excepting hotels and banks, contains no great capitalist industry, and the problems of public policy are so simple and so stable that an overwhelming majority can be expected to understand them and to agree about them. But if we can conclude that in such cases the classical doctrine approximates reality we have to add immediately that it does so not because it describes an effective mechanism of political decision but only because there are no great decisions to be made. Finally, the case of the United States may again be invoked in order to show that the classical doctrine sometimes appears to fit facts even in a society that is big and highly differentiated and in which there are great issues to decide provided the sting is taken out of them by favorable conditions. Until this country's entry into the First World War, the public mind was concerned mainly with the business of exploiting the economic possibilities of the environment. So long as this business was not seriously interfered with nothing mattered fundamentally to the average citizen who looked on the antics of politicians with good-natured contempt. Sections might get excited over the tariff, over silver, over local misgovernment, or over an occasional squabble with England. The people at large did not care much, except in the one case of serious disagreement which in fact produced national disaster, the Civil War.

And fourth, of course, politicians appreciate a phraseology that flatters the masses and offers an excellent opportunity not only for evading responsibility but also for crushing opponents in the name of the people.

Chapter XXII: Another Theory of Democracy

I: Competition for Political Leadership.

I think that most students of politics have by now come to accept the criticisms leveled at the classical doctrine of democracy in the preceding chapter. I also think that most of them agree, or will agree before long, in accepting another theory which is much truer to life and at the same time salvages much of what sponsors of the democratic method really mean by this term. Like the classical theory, it may be put into the nutshell of a definition.

It will be remembered that our chief troubles about the classical theory centered in the proposition that "the people hold a definite and rational opinion about every individual question and that they give effect to this opinion—in a democracy—by choosing "representatives" who will see to it that that opinion is carried out. Thus the selection of the representatives is made secondary to the primary purpose of the democratic arrangement which is to vest the power of deciding political issues in the electorate. Suppose we reverse the roles of these two elements and make the deciding of issues by the electorate secondary to the election of the men who are to do the deciding. To put it differently, we now take the view that the role of the people is to produce a government, or else an intermediate body which in turn will produce a national executive[23] or government. And we define: the democratic method is that institutional arrangement for arriving at political decisions in which individuals acquire the power to decide by means of a competitive struggle for the people's vote.

Defense and explanation of this idea will speedily show that, as to both plausibility of assumptions and tenability of propositions, it greatly improves the theory of the democratic process.

First of all, we are provided with a reasonably efficient criterion by which to distinguish democratic governments from others. We have seen that the classical theory meets with difficulties on that score because both the will and the good of the people may be, and in many historical instances have been, served just as well or better by governments that cannot be described as democratic according to any accepted usage of the term. Now we are in a somewhat better position partly because we are resolved to stress a *modus procedendi* the presence or absence of which it is in most cases easy to verify?[24]

For instance, a parliamentary monarchy like the English one fulfills the requirements of the democratic method because the monarch is practically constrained to appoint to cabinet office the same people as parliament would elect. A "constitutional" monarchy does not qualify to be called democratic because electorates and parliaments, while having all the other rights that electorates and parliaments have in parliamentary monarchies, lack the power to impose their choice as to the governing committee: the cabinet ministers are in this case servants of the monarch, in substance as well as in name, and can in principle be dismissed as well as appointed by him. Such an arrangement may satisfy the people. The electorate may reaffirm this fact by voting against any proposal for change. The monarch may be so popular as to be able to defeat any competition for the supreme office. But since no machinery is provided for making this competition effective the case does not come within our definition.

Second, the theory embodied in this definition leaves all the room we may wish to have for a proper recognition of the vital fact of leadership. The classical theory did not do this but, as we have seen, attributed to the electorate an altogether unrealistic degree of initiative which practically amounted to ignoring leadership. But collectives act almost exclusively by accepting leadership—this is the dominant mechanism of practically any collective action which is more than a reflex. Propositions about the working and the results of the democratic method that take account of this are bound to be infinitely more realistic than propositions which do not. They will not stop at the execution of a *volonté generalé* but will go some way toward showing how it emerges or how it is substituted or faked. What we have termed Manufactured Will is no longer outside the theory, an aberration for the absence of which we piously pray; it enters on the ground floor as it should.

Third, however, so far as there are genuine group-wise volitions at all—for instance the will of the unemployed to receive unemployment benefit or the will of other groups to help—our theory does not neglect them. On the contrary we are now able to insert them in exactly the role they actually play. Such volitions do not as a rule assert themselves directly. Even if strong and definite they remain latent, often for decades, until they are called to life by some political leader who turns them into political factors. This he does, or else his agents do it for him, by organizing these volitions, by working them up and by including eventually appropriate items in his competitive offering. The interaction between sectional interests and public opinion and the way in which they produce the pattern we call the political situation appear from this angle in a new and much clearer light.

Fourth, our theory is of course no more definite than is the concept of competition for leadership. This concept presents similar difficulties as the concept of competition in the economic sphere, with which it may be usefully compared. In economic life competition is never completely lacking, but hardly ever is it perfect.[25] Similarly, in political life there is always some competition, though perhaps only a potential one, for the allegiance of the people. To simplify matters we have restricted the kind of competition for leadership which is to define democracy, to free competition for a free vote. The justification for this is that democracy seems to imply a recognized method by which to conduct the competitive struggle, and that the electoral method is practically the only one available for communities of any size. But though this excludes many ways of securing leadership which should be excluded,[26] such as competition by military insurrection, it does not exclude the cases that are strikingly analogous to the economic phenomena we label "unfair" or "fraudulent" competition or restraint of competition. And we cannot exclude them because if we did we should be left with a completely unrealistic ideal.[27] Between this ideal case which does not exist and the cases in which all competition with the established leader is prevented by force, there is a continuous range of variation within which the democratic method of government shades off into the autocratic one by imperceptible steps. But if we wish to understand and not to philosophize, this is as it should be. The value of our criterion is not seriously impaired thereby.

Fifth, our theory seems to clarify the relation that subsists between democracy and individual freedom. If by the latter we mean the existence of a sphere of individual self-government the boundaries of which are historically variable—no society tolerates absolute freedom even of conscience and of speech, *no* society reduces that sphere to zero—the question clearly becomes a matter of degree. We have seen that the democratic method does not necessarily guarantee a greater amount of individual freedom than another political method would permit in similar circumstances. It may well be the other way round. But there is still a relation between the two. If, on principle at least, everyone is free to compete for political leadership[28] by presenting himself to the electorate, this will in most cases though not in all mean a considerable amount of freedom of discussion *for all*. In particular it will normally mean a considerable amount of freedom of the press. This relation between democracy and freedom is not absolutely stringent and can be tampered with. But, from the standpoint of the intellectual, it is nevertheless very important. At the same time, it is all there is to that relation.

Sixth, it should be observed that in making it the primary function of the electorate to produce a government (directly or through an intermediate body) I intended to include in this phrase also the function of evicting it. The one means simply the acceptance of a leader or a group of leaders, the other means simply the withdrawal of this acceptance. This takes care of an element the reader may have missed. He may have thought that the electorate controls as well as installs. But since electorates normally do not control their political leaders in any way except by refusing to reelect them or the parliamentary majorities that support them, it seems well to reduce our ideas about this control in the way indicated by our definition. Occasionally, spontaneous revulsions occur which upset a government or an individual minister directly or else enforce a certain course of action. But they are not only exceptional, they are, as we shall see, contrary to the spirit of the democratic method.

Seventh, our theory sheds much-needed light on an old controversy. Whoever accepts the classical doctrine of democracy and in consequence believes that the democratic method is to guarantee that issues be decided and policies framed according to the will of the people must be struck by the fact that, even if that will were undeniably real and definite, decision by simple majorities would in many cases distort it rather than give effect to it. Evidently the will of the majority is the will of the majority and not the will of "the people." The latter is a mosaic that the former completely fails to "represent." To equate both by definition is not to solve the problem. Attempts at real solutions have however been made by the authors of the various plans for Proportional Representation.

These plans have met with adverse criticism on practical grounds. It is in fact obvious not only that proportional representation will offer opportunities for all sorts of idiosyncrasies to assert themselves but also that it may prevent democracy from producing efficient governments and thus prove a danger in times of stress.[29] But before concluding that democracy becomes unworkable if its principle is carried out consistently, it is just as well to ask ourselves whether this principle really implies proportional representation. As a matter of fact it does not. If acceptance of leadership is the true function of the electorate's vote, the case for proportional representation collapses because its premises are no longer binding. The principle of democracy then merely means that the reins of government should be handed to those who command more support than do any of the competing individuals or teams. And this in turn seems to assure the standing of the majority system within the logic of the democratic method, although we might still condemn it on grounds that lie outside of that logic [. . .].

NOTES

1. The official theory of the functions of a cabinet minister holds in fact that he is appointed in order to see to it that in his department the will of the people prevails.

2. The very meaning of "greatest happiness" is open to serious doubt. But even if this doubt could be removed and definite meaning could be attached to the sum total of economic satisfaction of a group of people, that maximum would still be relative to given situations and valuations, which it might be impossible to alter, or compromise on, in a democratic way.

3. This accounts for the strongly equalitarian character both of the classical doctrine of democracy and of popular democratic beliefs. It will be pointed out later on how Equality may acquire the status of an ethical postulate. As a factual statement about human nature, it cannot be true in any conceivable sense. In recognition of this the postulate itself has often been reformulated so as to mean "equality of opportunity." But, disregarding even the difficulties inherent in the word *opportunity*, this reformulation does not help us much because it is actual and not potential equality of performance in matters of political behavior that is required if each man's vote is to carry the same weight in the decision of issues. It should be noted in passing that democratic phraseology has been instrumental in fostering the association of inequality of any kind with "injustice," which is so important an element in the psychic pattern of the unsuccessful and in the arsenal of the politician who uses him. One of the most curious symptoms of this was the Athenian institution of ostracism or rather the use to which it was sometimes put. Ostracism consisted in banishing an individual by popular vote, not necessarily for any particular reason: it sometimes served as a method of eliminating an uncomfortably prominent citizen who was felt to "count for more than one."

4. This term is here being used in its original sense and not in the sense which it is rapidly acquiring at present and which suggests the definition: propaganda is any statement emanating from a source that we do not like. I suppose that the term derives from the name of the committee of cardinals which deals with matters concerning the spreading of the Catholic faith, the *congregatio de propaganda fide*. In itself therefore it does not carry any derogatory meaning and in particular it does not imply distortion of facts. One can make propaganda, for instance, for a scientific method. It simply means the presentation of facts and arguments with a view to influencing people's actions or opinions in a definite direction.

5. The legislative bodies, cowed though they were, completely failed in fact to support Napoleon in this policy. And some of his most trusted paladins opposed it.

6. Other instances could in fact be adduced from Napoleon's practice. He was an autocrat who, whenever his dynastic interests and his foreign policy were not concerned, simply strove to do what he conceived the people wanted or needed. This is what the advice amounted to which he gave to Eugene Beauharnais concerning the latter's administration of northern Italy.

7. This is the title of the frank and charming book by one of the most lovable English radicals who ever lived, Graham Wallas. In spite of all that has since been written on the subject and especially in spite of all the detailed case studies that now make it possible to see so much more clearly, that book may still be recommended as the best introduction to political psychology. Yet, after having stated with admirable honesty the case against the uncritical ac-

ceptance of the classical doctrine, the author fails to draw the obvious conclusion. This is all the more remarkable because he rightly insists on the necessity of a scientific attitude of mind and because he does not fail to take Lord Bryce to task for having, in his book on the American commonwealth, professed himself "grimly" resolved to see some blue sky in the midst of clouds of disillusioning facts. Why, so Graham Wallas' seems to exclaim, what should we say of a meteorologist who insisted from the outset that he saw some blue sky? Nevertheless in the constructive part of his book he takes much the same ground.

8. The German term, *Massenpsychologie*, suggests a warning: the psychology of crowds must not be confused with the psychology of the masses. The former does not necessarily carry any class connotation and in itself has nothing to do with a study of the ways of thinking and feeling of, say, the working class.

9. In the above passage irrationality means failure to act rationally upon a given wish. It does not refer to the reasonableness of the wish itself in the opinion of the observer. This is important to note because economists in appraising the extent of consumers' irrationality sometimes exaggerate it by confusing the two things. Thus, a factory girl's finery may seem to a professor an indication of irrational behavior for which there is no other explanation but the advertiser's arts. Actually, it may be all she craves for. If so her expenditure on it may be ideally rational in the above sense.

10. This level differs of course not only as between epochs and places but also, at a given time and place, as between different industrial sectors and classes. There is no such thing as a universal pattern of rationality.

11. Rationality of thought and rationality of action are two different things. Rationality of thought does not always guarantee rationality of action. And the latter may be present without any conscious deliberation and irrespective of any ability to formulate the rationale of one's action correctly. The observer, particularly the observer who uses in interview and questionnaire methods, often overlooks this and hence acquires an exaggerated idea of the importance of irrationality in behavior. This is another source of those overstatements which we meet so often.

12. It should be observed that in speaking of definite and genuine volitions I do not mean to exalt them into ultimate data for all kinds of social analysis. Of course they are themselves the product of the social process and the social environment. All I mean is that they may serve as data for the kind of special-purpose analysis which the economist has in mind when he derives prices from tastes or wants that are "given" at any moment and need not be further analyzed each time. Similarly we may for our purpose speak of genuine and definite volitions that at any moment are given independently of attempts to manufacture them, although we recognize that these genuine volitions themselves are the result of environmental influences in the past, propagandist influences included. This distinction between genuine and manufactured will (see below) is a difficult one and cannot be applied in all cases and for all purposes. For our purpose however it is sufficient to point to the obvious common-sense case which can be made for it.

13. The reason why the Benthamites so completely overlooked this is that they did not consider the possibilities of mass corruption in modern capitalism. Committing in their political theory the same error which they committed in their economic theory, they felt no compunction about postulating that "the people" were the best judges of their own individual interests and that these must necessarily coincide with the interests of all the people taken together. Of course this was made easier for them because actually though not intentionally they philosophized in terms of bourgeois interests which had more to gain from a parsimonious state than from any direct bribes.

14. William James' "pungent sense of reality." The relevance of this point has been particularly emphasized by Graham Wallas.

15. It will help to clarify the point if we ask ourselves why so much more intelligence and clear-headedness show up at a bridge table than in, say, political discussion among non-politicians. At the bridge table we have a definite task; we have rules that discipline us; success and failure are clearly defined; and we are prevented from behaving irresponsibly because every mistake we make will not only immediately tell but also be immediately allocated to us. These conditions, by their failure to be fulfilled for the political behavior of the ordinary citizen, show why it is that in politics he lacks all the alertness and the judgment he may display in his profession.

16. See ch. xii.

17. The importance of such bursts cannot be doubted. But it is possible to doubt their genuineness. Analysis will show in many instances that they are induced by the action of some group and do not spontaneously arise from the people. In thiscase they enter into a (second) class of phenomena which we are about to deal with. Personally, I do believe that genuine instances exist. But I cannot be sure thatmore thorough analysis would not reveal some psycho-technical effort at the bottom of them.

18. Selective information, if in itself correct, is an attempt to lie by speaking the truth.

19. Possibly they might show more clearly if issues were more frequently decided by referendum. Politicians presumably know why they are almost invariably hostile to that institution.

20. Observe the analogy with socialist belief which also is a substitute for Christian belief to some and a complement of it to others.

21. It might be objected that, however difficult it may be to attach *a general* meaning to the word Equality, such meaning can be unraveled from its context in most if not all cases. For instance, it may be permissible to infer from the circumstances in which the Gettysburg address was delivered that by the "proposition that all men are created free and equal," Lincoln simply meant equality of legal status versus the kind of inequality that is implied in the recognition of slavery. This meaning would be definite enough. But if we ask why that proposition—"every man is by nature exactly like every other man," then we can only fall back upon the divine sanction supplied by Christian belief. This solution is conceivably implied in the word "created."

22. It might seem that an exception should be made for oppositions that issue into frankly autocratic regimes. But even most of these rose, as a matter of history, in democratic ways and based their rule on the approval of the people. Caesar was not killed by plebeians. But the aristocratic oligarchs who did kill him also used democratic phrases.

23. The insincere word "executive" really points in the wrong direction. It ceases however to do so if we use it in the sense in which we speak of the "executives" of a business corporation who also do a great deal more than "execute" the will of stockholders.

24. See however the fourth point below.

25. In Part II we had examples of the problems which arise out of this.

26. It also excludes methods which should not be excluded, for instance, the acquisition of political leadership by the people's tacit acceptance of it or by election *quasi per inspirationem.* The latter differs from election by voting only by a technicality. But the former is not quite without importance even in modern politics; the sway held by a party boss *within his party is* often based on nothing but tacit acceptance of his leadership. Comparatively speaking however these are details which may, I think, be neglected in a sketch like this.

27. As in the economic field, *some* restrictions are implicit in the legal and moral principles of the community.

28. Free, that is, in the same sense in which everyone is free to start another textile mill.

29. The argument against proportional representation has been ably stated by Processor F. A. Hermens in "The Trojan Horse of Democracy," *Social Research*, November 1938.

CARL SCHMITT

EXCERPT FROM *THE CRISIS OF PARLIAMENTARY DEMOCRACY* (1923)

Carl Schmitt (1888–1985) was a German professor of law. He was one of the foremost interpreters of the idea of the liberal Rechtsstaat, *of a rule of law, as well as one of its fiercest critics. Schmitt belonged to the so called conservative revolution of the Weimar republic and ended up as "Kronjurist des Dritten Reiches." He became a Nazi party member in 1933 and was for a period president of the "Vereinigung Nationalsozialistischer Juristen." In 1945, he lost his professorship and was examined during the Nürnberg trials without being accused. Even if compromised by his Nazi involvement, Schmitt's writings have attracted a growing interest during the last decades, also among leftist thinkers, such as Chantal Mouffe, who is represented in this reader.*

Schmitt's political thought belongs to the "dark" tradition of thinkers, such as Machiavelli and Hobbes. For Schmitt, the essence of politics is the sovereign decision freed from all normative bonds, sovereignty being defined here with reference to a state of emergency: As he wrote in Political Theology *([1922] 1985), "Control over the emergency is in a very real sense the power to decide." A decade later, in* The Concept of the Political, *he argued that politics was grounded in the distinction between friends and enemies. The enemy is not necessarily bad or ugly, just the "other," the alien, but how the enemy is defined shapes and affirms the identity of a political collective.*

Schmitt developed this concept of the political in opposition to liberal constitutionalism whose insistence that political power be subjected to a system of norms, he saw as an empty "normativism," negating the very nature of the political. It was also outdated. The presupposed dualism of state and society was no longer valid as a result of the influence of organized interest groups on state on the one hand and state's expansion and intervention into society on the other.

The following text comes from his The Crisis of Parliamentary Democracy *([1923] 1986). Here, Schmitt attacks one of the core principles of a liberal constitution, namely that a free public sphere should form the basis for parliamentary proceedings. He argues that the idea of "government by discussion" relies on the rationalistic belief that the parliament is "the place in which particles of reason that strewn unequally among human beings gather themselves and bring public power under their control." However, the real existing public sphere and parliament are far from fulfilling this ideal synthesizing and controlling function.*

Chapter 2: The Principles of Parliamentarism

In the struggle between parliament and monarchy, a government that was decisively influenced by the representation of the people was called a parliamentary government, and the word was thus applied to a particular kind of executive. The meaning of the concept "parliamentarism" was thereby changed. "Parliamentary government" presupposes a parliament, and to demand such a government means that one begins with parliament as an existing institution in order to extend its powers, or, in the customary language of constitutionalism, the legislative should influence the executive. The fundamental concept of the parliamentary principle

cannot rest solely on the participation of parliament in government, and so far as
the question that interests us here is concerned, it cannot be expected that a discussion of this postulate of parliamentary government would produce much. We are
concerned here with the ultimate intellectual foundations of parliamentarism itself,
not with the extension of the power of parliament. Why has parliament been in
fact the *ultimum sapientiae* for many generations, and on what has the belief in this
institution rested for over a century? The demand that parliament must control the
government, and influence the selection of ministers who are responsible to it, assumes that belief.

The oldest justification for parliament, constantly repeated through the centuries,
takes into account an extreme "expedient"[1]: The people in its entirety must decide,
as was originally the case when all members of the community could assemble
themselves under the village tree. But for practical reasons it is impossible today for
everyone to come together at the same time in one place; it is also impossible to ask
everyone about every detail. Because of this, one helps oneself quite reasonably with
an elected committee of responsible people, and parliament is precisely that. So the
familiar scale originated: Parliament is a committee of the people, the government
is a committee of parliament. The notion of parliamentarism thereby appears to be
something essentially democratic. But in spite of all its coincidence with democratic
ideas and all the connections it has to them, parliamentarism is not democracy any
more than it is realized in the practical perspective of expediency. If for practical and
technical reasons the representatives of the people can decide instead of the people
themselves, then certainly a single trusted representative could also decide in the
name of the same people.[2] Without ceasing to be democratic, the argument would
justify an antiparliamentary Caesarism. Consequently, this cannot be specific to the
idea of parliamentarism, and the essential point is not that parliament is a committee of the people, a council of trusted men. There is even a contradiction here
in that parliament, as the first committee, is independent of the people throughout
the electoral period and is not usually subject to recall, whereas the parliamentary
government, the second committee, is always dependent on the trust of the first
committee and can therefore be recalled at any time.

The *ratio* of parliament rests, according to the apt characterization of Rudolf
Smend,[3] in a "dynamic-dialectic," that is, in a process of confrontation of differences and opinions, from which the real political will results. The essence of parliament is therefore public deliberation of argument and counterargument, public
debate and public discussion, parley, and all this without taking democracy into
account.[4] The absolutely typical chain of thought is to be found in the absolutely
typical representative of parliamentarism, in Guizot. Starting from right (as the opposite to might), he lists the essential characteristics of a system that guarantees the
rule of law: (1) that "the powers" are always forced to discuss and thereby to seek
the truth together; (2) that the openness of the whole of political life places "the
powers" under the citizens' control; and (3) that press freedom prompts citizens to
seek the truth for themselves and to make it known to "the powers."[5] Parliament is
accordingly the place in which particles of reason that are strewn unequally among
human beings gather themselves and bring public power under their control. This
appears a typical rationalist idea. Nevertheless it would be incomplete and inexact

to define modern parliament as an institution that has come into existence out of the rationalist spirit. Its ultimate justification and its obviousness to a whole epoch rests on the fact that this rationalism is not absolute and direct, but relative in a specific sense. Against Guizot's maxim, Mohl objected: Where is there any kind of certainty that the possessors of particles of reason are to be found precisely in parliament?[6] The answer lies in the notion of free competition and a preestablished harmony, which, certainly in the institution of parliament, as in politics itself, often appears in a hardly recognizable disguise.

It is essential that liberalism be understood as a consistent, comprehensive metaphysical system. Normally one only discusses the economic line of reasoning that social harmony and the maximization of wealth follow from the free economic competition of individuals, from freedom of contract, freedom of trade, free enterprise. But all this is only an application of a general liberal principle. It is exactly the same: That the truth can be found through an unrestrained clash of opinion and that competition will produce harmony. The intellectual core of this thought resides finally in its specific relationship to truth, which becomes a mere function of the eternal competition of opinions. In contrast to the truth, it means renouncing a definite result. In German thought the notion of eternal discussion was more accessible in the Romantic conception of an unending conversation,[7] and it may be remarked in passing that all the intellectual confusion of the conventional reading of German political Romanticism, which characterizes it as conservative and antiliberal, is revealed in precisely this connection. Freedom of speech, freedom of press, freedom of assembly, freedom of discussion, are not only useful and expedient, therefore, but really life-and-death questions for liberalism. Guizot's description placed particular emphasis on freedom of the press as the third characteristic of parliamentarism, after discussion and openness. One can easily see that freedom of the press is only a means for discussion and openness and not an independent factor. But since a free press is a typical means for the other characteristic features of liberalism, Guizot is quite justified in giving it particular emphasis.

Only if the central place of discussion in the liberal system is correctly recognized do the two political demands that are characteristic of liberal rationalism take on their proper significance with a scientific clarity above the confused atmosphere of slogans, political tactics, and pragmatic considerations: the postulate of openness in political life and the demand for a division of powers, or more specifically the theory of a balance of opposing forces from which truth will emerge automatically as an equilibrium. Because of the decisive importance of openness and especially of the power of public opinion in liberal thought, it appears that liberalism and democracy are identical here. In the theory of the division of powers, that is obviously not the case. These, on the contrary, are used by Hasbach in order to construct the sharpest contrast between liberalism and democracy.[8] A threefold division of powers, a substantial distinction between the legislative and the executive, the rejection of the idea that the plenitude of state power should be allowed to gather at any one point—all of this is in fact the antithesis of a democratic concept of identity. The two postulates are thus not simple equivalents. Of the many very different ideas connected to these two demands, only those that are essential for the understanding of the intellectual center of modern parliamentarism will be considered here.

1: Openness

The belief in public opinion has its roots in a conception that has not been properly emphasized in the enormous literature on public opinion, not even in Tönnies's great work.[9] It is less a question of public opinion than a question about the openness of opinions. This becomes clear when one identifies the historical contradiction from which these demands arise and have arisen, namely, the theory of state secrets, *Arcana rei publicae*, that dominates much of sixteenth- and seventeenthcentury literature. This theory of a great practice began with the literature on *Staatsraison*, the *ratio status* of which it is actually the core; its literary beginning is in Machiavelli and its high point in Paolo Sarpi. For a systematic and methodological treatment by German scholars, Arnold Clapmar's book can be mentioned as an example.[10] It is, generally speaking, a theory that treats the state and politics only as techniques for the assertion of power and its expansion. Against its Machiavellianism there arose a great anti-Machiavellian literature, which, shocked by the St. Bartholomew's Massacre (1572), boiled with indignation at the immorality of such principles. It answered the power ideal of political technique with the concept of law and justice. This was above all the argument of the Monarchomachian authors against princely absolutism.[11] In intellectual history this controversy is first of all only an example of the old struggle between might and right: The Machiavellian use of power is combated with a moral and legal ethos. But this description is incomplete because specific counterdemands gradually develop: precisely those two postulates of openness and the division of powers. These try to neutralize the concentration of power contained in absolutism through a system of the division of powers. The postulate of openness finds its specific opponent in the idea that *Arcana* belong to every kind of politics, political-technical secrets which are in fact just as necessary for absolutism as business and economic secrets are for an economic life that depends on private property and competition.

Cabinet politics, conducted by a few people behind closed doors, now appears something *eo ipso* evil, and as a result, the openness of political life seems to be right and good just because of its openness. Openness becomes an absolute value, although at first it was only a practical means to combat the bureaucratic, specialist-technical secret politics of absolutism. The elimination of secret politics and secret diplomacy becomes a wonder cure for every kind of political disease and corruption, and public opinion becomes a totally effective controlling force. Of course, public opinion attained this absolute character first in the eighteenth century, during the Enlightenment. The light of the public is the light of the Enlightenment, a liberation from superstition, fanaticism, and ambitious intrigue. In every system of Enlightened despotism, public opinion plays the role of an absolute corrective. The power of a despot can be all the greater as Enlightenment increases, for Enlightened public opinion makes the abuse of power impossible in itself. For the Enlightened, that can be taken for granted. Le Mercier de la Rivière developed the notion systematically.[12] Condorcet attempted to draw out its practical conclusions with an enthusiastic belief in freedom of speech and the press that is very moving when one remembers the experiences of recent generations: Where there is freedom of the press, the misuse of power is unthinkable; a single free newspaper would destroy the most powerful tyrant; the printing press is the basis of freedom, "the art that creates liberty."[13] Even Kant was in this respect only an expression of the political belief of his time, a belief in the progress of publicity and in the public's ability to enlighten itself inevitably, if it were only free to do so.[14] In England the fanatic of liberal rationality was Jeremy Bentham. Before him, argument in England had been essentially practical and pragmatic. Bentham proclaimed the significance of a free press from a liberal ideology: Freedom of public discussion, especially freedom of the press, is the most effective protection against political abuses, and "controlling power" is the real "check to arbitrary power" and so forth.[15] As this idea developed one comes across its contradiction of democracy once more. John Stuart Mill understood, with despairing concern, that a contradiction between democracy and freedom is possible and that the majority could crush minorities. Even the thought that a single person might be deprived of the opportunity to express his opinion set this positivist in an inexplicable uproar, because he considered it possible that this individual's expression of opinion might have come closest to the truth.[16]

Public opinion protected through freedom of speech, freedom of the press, freedom of assembly, and parliamentary immunities means freedom of opinion in liberal thought, with all the significance which the word *freedom* has in this system. Where the public can exercise pressure—through a single individual casting a vote, for example—here, at the transition of the private into the public, the contradictory demand for a secret ballot appears. Freedom of opinion is a freedom for private people; it is necessary for that competition of opinions in which the best opinion wins.

2: The division (balance) of powers

In modern parliamentarism the belief in public opinion is bound to a second, more organizational conception: the division or balance of different state activities and institutions. Here too the idea of competition appears, a competition from which the truth will emerge. That parliament assumes the role of the legislative in the division of powers and is limited to that role makes the rationalism which is at the heart of the theory of a balance of powers rather relative and, as will now be shown, it distinguishes this system from the absolute rationalism of the Enlightenment. One does not need to waste many words on the general meaning of the idea of balance. Of the images which typically recur in the history of political thought and state theory, and whose systematic investigation has not yet begun—for example, the state as a machine, the state as an organism, the king as the keystone of an arch, as a flag, or as the soul of a ship—the imagery of balance is most important for the modern age. Since the sixteenth century the image of a balance can be found in every aspect of intellectual life (Woodrow Wilson was certainly the first to acknowledge this in his speeches on freedom): a balance of trade in international economics, the European balance of power in foreign politics, the cosmic equilibrium of attraction and repulsion, the balance of the passions in the works of Malebranche and Shaftesbury, even a balanced diet is recommended by J. J. Moser. The importance for state theory of this universally employed conception is demonstrated by a few names: Harrington, Locke, Bolingbroke, Montesquieu, Mably, de Lolme, *The Federalist*, and the French National Assembly of 1789. To give just two modern examples: Maurice Hauriou, in his "Principes de droit public," applies the notion of equilibrium to every problem of the state and administration, and the enormous success of Robert Redslob's definition of parliamentary government (1918) demonstrates how powerful this theory is even today.[17]

Applied to the institution of parliament this general conception takes on a specific meaning. This has to be emphasized because it dominates even Rousseau's thought, although there it does not have this particular application to parliament.[18] Here, in parliament, there is a balance that assumes the moderate rationalism of this concept of the balance of powers. Under the suggestive influence of a compendium tradition, which Montesquieu's theory of the division of powers simplified,[19] one has become accustomed to seeing parliament as only a part of the state's functions, one part that is set against the others (executive and courts). Nevertheless, parliament should not be just a part of this balance, but precisely because it is the legislative, parliament should itself be balanced. This depends on a way of thinking that creates multiplicity everywhere so that an equilibrium created from the imminent dynamics of a system of negotiations replaces absolute unity. First through this processs can the legislative itself be balanced and mediated either in a bicameral system or through federalism; but even within a single chamber the balancing of outlooks and opinions functions as a consequence of this special kind of rationalism. An opposition belongs to the essence of parliament and every chamber, and there is actually a metaphysic of the two-party system. Normally a rather banal sentence is quoted, usually from Locke, to justify the balance of power theory.[20] It would be dangerous if the offices which make the laws were also to execute them; that would be too much temptation to the human desire for power. Therefore, neither the prince as head of the executive nor the parliament as legislative organ should be allowed to unite all state power in themselves. The first theories of the division and balance of power developed, after all, from an experience of the concentration of power in the Long Parliament of 1640.[21] But as soon as a justification in political theory was established, a constitutional theory with a constitutional concept of legislation appeared on the Continent. According to this, the institution of parliament must be understood as an essentially legislative state organ. Only this legislative concept justifies a notion that is scarcely understood today but which has held an absolutely dominant position in West European thought since the middle of the eighteenth century: that a constitution is identical with division of power. In article 16 of the Declaration of the Rights of Man and Citizens of 1789 can be found its most famous proclamation: "Any society in which the separation of powers and rights is not guaranteed has no constitution."[22] That the division of powers and a constitution are identical and that this defines the concept of a constitution even appears in German political thought from Kant to Hegel as a given. In consequence such a theory understands dictatorship not just as an antithesis of democracy but also essentially as the suspension of the division of powers, that is, as a suspension of the constitution, a suspension of the distinction between legislative and executive.[23]

3: The Concept of Law and Legislation in Parliamentarism

The parliamentary conception of legislation is already recognizable with the Monarchomachians. In his *Droit des Magistrats*, Beza writes: "One should not judge by cases, but by the law."[24] The *Vindiciae* of Junius Brutus was directed against the "pernicious doctrine" of Machiavelli, and displays not only a passionate feeling of justice but also a certain kind of rationalism. The author wanted to advance "mathematical ethics" and replace the concrete person of the king with an impersonal *authority* and a universal *reason*, which according to Aristotelian-scholastic tradition constitutes the essence of law. The king must obey the law as the body obeys the soul. The universal criterion of the law is deduced from the fact that law (in contrast to will or the command of a concrete person) is only *reason*, not desire, and that it has no *passions*, whereas a concrete person "is moved by a variety of particular passions."[25] In many different versions, but always with the essential characteristic of the "universal," this concept of legislation has become the foundation of constitutional theory. Grotius presents it in the scholastic form of the universal in contrast to the particular.[26] The whole theory of the *Rechtsstaat* rests on the contrast between law which is general and already promulgated, universally binding without exception, and valid in principle for all times, and a personal order which varies case to case according to particular concrete circumstances. In a well-known exposition, Otto Mayer talks about the inviolability of the law.[27] This conception of law is based on a rationalistic distinction between the (no longer universal but) general and the particular, and representatives of *Rechtsstaat* thinking believe that the general has a higher value, in itself, than the particular. This becomes especially clear in the juxtaposition of law and commission, which belongs to the center of Locke's argument. This classical theorist of the philosophy of the *Rechtsstaat*[28] is only one example of the controversy that has gone on for more than a century over the question of whether the impersonal law or the king personally is sovereign.[29] Even "the government of the United States of America can be designated with particular emphasis as a government of laws in contrast to a government of men."[30] The usual definition of sovereignty today rests on Bodin's recognition that it will always be necessary to make exceptions to the general rule in concrete circumstances, and that the sovereign is whoever decides what constitutes an exception.[31] The cornerstone, therefore, of constitutional and absolutist thought is a concept of law. Not of course the concept that in Germany one has called law in the formal sense ever since Laband,[32] according to which everything that comes into existence with the agreement of the popular assembly can be called law, but rather a principle that accords with certain logical attributes. The crucial distinction always remains whether the law is a general rational principle or a measure, a concrete decree, an order.

If only those regulations which have come into effect with the cooperation and participation of the popular assembly are called laws, then it is because the popular assembly, that is, the parliament, has taken its decisions according to a parliamentary method, considering arguments and counterarguments. As a consequence its decisions have a logically different character from that of commands which are only based on authority. This is expressed in the biting antitheses of Hobbes's definition of law: "Every man seeth, that some lawes are addressed to all the subjects in generall, some to particular Provinces; some to particular Vocations; and some to particular Men." To an absolutist it is obvious "that Law is not Counsell, but Command,"[33] essentially authority and not, as in the rationalist conception of the law in *Rechtsstaat* theories, truth and justice: *Autoritas, non Veritas facit Legem* ("Authority, not truth, makes the law"). Bolingbroke, who as a representative of the balance of powers theory of government thought in terms of the *Rechtsstaat*, formulated the

contrast as one of "Government by constitution" and "Government by will." He distinguished between constitution and government so that the constitution contained
a system of rules that is always and *at all times* valid, whereas government was what
actually occurred *at any time*; the one is unchanging, and the other changes with
time and circumstances.[34] The theory of law as the General Will (a will that is valuable as such because of its general character, in constrast to every particular will),
which dominated political thought throughout the seventeenth and eighteenth
centuries, can be understood as an expression of the concept of law in a *Rechtsstaat*.
Here, too, Condorcet is the typical representative of enlightened radicalism, for
whom everything concrete is only a case for the application of a general law. Every
activity, the whole life of the state, according to Condorcet, exhausts itself in law
and the application of law; even the executive has only the function "of pronounc-
ing a syllogism in which the law is the major premise; a more or less general fact
is the minor premise; and the conclusion is the application of the law." Justice is
not only, as Montesquieu said, "the mouth that pronounces the words of the law"
but the administration as well.[35] In the design of the Girondist constitution of 1793
this principle was to be firmly established in the distinguishing characteristic of the
law: "The characteristic that distinguishes the laws is to be found in their general-
ity and unlimited duration."[36] Even the executive should no longer command, but
only reason: "The agents of the executive do not command, they reason." The last
example of the central, systematic distinction of law and command is offered in
Hegel's argument about the legal character of a budget law: The so-called financial
law is, despite the cooperation of the corporations, essentially a government prerogative. It is thus inappropriately called a law because it embraces the widest, even
the complete, extent of government and the means of government. "A law passed
each year for only a year will seem unreasonable even to the common man who
distinguishes the substantial universality of a true law from that which is, by its
nature, only superficially general."[37]

4: Parliament Limited to Legislation

Law, *Veritas* in contrast to mere *Autoritas*, the generally correct norm in contrast to
the merely real and concrete order as Zitelmann argued in a brilliant formulation,[38]
as an imperative always contains an individual nontransferable moment; this idea
of law has always been conceived as something intellectual, unlike the executive,
which is essentially active. Legislation is *deliberare*, executive *agere*. This contrast too
has a history, one that begins with Aristotle. The rationalism of the French Enlightenment emphasized the legislative at the expense of the executive, and it found a
potent formula for the executive in the constitution of 5 Fructidor III (Title IX, 275):
"No armed force can deliberate."[39] The least doctrinaire explanation of this principle
is to be found in *The Federalist* (1788): The executive must be in the hand of a single
man because its energy and activity depend upon that; it is a general principle recognized by the best politicians and statesmen that legislation is deliberation and
therefore must be made by a larger assembly, while decision making and protection
of state secrets belong to the executive, things which "decline in the same measure
as the numbers increase." A few historical examples are given for this, and the argu-

ment of *The Federalist* then goes on: Let us set aside the uncertainty and confusion of historical reflection and affirm what reason and sound judgment tell us; the guarantee of civic freedom can only be logically implemented in the legislative, not in the executive; in the legislative the opposition of opinions and parties may hinder many useful and correct decisions, but the arguments of the minority do contain or reduce the excesses of the majority in this way. Different opinions are useful and necessary in the legislative; but not in the executive, where especially in times of war and disturbance action must be energetic; to this belongs a unity of decision.[40]

This moderate argument in *The Federalist* shows most clearly how little consideration was given in the balance theory to extending the rationalism that is authoritative in the legislative branch and parliament to the executive as well and thus dissolving it, too, into discussion. The rationalism of this theory even maintains a balance between the rational and the irrational (if this is what one calls things that are not accessible through rational discussion), and even here there is negotiation and a certain compromise, just as deism can be conceived as a metaphysical compromise.[41] By contrast, Condorcet's absolute rationalism negates the division of powers and destroys both its inherent negotiation and moderation of state powers and the independence of the parties. To his radicalism, the complicated balancing of the American constitution appeared subtle and difficult, a concession to the peculiarities of that land, one of those systems "where one must enforce the laws and in consequence truth, reason and justice,"[42] and where one must sacrifice "rational legislation" to the prejudices and stupidity of individual people. Such rationalism led to the elimination of balance and to a rational dictatorship. Both the American constitution and Condorcet identify law with truth; but the relative rationalism of the balance theory was limited to the legislative and logically limited again within parliament to a merely relative truth. A balance of opinions achieved through the contradiction and opposition of the parties can as a consequence never extend to absolute questions of an ideology, but can only concern things that are by their nature relative and therefore appropriate for this purpose. Contradictory oppositions eliminate parliamentarism, and parliamentary discussion assumes a common, indisputable foundation. Neither state power nor any kind of metaphysical conviction is allowed to appear immediately within its sphere; everything must be negotiated in a deliberately complicated process of balancing. Parliament is the place where one deliberates, that is, where a relative truth is achieved through discourse, in the discussion of argument and counterargument. Just as a multiplicity of powers is necessary for the state, so every parliamentary body needs multiple parties.

In German liberalism during the first half of the nineteenth century, these ideas were already bound up with historical thought. Surely the balance theory, with its elasticity and mediating capacity, could also integrate historical thought into its system. It is of great interest how the mechanical conception of balance was developed within nineteenth-century German liberalism in a peculiar way into a theory of organic agency and thus always retained, too, the possibility of accepting the prince as a preeminent person representing the unity of the state. While liberal discussion became an eternal conversation in German romanticism,[43] in the philosophical system of Hegel it is the self-development of consciousness out of positions and negations into always new syntheses. Hegel limited the Estates to a purely advisory role, and understood the function of corporative representation as that of bringing into existence "the public consciousness as an empirical universal, of which the thoughts and opinions of the many are particulars." The Estates are a mediating organ between the government and the people, which have only an advisory role in legislation; through the openness of their deliberations "the moment of formal freedom shall come into its right in respect of those members of civil society who are without any share in the executive," and general knowledge shall be extended and increased. "Through the opening of this opportunity to know . . . public opinion first reaches thoughts that are true and attains an insight into the situation and concept of the state and its affairs, and so first acquires ability to estimate these more rationally." Hence this kind of parliamentarism is an educational means, "and indeed one of the greatest."[44] On the value of openness and public opinion Hegel delivers a characteristic comment: "Estates Assemblies, open to the public, are a great spectacle and an excellent education for the citizens, and it is from them that the people learns best how to recognize the true character of its interests." The vitality of state interests first comes into existence in this way. "Public opinion is," for Hegel, "the unorganized way in which a people's opinions and wishes are made known." The theory of parties in German liberalism also contains a conception of organic life. There a distinction is made between parties and factions, in which the latter are caricatures of parties, whereas true parties are the expression of "living and multiple aspects of the public being . . . concerned with the proper disposition of public or state questions through a vigorous struggle."[45] Bluntschli, who took over F. Rohmer's theory of parties, says that a party cannot exist without an opposite party, that only the prince and civil servants (and these as such, not as private persons) are prohibited from membership in a party, because the state and its organs exist above the parties. "Constitutional law does not recognize parties; the calm and settled organization of the state is the common, firm order for everything, and it limits party business and party struggle. . . . Only if the movement of a new free life starts when politics begins do the parties appear." The parties are for him (following Rohmer) analogous to various stages of life. One also finds here a conception that Lorenz von Stein developed in its classic form: that contradictions belong to the life of the state just as they do to individual lives, and that these constitute the dynamic of something really living.[46]

On this point liberal thought merges with a specifically German organic theory and overcomes the mechanical conception of balance. But one could still hold onto the idea of parliamentarism with the help of this organic theory. As soon as there is a demand for parliamentary government, such as Mohl's, the idea of parliamentarism finds itself in a crisis because the perspective of a dialectic-dynamic process of discussion can certainly be applied to the legislative but scarcely to the executive. Only a universally applicable law, not a concrete order, can unite truth and justice through the balance of negotiations and public discussion. The old conception of parliament remained secure in these conclusions even in particular points, without their systematic interdependence being made clear. Bluntschli, for example, set out as an essential characteristic of modern parliament that it should not conclude its business in committees as the old corporative assembly had done.[47] That is completely correct; but this conclusion is derived from principles of openness and discussion that were no longer current.

5: The General Meaning of the Belief in Discussion

Openness and discussion are the two principles on which constitutional thought and parliamentarism depend in a thoroughly logical and comprehensive system. For the sense of justice of an entire historical epoch, they seemed to be essential and indispensable. What was to be secured through the balance guaranteed by openness and discussion was nothing less than truth and justice itself. One believed that naked power and force—for liberal, *Rechtsstaat* thinking, an evil in itself, "the way of beasts," as Locke said[48]—could be overcome through openness and discussion alone, and the victory of right over might achieved. There is an utterly typical expression for this way of thinking: "discussion in place of force." In this formulation, it comes from a man who was certainly not brilliant, not even important, but a typical adherent, perhaps, of the bourgeois monarchy. He summarized the warp and woof of the whole complex fabric of constitutional and parliamentary thought: All progress, including social progress, is realized "through representative institutions, that is, regulated liberty—through public discussion, that is, reason."[49]

The reality of parliamentary and party political life and public convictions are today far removed from such beliefs. Great political and economic decisions on which the fate of mankind rests no longer result today (if they ever did) from balancing opinions in public debate and counterdebate. Such decisions are no longer the outcome of parliamentary debate. The participation of popular representatives in government—parliamentary government—has proven the most effective means of abolishing the division of powers, and with it the old concept of parliamentarism. As things stand today, it is of course practically impossible not to work with committees, and increasingly smaller committees; in this way the parliamentary plenum gradually drifts away from its purpose (that is, from its public), and as a result it necessarily becomes a mere façade. It may be that there is no other practical alternative. But one must then at least have enough awareness of the historical situation to see that parliamentarism thus abandons its intellectual foundation and that the whole system of freedom of speech, assembly, and the press, of public meetings, parliamentary immunities and privileges, is losing its rationale. Small and exclusive committees of parties or of party coalitions make their decisions behind closed doors, and what representatives of the big capitalist interest groups agree to in the smallest committees is more important for the fate of millions of people, perhaps, than any political decision. The idea of modern parliamentarism, the demand for checks, and the belief in openness and publicity were born in the struggle against the secret politics of absolute princes. The popular sense of freedom and justice was outraged by arcane practices that decided the fate of nations in secret resolutions. But how harmless and idyllic are the objects of cabinet politics in the seventeenth and eighteenth centuries compared with the fate that is at stake today and which is the subject of all manner of secrets. In the face of this reality, the belief in a discussing public must suffer a terrible disillusionment. There are certainly not many people today who want to renounce the old liberal freedoms, particularly freedom of speech and the press. But on the European continent there are not many more who believe that these freedoms still exist where they could actually endanger the real holders of power. And the smallest number still believe that just laws and the right politics can be achieved through newspaper articles, speeches at demonstrations, and parliamentary debates. But that is the very belief in parliament. If in the actual circumstances of parliamentary business, openness and discussion have become an empty and trivial formality, then parliament, as it developed in the nineteenth century, has also lost its previous foundation and its meaning.

NOTES

1. Egon Zweig, *Die Lehre vom pouvoir constituant* (Tübingen: Mohr, 1909).

2. [Trans] Monarchists in the French National Assembly argued that a single man could be the representative of the people. See Karl Löwenstein, *Volk and Parlament nach der Staatstheorie der französischen Nationalversammlung von 1789* (Munich: Drei Masken Verlag, 1922).

3. Rudolf Smend, "Die Verschiebung der konstitutionellen Ordnung durch Verhältniswahl," in *Festgabe für Karl Bergbohm* [vol. 2] (Bonn: A. Marcus & E. Webers, 1919), 278; and Smend, "Die politische Gewalt im Verfassungsstaat and das Problem der Staatsform," in *Festgabe für Wilhelm Kahl* (Tübingen: Mohr, 1923), 22. [Both are reprinted in Smend, *Staatsrechtliche Abhandlungen* (Berlin: Duncker & Humblot, 1955, 1968), 60–88.—tr.]

4. As characteristic of this view the following can be mentioned: Adémar Esmein, *Éléments de droit constitutionnel* (Paris: Librairie de la Société du Recueil Général des Lois et des Arrets, 1909, 5th edition), 274: "Because the representative regime [by this he means parliamentarism] is essentially a regime of debate and free discussion." Further, in the seventh edition of the same work (Esmein-Nezard, 1921), vol. 1, 448, he explains all the institutions of parliamentary constitutional law today by noting that such a system "assumes the maximum liberty of decision and discussion in the legislative assembly." See also Harold Laski, *The Foundations of Sovereignty* [New York: Harcourt, Brace & Co., 1921], 36: "The fundamental hypothesis of government in a representative system is that it is government by discussion."

5. Guizot, *Histoire des origines du gouvernement représentatif en France*, vol. 2 (Paris: Didier, 1851), 14. This book arose from lectures that Guizot held from 1820 onward and often rewrote; it is the result of what an important scholar, an experienced politician, and an honorable man observed and thought in the years from 1814 to 1848. His theory of parliamentarism, inspired by the Anglo-Saxon spirit, Guizot called in the foreword (dated May 1851) "the faith and hope that have filled my life and which until lately have been the faith and hope of our times." The typical meaning of Guizot is well recognized by Hugo Krabbe, *Die moderne Staatsidee* (The Hague: Martinus Nijhof, 1919), 178. Because of its exhaustive summary, Krabbe cites Guizot's opinion of parliamentarism in full: "That is in addition the character of a system that nowhere acknowledges the legitimacy of absolute power to oblige all citizens constantly and without restriction to seek truth, reason, and justice, which have to check actual power. It is this which constitutes the representative system: (1) through discussion the powers-that-be are obliged to seek truth in common; (2) through publicity the powers are brought to this search under the eyes of the citizenry; (3) through freedom of the press the citizens themselves are brought to look for truth and to tell this to the powers-that-be." In the phrase *representative system, representative* refers to the representation of the (rational) people in parliament. The equation of parliamentarism and the representative system is characteristic of the confusion of the nineteenth century. The concept of representation has a deeper problematic that has not yet been fully recognized. For my purposes here it is enough to refer to parliamentarism and only briefly indicate the particular character of the true concept of representation: It belongs essentially to the sphere of publicity (in contrast to deputization, commission, mandate, and so forth, which are originally concepts of civil law), and it assumes a personal worth in the persons representing and represented and also in that person before whom representation is made (in contrast to the representation of

interests or management). To give a very clear example: In the eighteenth century a prince was represented before other princes by his ambassador (who must also be a nobleman), whereas economic and other sorts of business could be left to "agents." In the struggle of parliament with absolute monarchy, parliament appeared as the representative of the people (conceived as a unity). Where the people were represented, the king could preserve his worth only as the representative of the people (as in the French constitution of 1791). Where absolute monarchy asserted itself, it had to contest the possibility or even the admissibility of popular representation and tried for that reason to make parliament into a body for the representation of corporate interests (as, for example, in Germany during 1815–1848). When a "free" in contrast to an "imperative" mandate is identified as the particular characteristic of a "representative" assembly, then this is explicable in terms of a practically important peculiarity. In truth parliament is not the representative of the whole people simply because it is dependent on the voters, for the voters are not the whole people. Only gradually in the course of the nineteenth century, as one could no longer imagine the concept of a person and it became something objective, did one confuse the sum of current voters (or their majority) for the overriding total person of the people or nation, and thus one lost the sense of the representation of the people and of representation altogether. In the struggle for representation in Germany during 1815–1848, this confusion is already indescribable; and it can scarcely be determined whether parliament should represent the people before the king (so that two are represented in the state, the king and the people), or whether parliament in addition to the king is a representative of the nation (for instance in France, where according to the constitution of 1791 there were two representatives). The historical description of the French National Assembly of 1789 and of the German struggle for a "representative constitution" suffers from the misunderstanding of a concept so important as representation. That is true even of a book that is as valuable and as important as Karl Löwenstein, *Volk and Parlament nach der Staatstheorie der französischen Nationalversammlung von 1789* (Munich, 1922). On the concept of representation in German literature between 1815 and 1848, see Emil Gerber's Bonn dissertation, 1926.

6. Robert von Mohl, *Staatsrecht, Völkerrecht and Politik. Monographien vol. 1* (Tübingen: Verlag der H. Laupp'schen Buchhandlung, 1860–62), 5.

7. [Trans.] See Schmitt, *Politische Romantik* (Munich & Leipzig: Duncker & Humblot, 1919).

8. Wilhelm von Hasbach, *Die moderne Demokratie* (Jena: Gustav Fischer, 1913, 1921), and *Die parlamentarische Kabinettsregierung* (1919); see also Hasbach's article "Gewaltenteilung, Gewaltentrennung and gemischte Staatsform," *Vierteljahrsschrift für Sozial and Wirtschaftsgeschichte*, 13 (1916), 562.

9. Ferdinand Tönnies, *Kritik der öffentliche Meinung* (1922), 100.

10. There is more on this in my book on dictatorship, *Die Diktatur* (1921), 14ff.; see also Friedrich Meinecke, *Die Idee der Staatsräson* (Munich & Berlin: Oldenburg, 1924), and my review in the *Archiv für Sozialwissenschaft and Sozialpolitik*, 56 (1926), 226–234. [Schmitt refers here to Arnold Clapmar, *De Arcanis rerum publicarum* (Bremen, 1605). Schmitt's review of Meinecke was reprinted in Schmitt's *Positionen and Begriffe im Kampf mit Weimar, Genf, Versailles, 1923–39* (Hamburg: Hanseatische Verlag, 1940). Meinecke's Staatsräson has been translated as *Machiavellism: The Doctrine of Raison d'Etat and Its Place in Modern History* (London: Routledge, Kegan Paul, 1957). —tr.]

11. [Trans.] On the Monarchomachians see Harold Laski's introduction to the English translation of the *Vindiciae contra Tyrannos* of Junius Brutus: *A Defence of Liberty against Tyrants* (London: G. Bell & Sons, 1924). Laski comments that "at the bottom of [the Monarchomachians'] argument is an emphasis which no political philosophy can afford to neglect. In part it is the realisation that every state is built upon the consciences of men. . . . In part also it is the insistence that the state exists to secure for its members some agreed minimum

of civilization" (55). The Monarchomachian tradition originated in the massacre of Hugue-nots ordered by the Catholic monarch Catherine de Medici in September 1572; some two thousand French Protestants were murdered, and there followed a period of retaliation in other European countries in which Catholics were persecuted by Protestant monarchs, and Catholics by Protestants. On the Monarchomachians see also Albert Elkan, *Die Publizistik der Bartholomausnacht* (Heidelberg: Carl Winter, 1904), and Otto von Gierke, *Johannes Althusius and die Entwicklung der naturrechtlichen Staatstheorien* (Breslau, 1878), 3–4. Gierke's work has been translated as *The Development of Political Theory* (London: Allen & Unwin, 1939). Laski— and Schmitt here too—contrasts the *Vindiciae contra Tyrannos* with Bodin's *Les six livres de la République* (1576) as a text that upholds the concept of limited power against the unlimited sovereignty of absolute monarchs: he comments that in the late sixteenth century "Bodin was the innovator" while the *Vindiciae* upheld a medieval concept of the world governed by natural law (Laski, introduction to the *Vindiciae*, 47).

12. [Trans.] Economist and follower of Francois Quesnay, founder of the physiocrats, Le Mercier de la Rivière was counselor to Parlement before the revolution. In the years before the revolution he produced a series of tracts justifying the French monarch, and his most famous work, *L'Ordre naturel* (1767), justified the rights and property of the monarchy. He remained unrepentant throughout the Terror, and he died, persecuted, in 1793 or 1794. Cf. Lotte Silberstein, *Le Mercier de la Rivière and seine politischen Ideen* (Berlin: Emil Ebering, 1928).

13. Marquis de Condorcet in the "Discours sur les conventions nationales" (April 1, 1791) and also in the speech on monarchy and the republic (also 1791), in *Oeuvres*, vol. 11. The belief in the art of printing books is one of the characteristic signs of the revolutionary En-lightenment. An article from year one of the Republic, cited according to the *Citateur Repub-licain* (Paris, 1834), 97, enumerates the consequences: Every unfreedom, every burden, every obstacle to the general happiness will disappear, wars will cease and in their place wealth and surplus and virtue will appear—"such will be the benefits of printing."

14. See. Erich Kaufmann, *Kritik der neukantischen Rechtsphilosophie* (Tübingen: Mohr, 1921), 60–61.

15. In his work "On the Liberty of the Press and Public Discussion" (1821). [In *The Works of Jeremy Bentham*, ed. John Bowring, vol. 2 (Edinburgh: Tait, 1843), 275–297.—tr.]

16. [Tr.] J. S. Mill, *On Liberty* (1859).

17. Maurice Hauriou, *Précis de droit administratif et de droit public* (Paris, 1914); Redslob, *Die parlamentarische Regierung* (1918).

18. Rousseau talks about a balance of interests in the general will; cf. *Du contrat social*, Bk. II, chap. 9, sect. 4; Bk. II, chap. 11, note; Bk. 11, chap. 6, sect. 10; Bk. III, chap. 8, sect. 10; Bk. IV, chap. 4, sect. 25; Bk. V; see esp. Bk. I, chap. 8, sect. 2; Bk. II, chap. 6, sect. 10; Bk. III, chap. 8, sect. 10.

19. [Trans.] Montesquieu, *L'Esprit des lois* (1748); translated as *The Spirit of the Laws* (Chicago: Encyclopedia Britannica, 1952). On Montesquieu's political thought see the aptly named chapter "The British Constitution," in Kingsley Martin, *French Liberal Thought in the Eighteenth Century* (London: Phoenix, 1962), 147ff.

20. [Trans.] John Locke, *Two Treatises of Government* (1690), Second Treatise, sect. 172.

21. [Trans.] Cf. Thomas Hobbes, *Behemoth; or, The Long Parliament* (1679); a modern edi-tion was prepared by Ferdinand Tönnies (Cambridge: Cambridge University Press, 1889). On the Long Parliament and the English Civil War see Christopher Hill, *The Intellectual Origins of the English Revolution* (Oxford: Clarendon Press, 1965), and *God's Englishman: Oliver Cromwell and the English Revolution* (London: Weidenfeld & Nicholson, 1970).

22. [Trans.] Cf. Martin, *French Liberal Thought in the Eighteenth Century*, and "Acte constitu-tionnel du 24 Juin 1793, et Declaration des droit de l'homme et du citoyen," in Leon Duguit and Henry Monnier, *Les Constitutions et les principales lois politiques de la France depuis 1789* (Paris: Librairie Generate de Droit et de jurisprudence, 1915, 3d edition).

23. Cf. my book *Die Diktatur* (1921), 149.

24. Theodore de Beza, *Droit de Magistrats* (1574). ["The theory of Calvinist politics is here set forth with perfect clarity. To God alone does absolute power belong. Magistrates indeed have wide authority and they cannot be held to account by the people . . . but when the tyranny becomes intolerable, just remedies must be used against it. Not, however, by every member of the state. The ordinary citizen is bound by the conditions of his citizenship to submit . . . . There are, however, in each state a body of citizens whose function it is to see that the sovereign does his duty; in France the States-General is such a body of such men . . . . Royalty is, even though divine in nature, essentially dependent upon popular institution" (Laski, introduction to *Vindiciae contra Tyrannos*, 24–25). Beza's pamphlet was the first during the civil wars to assert the principle of popular sovereignty, and according to Laski, Beza can be considered the first Monarchomachian.—tr.]

25. Junius Brutus, *Vindiciae contra Tyrannos*. [Schmitt refers to pages 115–116 of an Edinburgh edition of 1579. See the English translation introduced by Laski (note 11).—tr.]

26. Grotius, *De jure belli ac Pacis*, Bk. I, chap. 3, sect. 6 (Amsterdam, 1631). Grotius also uses the comparison with mathematics in order to justify his negative estimation of particular facts.

27. [Tr.] Otto Mayer, *Deutsches Verwaltungsrecht* (Munich & Leipzig: Duncker & Humblot, 1895–96).

28. Erich Kaufmann's exposition of Locke in his *Untersuchungsausschluss and Staatsgerichthof* (Berlin: G. Stelka, 1920) is a perfect example of Locke's immediate and practical relevance today. Kaufmann's work must also be noted because of its importance for the material concept of law (*materielle Gesetzesbegriff*).

29. John Neville Figgis, *The Divine Right of Kings* (Cambridge: Cambridge University Press, 1914, 2d edition).

30. John Marshall's opinion appears as the motto of chapter 16 in James Beck's book on the American constitution. [Schmitt refers to the German translation of Beck, *The American Constitution* (Oxford: Oxford University Press, 1924), which appeared as *Die Verfassung der Vereinigten Staaten von Amerika* (Berlin: Walter de Gruyter, 1926). A foreword by Calvin Coolidge and an introduction by Walter Simons, interim president of the Weimar Republic and later chief justice of the German Supreme Court, appeared in the German edition. Chief Justice John Marshall established the principle of judicial review in the American constitution. In the last years of the Weimar Republic, Schmitt was involved in a debate with Hans Kelsen and others on the question of a "defender of the constitution." While Kelsen argued that judicial review would be the best solution to the question of which of the republic's governmental branches should be the authoritative interpreter of the constitution and thus its "defender," Schmitt, after briefly sharing this point of view, argued in *Der Hüter der Verfassung* (1931) that the Reichsprasident was best suited to defend the constitution. Cf. the 1931 version of this discussion with Schmitt's "Der Hüter der Verfassung," *Archiv des öffentlichen Rechts*, 16 (1929), 161–237. See also Bendersky, *Carl Schmitt: Theorist for the Reich* (Princeton: Princeton University Press, 1983), 112f1., and Ellen Kennedy, "Bendersky, Carl Schmitt: Theorist for the Reich," *History of Political Thought* 4 (1983): 582ff.; see also George Schwab, *The Challenge of the Exception* (Berlin: Duncker & Humblot, 1970), 80ff.—tr.]

31. *Politische Theologie*, 411. [Schmitt defines the sovereign as whoever decides the question of a state of exception ("Souverän ist, wer über den Ausnahmezustand entscheidet"). Cf. Pufendorf's discussion in *De jure naturae* (Bk. VII, chap. 6, sect. 8), quoted above. On Bodin see Julian H. Franklin's study, *Jean Bodin and the Rise of Absolutist Theory* (Cambridge: Cambridge University Press, 1973).—tr.]

32. [Trans.] Paul Laband was one of the founders of legal positivism in Germany. See Peter Oertzen, *Die soziale Funktion des staatsrechtlichen Postivismus* (Frankfurt: Suhrkamp Verlag,

1974), and Walter Wilhelm, *Zur juristischen Methodenlehre im 19. Jahrhundert. Die Herkunft der Methode Paul Labands aus der Privatrechtlichenwissenschaft* (Frankfurt: Klostermann, 1958).

33. *Leviathan*, chap. 26, p. 137 of the English edition of 1651. [Schmitt refers to the chapter "Of Civil Laws," in Hobbes, *Leviathan*, ed. Michael Oakeshott (Oxford: Blackwells, 1946).—tr.]

34. *Dissertation on Parties*, letter 10.

35. On this see the extremely interesting examination by Joseph Barthélemy, *Le rôle du pouvoir exécutif dans les republiques modernes* (Paris: Giard & Briere, 1906), 489. The citation above is taken from Condorcet's "Rapport sur le projet girondin," in *Archives parlementaires*, vol. 58, 583 (quoted by Barthelémy).

36. Titre VII, sect. II, art. 3, in "contrast" to laws the characteristic of decrees are "local or particular application, and the necessity of their being renewed after a certain period." The constitution of June 21, 1793 (articles 54 and 55), defined the concept of law in the usual way, according to subject matter. Leon Duguit and Henry Monnier, *Les Constitutions et les principales lois politiques de la France depuis 1789* (1915), 52.

37. G. W. F. Hegel, *Enzyklopädie*, sect. 544. [There were three editions of Hegel's *Enzyklopädie*; this paragraph does not appear in the first one (1817) but was included in Karl Rosenkranz's edition (Berlin: L. Heimann, 1870). The paragraph continues with a critical discussion of the concept of a check on government through the budget law. It concludes by rejecting the theory of balance of powers within the state as "a contradiction of the fixndamental idea of what a state is" (449).—tr.]

38. Ernst Zitelmann, *Irrtum and Rechtsgeschäft* (Leipzig: Duncker & Humblot, 1879).

39. [Tr.] Duguit and Monnier, *Les Constitutions*, 260.

40. Alexander Hamilton, *The Federalist Papers*, No. 70 (March 18, 1788). Montesquieu (*L'Esprit des lois*, Bk. XI, chap. 6) is also of the opinion that the executive must be in the hands of a single person because it requires immediate action; legislation by contrast can often better (as he cautiously puts it) be decided by many rather than by one man. On popular representation Montesquieu makes the characteristic remark that the great advantage of the representatives is that they "are able to discuss affairs. The people are not at all capable of that; and that is one of the great inconveniences of democracy." The distinction between legislation as advice and reflection and execution as action can be found again in Sieyès. Cf. his *Politische Schriften* (1796), vol. 2, 384.

41. That deism maintains that God is an otherworldly authority is of great importance for the conception of a balance of powers. It makes a difference whether a third person holds the balance or the balance derives from counterbalancing forces. Swift's remark in 1701 is typical of the first conception of balance (and important for Bolingbroke's theory of balance): "The 'balance of power' supposes three things: first, the part which is held, together with the hand that holds it; and then the two scales with whatever is weighed therein." I am grateful to Eduard Rosenbaum for calling my attention to this citation; cf. also *Weltwirtschaftliches Archiv*, 18 (1922), 423. [Schmitt's citation of Swift is taken from Eduard Rosenbaum's article "Eire Geschichte der Pariser Friendenskonferenz," which was a review of H. W. V. Temperley's *A History of the Peace Conference of Paris*, 5 vols. (London: Henry Frouda, Hodder & Stoughton, 1920-21).—tr.]

42. Condorcet, *Oeuvres*, vol. 13, 18.

43. [Trans.] Cf. Schmitt, *Politische Romantik* (1919).

44. G. W. F. Hegel, *Rechtsphilosophie* (1821), sects. 301, 314, 315, and see sects. 315 and 316 for the citations which follow in the text. [English citations are taken from T. M. Knox's translation, *Hegel's Philosophy of Right* (Oxford: Oxford University Press, 1973).—tr.]

45. Robert von Mohl, *Enzyklopädie der Staatswissenschaft* (Tübingen: Laupp'schen Buchhandlung, 1872), 655.

46. J. C. Bluntschli, "Parteien, politische," in Bluntschli and K. Brater, eds., *Deutsches-Staatswörterbuch*, vol. 7 (Stuttgart & Leipzig: Expedition des Staatswörterbuches, 1861), 717–747. On Lorenz von Stein see my *Politische Theologie*, 53. This explanation of the parties, which is characteristic for German liberalism, is also found in Friedrich Meinecke, *Staatsräson*, 525. [Schmitt's citation is inaccurate; the discussion of political parties is on pages 537–538. Meinecke argues here that political parties belong to the healthy political life of the state just as contradictions and pluralism belong to individual life. Although the argument appears characteristically liberal at this stage, Meinecke later notes that "parliamentarism only temporarily fills the statesman with Staatsrason; his attention soon turns to the next election" (538).—tr.]

47. J. K. Bluntschli, *Allgemeines Staatsrecht* (Stuttgart: J. G. Cotta'schen Buchhandlung, 1876, 5th edition). An interesting combination of the good old understanding of the principles of parliamentarism and modern misunderstandings is the article by Adolf Neumann-Hofer, "Die Wirksamkeit der Kommissionen in den Parlamenten," *Zeitschrift für Politik* 4 (1911): 51ff: He starts from the assumption that experience has shown that public discussion no longer takes place in popular assemblies, but he believes that in order to preserve discussion, the committees could become "discussion clubs" (64–65). On the misunderstanding of the concept of discussion here, see the preface, above. [On Robert von Mohl's argument for parliamentarism see his *Representativsystem* (1860), discussed in James J. Sheehan, *German Liberalism in the Nineteenth Century* (London: Methuen, 1982), 116, 385.—tr.]

48. [Tr.] Locke, *Two Treatises*, Second Treatise, sect. 172.

49. Eugene Forcade, *Études historiques* (Paris: Michel Levy, 1853), in a review of Lamartine's history of the revolution of 1848. Lamartine is also an example of the belief in discussion, which he contrasts with power and force. Both his *Sur la Politique Rationelle* (1831) and *Le Passé, le Présent, l'Avanir de la Republique* (1848) are inspired by this. He even thinks that the newspapers appear in the morning like a rising sun that dispels darkness! Victor Hugo's poetic description of the *Tribune* in his famous *Napoléon le Petit* is absolutely characteristic and of great importance as a symptom. The belief in discussion characterizes this epoch. Thus Hauriou, *Précis de droit constitutionnel* (Paris: Recueil Sirey, 1923), 198, 201, describes the age of parliamentarism as the age of discussion (*l'âge de la discussion*), and a staunch liberal such as Yves Guyot contrasts parliamentary government resting on discussion (for him, of course, a *gouvernement de discussion*) with the "atavism" of all politics that does not rest on discussion. Guyot, *Politique Parlementaire—Politique Atavique* (Paris, Felix Alcan, 1924). In this way parliamentarism becomes identical with freedom and culture altogether. L. Gumplowicz completely dissolves all these concepts: "The character and peculiarity of Asiatic culture is despotism; that of European culture, the parliamentary regime." Ludwig Gumplowicz, *Soziologie and Politik* (Leipzig: Duncker & Humblot, 1892), 116. [Schmitt refers to Alphonse Lamartine, Histoire de la Revolution de 1848 (Pans: Penotin, 1848).—tr.]

Section III

The Public Sphere Rediscovered

INTRODUCTION

After World War II, Communism survived in the Soviet Union and its extension to Eastern Europe and China made it appear a strong challenge to liberal democracy. At the same time, authoritarian regimes with direct ties to fascism in the '30s held power in Spain and Portugal until the mid-'70s, and Greece had a right-wing dictatorship between 1967 and 1974. The question of democracy therefore remained central to the Cold War era, but within an overall ideological ecology rather different from that of the 1920s and '30s. New types of social critique came to the fore, especially from about 1960. The idea of the public sphere was rediscovered and elaborated in a new, socially critical atmosphere.

The author of the first text in this section is Hannah Arendt, who in 1951 published *The Origins of Totalitarianism*, a study of Nazism and Stalinism that became a classic almost instantly. She spent her formative years as a scholar in Germany in the 1920s and early 30s, as did the Marxism-influenced critical theorists, such as Theodor Adorno and Walter Benjamin, associated with the Frankfurt School. Like them, she was Jewish, and had to flee Hitler's Germany. Although she introduced Benjamin to the English-speaking world as editor of the collection *Illuminations* (1968), philosophically she was very different from the Frankfurt School in her orientation. She was inspired not least by Martin Heidegger, and she constantly returned to the thinkers of Antiquity. In 1958, she published *The Human Condition*, in which she formulated a critique of modernity.

Arendt saw the public sphere as a sphere for human cultivation and self-realization and political life as the highest form of human life. However, Arendt cannot be unproblematically placed in any of the usual main traditions of political thought. She was a critic of representative democracy and strongly in favor of civic engagement and collective deliberation. At the same time, she defended fundamental liberal rights, including freedom of speech, and she opposed any construction of political community on the basis of tradition, customs, religion, race, or ethnicity.

Despite their differences, she was a source of inspiration for the Frankfurt School's leading representative from the late '60s onward, Jürgen Habermas, who in 1962 published his *Strukturwandel der Öffentlichkeit (The Structural Transformation of the Public Sphere)*, a book that would be formative for understanding of and debate about the public sphere for decades. It argued that space for the public use of reason and the force of the better argument that developed from the late seventeenth century on was of shrinking importance because the modern public sphere was crushed between the twin forces of the welfare state and the forces of commercialism. Public debate had become entertainment, in which predetermined positions fought for the support of a public that was no longer made up of active participants in public deliberation but of paying audiences for spectacular shows.

An early critique of Habermas was launched by the sociologist Oskar Negt and filmmaker Alexander Kluge in their *Öffentlichkeit und Erfahrung (Public Sphere and Experience)* ([1972] 1993), a work deeply marked by the new left movement of the late '60s and early '70s. They argue that Habermas' positive presentation of the classical bourgeois public sphere reflects the bourgeoisie's belief that the borders between the public and the private, between economy/work and the sphere of intimacy, between politics and art must be respected, divisions that the Labour Movement had also reproduced in its organizational structures and work. Against this, Negt and Kluge proposed a "counter public sphere," which they call the "proletarian public sphere" based on communication and learning in extreme situations of social and political struggle where they argue, the real connections between work, family life, and leisure activities are exposed and reflected upon.

In her article "Rethinking the Public Sphere," first published in 1990, Nancy Fraser developed another influential riposte to Habermas, grounded in feminism. She shows how certain groups were excluded from the public sphere on the basis of gender, property, and race, and argues that Habermas failed to examine other, competing public spheres. Fraser's distinction between strong and weak publics has been very influential. In the latter, deliberative practice consists of opinion making only, while the discourse in the former encompasses both opinion formation and decision-making. Fraser's intervention also marks the opening up of the theory of the public sphere to the challenges of an era of diversity, globalization, and digitization.

HANNAH ARENDT

EXCERPT FROM *THE HUMAN CONDITION* (1958)

Hannah Arendt (1906–1975) was born in Germany into a family of secular Jews. She studied philosophy with Martin Heidegger and Karl Jaspers and completed her doctoral dissertation in 1929. Forced to leave the country after the Nazi take-over in 1933, she lived for a while in Paris and later fled to the USA. She became a US citizen in 1950 and held academic positions at various US universities until her death in 1975.

The relations between politics and other spheres of human activity were a central concern in her writings. In the following excerpt from her book The Human Condition *(1958), she discusses the defining qualities of human action and the changing relations between the public and the private sphere from ancient Greece to the present.*

In Arendt's view, the fundamental human activities are (1) labor—activities necessary for the production and reproduction of life; (2) work—activities necessary for constructing a permanent human world; and (3) action—free, non-instrumental activities. Referring to the social topography of ancient Greece, she further distinguishes between two social spheres: Oikos (the "house"), the private sphere of the family and the household, the realm of necessity; and polis (the "city"), the public sphere of political discussion and communality, the realm of freedom and equality. Labor and work belong to oikos, while action is the activity of the polis. On the basis of this description, Arendt then develops a conception of participatory democracy that she contrasts with political life in modern societies.

According to Arendt, there was a strong connection between politics, individuality, and excellence in the Greek polis. Life in the public sphere was "permeated by a fiercely agonal spirit." Everybody had to distinguish themselves through unique deeds or achievements. To participate in the political community by acting and speaking, was to realize the full potential of human existence. However, from the Middle Age onward, the old social topography was transformed by "the rise of the social." Labor and work became a public matter. Consequently, the possibility of political action in the original Greek sense was lost and the borderline between the private and the political became blurred.

Though Arendt's conception of public life differs from most other theories in the field, her analyses of political action and her emphasis on the fundamental agonistic nature of the public sphere have attracted increasing attention.

Chapter II: The Public and the Private Realm

The Polis and the Household

[. . .] Although misunderstanding and equating the political and social realms is as old as the translation of Greek terms into Latin and their adaption to Roman–Christian thought, it has become even more confusing in modern usage and modern understanding of society. The distinction between a private and a public sphere of life corresponds to the household and the political realms, which have existed as distinct, separate entities at least since the rise of the ancient city-state; but the emergence of the social realm, which is neither private nor public, strictly speaking, is a relatively new phenomenon whose origin coincided with the emergence of the modern age and which found its political form in the nation-state.

What concerns us in this context is the extraordinary difficulty with which we, because of this development, understand the decisive division between the public and private realms, between the sphere of the *polis* and the sphere of household and family, and, finally, between activities related to a common world and those related to the maintenance of life, a division upon which all ancient political thought rested as self-evident and axiomatic. In our understanding, the dividing line is entirely blurred, because we see the body of peoples and political communities in the image of a family whose everyday affairs have to be taken care of by a gigantic, nation-wide administration of housekeeping. The scientific thought that corresponds to this development is no longer political science but "national economy" or "social economy" or *Volkswirtschaft*, all of which indicate a kind of "collective housekeeping";[1] the collective of families economically organized into the facsimile of one super-human family is what we call "society," and its political form of organization is called "nation."[2] We therefore find it difficult to realize that according to ancient thought on these matters, the very term "political economy" would have been a contradiction in terms: whatever was "economic," related to the life of the individual and the survival of the species, was a non-political, household affair by definition.[3]

Historically, it is very likely that the rise of the city-state and the public realm occurred at the expense of the private realm of family and household.[4] Yet the old sanctity of the hearth, though much less pronounced in classical Greece than in ancient Rome, was never entirely lost. What prevented the *polis* from violating the private lives of its citizens and made it hold sacred the boundaries surrounding each property was not respect for private property as we understand it, but the fact that without owning a house a man could not participate in the affairs of the world because he had no location in it which was properly his own.[5] Even Plato, whose political plans foresaw the abolition of private property and an extension of the public sphere to the point of annihilating private life altogether, still speaks with great reverence of Zeus Herkeios, the protector of border lines, and calls the *horoi*, the boundaries between one estate and another, divine, without seeing any contradiction.[6]

The distinctive trait of the household sphere was that in it men lived together because they were driven by their wants and needs. The driving force was life itself—the penates, the household gods, were, according to Plutarch, "the gods who make us live and nourish our body"[7]—which, for its individual maintenance and its survival as the life of the species needs the company of others. That individual maintenance should be the task of the man and species survival the task of the woman was obvious, and both of these natural functions, the labor of man to provide nourishment and the labor of the woman in giving birth, were subject to the same urgency of life. Natural community in the household therefore was born of necessity, and necessity ruled over all activities performed in it.

The realm of the *polis*, on the contrary, was the sphere of freedom, and if there was a relationship between these two spheres, it was a matter of course that the mastering of the necessities of life in the household was the condition for freedom of the *polis*. Under no circumstances could politics be only a means to protect society—a society of the faithful, as in the Middle Ages, or a society of property-owners, as in Locke, or a society relentlessly engaged in a process of acquisition, as in Hobbes, or a society of producers, as in Marx, or a society of jobholders, as in our own society, or a society of laborers, as in socialist and communist countries. In all these cases, it is the freedom (and in some instances so–called freedom) of society which requires and justifies the restraint of political authority. Freedom is located in the realm of the social, and force or violence becomes the monopoly of government.

What all Greek philosophers, no matter how opposed to *polis* life, took for granted is that freedom is exclusively located in the political realm, that necessity is primarily a prepolitical phenomenon, characteristic of the private household organization, and that force and violence are justified in this sphere because they are the only means to master necessity—for instance, by ruling over slaves—and to become free. Because all human beings are subject to necessity, they are entitled to violence toward others; violence is the prepolitical act of liberating oneself from the necessity of life for the freedom of world. This freedom is the essential condition of what the Greeks called felicity, *eudaimonia*, which was an objective status depending first of all upon wealth and health. To be poor or to be in ill health meant to be subject to physical necessity, and to be a slave meant to be subject, in addition, to manmade violence. This twofold and doubled "unhappiness" of slavery is quite independent of the actual subjective well-being of the slave. Thus, a poor free man preferred the insecurity of a daily-changing labor market to regular assured work, which, because it restricted his freedom to do as he pleased every day, was already felt to be servitude *(douleia)*, and even harsh, painful labor was preferred to the easy life of many household slaves.[8]

The prepolitical force, however, with which the head of the household ruled over the family and its slaves and which was felt to be necessary because man is a "social" before he is a "political animal," has nothing in common with the chaotic "state of nature" from whose violence, according to seventeenth-century political thought, men could escape only by establishing a government that, through a monopoly of power and of violence, would abolish the "war of all against all" by "keeping them all in awe."[9] On the contrary, the whole concept of rule and being ruled, of government and power in the sense in which we understand them as well as the regulated order attending them, was felt to be prepolitical and to belong in the private rather than the public sphere.

The *polis* was distinguished from the household in that it knew only "equals," whereas the household was the center of the strictest inequality. To be free meant both not to be subject to the necessity of life or to the command of another *and* not to be in command oneself. It meant neither to rule nor to be ruled.[10] Thus within the realm of the household, freedom did not exist, for the household head, its ruler, was considered to be free only in so far as he had the power to leave the household and enter the political realm, where all were equals. To be sure, this equality of the political realm has very little in common with our concept of equality: it meant to live among and to have to deal only with one's peers, and it presupposed the existence of "unequals" who, as a matter of fact, were always the majority of the population in a city-state.[11] Equality, therefore, far from being connected with justice, as in modern times, was the very essence of freedom: to be free meant to be free from the inequality present in rulership and to move in a sphere where neither rule nor being ruled existed.

However, the possibility of describing the profound difference between the modern and the ancient understanding of politics in terms of a clear–cut opposition ends here. In the modern world, the social and the political realms are much less distinct. That politics is nothing but a function of society, that action, speech, and thought are primarily superstructures upon social interest, is not a discovery of Karl Marx but on the contrary is among the axiomatic assumptions Marx accepted uncritically from the political economists of the modern age. This functionalization makes it impossible to perceive any serious gulf between the two realms; and this is not a matter of a theory or an ideology, since with the rise of society, that is, the rise of the "household" *(oikia)* or of economic activities to the public realm, housekeeping and all matters pertaining formerly to the private sphere of the family have become a "collective" concern.[12] In the modern world, the two realms indeed constantly flow into each other like waves in the never-resting stream of the life process itself.

The disappearance of the gulf that the ancients had to cross daily to transcend the narrow realm of the household and "rise" into the realm of politics is an essentially modern phenomenon. Such a gulf between the private and the public still existed somehow in the Middle Ages, though it had lost much of its significance and changed its location entirely. It has been rightly remarked that after the downfall of the Roman Empire, it was the Catholic Church that offered men a substitute for the citizenship which had formerly been the prerogative of municipal government.[13] The medieval tension between the darkness of everyday life and the grandiose splendor attending everything sacred, with the concomitant rise from the secular to the religious, corresponds in many respects to the rise from the private to the public in antiquity. The difference is of course very marked, for no matter how "worldly" the Church became, it was always essentially an otherworldly concern which kept the community of believers together. While one can equate the public with the religious only with some difficulty, the secular realm under the rule of feudalism was indeed in its entirety what the private realm had been in antiquity. Its hallmark was the absorption of all activities into the household sphere, where they had only private significance, and consequently the very absence of a public realm.[14]

It is characteristic of this growth of the private realm, and incidentally of the difference between the ancient household head and the feudal lord, that the feudal lord could render justice within the limits of his rule, whereas the ancient household head, while he might exert a milder or harsher rule, knew neither of laws nor justice outside the political realm.[15] The bringing of all human activities into the private realm and the modeling of all human relationships upon the example of the household reached far into the specifically medieval professional organizations in the cities themselves, the guilds, *confrèries*, and *compagnons*, and even into the early business companies, where "the original joint household would seem to be indicated by the very word 'company' *(companis)* . . . [and] such phrases as 'men who eat one bread,' 'men who have one bread and one wine.' "[16] The medieval concept of the "common good," far from indicating the existence of a political realm, recognizes only that private individuals have interests in common, material and spiritual, and that they can retain their privacy and attend to their own business only if one of them takes it upon himself to look out for this common interest. What distinguishes this essentially Christian attitude toward politics from the modern reality is not so much the recognition of a "common good" as the exclusivity of the private sphere and the absence of that curiously hybrid realm where private interests assume public significance that we call "society."

It is therefore not surprising that medieval political thought, concerned exclusively with the secular realm, remained unaware of the gulf between the sheltered life in the household and the merciless exposure of the *polis* and, consequently, of the virtue of courage as one of the most elemental political attitudes. What remains surprising is that the only postclassical political theorist who, in an extraordinary effort to restore its old dignity to politics, perceived the gulf and understood something of the courage needed to cross it was Machiavelli, who described it in the rise "of the Condottiere from low condition to high rank," from privacy to princedom, that is, from circumstances common to all men to the shining glory of great deeds.[17]

To leave the household, originally in order to embark upon some adventure and glorious enterprise and later simply to devote one's life to the affairs of the city, demanded courage because only in the household was one primarily concerned with one's own life and survival. Whoever entered the political realm had first to be ready to risk his life, and too great a love for life obstructed freedom, was a sure sign of slavishness.[18] Courage therefore became the political virtue par excellence, and only those men who possessed it could be admitted to a fellowship that was political in content and purpose and thereby transcended the mere togetherness imposed on all—slaves, barbarians, and Greeks alike through the urgencies of life.[19] The "good life," as Aristotle called the life of the citizen, therefore was not merely better, more carefree or nobler than ordinary life, but of an altogether different quality. It was "good" to the extent that by having mastered the necessities of sheer life, by being freed from labor and work, and by overcoming the innate urge of all living creatures for their own survival, it was no longer bound to the biological life process.

At the root of Greek political consciousness we find an unequaled clarity and articulateness in drawing this distinction. No activity that served only the purpose of making a living, of sustaining only the life process, was permitted to enter the political realm, and this at the grave risk of abandoning trade and manufacture to the industriousness of slaves and foreigners, so that Athens indeed became the "pensionopolis" with a "proletariat of consumers" which Max Weber so vividly described.[20] The true character of this *polis* is still quite manifest in Plato's and Aristotle's political philosophies, even if the borderline between household and *polis* is occasionally blurred, especially in Plato who, probably following Socrates, began to draw his examples and illustrations for the *polis* from everyday experiences in private life, but also in Aristotle when he, following Plato, tentatively assumed that at least the historical origin of the *polis* must be connected with the necessities of life and that only its content or inherent aim (*telos*) transcends life in the "good life."

These aspects of the teachings of the Socratic school, which soon were to become axiomatic to the point of banality, were then the newest and most revolutionary of all and sprang not from actual experience in political life but from the desire to be freed from its burden, a desire which in their own understanding the philosophers could justify only by demonstrating that even this freest of all ways of life was still connected with and subject to necessity. But the background of actual political experience, at least in Plato and Aristotle, remained so strong that the distinction between the spheres of household and political life was never doubted. Without mastering the necessities of life in the household, neither life nor the "good life" is possible, but politics is never for the sake of life. As far as the members of the *polis* are concerned, household life exists for the sake of the "good life" in the *polls*.

The Rise of the Social

   The emergence of society—the rise of housekeeping, its activities, problems, and organizational devices—from the shadowy interior of the household into the light of the public sphere, has not only blurred the old borderline between private and political, it has also changed almost beyond recognition the meaning of the two terms and their significance for the life of the individual and the citizen. Not only would we not agree with the Greeks that a life spent in the privacy of "one's own" (*idion*), outside the world of the common, is "idiotic" by definition, or with the Romans to whom privacy offered but a temporary refuge from the business of the *res publica;* we call private today a sphere of intimacy whose beginnings we may be able to trace back to late Roman, though hardly to any period of Greek antiquity, but whose peculiar manifoldness and variety were certainly unknown to any period prior to the modern age.

   This is not merely a matter of shifted emphasis. In ancient feeling the privative trait of privacy, indicated in the word itself, was all-important; it meant literally a state of being deprived of something, and even of the highest and most human of man's capacities. A man who lived only a private life, who like the slave was not permitted to enter the public realm, or like the barbarian had chosen not to establish such a realm, was not fully human. We no longer think primarily of deprivation when we use the word "privacy," and this is partly due to the enormous enrichment of the private sphere through modern individualism. However, it seems even more important that modern privacy is at least as sharply opposed to the social realm—unknown to the ancients who considered its content a private matter—as it is to the political, properly speaking. The decisive historical fact is that modern privacy in its most relevant function, to shelter the intimate, was discovered as the opposite not of the political sphere but of the social, to which it is therefore more closely and authentically related.

   The first articulate explorer and to an extent even theorist of intimacy was Jean-Jacques Rousseau who, characteristically enough, is the only great author still frequently cited by his first name alone. He arrived at his discovery through a rebellion not against the oppression of the state but against society's unbearable perversion of the human heart, its intrusion upon an innermost region in man which until then had needed no special protection. The intimacy of the heart, unlike the private household, has no objective tangible place in the world, nor can the society against which it protests and asserts itself be localized with the same certainty as the public space. To Rousseau, both the intimate and the social were, rather, subjective modes of human existence, and in his case, it was as though Jean-Jacques rebelled against a man called Rousseau. The modern individual and his endless conflicts, his inability either to be at home in society or to live outside it altogether, his ever-changing moods and the radical subjectivism of his emotional life, was born in this rebellion of the heart. The authenticity of Rousseau's discovery is beyond doubt, no matter how doubtful the authenticity of the individual who was Rousseau. The astonishing flowering of poetry and music from the middle of the eighteenth century until almost the last third of the nineteenth, accompanied by the rise of the novel, the only entirely social art form, coinciding with a no less striking decline of all the more public arts, especially architecture, is sufficient testimony to a close relationship between the social and the intimate.

The rebellious reaction against society during which Rousseau and the Romanticists discovered intimacy was directed first of all against the leveling demands of the social, against what we would call today the conformism inherent in every society. It is important to remember that this rebellion took place before the principle of equality, upon which we have blamed conformism since Tocqueville, had had the time to assert itself in either the social or the political realm. Whether a nation consists of equals or non-equals is of no great importance in this respect, for society always demands that its members act as though they were members of one enormous family which has only one opinion and one interest. Before the modern disintegration of the family, this common interest and single opinion was represented by the household head who ruled in accordance with it and prevented possible disunity among the family members.[21] The striking coincidence of the rise of society with the decline of the family indicates clearly that what actually took place was the absorption of the family unit into corresponding social groups. The equality of the members of these groups, far from being an equality among peers, resembles nothing so much as the equality of household members before the despotic power of the household head, except that in society, where the natural strength of one common interest and one unanimous opinion is tremendously enforced by sheer number, actual rule exerted by one man, representing the common interest and the right opinion, could eventually be dispensed with. The phenomenon of conformism is characteristic of the last stage of this modern development.

It is true that one-man, monarchical rule, which the ancients stated to be the organizational device of the household, is transformed in society—as we know it today, when the peak of the social order is no longer formed by the royal household of an absolute ruler—into a kind of no-man rule. But this nobody, the assumed one interest of society as a whole in economics as well as the assumed one opinion of polite society in the salon, does not cease to rule for having lost its personality. As we know from the most social form of government, that is, from bureaucracy (the last stage of government in the nation-state just as one-man rule in benevolent despotism and absolutism was its first), the rule by nobody is not necessarily no-rule; it may indeed, under certain circumstances, even turn out to be one of its cruelest and most tyrannical versions.

It is decisive that society, on all its levels, excludes the possibility of action, which formerly was excluded from the household. Instead, society expects from each of its members a certain kind of behavior, imposing innumerable and various rules, all of which tend to "normalize" its members, to make them behave, to exclude spontaneous action or outstanding achievement. With Rousseau, we find these demands in the salons of high society, whose conventions always equate the individual with his rank within the social framework. What matters is this equation with social status, and it is immaterial whether the framework happens to be actual rank in the half-feudal society of the eighteenth century, title in the class society of the nineteenth, or mere function in the mass society of today. The rise of mass society, on the contrary, only indicates that the various social groups have suffered the same absorption into one society that the family units had suffered earlier; with the emergence of mass society, the realm of the social has finally, after several centuries of development, reached the point where it embraces and controls all members of a given community equally and with equal strength. But society equalizes under all circumstances, and the victory of equality in the modern world is only the political and legal recognition of the fact that society has conquered the public realm, and that distinction and difference have become private matters of the individual.

This modern equality, based on the conformism inherent in society and possible only because behavior has replaced action as the foremost mode of human relationship, is in every respect different from equality in antiquity, and notably in the Greek city-states. To belong to the few "equals" (*homoioi*) meant to be permitted to live among one's peers; but the public realm itself, the *polis*, was permeated by a fiercely agonal spirit, where everybody had constantly to distinguish himself from all others, to show through unique deeds or achievements that he was the best of all (*aien aristeuein*).[22] The public realm, in other words, was reserved for individuality; it was the only place where men could show who they really and inexchangeably were. It was for the sake of this chance, and out of love for a body politic that made it possible to them all, that each was more or less willing to share in the burden of jurisdiction, defense, and administration of public affairs.

It is the same conformism, the assumption that men behave and do not act with respect to each other, that lies at the root of the modern science of economics, whose birth coincided with the rise of society and which, together with its chief technical tool, statistics, became the social science par excellence. Economics—until the modern age a not too important part of ethics and politics and based on the assumption that men act with respect to their economic activities as they act in every other respect[23]—could achieve a scientific character only when men had become social beings and unanimously followed certain patterns of behavior, so that those who did not keep the rules could be considered to be asocial or abnormal.

The laws of statistics are valid only where large numbers or long periods are involved, and acts or events can statistically appear only as deviations or fluctuations. The justification of statistics is that deeds and events are rare occurrences in everyday life and in history. Yet the meaningfulness of everyday relationships is disclosed not in everyday life but in rare deeds, just as the significance of a historical period shows itself only in the few events that illuminate it. The application of the law of large numbers and long periods to politics or history signifies nothing less than the wilful obliteration of their very subject matter, and it is a hopeless enterprise to search for meaning in politics or significance in history when everything that is not everyday behavior or automatic trends has been ruled out as immaterial.

However, since the laws of statistics are perfectly valid where we deal with large numbers, it is obvious that every increase in population means an increased validity and a marked decrease of "deviation." Politically, this means that the larger the population in any given body politic, the more likely it will be the social rather than the political that constitutes the public realm. The Greeks, whose city-state was the most individualistic and least conformable body politic known to us, were quite aware of the fact that the *polis*, with its emphasis on action and speech, could survive only if the number of citizens remained restricted. Large numbers of people, crowded together, develop an almost irresistible inclination toward despotism, be this the despotism of a person or of majority rule; and although statistics, that is, the mathematical treatment of reality, was unknown prior to the modern age, the social phenomena which make such treatment possible—great numbers, accounting for conformism, behaviorism, and automatism in human affairs—were precisely those traits which, in Greek self-understanding, distinguished the Persian civilization from their own.

The unfortunate truth about behaviorism and the validity of its "laws" is that the more people there are, the more likely they are to behave and the less likely to tolerate non-behavior. Statistically, this will be shown in the leveling out of fluctuation. In reality, deeds will have less and less chance to stem the tide of behavior, and events will more and more lose their significance, that is, their capacity to illuminate historical time. Statistical uniformity is by no means a harmless scientific ideal; it is the no longer secret political ideal of a society which, entirely submerged in the routine of everyday living, is at peace with the scientific outlook inherent in its very existence.

The uniform behavior that lends itself to statistical determination, and therefore to scientifically correct prediction, can hardly be explained by the liberal hypothesis of a natural "harmony of interests," the foundation of "classical" economics; it was not Karl Marx but the liberal economists themselves who had to introduce the "communistic fiction," that is, to assume that there is one interest of society as a whole which with "an invisible hand" guides the behavior of men and produces the harmony of their conflicting interests.[24] The difference between Marx and his forerunners was only that he took the reality of conflict, as it presented itself in the society of his time, as seriously as the hypothetical fiction of harmony; he was right in concluding that the "socialization of man" would produce automatically a harmony of all interests, and was only more courageous than his liberal teachers when he proposed to establish in reality the "communistic fiction" underlying all economic theories. What Marx did not—and, at his time, could not—understand was that the germs of communistic society were present in the reality of a national household, and that their full development was not hindered by any class-interest as such, but only by the already obsolete monarchical structure of the nation-state. Obviously, what prevented society from smooth functioning was only certain traditional remnants that interfered and still influenced the behavior of "backward" classes. From the viewpoint of society, these were merely disturbing factors in the way of a full development of "social forces"; they no longer corresponded to reality and were therefore, in a sense, much more "fictitious" than the scientific "fiction" of one interest.

A complete victory of society will always produce some sort of "communistic fiction," whose outstanding political characteristic is that it is indeed ruled by an "invisible hand," namely, by nobody. What we traditionally call state and government gives place here to pure administration—a state of affairs which Marx rightly predicted as the "withering away of the state," though he was wrong in assuming that only a revolution could bring it about, and even more wrong when he believed that this complete victory of society would mean the eventual emergence of the "realm of freedom"[25]

To gauge the extent of society's victory in the modern age, its early substitution of behavior for action and its eventual substitution of bureaucracy, the rule of nobody, for personal rulership, it may be well to recall that its initial science of economics, which substitutes patterns of behavior only in this rather limited field of human activity, was finally followed by the all-comprehensive pretension of the social sciences which, as "behavioral sciences," aim to reduce man as a whole, in all his activities, to the level of a conditioned and behaving animal. If economics is the science of society in its early stages, when it could impose its rules of behavior only on sections of the population and on parts of their activities, the rise of the "behavioral sciences" indicates clearly the final stage of this development, when mass society has devoured all strata of the nation and "social behavior" has become the standard for all regions of life.

Since the rise of society, since the admission of household and housekeeping activities to the public realm, an irresistible tendency to grow, to devour the older realms of the political and private as well as the more recently established sphere of intimacy, has been one of the outstanding characteristics of the new realm. This constant growth, whose no less constant acceleration we can observe over at least three centuries, derives its strength from the fact that through society it is the life process itself which in one form or another has been channeled into the public realm. The private realm of the household was the sphere where the necessities of life, of individual survival as well as of continuity of the species, were taken care of and guaranteed. One of the characteristics of privacy, prior to the discovery of the intimate, was that man existed in this sphere not as a truly human being but only as a specimen of the animal species man-kind. This, precisely, was the ultimate reason for the tremendous contempt held for it by antiquity. The emergence of society has changed the estimate of this whole sphere but has hardly transformed its nature. The monolithic character of every type of society, its conformism which allows for only one interest and one opinion, is ultimately rooted in the one-ness of man-kind. It is because this one-ness of man-kind is not fantasy and not even merely a scientific hypothesis, as in the "communistic fiction" of classical economics, that mass society, where man as a social animal rules supreme and where apparently the survival of the species could be guaranteed on a world-wide scale, can at the same time threaten humanity with extinction.

Perhaps the clearest indication that society constitutes the public organization of the life process itself may be found in the fact that in a relatively short time the new social realm transformed all modern communities into societies of laborers and jobholders; in other words, they became at once centered around the one activity necessary to sustain life. (To have a society of laborers, it is of course not necessary that every member actually be a laborer or worker—not even the emancipation of the working class and the enormous potential power which majority rule accords to it are decisive here—but only that all members consider whatever they do primarily as a way to sustain their own lives and those of their families.) Society is the form in which the fact of mutual dependence for the sake of life and nothing else assumes public significance and where the activities connected with sheer survival are permitted to appear in public.

Whether an activity is performed in private or in public is by no means a matter of indifference. Obviously, the character of the public realm must change in accordance with the activities admitted into it, but to a large extent the activity itself changes its own nature too. The laboring activity, though under all circumstances connected with the life process in its most elementary, biological sense, remained stationary for thousands of years, imprisoned in the eternal recurrence of the life process to which it was tied. The admission of labor to public stature, far from eliminating its character as a process—which one might have expected, remembering that bodies politic have always been designed for permanence and their laws always understood as limitations imposed upon movement—has, on the contrary, liberated this process from its circular, monotonous recurrence and transformed it into a swiftly progressing development whose results have in a few centuries totally changed the whole inhabited world.

The moment laboring was liberated from the restrictions imposed by its banishment into the private realm—and this emancipation of labor was not a consequence of the emancipation of the working class, but preceded it—it was as though the growth element inherent in all organic life had completely overcome and overgrown the processes of decay by which organic life is checked and balanced in nature's household. The social realm, where the life process has established its own public domain, has let loose an unnatural growth, so to speak, of the natural; and it is against this growth, not merely against society but against a constantly growing social realm, that the private and intimate, on the one hand, and the political (in the narrower sense of the word), on the other, have proved incapable of defending themselves.

What we described as the unnatural growth of the natural is usually considered to be the constantly accelerated increase in the productivity of labor. The greatest single factor in this constant increase since its inception has been the organization of laboring, visible in the so-called division of labor, which preceded the industrial revolution; even the mechanization of labor processes, the second greatest factor in labor's productivity, is based upon it. Inasmuch as the organizational principle itself clearly derives from the public rather than the private realm, division of labor is precisely what happens to the laboring activity under conditions of the public realm and what could never have happened in the privacy of the household.[26] In no other sphere of life do we appear to have attained such excellence as in the revolutionary transformation of laboring, and this to the point where the verbal significance of the word itself (which always had been connected with hardly bearable "toil and trouble," with effort and pain and, consequently, with a deformation of the human body, so that only extreme misery and poverty could be its source), has begun to lose its meaning for us.[27] While dire necessity made labor indispensable to sustain life, excellence would have been the last thing to expect from it.

Excellence itself, *aret* as the Greeks, *virtus* as the Romans would have called it, has always been assigned to the public realm where one could excel, could distinguish oneself from all others. Every activity performed in public can attain an excellence never matched in privacy; for excellence, by definition, the presence of others is always required, and this presence needs the formality of the public, constituted by one's peers, it cannot be the casual, familiar presence of one's equals or inferiors.[28] Not even the social realm—though it made excellence anonymous, emphasized the progress of mankind rather than the achievements of men, and changed the content of the public realm beyond recognition—has been able altogether to annihilate the connection between public performance and excellence. While we have become excellent in the laboring we perform in public, our capacity for action and speech has lost much of its former quality since the rise of the social realm banished these into the sphere of the intimate and the private. This curious discrepancy has not escaped public notice, where it is usually blamed upon an assumed time lag between our technical capacities and our general humanistic development or between the physical sciences, which change and control nature, and the social sciences, which do not yet know how to change and control society. Quite apart from other fallacies of the argument which have been pointed out so frequently that we need not repeat them, this criticism concerns only a possible change in the psychology of human beings—their so-called behavior patterns—not a change of the world they move in. And this psychological interpretation, for which the absence or presence of a public realm is as irrelevant as any tangible, worldly reality, seems rather doubtful in view of the fact that no activity can become excellent if the world does not provide a proper space for its exercise. Neither education nor ingenuity nor talent can replace the constituent elements of the public realm, which make it the proper place for human excellence.

The Public Realm: Common

The term "public" signifies two closely interrelated but not altogether identical phenomena:

It means, first, that everything that appears in public can be seen and heard by everybody and has the widest possible publicity. For us, appearance—something that is being seen and heard by others as well as by ourselves—constitutes reality. Compared with the reality which comes from being seen and heard, even the greatest forces of intimate life—the passions of the heart, the thoughts of the mind, the delights of the senses—lead an uncertain, shadowy kind of existence unless and until they are transformed, deprivatized and deindividualized, as it were, into a shape to fit them for public appearance.[29] The most current of such transformations occurs in storytelling and generally in artistic transposition of individual experiences. But we do not need the form of the artist to witness this transfiguration. Each time we talk about things that can be experienced only in privacy or intimacy, we bring them out into a sphere where they will assume a kind of reality which, their intensity notwithstanding, they never could have had before. The presence of others who see what we see and hear what we hear assures us of the reality of the world and ourselves, and while the intimacy of a fully developed private life, such as had never been known before the rise of the modern age and the concomitant decline of the public realm, will always greatly intensify and enrich the whole scale of subjective emotions and private feelings, this intensification will always come to pass at the expense of the assurance of the reality of the world and men.

Indeed, the most intense feeling we know of, intense to the point of blotting out all other experiences, namely, the experience of great bodily pain, is at the same time the most private and least communicable of all. Not only is it perhaps the only experience which we are unable to transform into a shape fit for public appearance, it actually deprives us of our feeling for reality to such an extent that we can forget it more quickly and easily than anything else. There seems to be no bridge from the most radical subjectivity, in which I am no longer "recognizable," to the outer world of life.[30] Pain, in other words, truly a borderline experience between life as "being among men" (*inter homines esse*) and death, is so subjective and removed from the world of things and men that it cannot assume an appearance at all.[31]

Since our feeling for reality depends utterly upon appearance and therefore upon the existence of a public realm into which things can appear out of the darkness of sheltered existence, even the twilight which illuminates our private and intimate lives is ultimately derived from the much harsher light of the public realm. Yet there are a great many things which cannot withstand the implacable, bright light of the constant presence of others on the public scene; there, only what is considered to be relevant, worthy of being seen or heard, can be tolerated, so that the irrelevant becomes automatically a private matter. This, to be sure, does not mean that private concerns are generally irrelevant; on the contrary, we shall see that there are very relevant matters which can survive only in the realm of the private. For instance, love, in distinction from friendship, is killed, or rather extinguished, the moment it is displayed in public. ("Never seek to tell thy love / Love that never told can be.") Because of its inherent worldlessness, love can only become false and perverted when it is used for political purposes such as the change or salvation of the world.

What the public realm considers irrelevant can have such an extraordinary and infectious charm that a whole people may adopt it as their way of life, without for that reason changing its essentially private character. Modern enchantment with "small things," though preached by early twentieth-century poetry in almost all European tongues, has found its classical presentation in the *petit bonheur* of the French people. Since the decay of their once great and glorious public realm, the French have become masters in the art of being happy among "small things," within the space of their own four walls, between chest and bed, table and chair, dog and cat and flowerpot, extending to these things a care and tenderness which, in a world where rapid industrialization constantly kills off the things of yesterday to produce today's objects, may even appear to be the world's last, purely humane corner. This enlargement of the private, the enchantment, as it were, of a whole people, does not make it public, does not constitute a public realm, but, on the contrary, means only that the public realm has almost completely receded, so that greatness has given way to charm everywhere; for while the public realm may be great, it cannot be charming precisely because it is unable to harbor the irrelevant.

Second, the term "public" signifies the world itself, in so far as it is common to all of us and distinguished from our privately owned place in it. This world, however, is not identical with the earth or with nature, as the limited space for the movement of men and the general condition of organic life. It is related, rather, to the human artifact, the fabrication of human hands, as well as to affairs which go on among those who inhabit the man-made world together. To live together in the world means essentially that a world of things is between those who have it in common, as a table is located between those who sit around it; the world, like every in-between, relates and separates men at the same time.

The public realm, as the common world, gathers us together and yet prevents our falling over each other, so to speak. What makes mass society so difficult to bear is not the number of people involved, or at least not primarily, but the fact that the world between them has lost its power to gather them together, to relate and to separate them. The weirdness of this situation resembles a spiritualistic seance where a number of people gathered around a table might suddenly, through some magic trick, see the table vanish from their midst, so that two persons sitting opposite each other were no longer separated but also would be entirely unrelated to each other by anything tangible.

Historically, we know of only one principle that was ever devised to keep a community of people together who had lost their interest in the common world and felt themselves no longer related and separated by it. To find a bond between people strong enough to replace the world was the main political task of early Christian philosophy, and it was Augustine who proposed to found not only the Christian "brotherhood" but all human relationships on charity. But this charity, though its worldlessness clearly corresponds to the general human experience of love, is at the same time clearly distinguished from it in being something which, like the world, is between men: "Even robbers have between them [*inter se*] what they call charity."[32] This surprising illustration of the Christian political principle is in fact very well chosen, because the bond of charity between people, while it is incapable of founding a public realm of its own, is quite adequate to the main Christian principle of worldlessness and is admirably fit to carry a group of essentially worldless people through the world, a group of saints or a group of criminals, provided only it is understood that the world itself is doomed and that every activity in it is undertaken with the proviso *quamdiu mundus durat* ("as long as the world lasts").[33] The unpolitical, non-public character of the Christian community was early defined in the demand that it should form *a corpus*, a "body," whose members were to be related to each other like brothers of the same family.[34] The structure of communal life was modeled on the relationships between the members of a family because these were known to be non-political and even antipolitical. A public realm had never come into being between the members of a family, and it was therefore not likely to develop from Christian community life if this life was ruled by the principle of charity and nothing else. Even then, as we know from the history and the rules of the monastic orders—the only communities in which the principle of charity as a political device was ever tried—the danger that the activities undertaken under "the necessity of present life" (*necessitas vitae praesentis*)[35] would lead by themselves, because they were performed in the presence of others, to the establishment of a kind of counterworld, a public realm within the orders themselves, was great enough to require additional rules and regulations, the most relevant one in our context being the prohibition of excellence and its subsequent pride.[36]

Worldlessness as a political phenomenon is possible only on the assumption that the world will not last; on this assumption, however, it is almost inevitable that worldlessness, in one form or another, will begin to dominate the political scene. This happened after the downfall of the Roman Empire and, albeit for quite other reasons and in very different, perhaps even more disconsolate forms, it seems to happen again in our own days. The Christian abstention from worldly things is by no means the only conclusion one can draw from the conviction that the human artifice, a product of mortal hands, is as mortal as its makers. This, on the contrary, may also intensify the enjoyment and consumption of the things of the world, all manners of intercourse in which the world is not primarily understood to be the *koinon*, that which is common to all. Only the existence of a public realm and the world's subsequent transformation into a community of things which gathers men together and relates them to each other depends entirely on permanence. If the world is to contain a public space, it cannot be erected for one generation and planned for the living only; it must transcend the life-span of mortal men.

Without this transcendence into a potential earthly immortality, no politics, strictly speaking, no common world and no public realm, is possible. For unlike the common good as Christianity understood it—the salvation of one's soul as a concern common to all—the common world is what we enter when we are born and what we leave behind when we die. It transcends our lifespan into past and future alike; it was there before we came and will outlast our brief sojourn in it. It is what we have in common not only with those who live with us, but also with those who were here before and with those who will come after us. But such a common world can survive the coming and going of the generations only to the extent that it appears in public. It is the publicity of the public realm which can absorb and make shine through the centuries whatever men may want to save from the natural ruin of time. Through many ages before us—but now not any more—men entered the public realm because they wanted something of their own or something they had in common with others to be more permanent than their earthly lives. (Thus, the curse of slavery consisted not only in being deprived of freedom and of visibility, but also in the fear of these obscure people themselves "that from being obscure they should pass away leaving no trace that they have existed.")[37] There is perhaps no clearer testimony to the loss of the public realm in the modern age than the almost complete loss of authentic concern with immortality, a loss somewhat overshadowed by the simultaneous loss of the metaphysical concern with eternity. The latter, being the concern of the philosophers and the *vita contemplativa*, must remain outside our present considerations. But the former is testified to by the current classification of striving for immortality with the private vice of vanity. Under modem conditions, it is indeed so unlikely that anybody should earnestly aspire to an earthly immortality that we probably are justified in thinking it is nothing but vanity.

The famous passage in Aristotle, "Considering human affairs, one must not . . . consider man as he is and not consider what is mortal in mortal things, but think about them [only] to the extent that they have the possibility of immortalizing," occurs very properly in his political writings.[38] For the *polis* was for the Greeks, as the *res publica* was for the Romans, first of all their guarantee against the futility of individual life, the space protected against this futility and reserved for the relative permanence, if not immortality, of mortals.

What the modern age thought of the public realm, after the spectacular rise of society to public prominence, was expressed by Adam Smith when, with disarming sincerity, he mentions "that unprosperous race of men commonly called men of letters" for whom "public admiration . . . makes always a part of their reward . . . , a considerable part . . . in the profession of physic; a still greater perhaps in that of law; in poetry and philosophy it makes almost the whole."[39] Here it is self-evident that public admiration and monetary reward are of the same nature and can become substitutes for each other. Public admiration, too, is something to be used and consumed, and status, as we would say today, fulfils one need as food fulfils another: public admiration is consumed by individual vanity as food is consumed by hunger. Obviously, from this viewpoint the test of reality does not lie in the public presence of others, but rather in the greater or lesser urgency of needs to whose existence or non-existence nobody can ever testify except the one who happens to suffer them. And since the need for food has its demonstrable basis of reality in the life process itself, it is also obvious that the entirely subjective pangs of hunger are more real than "vainglory," as Hobbes used to call the need for public admiration. Yet, even if these needs, through some miracle of sympathy, were shared by others, their very futility would prevent their ever establishing anything so solid and durable as a common world. The point then is not that there is a lack of public admiration for poetry and philosophy in the modern world, but that such admiration does not constitute a space in which things are saved from destruction by time. The futility of public admiration, which daily is consumed in ever greater quantities, on the contrary, is such that monetary reward, one of the most futile things there is, can become more "objective" and more real.

As distinguished from this "objectivity," whose only basis is money as a common denominator for the fulfilment of all needs, the reality of the public realm relies on the simultaneous presence of innumerable perspectives and aspects in which the common world presents itself and for which no common measurement or denominator can ever be devised. For though the common world is the common meeting ground of all, those who are present have different locations in it, and the location of one can no more coincide with the location of another than the location of two objects. Being seen and being heard by others derive their significance from the fact that everybody sees and hears from a different position. This is the meaning of public life, compared to which even the richest and most satisfying family life can offer only the prolongation or multiplication of one's own position with its attending aspects and perspectives. The subjectivity of privacy can be prolonged and multiplied in a family, it can even become so strong that its weight is felt in the public realm; but this family "world" can never replace the reality rising out of the sum total of aspects presented by one object to a multitude of spectators. Only where things can be seen by many in a variety of aspects without changing their identity, so that those who are gathered around them know they see sameness in utter diversity, can worldly reality truly and reliably appear.

Under the conditions of a common world, reality is not guaranteed primarily by the "common nature" of all men who constitute it, but rather by the fact that, differences of position and the resulting variety of perspectives notwithstanding, everybody is always concerned with the same object. If the sameness of the object can no longer be discerned, no common nature of men, least of all the unnatural conformism of a mass society, can prevent the destruction of the common world, which is usually preceded by the destruction of the many aspects in which it presents itself to human plurality. This can happen under conditions of radical isolation, where nobody can any longer agree with anybody else, as is usually the case in tyrannies. But it may also happen under conditions of mass society or mass hysteria, where we see all people suddenly behave as though they were members of one family, each multiplying and prolonging the perspective of his neighbor. In both instances, men have become entirely private, that is, they have been deprived of seeing and hearing others, of being seen and being heard by them. They are all imprisoned in the subjectivity of their own singular experience, which does not cease to be singular if the same experience is multiplied innumerable times. The end of the common world has come when it is seen only under one aspect and is permitted to present itself in only one perspective. [. . .]

NOTES

1. According to Gunnar Myrdal (*The Political Element in the Development of Economic Theory* [1953], p. xl), the "idea of Social Economy or collective housekeeping (*Volkswirtschaft*)" is one of the "three main foci" around which "the political speculation which has permeated economics from the very beginning is found to be crystallized."

2. This is not to deny that the nation-state and its society grew out of the medieval kingdom and feudalism, in whose framework the family and household unit have an importance unequalled in classical antiquity. The difference, however, is marked. Within the feudal framework, families and households were mutually almost independent, so that the royal household, representing a given territorial region and ruling the feudal lords as *primus inter pares*, did not pretend, like an absolute ruler, to be the head of one family. The medieval "nation" was a conglomeration of families; its members did not think of themselves as members of one family comprehending the whole nation.

3. The distinction is very clear in the first paragraphs of the Ps. Aristotelian *Economics*, because it opposes the despotic one-man rule (*mon-archia*) of the household organization to the altogether different organization of the *polis*.

4. In Athens, one may see the turning point in Solon's legislation. Coulanges rightly sees in the Athenian law that made it a filial duty to support parents the proof of the loss of paternal power (*op. cit.*, pp. 315–16). However, paternal power was limited only if it conflicted with the interest of the city and never for the sake of the individual family member. Thus the sale of children and the exposure of infants lasted throughout antiquity (see R. H. Barrow, *Slavery in the Roman Empire* [1928], p. 8: "Other rights in the *patria potestas* had become obsolete; but the right of exposure remained unforbidden till A.D. 374").

5. It is interesting for this distinction that there were Greek cities where citizens were obliged by law to share their harvest and consume it in common, whereas each of them had the absolute uncontested property of his soil. See Coulanges (*op. cit.*, p. 61), who calls this law "a singular contradiction"; it is no contradiction, because these two types of property had nothing in common in ancient understanding.

6. See *Laws* 842.

7. Quoted from Coulanges, *op. cit.*, p. 96; the reference to Plutarch is *Quaestiones Romanae* 51. It seems strange that Coulanges' one-sided emphasis on the underworld deities in Greek and Roman religion should have overlooked that these gods were not mere gods of the dead and the cult not merely a "death cult," but that this early earth-bound religion served life and death as two aspects of the same process. Life rises out of the earth and returns to it; birth and death are but two different stages of the same biological life over which the subterranean gods hold sway.

8. The discussion between Socrates and Eutherus in Xenophon's *Memorabilia* (ii. 8) is quite interesting: Eutherus is forced by necessity to labor with his body and is sure that his body will not be able to stand this kind of life for *very* long and also that in his old age he will be destitute. Still, he thinks that to labor is better than to beg. Whereupon Socrates proposes that he look for somebody "who is better off and needs an assistant." Eutherus replies that he could not bear servitude (*douleia*).

9. The reference is to Hobbes, *Leviathan*, Part I, ch. 13.

10. The most famous and the most beautiful reference is the discussion of the different forms of government in Herodotus (iii. 80–83), where Otanes, the defender of Greek equality (*isonomi*), states that he "wishes neither to rule nor to be ruled." But it is the same spirit in which Aristotle states that the life of a free man is better than that of a despot, denying freedom to the despot as a matter of course (*Politics* 1325a24). According to Coulanges, all Greek and Latin words which express some rulership over others, such as *rex, pater, anax,*

basileus, refer originally to household relationships and were names the slaves gave to their master (*op. cit.,* pp. 89 ff., 228).

11. The proportion varied and is certainly exaggerated in Xenophon's report from Sparta, where among four thousand people in the market place, a foreigner counted no more than sixty citizens (*Hellenica* iii. 35).

12. See Myrdal, *op. cit.:* "The notion that society, like the head of a family, keeps house for its members, is deeply rooted in economic terminology. . . .. In German *Volkswirtschaftslehre* suggests . . . that there is a collective subject of economic activity . . . with a common purpose and common values. In English, . . . 'theory of wealth' or 'theory of welfare' express similar ideas" (p. 140). "What is meant by a social economy whose function is social housekeeping? In the first place, it implies or suggests an analogy between the individual who runs his own or his family household and society. Adam Smith and James Mill elaborated this analogy explicitly. After J. S. Mill's criticism, and with the wider recognition of the distinction between practical and theoretical political economy, the analogy was generally less emphasized" (p. 143). The fact that the analogy was no longer used may also be due to a development in which society devoured the family unit until it became a full-fledged substitute for it.

13. R. H. Barrow, *The Romans* (1953), p. 194.

14. The characteristics which E. Levasseur (*Histoire des classes ouvrières et de l'industrie en France avant 1789* [1900]) finds for the feudal organization of labor are true for the whole of feudal communities: "Chacun vivait chez soi et vivait de soi-même, le noble sur sa seigneurie, le vilain sur sa culture, le citadin dans sa ville" (p. 229).

15. The fair treatment of slaves which Plato recommends in the *Laws* (777) has little to do with justice and is not recommended "out of regard for the [slaves], but more out of respect to ourselves." For the coexistence of two laws, the political law of justice and the household law of rule, see Wallon, *op. cit.,* II, 200: "La loi, pendant bien longtemps, donc . . . s'abstenait de pénétrer dans la famille, où elle reconnaissait l'empire d'une autre loi." Ancient, especially Roman, jurisdiction with respect to household matters, treatment *of* slaves, family relationships, etc., was essentially designed to restrain the otherwise unrestricted power of the household head; that there could be a rule of justice within the entirely "private" society of the slaves themselves was unthinkable—they were by definition outside the realm of the law and subject to the rule of their master. Only the master himself, in so far as he was also a citizen, was subject to the rules of laws, which for the sake of the city eventually even curtailed his powers in the household.

16. W. J. Ashley, *op. cit.,* p. 415.

17. This "rise" from one realm or rank to a higher is a recurrent theme in Machiavelli (see esp. *Prince,* ch. 6 about Hiero of Syracuse and ch. 7; and *Discourses,* Book II, ch. 13).

18. "By Solon's time slavery had come to be looked on as worse than death" (Robert Schlaifer, "Greek Theories of Slavery from Homer to Aristotle," *Harvard Studies in Classical Philology* [1936], XLVII). Since then, *philopsychia* ("love of life") and cowardice became identified with slavishness. Thus, Plato could believe he had demonstrated the natural slavishness of slaves by the fact that they had not preferred death to enslavement (*Republic* 386A). A late echo of this might still be found in Seneca's answer to the complaints of slaves: "Is freedom so close at hand, yet is there any one a slave?" (*Ep.* 77. 14) or in his *vita si moriendi virtus abest, servitus* est—"life is slavery without the virtue which knows how to die" (77. 13). To understand the ancient attitude toward slavery, it is not immaterial to remember that the majority of slaves were defeated enemies and that generally only a small percentage were born slaves. And while under the Roman Republic slaves were, on the whole, drawn from outside the limits of Roman rule, Greek slaves usually were of the same nationality as their masters; they had proved their slavish nature by not committing suicide, and since courage was the political virtue par excellence, they had thereby shown their "natural" unworthiness, their unfitness to be citizens. The attitude toward slaves changed in the Roman Empire, not only

because of the influence of Stoicism but because a much greater portion of the slave population were slaves by birth. But even in Rome, *labos is* considered to be closely connected with unglorious death by Vergil *(Aeneis* vi).

19. That the free man distinguishes himself from the slave through courage seems to have been the theme of a poem by the Cretan poet Hybrias: "My riches are spear and sword and the beautiful shield. . . . But those who do not dare to bear spear and sword and the beautiful shield that protects the body fall all down unto their knees with awe and address me as Lord and great King" (quoted from Eduard Meyer, *Die Sklaverei im Altertum* [1898], p. 22).

20. Max Weber, "Agrarverhältnisse im Altertum," *Gesammelte Aufsätse zur Sozial- und Wirtschaftsgeschichte* (1924), p. 147.

21. This is well illustrated by a remark of Seneca, who, discussing the usefulness of highly educated slaves (who know all the classics by heart) to an assumedly rather ignorant master, comments: "What the household knows the master knows" (Ep. 27. 6, quoted from Barrow, *Slavery in the Roman Empire*, p. 61).

22. *Aien aristeuein kai hypeirochon emmenai all n* ("always to be the best and to rise above others") is the central concern of Homer's heroes *(Iliad* vi. 208), and Homer was "the educator of Hellas."

23. "The conception of political economy as primarily a 'science' dates only from Adam Smith" and was unknown not only to antiquity and the Middle Ages, but also to canonist doctrine, the first "complete and economic doctrine" which "differed from modern economics in being an 'art' rather than a 'science' " (W. J. Ashley, *op. cit.,* pp. 379 ff.). Classical economics assumed that man, in so far as he is an active being, acts exclusively from self-interest and is driven by only one desire, the desire for acquisition. Adam Smith's introduction of an "invisible hand to promote an end which was no part of [anybody's] intention" proves that even this minimum of action with its uniform motivation still contains too much unpredictable initiative for the establishment of a science. Marx developed classical economics further by substituting group or class interests for individual and personal interests and by reducing these class interests to two major classes, capitalists and workers, so that he was left with one conflict, where classical economics had seen a multitude of contradictory conflicts. The reason why the Marxian economic system is more consistent and coherent, and therefore apparently so much more "scientific" than those of his predecessors, lies primarily in the construction of "socialized man," who is even less an acting being than the "economic man" of liberal economics.

24. That liberal utilitarianism, and not socialism, is "forced into an untenable 'communistic fiction' about the unity of society" and that "the communist fiction [is] implicit in most writings on economics" constitutes one of the chief theses of Myrdal's brilliant work *(op. cit.,* pp. 54 and 150). He shows conclusively that economics can be a science only if one assumes that one interest pervades society as a whole. Behind the "harmony of interests" stands always the "communistic fiction" of one interest, which may then be called welfare or commonwealth. Liberal economists consequently were always guided by a "communistic" ideal, namely, by "interest of society as a whole" (pp. 194–95). The crux of the argument is that this "amounts to the assertion that society must be conceived as a single subject. This, however, is precisely what cannot be conceived. If we tried, we would be attempting to abstract from the essential fact that social activity is the result of the intentions of several individuals" (p. 154).

25. For a brilliant exposition of this usually neglected aspect of Marx's relevance for modern society, see Siegfried Landshut, "Die Gegenwart im Lichte der Marxschen Lehre," *Hamburger Jahrbuch für Wirtschafts- und Gesellschaftspolitik,* Vol. 1 (1956).

26. Here and later I apply the term "division of labor" only to modern labor conditions where one activity is divided and atomized into innumerable minute manipulations, and not to the "division of labor" given in professional specialization. The latter can be so classified only under the assumption that society must be conceived as one single subject, the

fulfilment of whose needs are then subdivided by "an invisible hand" among its members. The same holds true, *mutatis mutandis*, for the odd notion of a division of labor between the sexes, which is even considered by some writers to be the most original one. It presumes as its single subject man-kind, the human species, which has divided its labors among men and women. Where the same argument is used in antiquity (see, for instance, Xenophon *Oeconomicus* vii. 22), emphasis and meaning are quite different. The main division is between a life spent indoors, in the household, and a life spent outside, in the world. Only the latter is a life fully worthy of man, and the notion of equality between man and woman, which is a necessary assumption for the idea of division of labor, is of course entirely absent (cf. n. 81). Antiquity seems to have known only professional specialization, which assumedly was predetermined by natural qualities and gifts. Thus work in the gold mines, which occupied several thousand workers, was distributed according to strength and skill. See J.-P. Vernant, "Travail et nature dans la Grece ancienne," *Journal de psychologie normale et pathologique*, Vol. LII, No. 1 (January-March, 1955).

27. All the European words for "labor," the Latin and English *labor*, the Greek *ponos*, the French *travail*, the German *Arbeit*, signify pain and effort and are also used for the pangs of birth. *Labor* has the same etymological root as *labare* ("to stumble under a burden"); *pons* and *Arbeit* have the same etymological roots as "poverty" *(penia* in Greek and *Armut* in German). Even Hesiod, currently counted among the few defenders of labor in antiquity, put *ponon alginoenta* ("painful labor") as first of the evils plaguing man (*Theogony* 226). For the Greek usage, see G. Herzog-Hauser, "*Ponos*," in Pauly-Wissowa. The German *Arbeit* and *arm* are both derived from the Germanic *arbma-*, meaning lonely and neglected, abandoned. See Kluge/ Götze, *Etymologisches Wörterbuch* (1951). In medieval German, the word is used to translate *labor, tribulatio, persecutio, adversitas, malum* (see Klara Vontobel, *Das Arbeitsethos des deutschen Protestantismus* [Dissertation, Bern, 1946]).

28. Homer's much quoted thought that Zeus takes away half of a man's excellence (*aret*) when the day of slavery catches him (*Odyssey* xvii. 320 ff.) is put into the mouth of Eumaios, a slave himself, and meant as an objective statement, not a criticism or a moral judgment. The slave lost excellence because he lost admission to the public realm, where excellence can show.

29. This is also the reason why it is impossible "to write a character sketch of any slave who lived. . . . Until they emerge into freedom and notoriety, they remain shadowy types rather than persons" (Barrow, *Slavery in the Roman Empire*, p. 156).

30. I use here a little-known poem on pain from Rilke's deathbed: The first lines of the untitled poem are: "Komm du, du letzter, den ich anerkenne, / heilloser Schmerz im leib- lichen Geweb"; and it concludes as follows: "Bin ich es noch, der da unkenntlich brennt? / Erinnerungen reiss ich nicht herein. / O Leben, Leben: Draussensein. / Und ich in Lobe. Niemand, der mich kennt."

31. On the subjectivity of pain and its relevance for all variations of hedonism and sen- sualism, see §§ 15 and 43. For the living, death is primarily dis-appearance. But unlike pain, there is one aspect of death in which it is as though death appeared among the living, and that is in old age. Goethe once remarked that growing old is "gradually receding from ap- pearance" (*stufenweises Zurücktreten aus der Erscheinung*); the truth of this remark as well as the actual appearance of this process of disappearing becomes quite tangible in the old-age self-portraits of the great masters—Rembrandt, Leonardo, etc.—in which the intensity of the eyes seems to illuminate and preside over the receding flesh.

32. Contra Faustum Manichaeum v. 5.

33. This is of course still the presupposition even of Aquinas' political philosophy (see *op. cit.* ii. 2. 181. 4).

34. The term *corpus rei publicae* is current in pre-Christian Latin, but has the connotation of the population inhabiting a *res publica*, a given political realm. The corresponding Greek term

s ma is never used in pre-Christian Greek in a political sense. The metaphor seems to occur for the first time in Paul (I Cor. 12: 12–27) and is current in all early Christian writers (see, for instance, Tertullian *Apologeticus* 39, or Ambrosius *De officiis ministrorum* iii. 3. 17). It became of the greatest importance for medieval political theory, which unanimously assumed that all men were *quasi unum corpus* (Aquinas *op. cit.* ii. 1. 81. 1). But while the early writers stressed the equality of the members, which are all equally necessary for the well-being of the body as a whole, the emphasis later shifted to the difference between the head and the members, to the duty of the head to rule and of the members to obey. (For the Middle Ages, see Anton-Hermann Chroust, "The Corporate Idea in the Middle Ages," *Review of Politics*, Vol. VIII [1947].)

35. Aquinas *op. cit.* ii. 2. 179. 2.

36. See Article 57 of the Benedictine rule, in Levasseur, *op. cit.*, *p.* 187: If one of the monks became proud of his work, he had to give it up.

37. Barrow (*Slavery in the Roman Empire*, p. 168), in an illuminating discussion of the membership of slaves in the Roman colleges, which provided, besides "good fellowship in life and the certainty of a decent burial . . . the crowning glory of an epitaph; and in this last the slave found a melancholy pleasure."

38. Nicomachean Ethics 1177b31.

39. *Wealth of Nations*, Book I, ch. 10 (pp. 120 and 95 of Vol. I of Everyman's ed.).

JÜRGEN HABERMAS

THE PUBLIC SPHERE: AN ENCYCLOPEDIA ARTICLE (1964)

Jürgen Habermas (b. 1929) published his Strukturwandel der Öffentlichkeit *in 1962. Two years later, a condensation of his argument appeared as an article in the "Fischer Lexicon"* Staat und Politik. *This short piece was eventually translated into English and published for the first time in the US journal* New German Critique *in 1974. It remained the only available text in English on the public sphere written by Habermas until* Structural Transformation *was translated in 1989. It is still very useful as an introduction and an overview.*

*The bourgeois or modern public sphere he outlines differs fundamentally from the repre-*sentative *public sphere in pre-modern, feudal societies. Here, power was inseparable from the ruling person, who represented God's power and will, and distinctions between a private and a public social realm and between state and society had not yet been developed. In contrast, the ideal of the bourgeois public sphere imagines a space to which all citizens have access. He identifies two public spheres (or two parts of the public sphere), the literary and the political. The former, typified by the role of the novel, interrogates the basic qualities and ethical dilemmas of the human condition. The latter is the space where "public opinion" is formed when citizens confer with "guaranteed rights of freedom of assembly and association and the freedom to express and publish their opinions—about matters of general interest."*

Habermas goes on to describe how this model of the political public sphere developed in actual historical contexts from the late seventeenth century on. He identifies the coffee houses of eighteenth-century London, where participants gathered as equals, disregarding their private social status, and the force of the better argument reigned, as coming closest to the ideal of the "bourgeois public sphere." But he also emphasises the central role of the early press as a forum for the public use of reason and identifies the later "transformation from a journalism of conviction to one of commerce" as a destructive invasion of "private interests." For Habermas this shift is part of a wider transformation of the public sphere into a field of competing private interests where political decisions come about through struggles and arcane dealings between large organizations and between these organized interests and the state. What remains, is a need for ritual legitimation through a form of pseudo publicness (publicity) or openness. The public sphere becomes re-feudalised: A space where power and decisions are presented to the public, not developed by the public.

1. The Concept

By "the public sphere" we mean first of all a realm of our social life in which something approaching public opinion can be formed. Access is guaranteed to all citizens. A portion of the public sphere comes into being in every conversation in which private individuals assemble to form a public body.[1] They then behave neither like business or professional people transacting private affairs, nor like members of a constitutional order subject to the legal constraints of a state bureaucracy. Citizens behave as a public body when they confer in an unrestricted fashion—that is, with the guarantee of freedom of assembly and association and the freedom to express and publish their opinions—about matters of general interest. In a large public body this kind of communication requires specific means for transmitting information and influencing those who receive it. Today newspapers and magazines, radio and television are the media of the public sphere. We speak of the political public sphere in contrast, for instance, to the literary one, when public discussion deals with objects connected to the activity of the state. Although state authority is so to speak the executor of the political public sphere, it is not a part of it.[2] To be sure, state authority is usually considered "public" authority, but it derives its task of caring for the well-being of all citizens primarily from this aspect of the public sphere. Only when the exercise of political control is effectively subordinated to the democratic demand that information be accessible to the public, does the political public sphere win an institutionalized influence over the government through the instrument of law-making bodies. The expression "public opinion" refers to the tasks of criticism and control which a public body of citizens informally—and, in periodic elections, formally as well—practices vis-à-vis the ruling structure organized in the form of a state. Regulations demanding that certain proceedings be public (*Publizitätsvorschriften*), for example those providing for open court hearings, are also related to this function of public opinion. The public sphere as a sphere which mediates between society and state, in which the public organizes itself as the bearer or public opinion, accords with the principle of the public sphere[3]—that principle of public information which once had to be fought for against the arcane policies of monarchies and which since that time has made possible the democratic control of state activities.

It is no coincidence that these concepts of the public sphere and public opinion arose for the first time only in the eighteenth century. They acquire their specific meaning from a concrete historical situation. It was at that time that the distinction of "opinion" from "opinion publique" and "public opinion" came about. Though mere opinions (cultural assumptions, normative attitudes, collective prejudices and values) seem to persist unchanged in their natural form as a kind of sediment of history, public opinion can by definition only come into existence when a reasoning public is presupposed. Public discussions about the exercise of political power which are both critical in intent and institutionally guaranteed have not always existed—they grew out of a specific phase of bourgeois society and could enter into the order of the bourgeois constitutional state only as a result of a particular constellation of interests.

2. History

There is no indication European society of the high middle ages possessed a public sphere as a unique realm distinct from the private sphere. Nevertheless, it was not coincidental that during that period symbols of sovereignty, for instance the princely seal, were deemed "public." At that time there existed a public representation of power. The status of the feudal lord, at whatever level of the feudal pyramid, was oblivious to the categories "public" and "private," but the holder of the position represented it publicly: he showed himself, presented himself as the embodiment of an ever present "higher" power. The concept of this representation has been maintained up to the most recent constitutional history. Regardless of the degree to which it has loosed itself from the old base, the authority of political power today still demands a representation at the highest level by a head of state. Such elements, however, derive from a pre-bourgeois social structure. Representation in the sense of a bourgeois public sphere,[4] for instance the representation of the nation or of particular mandates, has nothing to do with the medieval representative public sphere—a public sphere directly linked to the concrete existence of a ruler. As long as the prince and the estates of the realm still "are" the land, instead of merely functioning as deputies for it, they are able to "re-present"; they represent their power "before" the people, instead of for the people.

The feudal authorities (church, princes and nobility), to which the representative public sphere was first linked, disintegrated during a long process of polarization. By the end of the eighteenth century they had broken apart into private elements on the one hand, and into public on the other. The position of the church changed with the reformation: the link to divine authority which the church represented, that is, religion, became a private matter. So-called religious freedom came to insure what was historically the first area of private autonomy. The church itself continued its existence as one public and legal body among others. The corresponding polarization within princely authority was visibly manifested in the separation of the public budget from the private household expenses of a ruler. The institutions of public authority, along with the bureaucracy and the military, and in part also with the legal institutions, asserted their independence from the privatized sphere of the princely court. Finally, the feudal estates were transformed as well: the nobility became the organs of public authority, parliament and the legal institutions; while those occupied in trades and professions, insofar as they had already established urban corporations and territorial organizations, developed into a sphere of bourgeois society which would stand apart from the state as a genuine area of private autonomy.

The representative public sphere yielded to that new sphere of "public authority" which came into being with national and territorial states. Continuous state activity (permanent administration, standing army) now corresponded to the permanence of the relationships which with the stock exchange and the press had developed within the exchange of commodities and information. Public authority consolidated into a concrete opposition for those who were merly subject to it and who at first found only a negative definition of themselves within it. These were the "private individuals" who were excluded from public authority because they held no office. "Public" no longer referred to the "representative" court of a prince endowed with authority, but rather to an institution regulated according to competence, to an apparatus endowed with a monopoly on the legal exertion of authority. Private individuals subsumed in the state at whom public authority was directed now made up the public body.

Society, now a private realm occupying a position in opposition to the state, stood on the one hand as if in clear contrast to the state. On the other hand, that society had become a concern of public interest to the degree that the reproduction of life in the wake of the developing market economy had grown beyond the bounds of private domestic authority. *The bourgeois public sphere* could be understood as the sphere of private individuals assembled into a public body, which almost immediately laid claim to the officially regulated "intellectual newspapers" for use against the public authority itself. In those newspapers, and in moralistic and critical journals, they debated that public authority on the general rules of social intercourse in their fundamentally privatized yet publically relevant sphere of labor and commodity exchange.

3. The Liberal Model of the Public Sphere

The medium of this debate—public discussion—was unique and without historical precedent. Hitherto the estates had negotiated agreements with their princes, settling their claims to power from case to case. This development took a different course in England, where the parliament limited royal power, than it did on the continent, where the monarchies mediatized the estates. The third estate then broke with this form of power arrangement since it could no longer establish itself as a ruling group. A division of power by means of the delineation of the rights of the nobility was no longer possible within an exchange economy—private authority over capitalist property is, after all, unpolitical. Bourgeois individuals are private individuals. As such, they do not "rule." Their claims to power vis-à-vis public authority were thus directed not against the concentration of power, which was to be "shared." Instead, their ideas infiltrated the very principle on which the existing power is based. To the principle of the existing power, the bourgeois public opposed the principle of supervision—that very principle which demands that proceedings be made public (*Publizität*). The principle of supervision is thus a means of transforming the nature of power, not merely one basis of legitimation exchanged for another.

In the first modern constitutions the catalogues of fundamental rights were a perfect image of the liberal model of the public sphere: they guaranteed the society as a sphere of private autonomy and the restriction of public authority to a few functions. Between these two spheres, the constitutions further insured the existence of a realm of private individuals assembled into a public body who as citizens transmit the needs of bourgeois society to the state, in order, ideally, to transform political into "rational" authority within the medium of this public sphere. The general interest, which was the measure of such a rationality, was then guaranteed, according to the presuppositions of a society of free commodity exchange, when the activities of private individuals in the marketplace were freed from social compulsion and from political pressure in the public sphere.

At the same time, daily political newspapers assumed an important role. In the second half of the eighteenth century literary journalism created serious competition for the earlier news sheets which were mere compilations of notices. Karl Bücher characterized this great development as follows: "Newspapers changed from mere institutions for the publication of news into bearers and leaders of public opinion— weapons of party politics. This transformed the newspaper business. A new element emerged between the gathering and the publication of news: the editorial staff. But for the newspaper publisher it meant that he changed from a vendor of recent news to a dealer in public opinion." The publishers insured the newspapers a commercial basis, yet without commercializing them as such. The press remained an institution of the public itself, effective in the manner of a mediator and intensifier of public discussion, no longer a mere organ for the spreading of news but not yet the medium of a consumer culture.

This type of journalism can be observed above all during periods of revolution when newspapers of the smallest political groups and organizations spring up, for

instance in Paris in 1789. Even in the Paris of 1848 every half-way eminent politician organized his club, every other his journal: 450 clubs and over 200 journals
were established there between February and May alone. Until the permanent
legalization of a politically functional public sphere, the appearance of a political
newspaper meant joining the struggle for freedom and public opinion, and thus for
the public sphere as a principle. Only with the establishment of the bourgeois constitutional state was the intellectual press relieved of the pressure of its convictions.
Since then it has been able to abandon its polemical position and take advantage of
the earning possibilities of a commercial undertaking. In England, France, and the
United States the transformation from a journalism of conviction to one of commerce began in the 1830s at approximately the same time. In the transition from the
literary journalism of private individuals to the public services of the mass media
the public sphere was transformed by the influx of private interests, which received
special prominence in the mass media.

4. The Public Sphere in the Social Welfare State Mass Democracy

Although the liberal model of the public sphere is still instructive today with respect to the normative claim that information be accessible to the public,[5] it cannot
be applied to the actual conditions of an industrially advanced mass democracy
organized in the form of the social welfare state. In part the liberal model had
always included ideological components, but it is also in part true that the social
pre-conditions, to which the ideological elements could at one time at least be
linked, had been fundamentally transformed. The very forms in which the public
sphere manifested itself, to which supporters of the liberal model could appeal
for evidence, began to change with the Chartist movement in England and the
February revolution in France. Because of the diffusion of press and propaganda,
the public body expanded beyond the bounds of the bourgeoisie. The public
body lost not only its social exclusivity; it lost in addition the coherence created
by bourgeois social institutions and a relatively high standard of education. Conflicts hitherto restricted to the private sphere now intrude into the public sphere.
Group needs which can expect no satisfaction from a self-regulating market now
tend towards a regulation by the state. The public sphere, which must now mediate these demands, becomes a field for the competition of interests, competitions
which assume the form of violent conflict. Laws which obviously have come about
under the "pressure of the street" can scarcely still be understood as arising from
the consensus of private individuals engaged in public discussion. They correspond
in a more or less unconcealed manner to the compromise of conflicting private
interests. Social organizations which deal with the state act in the political public
sphere, whether through the agency of political parties or directly in connection
with the public administration. With the interweaving of the public and private
realm, not only do the political authorities assume certain functions in the sphere
of commodity exchange and social labor, but conversely social powers now assume
political functions. This leads to a kind of "refeudalization" of the public sphere.
Large organizations strive for political compromises with the state and with each
other, excluding the public sphere whenever possible. But at the same time the
large organizations must assure themselves of at least plebiscitary support from

the mass of the population through an apparent display of openness (*demonstrative Publizität⁶*).

The political public sphere of the social welfare state is characterized by a peculiar weakening of its critical functions. At one time the process of making proceedings public (Publizität) 46 was intended to subject persons or affairs to public reason, and to make political decisions subject to appeal before the court of public opinion. But often enough today the process of making public simply serves the arcane policies of special interests; in the form of "publicity" it wins public prestige for people or affairs, thus making them worthy of acclamation in a climate of non-public opinion. The very words "public relations work" (Öffentlichkeitsarbeit) betray the fact that a public sphere must first be arduously constructed case by case, a public sphere which earlier grew out of the social structure. Even the central relationship of the public, the parties and the parliament is affected by this change in function.

Yet this trend towards the weakening of the public sphere as a principle is opposed by the extension of fundamental rights in the social welfare state. The demand that information be accessible to the public is extended from organs of the state to all organizations dealing with the state. To the degree that this is realized, a public body of organized private individuals would take the place of the now-defunct public body of private individuals who relate individually to each other. Only these organized individuals could participate effectively in the process of public communication; only they could use the channels of the public sphere which exist within parties and associations and the process of making proceedings public (Publizität) which was established to facilitate the dealings of organizations with the state. Political compromises would have to be legitimized through this process of public communication. The idea of the public sphere, preserved in the social welfare state mass democracy, an idea which calls for a rationalization of power through the medium of public discussion among private individuals, threatens to disintegrate with the structural transformation of the public sphere itself. It could only be realized today, on an altered basis, as a rational reorganization of social and political power under the mutual control of rival organizations committed to the public sphere in their internal structure as well as in their relations with the state and each other.

NOTES

1. Habermas' concept of the public sphere is not to be equated with that of "the public," i.e. of the individuals who assemble. His concept is directed instead at the institution, which to be sure only assumes concrete form through the participation of people. It cannot, however, be characterized simply as a crowd. (This and the following notes by Peter Hohendahl.)

2. The state and the public sphere do not overlap, as one might suppose from casual language use. Rather they confront one another as opponents. Habermas designates that sphere as public which antiquity understood to be private, i.e. the sphere of non-governmental opinion making.

3. The principle of the public sphere could still be distinguished from an institution which is demonstrable in social history. Habermas thus would mean a model of norms and modes of behavior by means of which the very functioning of public opinion can be guaranteed for the first time. These norms and modes of behavior include: a) general accessibility, b) elimination of all privileges and c) discovery of general norms and rational legitimations.

4. The expression "represent" is used in a very specific sense in the following section, namely to "present oneself." The important thing to understand is that the medieval public sphere, if it even deserves this designation, is tied to the *personal*. The feudal lord and estates create the public sphere by means of their very presence.

5. Here it should be understood that Habermas considers the principle behind the bourgeois public sphere as indispensable, but not its historical form.

6. One must distinguish between Habermas' concept of "making proceedings public" *(Publizität)* and the "public sphere" *(Öffentlichkeit)*. The term *Publizität* describes the degree of public effect generated by a public act. Thus a situation can arise in which the form of public opinion making is maintained, while the substance of the public sphere has long ago been undermined.

OSKAR NEGT AND ALEXANDER KLUGE

EXCERPT FROM *PUBLIC SPHERE AND EXPERIENCE. TOWARD AN ANALYSIS OF THE BOURGEOIS AND PROLETARIAN PUBLIC SPHERE* (1972)

Oskar Negt (b. 1934) studied sociology at the Institute for Social Research, home of the "Frankfurt School." His doctoral work on Hegel and Comte was carried out under the supervision of Theodor Adorno. He worked as an assistant to Jürgen Habermas before he took a position in sociology at the University of Hannover, where he remained until he retired in 2002. Alexander Kluge (b. 1932) studied law, history, and music before completing his doctorate in law at the University of Frankfurt a.M. in 1956. He then worked as legal counselor to the Institute for Social Research and Adorno. He made his first films in the early 1960s and was a central figure in New German Cinema. After 1988, he produced a number of offbeat cultural programs for commercial television. He is also a prize-winning author.

Negt and Kluge's co-written book Public Sphere and Experience *([1972] 1993) is dedicated to Adorno. Though grounded in the '60s revival of Marxism, with its emphasis on social classes and class struggle, it is also marked by the "total" emancipatory interest typical of the '60s, which is anti-authoritarian and critical not only of Stalinism but also of traditional organizational forms in the labour movement. Negt and Kluge argue that an understanding of the real conditions of life in capitalist societies, not least of the relations between the "private," the social (especially work) and the political, is blocked by the organizational forms of bourgeois society, including the bourgeois public sphere and that these forms are reproduced in the labour movement, with its division between party (politics), unions (economy), and leisure/cultural organizations. Negt and Kluge's alternative, the "proletarian public sphere" does not refer to actual organizational forms but to processes of learning made possible in certain social situations where habits are broken and questions are asked about fundamental issues—typically a wildcat strike, or a workers' factory occupation. The term "counterpublic sphere" has a wider meaning, referring more generally to anti-bourgeois public spheres. Negt and Kluge also coined the term "public spheres of production" where the experience of everyday life provide the raw materials for the products of commercial mass media. Even so, they argue that it is a mistaken strategy to try to withdraw completely from either these commercial spaces or the bourgeois public sphere.*

Introduction to the Book

Federal elections, Olympic ceremonies, the actions of a commando unit, a theater premiere—all are considered public events. Other events of overwhelming public significance, such as childrearing, factory work, and watching television within one's own four walls, are considered private. The real social experiences of human beings, produced in everyday life and work, cut across such divisions.

We originally intended to write a book about the public sphere and the mass media. This would have examined the most advanced structural changes within the public sphere and the mass media, in particular the media cartel. The loss of a public sphere within the various sectors of the left, together with the restricted access of workers in their existing organizations to channels of communication, soon led us to ask whether there can be any effective forms of a counterpublic sphere against the bourgeois public sphere. This is how we arrived at the concept of the proletarian public sphere, which embodies an experiential interest that is quite distinct. The dialectic of bourgeois and proletarian public sphere is the subject of our book.

Historical fissures—crises, war, capitulation, revolution, counterrevolution—denote concrete constellations of social forces within which a proletarian public sphere develops. Since the latter has no existence as a ruling public sphere, it has to be reconstructed from such rifts, marginal cases, isolated initiatives. To study substantive attempts at a proletarian public sphere is, however, only one aim in our argument: the other is to investigate the contradictions emerging within advanced capitalist societies for their potential for a counterpublic sphere. We are aware of the danger that the concepts "proletarian experience" and "proletarian public sphere" can be reduced to idealistic platitudes. In a far more cautious tone, Jürgen Habermas speaks with regard to this of a "variant of a plebian public sphere that has, as it were, been suppressed within the historical process."[1]

During the past fifty years the concept "bourgeois" has repeatedly been devalued: but it is not possible to do away with it so long as the facade of legitimation created by the revolutionary bourgeoisie continues to determine the decaying postbourgeois forms of the public sphere. We use the word bourgeois as an invitation to the reader to reflect critically upon the social origins of the ruling concept of the public sphere. Only in this way can the fetishistic character of the latter be grasped and a materialistic concept be developed.

We are starting from the assumption that the concept proletarian is no less ambiguous than bourgeois. Nonetheless, it does refer to a strategic position that is substantively meshed with the history of the emancipation of the working class. The other reason we have chosen this concept is because it is not at present susceptible to absorption into the ruling discourse; it resists being categorized into the symbolic spectrum of the bourgeois public sphere, which so readily accommodates the concept of a critical public sphere. There are objective reasons for this. Fifty years of counterrevolution and restoration have exhausted the labor movement's linguistic resources. The word proletarian has, in the Federal Republic, taken on an attenuated, indeed an anachronistic, sense. Yet the real conditions it denotes belong to the present, and there is no other word for them. We believe it is wrong to allow words to become obsolete before there is a change in the objects they denote.[2]

Whereas it is self-evident that the bourgeois public sphere is not a reference point for bourgeois interests alone, it is not generally assumed that proletarian experience and its organization likewise form a crystallizing point: namely, for a public sphere that reflects the interests and experiences of the overwhelming majority of the population, insofar as these experiences and interests are real.[3] Proletarian life does not form a cohesive whole, but is characterized by the blocking of those elements that, in reality, hold it together. The horizon of social experience that reinforces the block of these coherent elements is the bourgeois public sphere.

What is striking about the prevailing interpretations of the concept of the public sphere is that they attempt to bring together a multitude of phenomena and yet exclude the two most important areas of life: the whole of the industrial apparatus and socialization in the family. According to these interpretations, the public sphere derives its substance from an intermediate realm that does not specifically express any particular life context *[Lebenszusammenhang]*, even though this public sphere allegedly represents the totality of society.

The weakness characteristic of virtually all forms of the bourgeois public sphere derives from this contradiction: namely, that the bourgeois public sphere excludes substantial life interests and nevertheless claims to represent society as a whole. To enable it to fulfill its own claims, it must be treated like the laurel tree in Brecht's *Stories from the Calendar*, about which Mr. K. says: it is trimmed to make it even more perfect and even rounder until there is nothing left of it. Since the bourgeois public sphere is not sufficiently grounded in substantive life interests, it remains compelled to ally itself with the more tangible interests of capitalist production. For the bourgeois public sphere, proletarian life remains a "thing-in-itself": it exerts an influence on the former, but without being understood.

The tendencies of the consciousness and programming industry, advertising, the publicity campaigns of firms and administrative apparatuses have altogether different roots. These—along with the advanced production process (itself a pseudo-public sphere)—overlay, as *new public spheres of production*, the classical public sphere. These public spheres of production are nonpublicly anchored: in contrast to the traditional form of public sphere, they work the raw material of everyday life and they derive their penetrative force directly from the capitalist production interest. By circumventing the intermediate realm of the traditional public sphere (the seasonal public sphere of elections, the formation of public opinion), they seek direct access to the private sphere of the individual. It is essential that the proletarian counterpublic sphere confronts these public spheres, which are permeated by the interests of capital, and does not merely see itself as the antithesis of the classical public sphere.

At stake is a practical, political experience of the working class: the working class must know how to deal with the bourgeois public sphere and must know what threats the latter poses, without allowing its own experiences to be defined by the latter's narrow horizons. The bourgeois public sphere is of no use as a medium for the crystallization of the particular experience of the working class—it is not even the real enemy. Since it came into being, the labor movement's motive has been to express politically proletarian interests in its own forms of public sphere. At the same time, the goal has been to contest the ruling class's enlistment of the state. Marx recognizes this when he describes the theft of wood as analogous to the propertied class's theft of the public sphere by appropriating the executive power of the latter without paying for it through engaging thousands of gendarmes, foresters, and soldiers for its own interests. If the masses try to fight a ruling class reinforced by the power of the public sphere, their struggle is hopeless; they are always simultaneously fighting against themselves, for the public sphere is constituted by them. It is so difficult to grasp this because the idea of the bourgeois public sphere—as "the bold fiction of a binding of all politically significant decision-making processes to the right, guaranteed by law, of citizens to shape their own opinions"[4]—has, since its inception, been ambivalent. The revolutionary bourgeoisie attempted, via the emphatic concept of public opinion, to fuse the whole of society into a unity. This remained as a goal. In reality, although this was not expressed in political terms, it was the value abstraction founded on commodity production that forced society together. The extent to which the public sphere holds society together was therefore never gauged. It seemed possible, however, that society could be founded on something other than commodity exchange and private property. In this way the idea of the bourgeois public sphere created, in the masses organized by it, an awareness of possible reforms and alternatives. This illusion repeats itself in every attempt at political stocktaking and mass mobilization that occurs within the categories of the bourgeois public sphere.

In the seventeenth and eighteenth centuries, after centuries of preparing public opinion, bourgeois society constituted the public sphere as a crystallization point of its experiences and ideologies. The "dictatorship of the bourgeoisie" articulates itself in the compartmentalizations, the *forms* of this public sphere. Whereas the bourgeois revolution initially makes a thoroughgoing attempt to overcome the limits of the capitalist mode of production, the forms-for instance, the forced separation of powers, the division between public and private, between politics and production, between everyday language and authentic social expression, between education, science, and art on the one hand and the interests and experiences of the masses on the other—prevent even the mere expressions of social criticism, of a counterpublic sphere, and of the emancipation of the majority of the population. There is no chance that the experiences and interests of the proletariat, in the broadest sense, will be able to organize themselves amid this splitting of all the interrelated qualitative elements of experience and social practice.

We do not claim in our book to be able to say what the content of proletarian experience is. But our political motive is to uncouple the investigation of the public sphere and the mass media from its naturally rooted context, where all it yields is a vast number of publications that merely execute variations on the compartmentalizations of the bourgeois public sphere. What we understand by "naturally rooted" is evident in the ambivalence—one that has never been examined—of the most important concepts associated with the keyword "public sphere": public opinion, law enforcement, freedom of information, the production of a public sphere, mass media, and so on. All of these concepts have developed historically and express specific interests. The contradictory nature of social development is sedimented in the contradictory nature of these concepts. The inquiry into the source of these concepts and who employs them tells us more about their content than do any excursions into philology or the history of ideas.

The bourgeois public sphere is anchored in the formal characteristics of communication: it can be represented in terms of a schema of continuous historical progression, insofar as one focuses on the ideas that are realized within it. But if, by contrast, one takes its real substance as one's point of departure, it is not unified at all, but rather the aggregate of individual spheres that are only abstractly related. Television, the press, the public sphere of interest groups and political parties, parliament, the military, public education, public chairs in the universities, the legal system, the churches, industry, and so on, are only seemingly fused into a general concept of the public sphere. In reality, this general overriding public sphere runs parallel to these fields as an idea, and is exploited by the interests contained within each sphere, especially by the organized interests of the production sector. What are overriding, however, are those spheres that derive from the production sector, which is constituted as nonpublic, as well as the overwhelming collective doubt—a by-product of the capitalist mode of production—in the production network's ability to legitimate itself. Both of these tendencies come together and combine with the manifestations of the classical public sphere, as these are united in the state and in parliament. For this reason, the classical public sphere, despite its state of decay, is anything but a mere illusion behind which one could come into direct contact with capitalist interests. This assumption is just as false as the opposing one that, within this aggregated public sphere, politics could make a decision that ran counter to the interests of capital.

To simplify our account, concrete examples have been restricted to two relatively recent mass media: the media cartel and television. We have not examined in detail other spheres such as the press, parliament, the public sphere of interest groups and political parties, trade unions, or science and research. Individual aspects of the proletarian public sphere are discussed in a series of commentaries following the main chapters.

It is our political interest in this book to provide a framework for discussion that will open the analytical concepts of political economy *downward*, toward the real experiences of human beings. Such a discussion cannot itself be conducted in the forms of the bourgeois or the traditional academic public sphere alone. It must have recourse to investigative work that brings together existing social experiences with newly acquired ones. It is plausible that such investigative work must, above all, concern itself with its own bases of production, the structures of the public sphere and of the mass media.

Frankfurt am Main, Summer 1972

Oskar Negt, Alexander Kluge

NOTES

1. Jürgen Habermas, *Strukturwandel der Öffentlichkeit* (Neuwied and Berlin, 1969), 8. Habermas's choice of the concept of a "plebeian" public sphere can be justified by the fact that, throughout its history, the proletariat has never attempted on its own to constitute a public sphere without including elements of the bourgeoisie or of the lumpen proletariat. It was the heterogeneous urban lower classes who undertook to form a public sphere appropriate to them during the French Revolution or during the French nineteenth-century class struggles that can be defined with the term "plebeian." Moreover, the inaccuracy of the concept that makes it so handy for historical analysis (it must be able to condense together entirely heterogeneous historical moments) is more evident in the term "plebeian" than in "proletarian," since the latter term seems to have a more specific analytical meaning. We have nonetheless chosen the designation *proletarian* public sphere because we believe that what is at issue here is not a variant of the bourgeois public sphere, but rather an entirely separate conceptualization of the overall social context, which has been established in history but has not been included within the parameters of the term public sphere. Thus, a plant where there is a strike or a factory that is being occupied is to be understood not as a variant of the plebeian public sphere, but rather as the essential core of a *conception of public sphere that is rooted in the production process.* The same difficulty would also arise if one were to speak of "the people" (*Volk*) (a term Habermas always uses in quotation marks), since this term is inadequate for expressing the quality of working people as producers. The dialectic between historical and systematic methods of analysis is of central importance for the method of analysis practiced here and in what follows. The systematic method seeks out precise concepts and terms that are analytically articulate and capable of distinguishing between phenomena. However, the

historical method of analysis must, in order to grasp real historical movement, repeatedly sublate the apparent precision of systematic concepts, especially their tendency toward exclusion. Therefore, our use of the concept of a proletarian public sphere can only be understood within this conceptual dialectic, and does not claim to be more precise than, for instance, the term "plebeian public sphere"—although this choice of an alternative term does indicate that an alternative set of interests is at issue.

2. It is not our intention as individual authors to replace central, historically developed concepts that, as real concepts, designate real-life circumstances that have not been sublated and that possess so little purely definitional character. The formation of new concepts here is a matter that will require collective effort. If historical situations really change, new words will come into being accordingly.

3. The concept of the proletarian public sphere is not one we originated. It has been used variously in the history of the labor movement, but frequently in an unspecific way. As regards the period following World War I, one peculiarity stands out that is significant for the way this concept is used, particularly with reference to the communist parties. The proletarian public sphere is not exactly that which could be characterized as the public sphere of the party. Anyone who appeals to the proletarian public sphere also appeals initially to the party, but is in fact addressing the masses. Here it is striking that the concept of public sphere that is used always puts forward the mobilization of the masses or of party members for specific decisions that cannot be realized within the organizational apparatuses or are controversial. Thus one speaks, for example, of actions "that are capable of seriously jeopardizing the status of our party in the eyes of the proletarian public sphere" (Hermann Weber, *Die Stalinisierung der KPD in der Weimarer Republik*, documentary appendix, Rote Texte, Reihe Arbeiterbewegung, n.d., p. 416). Appeals are made to the proletarian public sphere whenever it is a matter of implementing the decisions and analyses of a particular faction within the party leadership or of criticizing something that cannot be reconciled with the interests of the proletariat as a whole. However, this instrumentalizing appeal to the masses and their acclamation corresponds precisely to a principle of the bourgeois public sphere. The proletarian sphere does not function in this way. Here the concept has an almost spontaneous, ad hoc quality, which is attributed to the masses from without. The situation is characterized by a state of affairs in which party organization and the masses are no longer united by a common experiential context. An even more graphic example for the way in which the concept of proletarian public sphere is taken up can be seen in the action that was organized by Trotsky and his supporters to parallel the official October demonstration during a phase in the development of Soviet society in which there was in practice only little possibility of implementing Trotsky's Left Opposition. Lenin also refers in various ways to appealing to the party in order to put through specific decisions in opposition to the majority in the party leadership. In all of these cases, the proletariat is viewed as a totality, as the material carrier of a specific public sphere. For Marx, the concept of "the proletarian" resonates with a meaning content that is not reflected in sociological and political-economic definitions of the working class, although it constitutes their material foundation. In the proletariat there is concentrated the practical negation of the existing world that need only be conceptualized to become part of the history of the political emancipation of the working class. In the *Critique of Hegel's Philosophy of Right*, Marx remarks that all of the demands of the working class are forms of expression of the mode of existence of this class itself. "When the proletariat announces the dissolution of the existing social order, it only declares the secret of its own existence, for it is the effective dissolution of this order. When the proletariat demands the negation of private property, it only lays down as a principle for society what society has already made a principle for the proletariat, and what the latter already involuntarily embodies as the negative result of society" (in *The Marx-Engels Reader*, ed. Robert C. Tucker, trans. T. B. Bottomore [New York: W. W. Norton, 1972], 23).

4. Jürgen Habermas, Introduction to *Theory and Practice* (Frankfurt, 1971), 32.

NANCY FRASER

RETHINKING THE PUBLIC SPHERE: A CONTRIBUTION TO THE CRITIQUE OF ACTUALLY EXISTING DEMOCRACY (1992)

Nancy Fraser (b. 1947) is a professor of political and social science at The New School for Social Research in New York. Working within the tradition of critical theory, she has criticized Jürgen Habermas from a feminist perspective. In her writings, she tries to work out a concept of social justice that involves the two dimensions of economic redistribution and cultural recognition. According to Fraser, a just society is characterized by "parity of participation" in social life and in political decision-making.

The article selected for this volume was first published in Social Text *in 1990. It is, Fraser argues, a contribution to the criticism of the public sphere theory as well as to the reconstruction of the concept for a new historical epoch. Habermas' concept was developed for a "bourgeois society." Because this society has now given way to a "welfare state mass democracy," the liberal model of the public sphere is no longer feasible and Fraser sets out develop a model for this "post-bourgeois society."*

She identifies four issues that are central to Habermas' concept of the public sphere: Social equality as a necessary condition for political democracy; the question of competing publics versus a single comprehensive public sphere; the role of private interests and private matters in the public sphere; and whether a functioning democratic public sphere requires a sharp distinction between civil society and the state.

In her criticism of the last assumption Fraser develops the concepts of "strong" and "weak" publics. In Habermas' initial version, the public sphere is situated within civil society (opinion formation) and must be separated from the state (decision making) in order to fulfill its function as a counterweight to and a discursive check on the state. Such conceptualization is complicated with the emergence of parliamentary sovereignty because a parliament functions as a public sphere within the state. To conceptualize this situation, Fraser makes a distinction between "weak publics," referring to deliberative practice con-sisting only in opinion formation and not decision making, and "strong publics," that is parliaments whose discourse encompassed both opinion making and decision making.

Fraser's concepts of weak and strong publics were included by Habermas in Between Facts and Norms *([1992] 1996), and are addressed in contributions by Habermas and James Bohman in this reader.*

1 Introduction

Today in the United States we hear a great deal of ballyhoo about "the triumph of liberal democracy" and even "the end of history." Yet there is still quite a lot to object to in our own actually existing democracy, and the project of a critical theory of the limits of democracy in late-capitalist societies remains as relevant as ever. 'In fact, this project seems to me to have acquired a new urgency at a time when "liberal democracy" is being touted as the *ne plus ultra* of social systems for countries that are emerging from Soviet-style state socialism, Latin American military dictatorships, and southern African regimes of racial domination.

Those of us who remain committed to theorizing the limits of democracy in late-capitalist societies will find in the work of Jürgen Habermas an indispensable resource. I mean the concept of "the public sphere," originally elaborated in his 1962 book, *The Structural Transformation of the Public Sphere*, and subsequently resituated but never abandoned in his later work.[1]

The political and theoretical importance of this idea is easy to explain. Habermas's concept of the public sphere provides a way of circumventing some confusions that have plagued progressive social movements and the political theories associated with them. Take, for example, the longstanding failure in the dominant wing of the socialist and Marxist tradition to appreciate the full force of the distinction between the apparatuses of the state, on the one hand, and public arenas of citizen discourse and association, on the other. All too often it was assumed in this tradition that to subject the economy to the control of the socialist state was to subject it to the control of the socialist citizenry. Of course, that was not so. But the conflation of the state apparatus with the public sphere of discourse and association provided ballast to processes whereby the socialist vision became institutionalized in an authoritarianstatist form instead of in a participatory-democratic form. The result has been to jeopardize the very idea of socialist democracy.

A second problem, albeit one that has so far been much less historically momentous and certainly less tragic, is a confusion one encounters at times in contemporary feminisms. I mean a confusion that involves the use of the very same expression "the public sphere" but in a sense that is less precise and less useful than Habermas's. This expression has been used by many feminists to refer to everything that is outside the domestic or familial sphere. Thus "the public sphere" on this usage conflates at least three analytically distinct things: the state, the official economy of paid employment, and arenas of public discourse.[2] Now it should not be thought that the conflation of these three things is a merely theoretical issue. On the contrary, it has practical political consequences when, for example, agitational campaigns against misogynist cultural representations are confounded with programs for state censorship or when struggles to deprivatize housework and child care are equated with their commodification. In both these cases the result is to occlude the question of whether to subject gender issues to the logic of the market or of the administrative state is to promote the liberation of women.

The idea of "the public sphere" in Habermas's sense is a conceptual resource that can help overcome such problems. It designates a theater in modern societies in which political participation is enacted through the medium of talk. It is the space in which citizens deliberate about their common affairs, and hence an institutionalized arena of discursive interaction. This arena is conceptually distinct from the state; it is a site for the production and circulation of discourses that can in principle be critical of the state. The public sphere in Habermas's sense is also conceptually distinct from the official economy; it is not an arena of market relations but rather one of discursive relations, a theater for debating and deliberating rather than for buying and selling. Thus this concept of the public sphere permits us to keep in view the distinctions among state apparatuses, economic markets, and democratic associations, distinctions that are essential to democratic theory.

For these reasons I am going to take as a basic premise for this essay that something like Habermas's idea of the public sphere is indispensable to critical social theory and democratic political practice. I assume that no attempt to understand the limits of actually existing late-capitalist democracy can succeed without in some way or another making use of it. I assume that the same goes for urgently needed constructive efforts to project alternative models of democracy.

If you will grant me that the general idea of the public sphere is indispensable to critical theory, then I shall go on to argue that the specific form in which Habermas has elaborated this idea is not wholly satisfactory. On the contrary, I contend that his analysis of the public sphere needs to undergo some critical interrogation and reconstruction if it is to yield a category capable of theorizing the limits of actually existing democracy.

Let me remind you that the subtitle of *Structural Transformation* is "An Inquiry into a Category of Bourgeois Society." The object of the inquiry is the rise and decline of a historically specific and limited form of the public sphere, which Habermas calls the "liberal model of the bourgeois public sphere." The aim is to identify the conditions that made possible this type of public sphere and to chart their devolution. The upshot is an argument that under altered conditions of late-twentieth-century "welfare state mass democracy," the bourgeois or liberal model of the public sphere is no longer feasible. Some new form of public sphere is required to salvage that arena's critical function and to institutionalize democracy.

Oddly, Habermas stops short of developing a new, post-bourgeois model of the public sphere. Moreover, he never explicitly problematizes some dubious assumptions that underlie the bourgeois model. As a result, we are left at the end of *Structural Transformation* without a conception of the public sphere that is sufficiently distinct from the bourgeois conception to serve the needs of critical theory today.

That, at any rate, is the thesis I intend to argue. To make my case, I shall proceed as follows: I shall begin in section 2 by juxtaposing Habermas's account of the structural transformation of the public sphere with an alternative account that can be pieced together from some recent revisionist historiography. Then I shall identify four assumptions underlying the bourgeois conception of the public sphere, as Habermas describes it, that this newer historiography renders suspect. Next in the following four sections I shall examine each of these assumptions in turn. Finally, in a brief conclusion I shall draw together some strands from these critical discussions that point toward an alternative, postbourgeois conception of the public sphere.

2 The Public Sphere: Alternative Histories, Competing Conceptions

Let me begin by sketching some highlights of Habermas's account of the structural transformation of the public sphere. According to Habermas, the idea of a public sphere is that of a body of "private persons" assembled to discuss matters of "public concern" or "common interest." This idea acquired force and reality in early modern Europe in the constitution of "bourgeois public spheres" as counterweights to absolutist states. These publics aimed to mediate between society and the state by holding the state accountable to society via publicity. At first this meant requiring that information about state functioning be made accessible so that state activities would be subject to critical scrutiny and the force of public opinion. Later it meant transmitting the considered "general interest" of "bourgeois society" to the state via forms of legally guaranteed free speech, free press, and free assembly, and eventually through the parliamentary institutions of representative government.

Thus at one level the idea of the public sphere designated an institutional mechanism for rationalizing political domination by rendering states accountable to (some of) the citizenry.

At another level, it designated a specific kind of discursive interaction. Here the public sphere connoted an ideal of unrestricted rational discussion of public matters. The discussion was to be open and accessible to all, merely private interests were to be inadmissible, inequalities of status were to be bracketed, and discussants were to deliberate as peers. The result of such discussion would be public opinion in the strong sense of a consensus about the common good.

According to Habermas, the full utopian potential of the bourgeois conception of the public sphere was never realized in practice. The claim to open access in particular was not made good. Moreover, the bourgeois conception of the public sphere was premised on a social order in which the state was sharply differentiated from the newly privatized market economy; it was this clear separation of society and state that was supposed to underpin a form of public discussion that excluded "private interests." But these conditions eventually eroded as nonbourgeois strata gained access to the public sphere. Then "the social question" came to the fore, society was polarized by class struggle, and the public fragmented into a mass of competing interest groups. Street demonstrations and back room, brokered compromises among private interests replaced reasoned public debate about the common good. Finally, with the emergence of welfare-state mass democracy, society and the state became mutually intertwined; publicity in the sense of critical scrutiny of the state gave way to public relations, mass-mediated staged displays and the manufacture and manipulation of public opinion.

Now let me juxtapose to this sketch of Habermas's account an alternative account that I shall piece together from some recent revisionist historiography. Briefly, scholars like Joan Landes, Mary Ryan, and Geoff Eley contend that Habermas's account idealizes the liberal public sphere. They argue that, despite the rhetoric of publicity and accessibility, the official public sphere rested on indeed was importantly constituted by, a number of significant exclusions. For Landes, the key axis of exclusion is gender; she argues that the ethos of the new republican public sphere in France was constructed in deliberate opposition to that of a more woman-friendly salon culture that the republicans stigmatized as "artificial," "effeminate," and "aristocratic." Consequently, a new, austere style of public speech and behavior was promoted, a style deemed "rational," "virtuous," and "manly." In this way masculinist gender constructs were built into the very conception of the republican public sphere, as was a logic that led, at the height of Jacobin rule, to the formal exclusion of women from political life.[3] Here the republicans drew on classical traditions that cast femininity and publicity as oxymorons; the depth of such traditions can be gauged in the etymological connection between "public" and "pubic," a graphic trace of the fact that in the ancient world possession of a penis was a requirement for speaking in public. (A similar link is preserved, incidentally, in the etymological connection between "testimony" and "testicle."[4])

Extending Landes's argument, Geoff Eley contends that exclusionary operations were essential to liberal public spheres not only in France but also in England and Germany and that in all these countries gender exclusions were linked to other exclusions rooted in processes of class formation. In all these countries, he claims, the soil that nourished the liberal public sphere was "civil society," the emerging new congeries of voluntary associations that sprung up in what came to be known as "the age of societies." But this network of clubs and associations—philanthropic, civic, professional, and cultural—was anything but accessible to everyone. On the contrary, it was the arena, the training ground, and eventually the power base of a stratum of bourgeois men who were coming to see themselves as a "universal class" and preparing to assert their fitness to govern. Thus the elaboration of a distinctive culture of civil society and of an associated public sphere was implicated in the process of bourgeois class formation; its practices and ethos were markers of "distinction" in Pierre Bourdieu's sense, ways of defining an emergent elite, of setting it off from the older aristocratic elites it was intent on displacing on the one hand and from the various popular and plebeian strata it aspired to rule on the other.[5] Moreover, this process of distinction helps explain the exacerbation of sexism characteristic of the liberal public sphere; new gender norms enjoining feminine domesticity and a sharp separation of public and private spheres functioned as key signifiers of bourgeois difference from both higher and lower social strata. It is a measure of the eventual success of this bourgeois project that these norms later became hegemonic, sometimes imposed on, sometimes embraced by, broader segments of society.[6]

There is a remarkable irony here, one that Habermas's account of the rise of the public sphere fails fully to appreciate.[7] A discourse of publicity touting accessibility, rationality, and the suspension of status hierarchies is itself deployed as a strategy of distinction. Of course, in and of itself this irony does not fatally compromise the discourse of publicity; that discourse can be, indeed has been, differently deployed in different circumstances and contexts. Nevertheless, it does suggest that the relationship between publicity and status is more complex than Habermas intimates, that declaring a deliberative arena to be a space where extant status distinctions are bracketed and neutralized is not sufficient to make it so.

Moreover, the problem is not only that Habermas idealizes the liberal public sphere but also that he fails to examine other, nonliberal, nonbourgeois, competing public spheres. Or rather, it is precisely because he fails to examine these other public spheres that he ends up idealizing the liberal public sphere.[8] Mary Ryan documents the variety of ways in which nineteenth century North American women of various classes and ethnicities constructed access routes to public political life, even despite their exclusion from the official public sphere. In the case of elite bourgeois women, this involved building a counter civil society of alternative, woman-only, voluntary associations, including philanthropic and moral-reform societies. In some respects, these associations aped the all-male societies built by these women's fathers and grandfathers, yet in other respects the women were innovating, since they creatively used the heretofore quintessentially "private" idioms of domesticity and motherhood precisely as springboards for public activity. Meanwhile, for some less privileged women, access to public life came through participation in supporting roles in male-dominated working-class protest activities. Still other women found public outlets in street protests and parades. Finally, women's-rights advocates publicly contested both women's exclusion from the official public sphere and the privatization of gender politics.[9]

Ryan's study shows that even in the absence of formal political incorporation through suffrage, there were a variety of ways of accessing public life and a multiplicity of public arenas. Thus the view that women were excluded from the public sphere turns out to be ideological; it rests on a class- and gender-biased notion of publicity, one which accepts at face value the bourgeois public's claim to be *the* public. In fact, the historiography of Ryan and others demonstrates that the bourgeois public was never *the* public. On the contrary, virtually contemporaneous with the bourgeois public there arose a host of competing counterpublics, including nationalist publics, popular peasant publics, elite women's publics, and working-class publics. Thus there were competing publics from the start, not just in the late nineteenth and twentieth centuries, as Habermas implies.[10]

Moreover, not only were there always a plurality of competing publics, but the relations between bourgeois publics and other publics were always conflictual. Virtually from the beginning, counterpublics contested the exclusionary norms of the bourgeois public, elaborating alternative styles of political behavior and alternative norms of public speech. Bourgeois publics in turn excoriated these alternatives and deliberately sought to block broader participation. As Eley puts it, "the emergence of a bourgeois public was never defined solely by the struggle against absolutism and traditional authority, but . . . addressed the problem of popular containment as well. The public sphere was always constituted by conflict."[11]

In general, this revisionist historiography suggests a much darker view of the bourgeois public sphere than the one that emerges from Habermas's study. The exclusions and conflicts that appeared as accidental trappings from his perspective become constitutive in the revisionists' view. The result is a gestalt switch that alters the very meaning of the public sphere. We can no longer assume that the bourgeois conception of the public sphere was simply an unrealized utopian ideal; it was also a masculinist ideological notion that functioned to legitimate an emergent form of class rule. Therefore, Eley draws a Gramscian moral from the story: the official bourgeois public sphere is the institutional vehicle for a major historical transformation in the nature of political domination. This is the shift from a repressive mode of domination to a hegemonic one, from rule based primarily on acquiescence to superior force to rule based primarily on consent supplemented with some measure of repression.[12] The important point is that this new mode of political domination, like the older one, secures the ability of one stratum of society to rule the rest. The official public sphere, then, was, and indeed is, the prime institutional site for the construction of the consent that defines the new, hegemonic mode of domination.[13]

What conclusions should we draw from this conflict of historical interpretations? Should we conclude that the very concept of the public sphere is a piece of bourgeois, masculinist ideology so thoroughly compromised that it can shed no genuinely critical light on the limits of actually existing democracy? Or should we conclude rather that the public sphere was a good idea that unfortunately was not realized in practice but retains some emancipatory force? In short, is the idea of the public sphere an instrument of domination or a utopian ideal?

Well, perhaps both, but actually neither. I contend that both of those conclusions are too extreme and unsupple to do justice to the material I have been discussing.[14] Instead of endorsing either one of them, I want to propose a more nuanced alternative. I shall argue that the revisionist historiography neither undermines nor vindicates *the* concept of the public sphere *simpliciter*, but that it calls into question four assumptions that are central to the *bourgeois, masculinist* conception of the public sphere, at least as Habermas describes it. These are as follows:

- The assumption that it is possible for interlocutors in a public sphere to bracket status differentials and to deliberate *as if* they were social equals; the assumption, therefore, that societal equality is not a necessary condition for political democracy
- The assumption that the proliferation of a multiplicity of competing publics is necessarily a step away from, rather than toward, greater democracy, and that a single, comprehensive public sphere is always preferable to a nexus of multiple publics
- The assumption that discourse in public spheres should be restricted to deliberation about the common good, and that the appearance of private interests and private issues is always undesirable
- The assumption that a functioning democratic public sphere requires a sharp separation between civil society and the state

Let me consider each of these in turn.

3 Open Access, Participatory Parity, and Social Equality

Habermas's account of the bourgeois conception of the public sphere stresses its claim to be open and accessible to all. Indeed, this idea of open access is one of the central meanings of the norm of publicity. Of course, we know both from revisionist history and from Habermas's account that the bourgeois public's claim to full accessibility was not in fact realized. Women of all classes and ethnicities were excluded from official political participation on the basis of gender status, while plebeian men were formally excluded by property qualifications. Moreover, in many cases women and men of racialized ethnicities of all classes were excluded on racial grounds.

What are we to make of this historical fact of the nonrealization in practice of the bourgeois public sphere's ideal of open access? One approach is to conclude that the ideal itself remains unaffected, since it is possible in principle to overcome these exclusions. And in fact, it was only a matter of time before formal exclusions based on gender, property, and race were eliminated.

This is convincing enough as far as it goes, but it does not go far enough. The question of open access cannot be reduced without remainder to the presence or absence of formal exclusions. It requires us to look also at the process of discursive interaction within formally inclusive public arenas. Here we should recall that the bourgeois conception of the public sphere requires bracketing inequalities of status. This public sphere was to be an arena in which interlocutors would set aside such characteristics as differences in birth and fortune and speak to one another as if they were social and economic peers. The operative phrase here is "as if." In fact, the social inequalities among the interlocutors were not eliminated but only bracketed.

But were they really effectively bracketed? The revisionist historiography suggests they were not. Rather, discursive interaction within the bourgeois public sphere was governed by protocols of style and decorum that were themselves correlates and markers of status inequality. These functioned informally to marginalize women and members of the plebeian classes and to prevent them from participating as peers.

Here we are talking about informal impediments to participatory parity that can persist even after everyone is formally and legally licensed to participate. That these constitute a more serious challenge to the bourgeois conception of the public sphere can be seen from a familiar contemporary example. Feminist research has documented a syndrome that many of us have observed in faculty meetings and other mixed-sex deliberative bodies: men tend to interrupt women more than women interrupt men; men also tend to speak more than women, taking more turns and longer turns; and women's interventions are more often ignored or not responded to than men's. In response to the sorts of experiences documented in this research, an important strand of feminist political theory has claimed that deliberation can serve as a mask for domination. Theorists like Jane Mansbridge have argued that "the transformation of 'I' into 'we' brought about through political deliberation can easily mask subtle forms of control. Even the language people use as they reason together usually favors one way of seeing things and discourages others. Subordinate groups sometimes cannot find the right voice or words to express their thoughts, and when they do, they discover they are not heard. [They] are silenced, encouraged to keep their wants inchoate, and heard to say 'yes' when what they have said is 'no.'[15] Mansbridge rightly notes that many of these feminist insights into ways in which deliberation can serve as a mask for domination extend beyond gender to other kinds of unequal relations, like those based on class or ethnicity. They alert us to the ways in which social inequalities can infect deliberation, even in the absence of any formal exclusions.

Here I think we encounter a very serious difficulty with the bourgeois conception of the public sphere. Insofar as the bracketing of social inequalities in deliberation means proceeding as if they don't exist when they do, this does not foster participatory parity. On the contrary, such bracketing usually works to the advantage of dominant groups in society and to the disadvantage of subordinates. In most cases it would be more appropriate to *unbracket* inequalities in the sense of explicitly thematizing them—a point that accords with the spirit of Habermas's later communicative ethics.

The misplaced faith in the efficacy of bracketing suggests another flaw in the bourgeois conception. This conception assumes that a public sphere is or can be a space of zero degree culture, so utterly bereft of any specific ethos as to accommodate with perfect neutrality and equal ease interventions expressive of any and every cultural ethos. But this assumption is counterfactual, and not for reasons that are merely accidental. In stratified societies, unequally empowered social groups tend to develop unequally valued cultural styles. The result is the development of powerful informal pressures that marginalize the contributions of members of subordinated groups both in everyday contexts and in official public spheres.[16] Moreover, these pressures are amplified, rather than mitigated, by the peculiar political economy of the bourgeois public sphere. In this public sphere the media that constitute the material support for the circulation of views are privately owned and operated for profit. Consequently, subordinated social groups usually lack equal access to the material means of equal participation.[17] Thus political economy enforces structurally what culture accomplishes informally.

If we take these considerations seriously, then we should be led to entertain serious doubts about a conception of the public sphere that purports to bracket, rather than to eliminate, structural social inequalities. We should question whether it is possible even in principle for interlocutors to deliberate *as if* they were social peers in specially designated discursive arenas when these discursive arenas are situated in a larger societal context that is pervaded by structural relations of dominance and subordination.

What is at stake here is the autonomy of specifically political institutions vis-à-vis the surrounding societal context. Now one salient feature that distinguishes liberalism from some other political-theoretical orientations is that liberalism assumes the autonomy of the political in a very strong form. Liberal political theory assumes that it is possible to organize a democratic form of political life on the basis of socioeconomic and sociosexual structures that generate systemic inequalities. For liberals, then, the problem of democracy becomes the problem of how to insulate political processes from what are considered to be nonpolitical or prepolitical processes, those characteristic, for example, of the economy, the family, and informal everyday life. The problem for liberals is thus how to strengthen the barriers separating political institutions that are supposed to instantiate relations of equality from economic, cultural, and sociosexual institutions that are premised on systemic relations of inequality.[18] Yet the weight of circumstance suggests that to have a public sphere in which interlocutors can deliberate as peers, it is not sufficient merely to bracket social inequality. Instead, a necessary condition for participatory parity is that systemic social inequalities be eliminated. This does not mean that everyone must have exactly the same income, but it does require the sort of rough equality that is inconsistent with systemically generated relations of dominance and subordination. *Pace* liberalism, then, political democracy requires substantive social equality.[19]

I have been arguing that the bourgeois conception of the public sphere is inadequate insofar as it supposes that social equality is not a necessary condition for participatory parity in public spheres. What follows from this for the critique of actually existing democracy? One task for critical theory is to render visible the ways in which societal inequality infects formally inclusive existing public spheres and taints discursive interaction within them.

4 Equality, Diversity, and Multiple Publics

So far I have been discussing what we might call "intrapublic relations," that is, the character and quality of discursive interactions within a given public sphere. Now I want to consider what we might call "interpublic relations," that is, the character of interactions among different publics.

Let me begin by recalling that Habermas's account stresses the singularity of the bourgeois conception of the public sphere, its claim to be *the* public arena, in the singular. In addition, his narrative tends in this respect to be faithful to that conception, since it casts the emergence of additional publics as a late development signaling fragmentation and decline. This narrative, then, like the bourgeois conception itself, is informed by an underlying evaluative assumption, namely, that the institutional confinement of public life to a single, overarching public sphere is a positive and desirable state of affairs, whereas the proliferation of a multiplicity of publics represents a departure from, rather than an advance toward, democracy. It is this normative assumption that I now want to scrutinize. In this section I shall assess the relative merits of a single, comprehensive public versus multiple publics in two kinds of modern societies: stratified societies and egalitarian multicultural societies.[20]

First, let me consider the case of stratified societies, by which I mean societies whose basic institutional framework generates unequal social groups in structural relations of dominance and subordination. I have already argued that in such societies, full parity of participation in public debate and deliberation is not within the reach of possibility. The question to be addressed here then is, What form of public life comes closest to approaching that ideal? What institutional arrangements will best help narrow the gap in participatory parity between dominant and subordinate groups?

I contend that in stratified societies, arrangements that accommodate contestation among a plurality of competing publics better promote the ideal of participatory parity than does a single, comprehensive, overarching public. This follows from the argument of the previous section. There I argued that it is not possible to insulate special discursive arenas from the effects of societal inequality and that where societal inequality persists, deliberative processes in public spheres will tend to operate to the advantage of dominant groups and to the disadvantage of subordinates. Now I want to add that these effects will be exacerbated where there is only a single, comprehensive public sphere. In that case, members of subordinated groups would have no arenas for deliberation among themselves about their needs, objectives, and strategies. They would have no venues in which to undertake communicative processes that were not, as it were, under the supervision of dominant groups. In this situation they would be less likely than otherwise to "find the right voice or words to express their thoughts" and more likely than otherwise "to keep their wants inchoate." This would render them less able than otherwise to articulate and defend their interests in the comprehensive public sphere. They would be less able than otherwise to expose modes of deliberation that mask domination by, in Mansbridge's words, "absorbing the less powerful into a false 'we' that reflects the more powerful."

This argument gains additional support from revisionist historiography of the public sphere, up to and including that of very recent developments. This historiography records that members of subordinated social groups—women, workers, peoples of color, and gays and lesbians—have repeatedly found it advantageous to constitute alternative publics. I propose to call these *subaltern counterpublics* in order to signal that they are parallel discursive arenas where members of subordinated social groups invent and circulate counterdiscourses to formulate oppositional interpretations of their identities, interests, and needs.[21] Perhaps the most striking example is the late-twentieth-century U.S. feminist subaltern counterpublic, with its variegated array of journals, bookstores, publishing companies, film and video distribution networks, lecture series, research centers, academic programs, conferences, conventions, festivals, and local meeting places. In this public sphere, feminist women have invented new terms for describing social reality, including "sexism," "the double shift," "sexual harassment," and "marital, date, and acquaintance rape." Armed with such language, we have recast our needs and identities, thereby reducing, although not eliminating, the extent of our disadvantage in official public spheres.[22]

Let me not be misunderstood. I do not mean to suggest that subaltern counterpublics are always necessarily virtuous. Some of them, alas, are explicitly antidemocratic and antiegalitarian, and even those with democratic and egalitarian intentions are not always above practicing their own modes of informal exclusion and marginalization. Still, insofar as these counterpublics emerge in response to exclusions within dominant publics, they help expand discursive space. In principle, assumptions that were previously exempt from contestation will now have to be publicly argued out. In general, the proliferation of subaltern counterpublics means a widening of discursive contestation, and that is a good thing in stratified societies.

I am emphasizing the contestatory function of subaltern counterpublics in stratified societies in part to complicate the issue of separatism. In my view, the concept of a counterpublic militates in the long run against separatism because it assumes *a publicist* orientation. Insofar as these arenas are *publics*, they are by definition not enclaves, which is not to deny that they are often involuntarily enclav*ed*. After all, to interact discursively as a member of public, subaltern or otherwise, is to aspire to disseminate one's discourse to ever widening arenas. Habermas captures well this aspect of the meaning of publicity when he notes that, however limited a public may be in its empirical manifestation at any given time, its members understand themselves as part of a potentially wider public, that indeterminate, empirically counterfactual body we call "the public at large." The point is that in stratified societies, subaltern counterpublics have a dual character. On the one hand, they function as spaces of withdrawal and regroupment; on the other hand, they also function as bases and training grounds for agitational activities directed toward wider publics. It is precisely in the dialectic between these two functions that their emancipatory potential resides. This dialectic enables subaltern counterpublics partially to offset, although not wholly to eradicate, the unjust participatory privileges enjoyed by members of dominant social groups in stratified societies.

So far I have been arguing that, although in stratified societies the ideal of participatory parity is not fully realizable, it is more closely approximated by arrangements that permit contestation among a plurality of competing publics than by a single, comprehensive public sphere. Of course, contestation among competing publics supposes interpublic discursive interaction. How, then, should we understand such interaction? Geoff Eley suggests that we think of the public sphere (in stratified societies) as "the structured setting where cultural and ideological contest or negotiation among a variety of publics takes place."[23] This formulation does justice to the multiplicity of public arenas in stratified societies by expressly acknowledging the presence and activity of "a variety of publics." At the same time, it also does justice to the fact that these various publics are situated in a single "structured setting" that advantages some and disadvantages others. Finally, Eley's formulation does justice to the fact that in stratified societies the discursive relations among differentially empowered publics are as likely to take the form of contestation as that of deliberation.

Let me now consider the relative merits of multiple publics versus a single public for egalitarian, multicultural societies. By "egalitarian societies" I mean nonstratified societies, societies whose basic framework does not generate unequal social groups in structural relations of dominance and subordination. Egalitarian societies, therefore, are societies without classes and without gender or racial divisions of labor. However, they need not be culturally homogeneous. On the contrary, provided such societies permit free expression and association, they are likely to be inhabited by social groups with diverse values, identities, and cultural styles, and hence to be multicultural. My question is, Under conditions of cultural diversity in the absence of structural inequality, would a single, comprehensive public sphere be preferable to multiple publics?

To answer this question, we need to take a closer look at the relationship between public discourse and social identities. *Pace* the bourgeois conception, public spheres are not only arenas for the formation of discursive opinion; in addition, they are arenas for the formation and enactment of social identities.[24] This means that participation is not simply a matter of being able to state propositional contents that are neutral with respect to form of expression. Rather, as I argued in the previous section, participation means being able to speak in one's own voice, and thereby simultaneously to construct and express one's cultural identity through idiom and style.[25] Moreover, as I also suggested, public spheres themselves are not spaces of zero-degree culture, equally hospitable to any possible form of cultural expression. Rather, they consist in culturally specific institutions, including, for example, various journals and various social geographies of urban space. These institutions may be understood as culturally specific rhetorical lenses that filter and alter the utterances they frame; they can accommodate some expressive modes and not others.[26]

It follows that public life in egalitarian, multicultural societies cannot consist exclusively in a single, comprehensive public sphere. That would be tantamount to filtering diverse rhetorical and stylistic norms through a single, overarching lens. Moreover, since there can be no such lens that is genuinely culturally neutral, it would effectively privilege the expressive norms of one cultural group over others and thereby make discursive assimilation a condition for participation in public debate. The result would be the demise of multiculturalism (and the likely demise of social equality). In general, then, we can conclude that the idea of an egalitarian, multicultural society only makes sense if we suppose a plurality of public arenas in which groups with diverse values and rhetorics participate. By definition, such a society must contain a multiplicity of publics.

However, this need not preclude the possibility of an additional, more comprehensive arena in which members of different, more limited publics talk across lines of cultural diversity. On the contrary, our hypothetical egalitarian, multicultural society would surely have to entertain debates over policies and issues affecting everyone. The question is, Would participants in such debates share enough in the way of values, expressive norms, and therefore protocols of persuasion to lend their talk the quality of deliberations aimed at reaching agreement through giving reasons?

In my view, this is better treated as an empirical question than as a conceptual question. I see no reason to rule out in principle the possibility of a society in which social equality and cultural diversity coexist with participatory democracy. I certainly hope there can be such a society. That hope gains some plausibility if we consider that, however difficult it may be, communication across lines of cultural difference is not in principle impossible, although it will certainly become impossible if one imagines that it requires bracketing of differences. Granted, such communication requires multicultural literacy, but that, I believe, can be acquired through practice. In fact, the possibilities expand once we acknowledge the complexity of cultural identities. *Pace* reductive, essentialist conceptions, cultural identities are woven of many different strands, and some of these strands may be common to people whose identities otherwise diverge, even when it is the divergences that are most salient.[27] Likewise, under conditions of social equality, the porousness, outer-directedness, and open-endedness of publics could promote intercultural communication. After all, the concept of a public presupposes a plurality of perspectives among those who participate within it, thereby allowing for internal differences and antagonisms and discouraging reified blocs.[28] In addition, the unbounded character and publicist orientation of publics allows people to participate in more than one public, and it allows memberships of different publics partially to overlap. This in turn makes intercultural communication conceivable in principle. All told, then, there do not seem to be any conceptual (as opposed to empirical) barriers to the possibility of a socially egalitarian, multicultural society that is also a participatory democracy. But this will necessarily be a society with many different publics, including at least one public in which participants can deliberate as peers across lines of difference about policy that concerns them all.

In general, I have been arguing that the ideal of participatory parity is better achieved by a multiplicity of publics than by a single public. This is true both for stratified societies and for egalitarian, multicultural societies, albeit for different reasons. In neither case is my argument intended as a simple postmodern celebration of multiplicity. Rather, in the case of stratified societies, I am defending subaltern counterpublics formed under conditions of dominance and subordination. In the other case, by contrast, I am defending the possibility of combining social equality, cultural diversity, and participatory democracy.

What are the implications of this discussion for a critical theory of the public sphere in actually existing democracy? Briefly, we need a critical political sociology of a form of public life in which multiple but unequal publics participate. This means theorizing about the contestatory interaction of different publics and identifying the mechanisms that render some of them subordinate to others.

5 Public Spheres, Common Concerns, and Private Interests

I have argued that in stratified societies, like it or not, subaltern counterpublics stand in a contestatory relationship to dominant publics. One important object of such interpublic contestation is the appropriate boundaries of the public sphere. Here the central questions are, What counts as a public matter? What, in contrast, is private? This brings me to a third set of problematic assumptions underlying the bourgeois conception of the public sphere, namely, assumptions concerning the appropriate scope of publicity in relation to privacy.

Let me remind you that it is central to Habermas's account that the bourgeois public sphere was to be a discursive arena in which "private persons" deliberated about "public matters." There are several different senses of "private" and "public" in play here. "Public," for example, can mean (1) state-related, (2) accessible to everyone, (3) of concern to everyone, and (4) pertaining to a common good or shared interest. Each of these corresponds to a contrasting sense of "private." In addition, there are two other senses of "private" hovering just below the surface here: (5) pertaining to private property in a market economy and (6) pertaining to intimate domestic or personal life, including sexual life.

I have already talked at length about the sense of "public" as open or accessible to all. Now I want to examine some of the other senses, beginning with (3), of concern to everyone.[29] This is ambiguous between what objectively affects or has an impact on everyone as seen from an outsider's perspective, and the possibility of what is recognized as a matter of common concern by participants. The idea of a public sphere as an arena of collective self-determination does not sit well with approaches that would appeal to an outsider's perspective to delimit its proper boundaries. Thus it is the second, participant's perspective that is relevant here. Only participants themselves can decide what is and what is not of common concern to them. However, there is no guarantee that all of them will agree. For example, until quite recently, feminists were in the minority in thinking that domestic violence against women was a matter of common concern and thus a legitimate topic of public discourse. The great majority of people considered this issue to be a private matter between what was assumed to be a fairly small number of heterosexual couples (and perhaps the social and legal professionals who were supposed to deal with them). Then feminists formed a subaltern counterpublic from which we disseminated a view of domestic violence as a widespread systemic feature of male-dominated societies. Eventually, after sustained discursive contestation, we succeeded in *making* it a common concern.

The point is that there are no naturally given, a priori boundaries here. What will count as a matter of common concern will be decided precisely through discursive contestation. It follows that no topics should be ruled off limits in advance of such contestation. On the contrary, democratic publicity requires positive guarantees of opportunities for minorities to convince others that what in the past was not public in the sense of being a matter of common concern should now become so.[30]

What, then, of the sense of "publicity" as pertaining to a common good or shared interest? This is the sense that is in play when Habermas characterizes the bourgeois public sphere as an arena in which the topic of discussion is restricted to the "common good" and in which discussion of "private interests" is ruled out. This is a view of the public sphere that we would today call civic-republican, as opposed to liberal-individualist. Briefly, the civic-republican model stresses a view of politics as people reasoning together to promote a common good that transcends the mere sum of individual preferences. The idea is that through deliberation the members of the public can come to discover or create such a common good. In the process of their deliberations, participants are transformed from a collection of self-seeking, private individuals into a public-spirited collectivity, capable of acting together in the common interest. On this view, private interests have no proper place in the political public sphere. At best, they are the prepolitical starting point of deliberation, to be transformed and transcended in the course of debate.[31]

This civic-republican view of the public sphere is in one respect an improvement over the liberal-individualist alternative. Unlike the latter, it does not assume that people's preferences, interests, and identities are given exogenously in advance of public discourse and deliberation. It appreciates, rather, that preferences, interests, and identities are as much outcomes as antecedents of public deliberation; indeed, they are discursively constituted in and through it. However, the civic-republican view contains a very serious confusion, one that blunts its critical edge. This view conflates the ideas of deliberation and the common good by assuming that deliberation must be deliberation *about* the common good. Consequently, it limits deliberation to talk framed from the standpoint of a single, all-encompassing "we," thereby ruling claims of self-interest and group interest out of order. Yet, as Jane Mansbridge has argued, this works against one of the principal aims of deliberation, namely, to help participants clarify their interests, even when those interests turn out to conflict. "Ruling self-interest [and group interest] out of order makes it harder for any participant to sort out what is going on. In particular, the less powerful may not find ways to discover that the prevailing sense of "we" does not adequately include them."[32]

In general, there is no way to know in advance whether the outcome of a deliberative process will be the discovery of a common good in which conflicts of interest evaporate as merely apparent or the discovery that conflicts of interest are real and the common good is chimerical. But if the existence of a common good cannot be presumed in advance, then there is no warrant for putting any strictures on what sorts of topics, interests, and views are admissible in deliberation.[33]

This argument holds even in the best-case scenario of societies whose basic institutional frameworks do not generate systemic inequalities; even in such relatively egalitarian societies, we cannot assume in advance that there will be no real conflicts of interest. How much more pertinent, then, the argument is to stratified societies, which are traversed with pervasive relations of inequality. After all, when social arrangements operate to the systemic profit of some groups of people and to the systemic detriment of others, there are prima facie reasons for thinking that the postulation of a common good shared by exploiters and exploited may well be a mystification. Moreover, any consensus that purports to represent the common good in this social context should be regarded with suspicion, since this consensus will have been reached through deliberative processes tainted by the effects of dominance and subordination.

In general, critical theory needs to take a harder, more critical look at the terms "private" and "public." These terms, after all, are not simply straightforward designations of societal spheres; they are cultural classifications and rhetorical labels. In political discourse they are powerful terms frequently deployed to delegitimate some interests, views, and topics and to valorize others.

This brings me to two other senses of "private," which often function ideologically to delimit the boundaries of the public sphere in ways that disadvantage subordinate social groups. These are sense (5), pertaining to private property in a market economy, and sense (6), pertaining to intimate domestic or personal life, including sexual life. Each of these senses is at the center of a rhetoric of privacy that has historically been used to restrict the universe of legitimate public contestation.

The rhetoric of domestic privacy would exclude some issues and interests from public debate by personalizing and/or familializing them; it casts these as private, domestic or personal, familial matters in contradistinction to public, political matters. The rhetoric of economic privacy, in contrast, would exclude some issues and interests from public debate by economizing them; the issues in question here are cast as impersonal market imperatives or as "private" ownership prerogatives or as technical problems for managers and planners, all in contradistinction to public, political matters. In both cases, the result is to enclave certain matters in specialized discursive arenas and thereby to shield them from broadly based debate and contestation. This usually works to the advantage of dominant groups and individuals and to the disadvantage of their subordinates.[34] If wife battering, for example, is labeled a "personal" or "domestic" matter and if public discourse about it is channeled into specialized institutions associated with, say, family law, social work, and the sociology and psychology of "deviance," then this serves to reproduce gender dominance and subordination. Similarly, if questions of workplace democracy are labeled "economic" or "managerial" problems and if discourse about these questions is shunted into specialized institutions associated with, say, "industrial relations" sociology, labor law, and "management science," then this serves to perpetuate class (and usually also gender and race) dominance and subordination.

This shows once again that the lifting of formal restrictions on public-sphere participation does not suffice to ensure inclusion in practice. On the contrary, even after women and workers have been formally licensed to participate, their participation may be hedged by conceptions of economic privacy and domestic privacy that delimit the scope of debate. These notions, therefore, are vehicles through which gender and class disadvantages may continue to operate subtextually and informally, even after explicit, formal restrictions have been rescinded.

6 Strong Publics, Weak Publics: On Civil Society and the State

Let me turn now to my fourth and last assumption underlying the bourgeois conception of the public sphere, namely, the assumption that a functioning democratic public sphere requires a sharp separation of civil society and the state. This assumption is susceptible to two different interpretations, according to how one understands the expression "civil society."

If one takes that expression to mean a privately ordered, capitalist economy, then to insist on its separation from the state is to defend classical liberalism. The claim would be that a system of limited government and laissez-faire capitalism is a necessary precondition for a well-functioning public sphere.

We can dispose of this (relatively uninteresting) claim fairly quickly by drawing on some arguments of the previous sections. I have already shown that participatory parity is essential to a democratic public sphere and that rough socioeconomic equality is a precondition of participatory parity. Now I need only add that laissez-faire capitalism does not foster socioeconomic equality and that some form of politically regulated economic reorganization and redistribution is needed to achieve that end. Likewise, I have also shown that efforts to "privatize" economic issues and to cast them as off-limits with respect to state activity impede, rather than promote, the sort of full and free discussion built into the idea of a public sphere. It follows from these considerations that a sharp separation of (economic) civil society and the state is not a necessary condition for a well-functioning public sphere. On the contrary and *pace* the bourgeois conception, it is precisely some sort of interimbrication of these institutions that is needed.[35]

However, there is also a second, more interesting interpretation of the bourgeois assumption that a sharp separation of civil society and the state is necessary to a working public sphere, one that warrants more extended examination. In this interpretation, "civil society" means the nexus of nongovernmental or "secondary" associations that are neither economic nor administrative. We can best appreciate the force of the claim that civil society in this sense should be separate from the state if we recall Habermas's definition of the liberal public sphere as a "body of private persons assembled to form a public." The emphasis here on "private persons" signals (among other things) that the members of the bourgeois public are not state officials and that their participation in the public sphere is not undertaken in any official capacity. Accordingly, their discourse does not eventuate in binding, sovereign decisions authorizing the use of state power; on the contrary, it eventuates in "public opinion," critical commentary on authorized decision-making that transpires elsewhere. The public sphere, in short, is not the state; it is rather the informally mobilized body of nongovernmental discursive opinion that can serve as a counterweight to the state. Indeed, in the bourgeois conception, it is precisely this extragovernmental character of the public sphere that confers an aura of independence, autonomy, and legitimacy on the "public opinion" generated in it.

Thus the bourgeois conception of the public sphere supposes the desirability of a sharp separation of (associational) civil society and the state. As a result, it promotes what I shall call *weak publics*, publics whose deliberative practice consists exclusively in opinion formation and does not also encompass decision making. Moreover, the bourgeois conception seems to imply that an expansion of such publics' discursive authority to encompass decision making as well as opinion making would threaten the autonomy of public opinion, for then the public would effectively become the state, and the possibility of a critical discursive check on the state would be lost.

That, at least, is suggested by Habermas's initial formulation of the bourgeois conception. In fact, the issue becomes more complicated as soon as we consider the emergence of parliamentary sovereignty. With that landmark development in the history of the public sphere, we encounter a major structural transformation, since a sovereign parliament functions as a public sphere *within* the state. Moreover, sovereign parliaments are what I shall call *strong publics*, publics whose discourse encompasses both opinion formation and decision making. As a locus of public deliberation culminating in legally binding decisions (or laws), parliament was to be the site for the discursive authorization of the use of state power. With the achievement of parliamentary sovereignty, therefore, the line separating (associational) civil society and the state is blurred.

Clearly, the emergence of parliamentary sovereignty and the consequent blurring of the separation between (associational) civil society and the state represents a democratic advance over earlier political arrangements. This is because, as the terms "strong public" and "weak public" suggest, the force of public opinion is strengthened when a body representing it is empowered to translate such "opinion" into authoritative decisions. At the same time, there remain important questions about the relation between parliamentary strong publics and the weak publics to which they are supposed to be accountable. In general, these developments raise some interesting and important questions about the relative merits of weak and strong publics and about the respective roles that institutions of both kinds might play in a democratic and egalitarian society.

One set of questions concerns the possible proliferation of strong publics in the form of self-managing institutions. In self-managed workplaces, child-care centers, or residential communities, for example, internal institutional public spheres could be arenas both of opinion formation and decision making. This would be tantamount to constituting sites of direct or quasi-direct democracy, wherein all those engaged in a collective undertaking would participate in deliberations to determine its design and operation.[36] However, this would still leave open the relationship between such internal public spheres cum decision-making bodies and those external publics to which they might also be deemed accountable. The question of that relationship becomes important when we consider that people affected by an undertaking in which they do not directly participate as agents may nonetheless have a stake in its *modus operandi;* they therefore also have a legitimate claim to a say in its institutional design and operation.

Here we are again broaching the issue of accountability. What institutional arrangements best ensure the accountability of democratic decision-making bodies (strong publics) to *their* (external, weak, or, given the possibility of hybrid cases, weak*er*) publics?[37] Where in society are direct democracy arrangements called for, and where are representative forms more appropriate? How are the former best articulated with the latter? More generally, what democratic arrangements best institutionalize coordination among different institutions, including coordination among their various coimplicated publics? Should we think of central parliament as a strong superpublic with authoritative discursive sovereignty over basic societal ground rules and coordination arrangements? If so, does that require the assumption of a single weak(er) external superpublic (in addition to, not instead of, various other smaller publics)? In any event, given the inescapable global interdependence manifest in the international division of labor within a single shared planetary biosphere, does it make sense to understand the nation-state as the appropriate unit of sovereignty?

I do not know the answers to most of these questions, and I am unable to explore them further in this essay. However, the possibility of posing them, even in the absence of full, persuasive answers, enables us to draw one salient conclusion: any conception of the public sphere that requires a sharp separation between (associational) civil society and the state will be unable to imagine the forms of self-management, interpublic coordination, and political accountability that are essential to a democratic and egalitarian society. The bourgeois conception of the public sphere, therefore, is not adequate for contemporary critical theory. What is needed, rather, is a postbourgeois conception that can permit us to envision a greater role for (at least some) public spheres than mere autonomous opinion formation removed from authoritative decision making. A postbourgeois conception would enable us to think about strong *and* weak publics, as well as about various hybrid forms. In addition, it would allow us to theorize the range of possible relations among such publics, which would expand our capacity to envision democratic possibilities beyond the limits of actually existing democracy.

7 Conclusion: Rethinking the Public Sphere

Let me conclude by recapitulating what I believe I have accomplished in this essay. I have shown that the bourgeois conception of the public sphere as described by Habermas is not adequate for the critique of the limits of actually existing democracy in late-capitalist societies. At one level, my argument undermines the bourgeois conception as a normative ideal. I have shown first that an adequate conception of the public sphere requires not merely the bracketing, but rather the elimination, of social inequality. Second, I have shown that a multiplicity of publics is preferable to a single public sphere both in stratified societies and egalitarian societies. Third, I have shown that a tenable conception of the public sphere must countenance not the exclusion, but the inclusion, of interests and issues that bourgeois, masculinist ideology labels "private" and treats as inadmissible. Finally, I have shown that a defensible conception must allow both for strong publics and for weak publics and that it should help theorize the relations among them. In sum, I have argued against four constitutive assumptions of the bourgeois conception of the public sphere; at the same time, I have identified some corresponding elements of a new, postbourgeois conception.

At another level, my argument enjoins four corresponding tasks on the critical theory of actually existing democracy. First, this theory should render visible the ways in which social inequality taints deliberation within publics in late-capitalist societies. Second, it should show how inequality affects relations among publics in late-capitalist societies, how publics are differentially empowered or segmented, and how some are involuntarily enclaved and subordinated to others. Next, a critical theory should expose ways in which the labeling of some issues and interests as "private" limits the range of problems, and of approaches to problems, that can be widely contested in contemporary societies. Finally, the theory should show how the overly weak character of some public spheres in late-capitalist societies denudes "public opinion" of practical force.

In all these ways the theory should expose the limits of the specific form of democracy we enjoy in late-capitalist societies. Perhaps it can thereby help inspire us to try to push back those limits, while also cautioning people in other parts of the world against heeding the call to install them.

Acknowledgments

I am grateful for helpful comments from Craig Calhoun, Joshua Cohen, Nancy J. Hirschmann, Tom McCarthy, Moishe Postone, Baukje Prins, David Schweikart, and Rian Voet. I also benefitted from the inspiration and stimulation of participants in the conference on "Habermas and the Public Sphere," University of North Carolina, Chapel Hill, September 1989.

NOTES

1. Jürgen Habermas, *The Structural Transformation of the Public Sphere: An Inquiry into a Category of Bourgeois Society*, trans. Thomas Burger with Frederick Lawrence (Cambridge:

MIT Press, 1989). For Habermas's later use of the category of the public sphere, see Jürgen Habermas, *The Theory of Communicative Action, vol. 2, Lifeworld and System: A Critique of Functionalist Reason,* trans. Thomas McCarthy (Boston: Beacon Press, 1987). For a critical secondary discussion of Habermas's later use of the concept, see Nancy Fraser, "What's Critical About Critical Theory? The Case of Habermas and Gender," in *Unruly Practices: Power, Discourse, and Gender in Contemporary Social Theory,* ed. N. Fraser (University of Minnesota Press, 1989).

2. Throughout this paper I refer to paid workplaces, markets, credit systems, etc. as *official*-economic institutions so as to avoid the androcentric implication that domestic institutions are not also economic. For a discussion of this issue, see Nancy Fraser, "What's Critical about Critical Theory? The Case of Habermas and Gender."

3. Joan Landes, *Women and the Public Sphere in the Age of the French Revolution* (Ithaca: Cornell University Press, 1988).

4. For the "public"/"pubic" connection, see the *Oxford English Dictionary* (2nd ed., 1989), entry for "public." For the "testimony"/"testicle" connection, see Lucie White, "Subordination, Rhetorical Survival Skills, and Sunday Shoes: Notes on the Hearing of Mrs. G.," *Buffalo Law Review* 38, no. 1 (Winter 1990): 6.

5. Pierre Bourdieu, *Distinction: A Social Critique of the Judgment of Pure Taste* (Cambridge: Harvard University Press, 1979).

6. Geoff Eley, "Nations, Publics, and Political Cultures: Placing Habermas in the Nineteenth Century," in *Habermas and the Public Sphere,* ed. Craig Calhoun. See also Leonore Davidoff and Catherine Hall, *Family Fortunes: Men and Women of the English Middle Class, 1780–1850* (Chicago: University of Chicago Press, 1987).

7. Habermas does recognize that the issue of gender exclusion is connected to a shift from aristocratic to bourgeois public spheres, but, as I argue below, he fails to register its full implications.

8. I do not mean to suggest that Habermas is unaware of the existence of public spheres other than the bourgeois one; on the contrary, in the Preface to *Structural Transformation* (p. xviii) he explicitly states that his object is the liberal model of the bourgeois public sphere and that therefore he will discuss neither "the plebeian public sphere" (which he understands as an ephemeral phenomenon that existed "for just one moment" during the French Revolution) nor "the plebiscitary-acclamatory form of regimented public sphere characterizing dictatorships in highly developed industrial societies." My point is that, although Habermas acknowledges that there were alternative public spheres, he assumes that it is possible to understand the character of the bourgeois public by looking at it alone in isolation from its relations to other, competing publics. This assumption is problematic. In fact, as I shall demonstrate, an examination of the bourgeois public's relations to alternative publics challenges the bourgeois conception of the public sphere.

9. Mary P. Ryan, *Women in Public: Between Banners and Ballots, 1825–1880* (Baltimore: John Hopkins University Press, 1990) and "Gender and Public Access: Women's Politics in Nineteenth Century America," in *Habermas and the Public Sphere,* ed. Craig Calhoun.

10. Geoff Eley, "Nations, Publics, and Political Cultures."

11. Geoff Eley, "Nations, Publics, and Political Cultures."

12. I am leaving aside whether one should speak here not of consent *tout court* but rather of "something approaching consent," "something appearing as consent," or "something constructed as consent" in order to leave open the possibility of degrees of consent.

13. The public sphere produces consent via circulation of discourses that construct the common sense of the day and represent the existing order as natural and/or just, but not simply as a ruse that is imposed. Rather, the public sphere in its mature form includes sufficient participation and sufficient representation of multiple interests and perspectives to permit most people most of the time to recognize themselves in its discourses. People who

are ultimately disadvantaged by the social construction of consent nonetheless manage to find in the discourses of the public sphere representations of their interests, aspirations, life problems, and anxieties that are close enough to resonate with their own lived self-representations, identities, and feelings. Their consent to hegemonic rule is secured when their culturally constructed perspectives are taken up and articulated with other culturally constructed perspectives in hegemonic sociopolitical projects.

14. Here I want to distance myself from a certain overly facile line of argument that is sometimes made against Habermas. This is the line that ideological functions of public spheres in class societies simply undermine the normative notion as an ideal. This I take to be a non sequitur, since it is always possible to reply that under other conditions, say, the abolition of classes, genders, and other pervasive axes of inequality, the public sphere would no longer have this function but would instead be an institutionalization of democratic interaction. Moreover, as Habermas has often pointed out, even in existing class societies, the significance of the public sphere is not entirely exhausted by its class function. On the contrary, the idea of the public sphere also functions here and now as a norm of democratic interaction that we use to criticize the limitations of actually existing public spheres. The point here is that even the revisionist story and the Gramscian theory that cause us to doubt the value of the public sphere are themselves only possible because of it. It is the idea of the public sphere that provides the conceptual condition of possibility for the revisionist critique of its imperfect realization.

15. Jane Mansbridge, "Feminism and Democracy," *The American Prospect,* no. 1 (Spring 1990): 127.

16. In *Distinction* Pierre Bourdieu has theorized these processes in an illuminating way in terms of the concept of "class habitus."

17. As Habermas notes, this tendency is exacerbated with the concentration of media ownership in late-capitalist societies. For the steep increase in concentration in the United States in the late twentieth century, see Ben H. Bagdikian, *The Media Monopoly* (Boston: Beacon Press, 1983) and "Lords of the Global Village," *The Nation* (June 12, 1989). This situation contrasts in some respects with countries with television owned and operated by the state. But even there it is doubtful that subordinated groups have equal access. Moreover, political and economic pressures have recently encouraged privatization of media in several of these countries. In part, this reflects the problems of state networks having to compete for "market share" with private channels airing U.S.-produced mass entertainment.

18. This is the spirit behind, for example, proposals for reforms of election-campaign financing aimed at preventing the intrusion of economic dominance into the public sphere. Needless to say, within a context of massive societal inequality, it is far better to have such reforms than not to have them. However, in light of the sorts of informal effects of dominance and inequality discussed above, one ought not to expect too much from them. The most thoughtful recent defense of the liberal view comes from someone who in other respects is not a liberal. See Michael Walzer, *Spheres of Justice: A Defense of Pluralism and Equality* (New York: Basic Books, 1983). Another very interesting approach has been suggested by Joshua Cohen. In response to an earlier draft of this essay, he argued that policies designed to facilitate the formation of social movements, secondary associations, and political parties would better foster participatory parity than would policies designed to achieve social equality, since the latter would require redistributive efforts that carry "deadweight losses." I certainly support the sort of policies that Cohen recommends, as well as his more general aim of an "associative democracy." The sections of this paper on multiple publics and strong publics make a case for related arrangements. However, I am not persuaded by the claim that these policies can achieve participatory parity under conditions of social inequality. That claim seems to me to be another variant of the liberal view of the autonomy of the political, which Cohen otherwise claims to reject. See Joshua Cohen, "Comments on Nancy

Fraser's 'Rethinking the Public Sphere' " (unpublished manuscript presented at the meetings of the American Philosophical Association, Central Division, New Orleans, April 1990).

19. My argument draws on Karl Marx's still unsurpassed critique of liberalism in section 1 of "On the Jewish Question." Hence the allusion to Marx in the title of this essay.

20. My argument in this section is deeply indebted to Joshua Cohen's perceptive comments on an earlier draft of this paper in "Comments on Nancy Fraser's 'Rethinking the Public Sphere.'"

21. I have coined this expression by combining two terms that other theorists have recently effectively used for purposes consonant with my own. I take the term "subaltern" from Gayatri Spivak, "Can the Subaltern Speak?" in *Marxism and the Interpretation of Culture*, ed. Cary Nelson and Larry Grossberg (Chicago: University of Illinois Press, 1988), pp. 271–313. I take the term "counterpublic" from Rita Felski, *Beyond Feminist Aesthetics* (Cambridge: Harvard University Press, 1989).

22. For an analysis of the political import of oppositional feminist discourses about needs, see Nancy Fraser, "Struggle over Needs: Outline of a Socialist-Feminist Critical Theory of Late-Capitalist Political Culture, " in Fraser, *Unruly Practices*.

23. Geoff Eley, "Nations, Publics, and Political Cultures." Eley goes on to explain that this is tantamount to "extend[ing] Habermas's idea of the public sphere toward the wider public domain where authority is not only constituted as rational and legitimate, but where its terms are contested, modified, and occasionally overthrown by subaltern groups."

24. It seems to me that public discursive arenas are among the most important and under-recognized sites in which social identities are constructed, deconstructed, and reconstructed. My view stands in contrast to various psychoanalytic accounts of identity formation, which neglect the formative importance of post-Oedipal discursive interaction outside the nuclear family and which therefore cannot explain identity shifts over time. It strikes me as unfortunate that so much of contemporary feminist theory has taken its understanding of social identity from psychoanalytic models, while neglecting to study identity construction in relation to public spheres. The revisionist historiography of the public sphere discussed earlier can help redress the imbalance by identifying public spheres as loci of identity reconstruction. For an account of the discursive character of social identity and a critique of Lacanian psychoanalytic approaches to identity, see Nancy Fraser, "The Uses and Abuses of French Discourse Theories for Feminist Politics," *Boundary 2*, 17, no. 2 (Summer 1990): 82–101.

25. For another statement of this position, see Nancy Fraser, "Toward a Discourse Ethic of Solidarity," *Praxis International 5*, no. 4 (January 1986): 425–429. See also Iris Young, "Impartiality and the Civic Public: Some Implications of Feminist Critiques of Moral and Political Theory" in *Feminism as Critique*, ed. Seyla Benhabib and Drucilla Cornell (Minneapolis: University of Minnesota Press, 1987), pp. 56–76.

26. For an analysis of the rhetorical specificity of one historical public sphere, see Michael Warner, *The Letters of the Republic: Publication and the Public Sphere in Eighteenth Century America* (Cambridge: Harvard University Press, 1990).

27. One could say that at the deepest level, everyone is *mestizo*. The best metaphor here may be Wittgenstein's idea of family resemblances, or networks of crisscrossing, overlapping differences and similarities, no single thread of which runs continuously throughout the whole. For an account that stresses the complexity of cultural identities and the salience of discourse in their construction, see Nancy Fraser, "The Uses and Abuses of French Discourse Theories for Feminist Politics." For accounts that draw on concepts of *métissage*, see Gloria Anzaldua, *Borderlands: La Frontera* (1987) and Francoise Lionnet, *Autobiographical Voices: Race, Gender, Self-Portraiture* (Ithaca: Cornell University Press, 1989).

28. In these respects, the concept of a public differs from that of a community. "Community" suggests a bounded and fairly homogeneous group, and it often connotes consensus. "Public," in contrast, emphasizes discursive interaction that is in principle unbounded and

open-ended, and this in turn implies a plurality of perspectives. Thus, the idea of a public can accommodate internal differences, antagonisms, and debates better than that of a community. For an account of the connection between publicity and plurality, see Hannah Arendt, *The Human Condition* (Chicago: University of Chicago Press, 1958). For a critique of the concept of community, see Iris Young, "The Ideal of Community and the Politics of Difference," in *Feminism and Postmodernism*, ed. Linda J. Nicholson (New York: Routledge, Chapman and Hall, 1989), pp. 300–323.

29. In this essay I do not directly discuss sense (1), state-related. However, in the next section of this essay I consider some issues that touch on that sense.

30. This is the equivalent in democratic theory of a point that Paul Feyerabend has argued in the philosophy of science. See Feyerabend, *Against Method* (New York: Verso, 1988).

31. In contrast, the liberal-individualist model stresses the view of politics as the aggregation of self-interested, individual preferences. Deliberation in the strict sense drops out altogether. Instead, political discourse consists in registering individual preferences and in bargaining, looking for formulas that satisfy as many private interests as possible. It is assumed that there is no such thing as the common good over and above the sum of all the various individual goods, and so private interests are the legitimate stuff of political discourse.

32. Jane Mansbridge, "Feminism and Democracy," p. 131.

33. This point, incidentally, is in the spirit of a strand of Habermas's recent normative thought, which stresses the procedural, as opposed to the substantive, definition of a democratic public sphere; here the public sphere is defined as an arena for a certain type of discursive interaction, not as an arena for dealing with certain types of topics and problems. There are no restrictions, therefore, on what may become a topic of deliberation. See Seyla Benhabib's account of this radical proceduralist strand of Habermas's thought and her defense of it as the strand that renders his view of the public sphere superior to alternative views: Benhabib, "Models of Public Space: Hannah Arendt, the Liberal Tradition, and Jürgen Habermas," in *Habermas and the Public Sphere*, ed. Craig Calhoun.

34. Usually, but not always. As Josh Cohen has argued, exceptions are the uses of privacy in *Roe v. Wade*, the U.S. Supreme Court decision legalizing abortion, and in Justice Blackmun's dissent in *Bowers*, the decision upholding state antisodomy laws. These examples show that the privacy rhetoric is multivalent rather than univocally and necessarily harmful. On the other hand, there is no question but that the weightier tradition of privacy argument has buttressed inequality by restricting debate. Moreover, many feminists have argued that even the "good" privacy uses have some serious negative consequences in the current context and that gender domination is better challenged in this context in other terms. For a defense of privacy talk, see Joshua Cohen, "Comments on Nancy Fraser's 'Rethinking the Public Sphere.'"

35. There are many possibilities here, including such mixed forms as market socialism.

36. I use the expression "quasi-direct democracy" to signal the possibility of hybrid forms of self-management involving the democratic designation of representatives, managers, or planners held to strict standards of accountability through, for example, recall.

37. By "hybrid possibilities" I mean arrangements involving very strict accountability of representative decision-making bodies to their external publics through veto and recall rights. Such hybrid forms might be desirable in some circumstances, though certainly not all.

Section IV

The Public Sphere and Models of Democracy

INTRODUCTION

This section addresses the so called the deliberative turn that has taken place within democratic theory since the 1980s. The revival of the role of public discussion can be seen as a reaction to predominant images of politically passive citizens that developed after World War II. The social and political climate in the post-war era inspired elitist theories of democracy, as well as economic theories, where political processes were modeled on rational-choice assumptions. Both approaches reduced the role of active public deliberation by citizens. Critics set out to address both the theoretical anomalies in these models and the growing popular alienation from the political establishment. In the context of what Jürgen Habermas saw as a "legitimation crisis" in Western liberal democracies, they embarked on a rethinking and a revival of the normative dimension of democracy.

Although deliberative democratic theories come in different versions, some core elements can be identified: They all refer to the idea that legitimate lawmaking issues from the public deliberation among free and equal citizens, or more broadly to decision making by means of arguments offered by and to participants who are committed to the values of rationality and impartiality. Deliberative democrats define the essence of democratic legitimacy in terms of the ability or opportunity of all citizens to contribute to collective decisions by engaging in authentic deliberation about its justifications, its implications, and the possible alternatives.

The idea of deliberative democracy evokes ideals of rational legislation, participatory democracy, and consensual forms of self-government. But how can the public deliberation of citizens influence political outcomes? What is the relation between deliberation and decisions in time-constrained political settings? What are the proper institutional requirements for public deliberation on what constitutes the public interest or common good? Is consensus on central political issues possible, or even desirable, in modern pluralistic societies? The essays selected for this section discuss these key questions and the related issue of the role of deliberation and the public sphere in different conceptions and models of democracy.

The first essay spells out how political behavior differs from market behavior. Jon Elster argues against a narrow instrumental model of politics, as well as against a republican model which presents political activity as a goal in itself. Although critical of the deliberative model of politics in its strong consensual version, Elster sees public arguing as central to democratic politics. What emerges from his discussion is a picture of politics as "public in nature and instrumental in purpose."

Jürgen Habermas also seeks to combine two dominant conceptions of democracy: the participatory features of democracy found in civic republicanism and the central role of individual rights, institutions and law found in liberalism. Building on the notion of a deliberative procedure, Habermas develops a model of "the circulation of power," where social and economic power is to be disciplined by the "communicative power" of the public sphere. The network of different public spheres in civil society is given a vital role in formulating social problems, needs, and solutions. These are addressed to political parties and institutions, whose actions and problem solving in turn must be defended and legitimated before the public.

But what issues should enter democratic institutions? From the position of political liberalism, John Rawls argues that the plurality of worldviews and competing conceptions of the good in modern societies place restrictions on deliberation and the public use of reason. Public reason proper is restricted to reasoning in the forums of politics and jurisprudence, involving "constitutional essentials" and questions of basic justice. This is separate from what Rawls conceptualizes as non-public reasoning in the "background culture."

Rawls and Habermas hold that democratic procedures require norms of reasonableness and communicative rationality. With his notion of public opinion as a mere sensor for the political system, Niklas Luhmann's system theory represents a radical alternative to normative conceptions of democracy and public deliberation. Although stripped of normative bearings by Luhmann, his ideas of the public sphere as an arena for the detection of problems affecting the whole of society plays an important part in Habermas' discourse theory of democracy.

JON ELSTER

THE MARKET AND THE FORUM: THREE VARIETIES OF POLITICAL THEORY (1986)

Jon Elster (b. 1940), born in Norway, but working for most of his professional life in the United States and now professor at the Collège de France in Paris, is one of the most influential theorists currently writing in the social and political sciences, celebrated for his attempts to reconstitute a range of core problems in books such as Ulysses and the Sirens *(1979),* Sour Grapes *(1983),* Alchemies of the Mind *(1999), and* Explaining Social Behavior *(2007), where he sums up much of his work and provides an account of the nature of explanation in the social sciences.*

In the article reprinted here, he argues that rational-choice theory, which has enjoyed considerable currency among social scientists, and which Elster has commented on extensively in his work, reduces political action to the "totality of individuals queuing up for the election booth." By presenting voters as atomized subjects making personal choices between competing parties and programs, it equates them with consumers selecting commodities in the marketplace. He rejects this privatized market-driven view of democratic politics, arguing that it is "hopelessly inadequate" in addressing the allocation and redistribution of collective resources and ensuring just outcomes that strike a balance between individual interests and the common good. To achieve this he argues, the political sphere must be seen, first and foremost, as a forum, a public and open activity, in which citizenship, in its full sense, can only be realized through participation in collective deliberation. At the same time, he rejects the position, advanced most forcefully by Hannah Arendt, that sees participation primarily as a means of educating the participants. For Elster, any personal benefits gained from participation can only ever be by-products. Because political debate is defined by its concern with "what to do" it's main aim must always be adjudicating between competing positions and proposals and arriving at substantive decisions. Further, for Elster the urgent need to address key issues requires deliberation to be focused and time limited, conditions that preclude any idealized commitment to a "leisurely style of philosophical argument in which it may be better to travel hopefully than to arrive."

I want to compare three views of politics generally, and of the democratic system more specifically. I shall first look at social choice theory, as an instance of a wider class of theories with certain common features. In particular, they share the conception that the political process is instrumental rather than an end in itself, and the view that the decisive political act is a private rather than a public action, viz. the individual and secret vote. With these usually goes the idea that the goal of politics is the optimal compromise between given, and irreducibly opposed, private interests. The other two views arise when one denies, first, the private character of political behaviour and then, secondly, goes on also to deny the instrumental nature of politics. According to the theory of Jürgen Habermas, the goal of politics should be rational agreement rather than compromise, and the decisive political act is that of engaging in public debate with a view to the emergence of a consensus. According to the theorists of participatory democracy, from John Stuart Mill to Carole Pateman, the goal of politics is the transformation and education of the participants. Politics, on this view, is an end in itself—indeed many have argued that it represents the good life for man. I shall discuss these views in the order indicated. I shall present them in a somewhat stylized form, but my critical comments will not I hope, be directed to strawmen.

I

Politics, it is usually agreed, is concerned with the common good, and notably with the cases in which it cannot be realized as the aggregate outcome of individuals pursuing their private interests. In particular, uncoordinated private choices may lead to outcomes that are worse for all than some other outcome that could have been attained by coordination. Political institutions are set up to remedy such *market failures*, a phrase that can be taken either in the static sense of an inability to provide public goods or in the more dynamic sense of a breakdown of the self-regulating properties usually ascribed to the market mechanism.[1] In addition there is the redistributive task of politics—moving along the Pareto-optimal frontier once it has been reached.[2] According to the first view of politics, this task is inherently one of interest struggle and compromise. The obstacle to agreement is not only that most individuals want redistribution to be in their favour, or at least not in their disfavour.[3] More basically consensus is blocked because there is no reason to expect that individuals will converge in their views on what constitutes a just redistribution.

I shall consider social choice theory as representative of the private-instrumental view of politics, because it brings out supremely well the logic as well as the limits of that approach. Other varieties, such as the Schumpeterian or neo-Schumpeterian theories, are closer to the actual political process, but for that reason also less suited to my purpose. For instance, Schumpeter's insistence that voter preferences are shaped and manipulated by politicians[4] tends to blur the distinction, central to my analysis, between politics as the aggregation of given preferences and politics as the transformation of preferences through rational discussion. And although the neo-Schumpeterians are right in emphasizing the role of the political parties in the preference-aggregation process,[5] I am not here concerned with such mediating mechanisms. In any case, political problems also arise within the political parties, and so my discussion may be taken to apply to such lower-level political processes. In fact, much of what I shall say makes better sense for politics on a rather small scale—within the firm, the organization or the local community—than for nationwide political systems.

In very broad outline, the structure of social choice theory is as follows.[6] (1) We begin with a *given* set of agents, so that the issue of a normative justification of political boundaries does not arise. (2) We assume that the agents confront a *given* set of alternatives, so that for instance the issue of agenda manipulation does not arise. (3) The agents are supposed to be endowed with preferences that are similarly *given* and not subject to change in the course of the political process. They are, moreover, assumed to be causally independent of the set of alternatives. (4) In the standard version, which is so far the only operational version of the theory, preferences are assumed to be purely ordinal, so that it is not possible for an individual to express the intensity of his preferences, nor for an outside observer to compare preference intensities across individuals. (5) The individual preferences are assumed to be defined over all pairs of individuals, i.e., to be complete, and to have the formal property of transitivity, so that preference for A over B and for B over C implies preference for A over C.

Given this setting, the task of social choice theory is to arrive at a social preference ordering of the alternatives. This might appear to require more than is needed: why not define the goal as one of arriving at the choice of one alternative? There is, however, usually some uncertainty as to which alternatives are really feasible, and so it is useful to have an ordering if the top-ranked alternative proves unavailable. The ordering should satisfy the following criteria. (6) Like the individual preferences, it should be complete and transitive. (7) It should be Pareto-optimal, in the sense of never having one option socially preferred to another which is individually preferred by everybody. (8) The social choice between two given options should depend only on how the individuals rank these two options, and thus not be sensitive to changes in their preferences concerning other options. (9) The social preference ordering should respect and reflect individual preferences, over and above the condition of Pareto-optimality. This idea covers a variety of notions, the most important of which are *anonymity* (all individuals should count equally), *nondictatorship (a fortiori* no single individual should dictate the social choice), *liberalism* (all individuals should have some private domain within which their preferences are decisive), and *strategy-proofness* (it should not pay to express false preferences).

The substance of social choice theory is given in a series of impossibility and uniqueness theorems, stating either that a given subset of these conditions is incapable of simultaneous satisfaction or that they uniquely describe a specific method for aggregating preferences. Much attention has been given to the impossibility theorems, yet from the present point of view these are not of decisive importance. They stem largely from the paucity of allowable information about the preferences, i.e., the exclusive focus on ordinal preferences.[7] True, at present we do not quite know how to go beyond ordinality. Log-rolling and vote-trading may capture some of the cardinal aspects of the preferences, but at some cost.[8] Yet even should the conceptual and technical obstacles to intra- and inter-individual comparison of preference intensity be overcome,[9] many objections to the social choice approach would remain. I shall discuss two sets of objections, both related to the assumption of given preferences. I shall argue, first, that the preferences people choose to express may not be a good guide to what they really prefer; and secondly that what they really prefer may in any case be a fragile foundation for social choice.

In actual fact, preferences are never 'given,' in the sense of being directly observable. If they are to serve as inputs to the social choice process, they must somehow be *expressed* by the individuals. The expression of preferences is an action, which presumably is guided by these very same preferences.[10] It is then far from obvious that the individually rational action is to express these preferences as they are. Some methods for aggregating preferences are such that it may pay the individual to express false preferences, i.e., the outcome may in some cases be better according to his real preferences if he chooses not to express them truthfully. The condition for strategy-proofness for social choice mechanisms was designed expressly to exclude this possibility. It turns out, however, that the systems in which honesty always pays are rather unattractive in other respects.[11] We then have to face the possibility that even if we require that the social preferences be Pareto-optimal with respect to the expressed preferences, they might not be so with respect to the real ones.

Strategy-proofness and collective rationality, therefore, stand and fall together. Since it appears that the first must fall, so must the second. It then becomes very difficult indeed to defend the idea that the outcome of the social choice mechanism represents the common good, since there is a chance that everybody might prefer some other outcome.

Amos Tversky has pointed to another reason why choices—or expressed preferences—cannot be assumed to represent the real preferences in all cases.[12] According to his "concealed preference hypothesis," choices often conceal rather than reveal underlying preferences. This is especially so in two sorts of cases. First, there are the cases of anticipated regret associated with a risky decision. Consider the following example (from Tversky):

On her twelfth birthday, Judy was offered a choice between spending the weekend with her aunt in the city *(C)*, or having a party for all her friends. The party could take place either in the garden *(GP)* or inside the house *(HP)*. A garden party would be much more enjoyable, but there is always the possibility of rain, in which case an inside party would be more sensible. In evaluating the consequences of the three options, Judy notes that the weather condition does not have a significant effect on *C*. If she chooses the party, however, the situation is different. A garden party will be a lot of fun if the weather is good, but quite disastrous if it rains, in which case an inside party will be acceptable. The trouble is that Judy expects to have a lot of regret if the party is to be held inside and the weather is very nice.

Now, let us suppose that for some reason it is no longer possible to have an outside party. In this situation, there is no longer any regret associated with holding an inside party in good weather because (in this case) Judy has no other place for holding the party. Hence, the elimination of an available course of action (holding the party outside) removes the regret associated with an inside party, and increases its overall utility. It stands to reason, in this case, that if Judy was indifferent between *C* and *HP*, in the presence of *GP*, she will prefer *HP* to *C* when *GP* is eliminated.

What we observe here is the violation of condition (8) above, the so-called "independence of irrelevant alternatives." The expressed preferences depend causally on the set of alternatives. We may assume that the real preferences, defined over the set of possible outcomes, remain constant, contrary to the case to be discussed below. Yet the preferences over the *pairs* (choice, outcome) depend on the set of available choices, because the "costs of responsibility" differentially associated with various such pairs depend on what else one "could have done." Although Judy could not have escaped her predicament by deliberately making it physically impossible to have an outside party,[13] she might well have welcomed an event outside her control with the same consequence.

The second class of cases in which Tversky would want to distinguish the expressed preferences from the real preferences concerns decisions that are unpleasant rather than risky. For instance, "society may prefer to save the life of one person rather than another, and yet be unable to make this choice." In fact, losing both lives through inaction may be preferred to losing only one life by deliberate action. Such examples are closely related to the problems involved in act utilitarianism versus outcome utilitarianism.[14] One may well judge that it would be a good thing if state *A* came about, and yet not want to be the person by whose agency it comes about. The reasons for not wanting to be that person maybe quite respectable, or they may not. The latter would be the case if one were afraid of being blamed by the relatives of the person who was deliberately allowed to die, or if one simply confused the causal and the moral notions of responsibility. In such cases the expressed preferences might lead to a choice that in a clear sense goes against the real preferences of the people concerned.

A second, perhaps more basic, difficulty is that the real preferences themselves might well depend causally on the feasible set. One instance is graphically provided by the fable of the fox and the sour grapes.[15] For the "ordinal utilitarian," as Arrow for instance calls himself,[16] there would be no welfare loss if the fox were excluded from consumption of the grapes, since he thought them sour anyway. But of course the cause of his holding them to be sour was his conviction that he would in any case be excluded from consuming them, and then it is difficult to justify the allocation by invoking his preferences. Conversely, the phenomenon of "counter-adaptive preferences" —the grass is always greener on the other side of the fence, and the forbidden fruit always sweeter—is also baffling for the social choice theorist, since it implies that such preferences, if respected, would not be satisfied—and yet the whole point of respecting them would be to give them a chance of satisfaction.

Adaptive and counter-adaptive preferences are only special cases of a more general class of desires, those which fail to satisfy some substantive criterion for acceptable preferences, as opposed to the purely formal criterion of transitivity. I shall discuss these under two headings: autonomy and morality.

Autonomy characterizes the way in which preferences are shaped rather than their actual content. Unfortunately I find myself unable to give a positive characterization of autonomous preferences, so I shall have to rely on two indirect approaches. First, autonomy is for desires what judgment is for belief. The notion of judgment is also difficult to define formally, but at least we know that there are persons who have this quality to a higher degree than others: people who are able to take account of vast and diffuse evidence that more or less clearly bears on the problem at hand, in such a way that no element is given undue importance. In such people the process of belief formation is not disturbed by defective cognitive processing, nor distorted by wishful thinking and the like. Similarly, autonomous preferences are those that have not been shaped by irrelevant causal processes—a singularly unhelpful explanation. To improve somewhat on it, consider, secondly, a short list of such irrelevant causal processes. They include adaptive and counter-adaptive preferences, conformity and anti-conformity, the obsession with novelty and the equally unreasonable resistance to novelty. In other words, preferences may be shaped by adaptation to what is possible, to what other people do or to what one has been doing in the past—or they may be shaped by the desire to differ as much as possible from these. In all of these cases the source of preference change is not in the person, but outside him—detracting from his autonomy.

Morality, it goes without saying, is if anything even more controversial. (Within the Kantian tradition it would also be questioned whether it can be distinguished at all from autonomy.) Preferences are moral or immoral by virtue of their content, not by virtue of the way in which they have been shaped. Fairly uncontroversial examples of unethical preferences are spiteful and sadistic desires, and arguably also the desire for positional goods, i.e., goods such that it is logically impossible for more than a few to possess them.[17] The desire for an income twice the average can lead to less welfare for everybody, so that such preferences fail to pass the Kantian generalization test.[18] Also they are closely linked to spite, since one way of getting more than others is to take care that they get less—indeed this may often be a more efficient method than trying to excel.[19]

To see how the lack of autonomy may be distinguished from the lack of moral worth, let me use *conformity* as a technical term for a desire caused by a drive to be like other people, and *conformism* for a desire to be like other people, with anti-conformity and anti-conformism similarly defined. Conformity implies that other people's desires enter into the causation of my own, conformism that they enter irreducibly into the description of the object of my desires. Conformity may bring about conformism, but it may also lead to anti-conformism, as in Theodore Zeldin's comment that among the French peasantry "prestige is to a great extent obtained from conformity with traditions (so that the son of a non-conformist might be expected to be one too."[20] Clearly, conformity may bring about desires that are morally laudable, yet lacking in autonomy. Conversely, I do not see how one could rule out on a *priori* grounds the possibility of autonomous spite, although I would welcome a proof that autonomy is incompatible not only with anti-conformity, but also with anti-conformism.

We can now state the objection to the political view underlying social choice theory. It is, basically, that it embodies a confusion between the kind of behaviour that is appropriate in the market place and that which is appropriate in the forum. The notion of consumer sovereignty is acceptable because, and to the extent that, the consumer chooses between courses of action that differ only in the way they affect him. In political choice situations, however, the citizen is asked to express his preference over states that also differ in the way in which they affect other people. This means that there is no similar justification for the corresponding notion of the citizen's sovereignty, since other people may legitimately object to social choice governed by preferences that are defective in some of the ways I have mentioned. A social choice mechanism is capable of resolving the market failures that would result from unbridled consumer sovereignty, but as a way of redistributing welfare it is hopelessly inadequate. If people affected each other only by tripping over each other's feet, or by dumping their garbage into one another's backyards, a social choice mechanism might cope. But the task of politics is not only to eliminate inefficiency, but also to create justice—a goal to which the aggregation of prepolitical preferences is a quite incongruous means.

This suggests that the principles of the forum must differ from those of the market. A long-standing tradition from the *Greek polis* onwards suggests that politics must be an open and public activity, as distinct from the isolated and private expression of preferences that occurs in buying and selling. In the following sections I look at two different conceptions of public politics, increasingly removed from the market theory of politics. Before I go on to this, however, I should briefly consider an objection that the social choice theorist might well make to what has just been said. He could argue that the only alternative to the aggregation of given preferences is some kind of censorship or paternalism. He might agree that spiteful and adaptive preferences are undesirable, but he would add that any institutional mechanism for eliminating them would be misused and harnessed to the private purposes of power-seeking individuals. Any remedy, in fact, would be worse than the disease. This objection assumes (i) that the only alternative to aggregation of given preferences is censorship, and (ii) that censorship is always objectionable. Robert Goodin, in his contribution to this volume, challenges the second assumption, by arguing that laundering or filtering of preferences by self-censorship is an acceptable alternative to aggregation. I shall now discuss a challenge to the first assumption, viz. the idea of a *transformation* of preferences through public and rational discussion.

II

Today this view is especially associated with the writings of Jürgen Habermas on "the ethics of discourse" and "the ideal speech situation." As mentioned above, I shall present a somewhat stylized version of his views, although I hope they bear some resemblance to the original.[21] The core of the theory, then, is that rather than aggregating or filtering preferences, the political system should be set up with a view to changing them by public debate and confrontation. The input to the social choice mechanism would then not be the raw, quite possibly selfish or irrational, preferences that operate in the market, but informed and other-regarding preferences. Or rather, there would not be any need for an aggregating mechanism, since a rational discussion would tend to produce unanimous preferences. When the private and idiosyncratic wants have been shaped and purged in public discussion about the public good, uniquely determined rational desires would emerge. Not optimal compromise, but unanimous agreement is the goal of politics on this view.

There appear to be two main premises underlying this theory. The first is that there are certain arguments that simply cannot be stated publicly. In a political debate it is pragmatically impossible to argue that a given solution should be chosen just because it is good for oneself. By the very act of engaging in a public debate—by arguing rather than bargaining—one has ruled out the possibility of invoking such reasons.[22] To engage in discussion can in fact be seen as one kind of self-censorship, a pre-commitment to the idea of rational decision. Now, it might well be thought that this conclusion is too strong. The first argument only shows that in public debate one has to pay some lip-service to the common good. An additional premise states that over time one will in fact come to be swayed by considerations about the common good. One cannot indefinitely praise the common good "du bout des lèvres," for—as argued by Pascal in the context of the wager—one will end up having the preferences that initially one was faking.[23] This is a psychological, not a conceptual premise. To explain why going through the motions of rational discussion should tend to bring about the real thing, one might argue that people tend to bring what they mean into line with what they say in order to reduce dissonance, but this is a dangerous argument to employ in the present context. Dissonance reduction does not tend to generate autonomous preferences. Rather one would have to invoke the power of reason to break down prejudice and selfishness. By speaking with the voice of reason, one is also exposing oneself to reason.

To sum up, the conceptual impossibility of expressing selfish arguments in a debate about the public good, and the psychological difficulty of expressing other-regarding preferences without ultimately coming to acquire them, jointly bring it about that public discussion tends to promote the common good. The *volonté générale*, then, will not simply be the Pareto-optimal realization of given (or expressed) preferences,[24] but the outcome of preferences that are themselves shaped by a concern for the common good. For instance, by mere aggregation of given preferences one would be able to take account of some negative externalities, but not of those affecting future generations. A social choice mechanism might prevent persons now living from dumping their garbage into one another's backyards, but not from dumping it on the future. Moreover, considerations of distributive justice within the Pareto constraint would now have a more solid foundation, especially as one would also be able to avoid the problem of strategy-proofness. By one stroke one would achieve more rational preferences, as well as the guarantee that they will in fact be expressed.

I now want to set out a series of objections—seven altogether—to the view stated above. I should explain that the goal of this criticism is not to demolish the theory, but to locate some points that need to be fortified. I am, in fact, largely in sympathy with the fundamental tenets of the view, yet fear that it might be dismissed as Utopian, both in the sense of ignoring the problem of getting from here to there, and in the sense of neglecting some elementary facts of human psychology.

The *first objection* involves a reconsideration of the issues of paternalism. Would it not, in fact, be unwarranted interference to impose on the citizens the obligation to participate in political discussion? One might answer that there is a link between the right to vote and the obligation to participate in discussion, just as rights and duties are correlative in other cases. To acquire the right to vote, one has to perform certain civic duties that go beyond pushing the voting button on the television set. There would appear to be two different ideas underlying this answer. First, only those should have the right to vote who are sufficiently *concerned* about politics to be willing to devote some of their resources—time in particular—to it. Secondly, one should try to favour *informed* preferences as inputs to the voting process. The first argument favours participation and discussion as a sign of interest, but does not give it an instrumental value in itself. It would do just as well, for the purpose of this argument, to demand that people should pay for the right to vote. The second argument favours discussion as a means to improvement—it will not only select the right people, but actually make them more qualified to participate.

These arguments might have some validity in a near-ideal world, in which the concern for politics was evenly distributed across all relevant dimensions, but in the context of contemporary politics they miss the point. The people who survive a high threshold for participation are disproportionately found in a privileged part of the population. At best this could lead to paternalism, at worst the high ideals of rational discussion could create a self-elected elite whose members spend time on politics because they want power, not out of concern for the issues. As in other cases, to be discussed later, the best can be the enemy of the good. I am not saying that it is impossible to modify the ideal in a way that allows both for rational discussion and for low-profile participation, only that any institutional design must respect the tradeoff between the two.

My *second objection* is that even assuming unlimited time for discussion, unanimous and rational agreement might not necessarily ensue. Could there not be legitimate and unresolvable differences of opinions over the nature of the common good? Could there not even be a plurality of ultimate values?

I am not going to discuss this objection, since it is in any case preempted by the *third objection*. Since there are in fact always time constraints on discussions—often the stronger the more important the issues—unanimity will rarely emerge. For any constellation of preferences short of unanimity, however, one would need a social choice mechanism to aggregate them. One can discuss only for so long, and then one has to make a decision, even if strong differences of opinion should remain. This objection, then, goes to show that the transformation of preferences can never do more than supplement the aggregation of preferences, never replace it altogether.

This much would no doubt be granted by most proponents of the theory. True, they would say, even if the ideal speech situation can never be fully realized, it will nevertheless improve the outcome of the political process if one goes some way towards it. The *fourth objection* questions the validity of this reply. In some cases a little discussion can be a dangerous thing, worse in fact than no discussion at all, viz. if it makes some but not all persons align themselves on the common good. The following story provides an illustration:

Once upon a time two boys found a cake. One of them said, "Splendid! I will eat the cake." The other one said, "No, that is not fair! We found the cake together, and we should share and share alike, half for you and half for me." The first boy said, "No, I should have the whole cake!" Along came an adult who said, "Gentlemen, you shouldn't fight about this: you should *compromise*. Give him three quarters of the cake."[25]

What creates the difficulty here is that the first boy's preferences are allowed to count twice in the social choice mechanism suggested by the adult: once in his expression of them and then again in the other boy's internalized ethic of sharing. And one can argue that the outcome is socially inferior to that which would have emerged had they both stuck to their selfish preferences. When Adam Smith wrote that he had never known much good done by those who affected to trade for the public good, he may only have had in mind the harm that can be done by *unilateral* attempts to act morally. The categorical imperative itself may be badly served by people acting unilaterally on it.[26] Also, an inferior outcome may result if discussion brings about partial adherence to morality in all participants rather than full adherence in some and none in others, as in the story of the two boys. Thus Serge Kolm argues that economies with moderately altrustic agents tend to work less well than economies where either everybody is selfish or everybody is altruistic.[27]

A *fifth objection* is to question the implicit assumption that the body politic as a whole is better or wiser than the sum of its parts. Could it not rather be the case that people are made more, not less, selfish and irrational by interacting politically? The cognitive analogy suggests that the rationality of beliefs may be positively as well as negatively affected by interaction. On the one hand there is what Irving Janis has called "group-think," i.e., mutually reinforcing bias.[28] On the other hand there certainly are many ways in which people can, and do, pool their opinions and supplement each other to arrive at a better estimate.[29] Similarly autonomy and morality could be enhanced as well as undermined by interaction. Against the pessimistic view of Reinhold Niebuhr that individuals in a group show more unrestrained egoism than in their personal relationships,[30] we may set Hannah Arendt's optimistic view:

American faith was not all based on a semireligious faith in human nature, but on the contrary, on the possibility of checking human nature in its singularity, by virtue of human bonds and mutual promises. The hope for man in his singularity lay in the fact that not man but men inhabit the earth and form a world between them. It is human worldliness that will save men from the pitfalls of human nature.[31]

Niebuhr's argument suggests an aristocratic disdain of the *mass*, which transforms individually decent people—to use a characteristically condescending phrase—into an unthinking horde. While rejecting this as a general view, one should equally avoid the other extreme, suggested by Arendt. Neither the Greek nor the American assemblies were the paradigms of discursive reason that she makes them out to be. The Greeks were well aware that they might be tempted by demagogues, and in fact took extensive precautions against this tendency.[32] The American town surely has not always been the incarnation of collective freedom, since on occasion it could also serve as the springboard for witch hunts. The mere decision to engage in rational discussion does not ensure that the transactions will in fact be conducted rationally, since much depends on the structure and the framework of the proceedings. The random errors of selfish and private preferences may to some extent cancel each other out and thus be less to be feared than the massive and coordinated errors that may arise through group-think. On the other hand, it would be excessively stupid to rely on mutually compensating vices to bring about public benefits as a general rule. I am not arguing against the need for public discussion, only for the need to take the question of institutional and constitutional design very seriously.

A *sixth objection* is that unanimity, were it to be realized, might easily be due to conformity rather than to rational agreement. I would in fact tend to have more confidence in the outcome of a democratic decision if there was a minority that voted against it, than if it was unanimous. I am not here referring to people expressing the majority preferences against their real ones, since I am assuming that something like the secret ballot would prevent this. I have in mind that people may come to change their real preferences, as a result of seeing which way the majority goes. Social psychology has amply shown the strength of this bandwagon effect,[33] which in political theory is also known as the "chameleon" problem.[34] It will not do to argue that the majority to which the conformist adapts his view is likely to pass the test of rationality even if his adherence to it does not, since the majority could well be made up of conformists each of whom would have broken out had there been a minority he could have espoused.

To bring the point home, consider a parallel case of non-autonomous preference formation. We are tempted to say that a man is free if he can get or do whatever it is that he wants to get or do. But then we are immediately faced with the objection that perhaps he only wants what he can get, as the result of some such mechanism as "sour grapes."[35] We may then add that, other things being equal, the person is freer the more things he wants to do which he is not free to do, since these show that his wants are not in general shaped by adaptation to his possibilities. Clearly, there is an air of paradox over the statement that a man's freedom is greater the more of his desires he is not free to realize, but on reflection the paradox embodies a valid argument. Similarly, it is possible to dissolve the air of paradox attached to the view that a collective decision is more trustworthy if it is less than unanimous.

My *seventh objection* amounts to a denial of the view that the need to couch one's argument in terms of the common good will purge the desires of all selfish arguments. There are in general many ways of realizing the common good, if by that phrase we now only mean some arrangement that is Pareto-superior to uncoordinated individual decisions. Each such arrangement will, in addition to promoting the general interest, bring an extra premium to some specific group, which will then have a strong interest in that particular arrangement.[36] The group may then come to prefer the arrangement because of that premium, although it will argue for it in terms of the common good. Typically the arrangement will be justified by a causal theory—an account, say, of how the economy works—that shows it to be not only *a* way, but the only way of promoting the common good. The economic theories underlying the early Reagan administration provide an example. I am not imputing insincerity to the proponents of these views, but there may well be an element of wishful thinking. Since social scientists disagree so strongly among themselves as to how societies work, what could be more human than to pick on a theory that uniquely justifies the arrangement from which one stands to profit? The opposition between general interest and special interests is too simplistic, since the private benefits may causally determine the way in which one conceives of the common good.

These objections have been concerned to bring out two main ideas. First, one cannot assume that one will in fact approach the good society by acting as if one had already arrived there. The fallacy inherent in this "approximation assumption"[37] was exposed a long time ago in the economic "theory of the second best":

It is *not* true that a situation in which more, but not all, of the optimum conditions are fulfilled is necessarily, or is even likely to be, superior to a situation in which fewer are fulfilled. It follows, therefore, that in a situation in which there exist many constraints which prevent the fulfilment of the Paretian optimum conditions, the removal of any one constraint may affect welfare or efficiency either by raising it, by lowering it or by leaving it unchanged.[38]

The ethical analogue is not the familiar idea that some moral obligations may be suspended when other people act non-morally.[39] Rather it is that the nature of the moral obligation is changed in a non-moral environment. When others act non-morally, there may be an obligation to deviate not only from what they do, but also from the behaviour that would have been optimal if adopted by everybody.[40] In particular, a little discussion, like a little rationality or a little socialism, may be a dangerous thing.[41] If, as suggested by Habermas, free and rational discussion will only be possible in a society that has abolished political and economic domination, it is by no means obvious that abolition can be brought about by rational argumentation. I do not want to suggest that it could occur by force—since the use of force to end the use of force is open to obvious objections. Yet something like irony, eloquence or propaganda might be needed, involving less respect for the interlocutor than what would prevail in the ideal speech situation.

As will be clear from these remarks, there is a strong tension between two ways of looking at the relation between political ends and means. On the one hand, the means should partake of the nature of the ends, since otherwise the use of unsuitable means might tend to corrupt the end. On the other hand, there are dangers involved in choosing means immediately derived from the goal to be realized, since in a non-ideal situation these might take us away from the end rather than towards it. A delicate balance will have to be struck between these two, opposing considerations. It is in fact an open question whether there exists a ridge along which we can move to the good society, and if so whether it is like a knife-edge or more like a plateau.

The second general idea that emerges from the discussion is that even in the good society, should we hit upon it, the process of rational discussion could be fragile, and vulnerable to adaptive preferences, conformity, wishful thinking and the like.

To ensure stability and robustness there is a need for structures—political institutions or constitutions—that could easily reintroduce an element of domination. We would in fact be confronted, at the political level, with a perennial dilemma of individual behaviour. How is it possible to ensure at the same time that one is bound by rules that protect one from irrational or unethical behaviour—and that these rules do not turn into prisons from which it is not possible to break out even when it would be rational to do so?[42]

III

It is clear from Habermas's theory, I believe, that rational political discussion has an *object* in terms of which it makes sense.[43] Politics is concerned with substantive decision-making, and is to that extent instrumental. True, the idea of instrumental politics might also be taken in a more narrow sense, as implying that the political process is one in which individuals pursue their selfish interests, but more broadly understood it implies only that political action is primarily a means to a non-political end, only secondarily, if at all, an end in itself. In this section I shall consider theories that suggest a reversal of this priority, and that find the main point of politics in the educative or otherwise beneficial effects on the participants. And I shall try to show that this view tends to be internally incoherent, or self-defeating. The benefits of participation are by-products of political activity. Moreover, they are *essentially* by-products, in the sense that any attempt to turn them into the main purpose of such activity would make them evaporate.[44] It can indeed be highly satisfactory to engage in political work, but only on the condition that the work is defined by a serious purpose which goes beyond that of achieving this satisfaction. If that condition is not fulfilled, we get a narcissistic view of politics—corresponding to various consciousness-raising activities familiar from the last decade or so.

My concern, however, is with political theory rather than with political activism. I shall argue that certain types of arguments for political institutions and constitutions are self-defeating, since they justify the arrangement in question by effects that are essentially byproducts. Here an initial and important distinction must be drawn between the task of justifying a constitution *ex ante* and that of evaluating it *ex post* and at a distance. I argue below that Tocqueville, when assessing the American democracy, praised it for consequences that are indeed by-products. In his case, this made perfectly good sense as an analytical attitude adopted after the fact and at some distance from the system he was examining. The incoherence arises when one invokes the same arguments before the fact, in public discussion. Although the constitution-makers may secretly have such side effects in mind, they cannot coherently invoke them in public.

Kant proposed a *transcendental formula of public right*: "All actions affecting the rights of other human beings are wrong if their maxim is not compatible with their being made public."[45] Since Kant's illustrations of the principle are obscure, let me turn instead to John Rawls, who imposes a similar condition of publicity as a constraint on what the parties can choose in the original position.[46] He argues, moreover, that this condition tends to favour his own conception of justice, as compared to that of the utilitarians.[47] If utilitarian principles of justice were openly adopted, they would entail some loss of self-esteem, since people would feel that they were not fully being treated as ends in themselves. Other things being equal, this would also lead to a loss in average utility. It is then conceivable that public adoption of Rawls's two principles of justice would bring about a higher average utility than public adoption of utilitarianism, although a lower average than under a secret utilitarian constitution introduced from above. The latter possibility, however, is ruled out by the publicity constraint. A utilitarian could not then advocate Rawls's two principles on utilitarian grounds, although he might well applaud them on such grounds. The fact that the two principles maximize utility would essentially be a by-product, and if chosen on the grounds that they are utility-maximizing they would no longer be so. Utilitarianism, therefore, is self-defeating in Kant's sense: "it essentially lacks openness."[48]

Derek Parfit has raised a similar objection to act consequentialism (AC) and suggested how it could be met:

This gives to all one common aim: the best possible outcome. If we try to achieve this, we may often fail. Even when we succeed, the fact that we are disposed to try might make the outcome worse. AC might thus be indirectly self-defeating. What does this show? A consequentialist might say: "It shows that AC should be only one part of our moral theory. It should be the part that covers successful acts. When we are certain to succeed, we should aim for the best possible outcome. Our wider theory should be this: we should have the aim and dispositions having which would make the outcome best. This wider theory would not be self-defeating. So the objection has been met."[49]

Yet there is an ambiguity in the word "should" in the penultimate sentence, since it is not clear whether we are told that it is good to have certain aims and dispositions, or that we should aim at having them. The latter answer immediately raises the problem that having certain aims and dispositions—i.e., being a certain kind of person—is essentially a by-product. When instrumental rationality is self-defeating, we cannot decide on instrumentalist grounds to take leave of it—no more than we can fall asleep by deciding not to try to fall asleep. Although spontaneity may be highly valuable on utilitarian grounds, "you cannot both genuinely possess this kind of quality and also reassure yourself that while it is free and creative and uncalculative, it is also acting for the best."[50]

Tocqueville, in a seeming paradox, suggested that democracies are less suited than aristocracies to deal with long-term planning, and yet are superior in the long-run to the latter. The paradox dissolves once it is seen that the first statement involves time at the level of the actors, the second at the level of the observer. On the one hand, "a democracy finds it difficult to coordinate the details of a great undertaking and to fix on some plan and carry it through with determination in spite of obstacles. It has little capacity for combining measures in secret and waiting patiently for the result."[51] On the other hand, "in the long run government by democracy should increase the real forces of a society, but it cannot immediately assemble at one point and at a given time, forces as great as those at the disposal of an aristocratic government."[52] The latter view is further elaborated in a passage from the chapter on "The Real Advantages Derived by American Society from Democratic Government":

That constantly renewed agitation introduced by democratic government into political life passes, then, into civil society. Perhaps, taking everything into consideration, that is the greatest advantage of democratic government, and I praise it much more on account of what it causes to be done than for what it does. It is incontestable that the people often manage public affairs very badly, but their concern therewith is bound to extend their mental horizon and to shake them out of the rut of ordinary routine . . . Democracy does not provide a people with the most skillful of governments, but it does that which the most skillful government often cannot do: it spreads throughout the body social a restless activity, superabundant force, and energy never found elsewhere, which, however little favoured by circumstances, can do wonders. Those are its true advantages.[53]

The advantages of democracies, in other words, are mainly and essentially by-products. The avowed aim of democracy is to be a good system of government, but Tocqueville argues that it is inferior in this respect to aristocracy, viewed purely as a decision-making apparatus. Yet the very activity of governing democratically has as a by-product a certain energy and restlessness that benefits industry and generates prosperity. Assuming the soundness of this observation, could it ever serve as a public justification for introducing democracy in a nation that had not yet acquired it? The question is somewhat more complex than one might be led to think from what I have said so far, since the quality of the decisions is not the only consideration that is relevant for the choice of a political system. The argument from *justice* could also be decisive. Yet the following conclusion seems inescapable: if the system has no inherent advantage in terms of justice or efficiency, one cannot coherently and publicly advocate its introduction because of the side effects that would follow in its wake. There must be a *point* in democracy as such. If people are motivated by such inherent advantages to throw themselves into the system, other benefits may ensue—but the latter cannot by themselves be the motivating force. If the democratic method is introduced in a society solely because of the side effects on economic prosperity, and no one believes in it on any other ground, it will not produce them.

Tocqueville, however, did not argue that political activity is an end in itself. The justification for democracy is found in its effects, although not in the intended ones, as the strictly instrumental view would have it. More to the point is Tocqueville's argument for the jury system: "I do not know whether a jury is useful to the litigants, but I am sure that it is very good for those who have to decide the case. I regard it as one of the most effective means of popular education at society's disposal."[54] This is still an instrumental view, but the gap between the means and the end is smaller. Tocqueville never argued that the effect of democracy was to make politicians prosperous, only that it was conducive to general prosperity. By contrast, the justification of the jury system is found in the effect on the jurors themselves. And, as above, that effect would be spoilt if they believed that the impact on their own civic spirit was the main point of the proceedings.

John Stuart Mill not only applauded but advocated democracy on the ground of such educative effects on the participants. In current discussion he stands out both as an opponent of the purely instrumental view of politics, that of his father James Mill,[55] and as a forerunner of the theory of participatory democracy.[56] In his theory the gap between means and ends in politics is even narrower, since he saw political activity not only as a means to self-improvement, but also as a source of satisfaction and thus a good in itself. As noted by Albert Hirschman, this implies that "the benefit of collective action for an individual is not the difference between the hoped-for result and the effort furnished by him or her, but the *sum* of these two magnitudes."[57] Yet this very way of paraphrasing Mill's view also points to a difficulty. Could it really be the case that participation would yield a benefit even when the hoped-for results are nil, as suggested by Hirschman's formula? Is it not rather true that the effort is itself a function of the hoped-for result, so that in the end the latter is the only independent variable? When Mill refers, critically, to the limitations of Bentham, whose philosophy "can teach the means of organising and regulating the merely *business* part of the social arrangement,"[58] he seems to be putting the cart before the horse. The non-business part of politics may be the more valuable, but the value is contingent on the importance of the business part.

For a fully developed version of the non-instrumental theory of politics, we may go to the work of Hannah Arendt. Writing about the distinction between the private and the public realm in ancient Greece, she argues that:

> Without mastering the necessities of life in the household, neither life nor the "good life" is possible, but politics is never for the sake of life. As far as the members of the *polis* are concerned, household life exists for the sake of the "good life" in the *polis*.[59]
>
> The public realm . . . was reserved for individuality; it was the only place where men could show who they really and inexchangeably were. It was for the sake of this chance, and out of love for a body politic that it made it possible to them all, that each was more or less willing to share in the burden of jurisdiction, defence and administration of public affairs.[60]

Against this we may set the view of Greek politics found in the work of M. I. Finley. Asking why the Athenian people claimed the right of every citizen to speak and make proposals in the Assembly, yet left its exercise to a few, he finds that "one part of the answer is that the *demos* recognised the instrumental role of political rights and were more concerned in the end with the substantive decisions, were content with their power to select, dismiss and punish their political leaders."[61] Elsewhere he writes, even more explicitly: "Then, as now, politics was instrumental for most people, not an interest or an end in itself."[62] Contrary to what Arendt suggests, the possession or the possibility of exercising a political right may be more important than the actual exercise. Moreover, even the exercise derives its value from the decisions to be taken. Writing about the American town assemblies, Arendt argues that the citizens participated "neither exclusively because of duty nor, and even less, to serve their own interests but most of all because they enjoyed the discussions, the deliberations, and the making of decisions."[63] This, while not putting the cart before the horse, at least places them alongside each other. Although discussion and deliberation in other contexts may be independent sources of enjoyment, the satisfaction one derives from *political* discussion is parasitic on decision-making. Political debate is about what to do—not about what ought to be the case. It is defined by this practical purpose, not by its subject-matter.

Politics in this respect is on a par with other activities such as art, science, athletics or chess. To engage in them may be deeply satisfactory, if you have an independently defined goal such as "getting it right" or "beating the opposition." A chess player who asserted that he played not to win, but for the sheer elegance of the game, would be in narcissistic bad faith—since there is no such thing as an elegant way of losing, only elegant and inelegant ways of winning. When the artist comes to believe that the process and not the end result is his real purpose, and that defects and irregularities are valuable as reminders of the struggle of creation, he similarly forfeits any claim to our interest. The same holds for E. P. Thompson, who, when asked whether he really believed that a certain rally in Trafalgar Square would have any impact at all, answered: 'That's not really the point, is it? The point is, it shows that democracy's alive . . . A rally like that gives us self-respect. Chartism was terribly good for the Chartists, although they never got the Charter."[64] Surely, the Chartists, if asked whether they thought they would ever get the Charter, would not have answered: "That's not really the point, is it?" It was because they believed they might get the Charter that they engaged in the struggle for it with the seriousness of purpose that also brought them self- respect as a side effect.[65]

IV

I have been discussing three views concerning the relation between economics and politics, between the market and the forum. One extreme is "the economic theory of democracy," most outrageously stated by Schumpeter, but in essence also underlying social choice theory. It is a market theory of politics, in the sense that the act of voting is a private act similar to that of buying and selling. I cannot accept, therefore, Alan Ryan's argument that "On any possible view of the distinction between private and public life, voting is an element in one's public life."[66] The very distinction between the secret and the open ballot shows that there is room for a private-public distinction within politics. The economic theory of democracy, therefore, rests on the idea that the forum should be like the market, in its purpose as well as in its mode of functioning. The purpose is defined in economic terms, and the mode of functioning is that of aggregating individual decisions.

At the other extreme there is the view that the forum should be completely divorced from the market, in purpose as well as in institutional arrangement. The forum should be more than the distributive totality of individuals queuing up for the election booth. Citizenship is a quality that can only be realized in public, i.e., in a collective joined for a common purpose. This purpose, moreover, is not to facilitate life in the material sense. The political process is an end in itself, a good or even the supreme good for those who participate in it. It may be applauded because of the educative effects on the participants, but the benefits do not cease once the education has been completed. On the contrary, the education of the citizen leads to a preference for public life as an end in itself. Politics on this view is not *about* anything. It is the agonistic display of excellence,[67] or the collective display of solidarity, divorced from decision-making and the exercise" of influence on events.

In between these extremes is the view I find most attractive. One can argue that the forum should differ from the market in its mode of functioning, yet be concerned with decisions that ultimately deal with economic matters. Even higher-order political decisions concern lower-level rules that are directly related to economic matters. Hence constitutional arguments about how laws can be made and changed, constantly invoke the impact of legal stability and change on economic affairs. It is the concern with substantive decisions that lends the urgency to political debates. The ever-present constraint of *time* creates a need for focus and concentration that cannot be assimilated to the leisurely style of philosophical argument in which it may be better to travel hopefully than to arrive. Yet within these constraints arguments form the core of the political process. If thus defined as public in nature, and instrumental in purpose, politics assumes what I believe to be its proper place in society.

References

Ainslie, G. (1982) "A behavioral economic approach to the defense mechanisms," *Social Science Information* 21, 735–80.

Arendt, H. (1958) *The Human Condition*, Chicago: University of Chicago Press.

Arendt, H. (1973) *On Revolution*, Harmondsworth: Pelican Books.

Arrow, K. (1963) *Social Choice and Individual Values*, New York: Wiley.

Arrow, K. (1973) "Some ordinal-utilitarian notes on Rawls's theory of justice," *Journal of Philosophy* 70, 245–63.

Asch, S. (1956) "Studies of independence and conformity: I. A minority of one against a unanimous majority," *Psychology Monographs* 70.

Barry, B. (1978) "Comment," in S. Benn *et al.* (eds.), *Political Participation*, Canberra: Australian National University Press, pp. 37–48.

Berlin, I. (1969) *Two Concepts of Liberty*, Oxford: Oxford University Press.

d'Aspremont, C. and Gevers, L. (1977) "Equity and the informational basis of collective choice," *Review of Economic Studies* 44, 199–210.

Downs, A. (1957) *An Economic Theory of Democracy*, New York: Harper.

Elster, J. (1978) *Logic and Society*, Chichester: Wiley.

Elster, J. (1979) *Ulysses and the Sirens*, Cambridge: Cambridge University Press.

Elster, J. (1983a) *Explaining Technical Change*, Cambridge: Cambridge University Press; Oslo: Universitetsforlaget.

Elster, J. (1983b) *Sour Grapes*, Cambridge: Cambridge University Press.

Finley, M. I. (1973) *Democracy: Ancient and Modern*, London: Chatto and Windus.

Finley, M. I. (1976) "The freedom of the citizen in the Greek world," reprinted as Ch.5 in M. I. Finley, *Economy and Society in Ancient Greece*, London: Chatto and Windus 1981.

Finley, M. I. (1981) "Politics," in M. I. Finley (ed.), *The Legacy of Greece*, Oxford: Oxford University Press, pp. 22—36.

Føllesdal, D. and Hilpinen, R. (1971) "Deontic logic: an introduction," in R. Hilpinen (ed.), *Deontic Logic: Introductory and Systematic Readings*, Dordrecht: Reidel, pp. 1–35.

Goldman, A. (1972) "Toward a theory of social power," *Philosophical Studies* 23, 221–68.

Haavelmo, T. (1970) "Some observations on welfare and economic growth," in W. A. Eltis, M. Scott and N. Wolfe (eds.), *Induction, Growth and Trade: Essays in Honour of Sir Roy Harrod*, Oxford: Oxford University Press, pp. 65–75.

Habermas, J. (1982) Diskursethik—notizen zu einem Begründingsprogram. Mimeographed.

Hammond, P. (1976) "Why ethical measures need interpersonal comparisons," *Theory and Decision* 7, 263–74.

Hansson, B. (1970) "An analysis of some deontic logics," *Nous* 3, 373–98.

Hirsch, F. (1976) *Social Limits to Growth*, Cambridge, Mass.: Harvard University Press.

Hirschman, A. (1982) *Shifting Involvements*, Princeton: Princeton University Press.

Hogarth, R. M. (1977) "Methods for aggregating opinions," in H. Jungermann and G. de Zeeuw (eds.), *Decision Making and Change in Human Affairs*, Dordrecht: Reidel, pp. 231–56.

Janis, I. (1972) *Victims of Group-Think*, Boston: Houghton Mifflin.

Kant, I. (1795) *Perpetual Peace*, in H. Reiss (ed.), *Kant's Political Writings*, Cambridge: Cambridge University Press.

Kelly, J. (1978) *Arrow Impossibility Theorems*, New York: Academic Press.

Koim, S.-C. (1977) *La transition socialiste*, Paris: Editions du Cerf.

Koim, S.-C. (1981a) "Altruismes et efficacités," *Social Science Information* 20, 293–354.

Koim, S.-C. (1981b) "Efficacité et altruisme," *Revue Economique* 32, 5–31.

Lehrer, K. (1978) "Consensus and comparison. A theory of social rationality," in C. A. Hooker, J. J. Leach and E. F. McClennen (eds.), *Foundations and Applications of Decision Theory*. Vol. 1: *Theoretical Foundations*, Dordrecht: Reidel, pp. 283–310.

Lipsey, R. G. and Lancaster, K. (1956–57) "The general theory of the second-best," *Review of Economic Studies* 24, 11–32.

Lively, J. (1975) *Democracy*. Oxford: Blackwell.

Lyons, D. (1965) *Forms and Limits of Utilitarianism*, Oxford, Oxford University Press.

Margalit, A. (1983) "Ideals and second bests," in S. Fox (ed.), *Philosophy for Education*, Jerusalem: Van Leer Foundation, pp. 77—90.

Midgaard, K. (1980) "On the significance of language and a richer concept of rationality," in L. Lewin and E. Vedung (eds.), *Politics as Rational Action*, Dordrecht: Reidel, pp. 83—97.

Mill, J. S. (1859) "Bentham," in J. S. Mill, *Utilitarianism*, London: Fontana Books (1962), pp. 78–125.

Niebuhr, R. (1932) *Moral Man and Immoral Society*, New York: Scribner's.

Parfit, D. (1981) "Prudence, morality and the prisoner's dilemma," *Proceedings of the British Academy*, Oxford: Oxford University Press.

Pateman, C. (1970) *Participation and Democratic Theory*, Cambridge: Cambridge University Press.

Pattanaik, P. (1978) *Strategy and Group Choice*, Amsterdam: North—Holland.

Rawls, J. (1971) *A Theory of Justice*, Cambridge, Mass.: Harvard University Press.

Riker, W. and Ordeshook, P. C. (1973) *An Introduction to Positive Political Theory*, Englewood Cliffs, N.J.: Prentice Hall.

Runciman, W. G. and Sen, A. (1965) "Games, justice and the general will," *Mind* 74, 554–62.

Ryan, A. (1972) "Two concepts of politics and democracy: James and John Stuart Mill," in M. Fleisher (ed.), *Machiavelli and the Nature of Political Thought*, London: Croom Helm, pp. 76–113.

Samuelson, P. (1950) "The evaluation of real national income," *Oxford Economic Papers* 2, 1–29.

Schelling, T. C. (1980) "The intimate contest for self-command," *The Public Interest* 60, 94–118.

Schotter, A. (1981) *The Economic Theory of Social Institutions*, Cambridge: Cambridge University Press.

Schumpeter, J. (1939) *Business Cycles*, New York: McGraw-Hill.

Schumpeter, J. (1961) *Capitalism, Socialism and Democracy*. London: Allen and Unwin.

Sen, A. K. (1970) *Collective Choice and Social Welfare*, San Francisco: Holden–Day.

Sen, A. K. (1976) "Liberty, unanimity and rights," *Economica* 43, 217–45.

Sen, A. K. (1979) "Utilitarianism and welfarism," *Journal of Philosophy* 76, 463–88.

Sobel, J. H. (1967) "'Everyone,' consequences and generalization arguments," *Inquiry* 10, 373–404.

Smullyan, R. (1980) *This Book Needs No Title*, Englewood Cliffs, N.J.: Prentice Hall.

Tocqueville, A. de (1969) *Democracy in America*, New York: Anchor Books.

Tversky, A. (1981) "Choice, preference and welfare: some psychological observations," paper presented at a colloquium on "Foundations of social choice theory," Ustaoset (Norway).

Williams, B. A. O. (1973) "A critique of utilitarianism," in J. J. C. Smart and B. A. O. Williams, *Utilitarianism: For and Against*, Cambridge: Cambridge University Press, pp. 77–150.

Veyne, P. (1976) *Le pain et le cirque*, Paris: Seuil.

Zeldin, T. (1973) *France 1848–1945*, Vol. 1, Oxford: Oxford University Press.

NOTES

1. Elster (1978, Ch. 5) refers to these two varieties of market failure as *suboptimality* and *counterfinality* respectively, linking them both to collective action.

2. This is a simplification. First, as argued in Samuelson (1950), there may be political constraints that prevent one from attaining the Pareto-efficient frontier. Secondly, the very existence of several points that are Pareto-superior to the *status quo*, yet involve differential benefits to the participants, may block the realization of any of them.

3. Hammond (1976) offers a useful analysis of the consequences of selfish preferences over income distributions, showing that "without interpersonal comparisons of some kind, any social preference ordering over the space of possible income distributions must be dictatorial."

4. Schumpeter (1961, p. 263): "the will of the people is the product and not the motive power of the political process." One should not, however, conclude (as does Lively 1975, p. 38) that Schumpeter thereby abandons the market analogy, since on his view (Schumpeter 1939, p. 73) consumer preferences are no less manipulable (with some qualifications stated in Elster 1983a, Ch. 5).

5. See in particular Downs (1957).

6. For fuller statements, see Arrow (1963), Sen (1970), and Kelly (1978), as well as the contribution of Aanund Hylland to the present volume.

7. Cf. d'Aspremont and Gevers (1977).

8. Riker and Ordeshook (1973, pp. 112–13).

9. Cf. the contributions of Donald Davidson and Allan Gibbard to the present volume.

10. Presumably, but not obviously, since the agent might have several preference orderings and rely on higher-order preferences to determine which of the first-order preferences to express, as suggested for instance by Sen (1976).

11. Pattanaik (1978) offers a survey of the known results. The only strategy-proof mechanisms for social choice turn out to be the dictatorial one (the dictator has no incentive to misrepresent his preferences) and the randomizing one of getting the probability that a given option will be chosen equal to the proportion of voters that have it as their first choice.

12. Tversky (1981).

13. Cf. Elster (1979, Ch. II) or Schelling (1980) for the idea of deliberately restricting one's feasible set to make certain undesirable behaviour impossible at a later time. The reason this does not work here is that the regret would not be eliminated.

14. Cf. for instance Williams (1973) or Sen (1979).

15. Cf. Elster (1983b, Ch. III) for a discussion of this notion.

16. Arrow (1973).

17. Hirsch (1976).

18. Haavelmo (1970) offers a model in which everybody may suffer a loss of welfare by trying to keep up with the neighbours.

19. One may take the achievements of others as a parameter and one's own as the control variable, or conversely try to manipulate the achievements of others so that they fall short of one's own. The first of these ways of realizing positional goods is clearly less objectionable than the second, but still less pure than the non-comparative desire for a certain standard of excellence.

20. Zeldin (1973, p. 134).

21. I rely mainly on Habermas (1982). I also thank Helge Høibraaten, Rune Slagstad, and Gunnar Skirbekk for having patiently explained to me various aspects of Habermas's work.

22. Midgaard (1980).

23. For Pascal's argument, cf. Elster (1979, Ch. II. 3).

24. As suggested by Runciman and Sen (1965).

25. Smullyan (1980, p. 56).

26. Sobel (1967).

27. Koim (1981a, b).

28. Janis (1972).
29. Cf. Hogarth (1977) and Lehrer (1978).
30. Niebuhr (1932, p. 11).
31. Arendt (1973, p. 174).
32. Finley (1973); see also Elster (1979, Ch. II. 8).
33. Asch (1956) is a classic study.
34. See Goldman (1972) for discussion and further references.
35. Berlin (1969, p. xxxviii); cf. also Elster (1983b, Ch. III.3).
36. Schotter (1981, pp. 26ff., pp. 43 ff.) has a good discussion of this predicament.
37. Margalit (1983).
38. Lipsey and Lancaster (1956–57, p. 12).
39. This is the point emphasized in Lyons (1965).
40. Cf. Hansson (1970) as well as Føllesdal and Hilpinen (1971) for discussions of "conditional obligations" within the framework of deontic logic. It does not appear, however, that the framework can easily accommodate the kind of dilemma I am concerned with here.
41. Cf. for instance Koim (1977) concerning the dangers of a piecemeal introduction of socialism—also mentioned by Margalit (1983) as an objection to Popper's strategy for piecemeal social engineering.
42. Cf. Ainslie (1982) and Elster (1979, Ch. II.9).
43. Indeed, Habermas (1982) is largely concerned with maxims for *action*, not with the evaluation of states of affairs.
44. Cf. Elster (1983b, Ch. III) for a discussion of the notion that some psychological or social states are essentially by-products of actions undertaken for some other purpose.
45. Kant (1795, p. 126).
46. Rawls (1971, p. 133).
47. Rawls (1971, pp. 177 ff., esp. p. 181).
48. Williams (1973, p. 123).
49. Parfit (1981, p. 554).
50. Williams (1973, p. 131); also Elster (1983b, Ch. II.3).
51. Tocqueville (1969, p. 229).
52. Tocqueville (1969, p. 224).
53. Tocqueville (1969, pp. 243–4).
54. Tocqueville (1969, p. 275).
55. Cf. Ryan (1972). His contrast between 'two concepts of democracy' corresponds in part to the distinction between the first and the second of the theories discussed here, in part to the distinction between the first and the third, as he does not clearly separate the public conception of politics from the non-instrumental one.
56. Pateman (1970, p. 29).
57. Hirschman (1982, p. 82).
58. Mill (1859, p. 105).
59. Arendt (1958, p. 37).
60. Arendt (1958, p. 41).
61. Finley (1976, p. 83).
62. Finley (1981, p. 31).
63. Arendt (1973, p. 119).
64. *Sunday Times*, 2 November 1980.
65. Cf. also Barry (1978, p. 47).
66. Ryan (1972, p. 105).
67. Veyne (1976) makes a brilliant statement of this non-instrumental attitude among the elite of the Ancient World.

NIKLAS LUHMANN

SOCIETAL COMPLEXITY AND PUBLIC OPINION (1981)

Niklas Luhmann (1927–1998) studied law in Freiburg and worked in public administration for ten years before receiving a scholarship to Harvard in 1962 and spending a year with the sociologist Talcott Parsons. In 1968, he was appointed professor of sociology at the newly established University of Bielefeld, where he taught until his retirement. Before his appointment, he was asked about his research projects. His reply was: "The theory of modern society. Duration 30 years; no costs." In 1997, just before his death, he published Die Gesellschaft der Gesellschaft, *a two-volume summary of his work as a social theorist. Around this work are clustered a series of investigations of different social systems (law, economy, science, politics), starting with a general outline of his version of systems theory (Social Systems [1984] 1995). Posthumously, a number of additional manuscripts have been published.*

Luhmann's key concept is "system." A system differentiates itself from its environment and constantly struggles to reduce complexity, both the complexity of the environment and its own complexity. Social systems are systems of communication and operate according to different dichotomous codes (pay/not pay, position/opposition, legal/illegal, true/false, healthy/unhealthy, etc.). Each system is self-regulating (or in Luhmann's term "autopoetic"; "self-creating"), with different systems providing environments for each other.

Around 1970, Luhmann engaged in a famous debate with Jürgen Habermas on the prospects and limits of systems theory (Gesellschaftstheorie oder Sozialtechnologie?). In 1992–1993, they both published works on modern law continuing their controversy. While Luhmann describes the legal order from an objectifying, system theoretical point of view, Habermas tries to reconstruct the "normative content" of modern law by means of his discourse theory.

In the following text, Luhmann applies systems theory to "public opinion" with the consequence that this concept loses its normative connotations. Luhmann understands "public opinion" as an ongoing process of communication that structures attention and selects issues. Its primary function is, like a mirror, to make possible the political system's self-observation. With an implicit address to Habermas, Luhmann stresses that this conceptualization forces us to give up "expectations of rationality" and "hopes for a revitalization of a civic-republican life."

I

Like so many political concepts the concept of public opinion stands under the spell of a long tradition. The distinctive character it still possesses today can be traced back to the eighteenth century. Previously it had long been part of political theory that the prince's fortress lies in the hearts of his people[1] and that he must heed the opinion of his subordinates.[2] And the list of the prince's virtues always reflected the people's expectations. Until the eighteenth century, however, the conceptual development of these ideas had been determined and obstructed by two different distinctions: by the old (not least of all legal) distinction of public and private and by the distinction of public and secret.[3] This obfuscated the status of the counter concept of "public." The private individual was presented as the *civis* of the *res publica*. But at the same time the essence of important things in nature and in the civil republic were also viewed as "secret." And more than two centuries of scholarly endeavor was needed to eliminate this semantics of the secret.

It was not until the eighteenth century that both distinctions were brought together and only then, in the last third of this century, did the modern concept of public opinion arise as the "secret" sovereign and as the invisible authority[4] of political society. Public opinion was stylized as a paradox, as the invisible power of the visible. And in this semantic form it became the culminating idea of the political system. For the first time the result of communication itself was taken as substantive,[5] and thereby became the medium of further communication. This fusing of two distinctions into one was purchased at the cost of a severe overloading of the concept which was accompanied with an equally strong idealized concept of the individual. For those who advocated this new idea, public opinion itself now assumed the task of censorship and exercised it objectively and impartially. While more conservative authors looked upon this impartiality with skepticism because it appeared to them one-sidedly directed towards critique and change.[6]

Equipped with this disputed semantics, one entered the world of the modern state, of the establishment of constitutions, and so of the distinction of state and society. Equipped with this semantics, and with strong words, one demanded a freedom of the press.[7] Complexity was never mentioned. And it was not until today that authors have come to the conclusion that the problem of complexity had already covertly guided the pens (or better: the presses) at that time.[8]

Actually this was not exactly the case. Otherwise one would never have been able to form a clear concept of public opinion as the opinions of individuals (at least of literate and thereby enlightened individuals). Otherwise one would not have been able very well to attribute to public opinion the function of a kind of arbiter in the political domain. And, above all, one would not have been able to expect that a consensus of public opinion—measured by what actual persons actually think—could ever arise. Talk of "public opinion" causes a misunderstanding of the problem of complexity within the concept. If one raises the empirical question, which concrete states and operations of which psychical and social systems are the source of this opinion, the concept in its conventional understanding dissolves. This does not have to mean that it must be abandoned. But it needs a reconstruction starting from a radical beginning. Only in this way can one validate the empirical reference and claims of precision of contemporary social sciences. And only in this way can one extract political implications from the concept that are explainable only through its history and which today cannot be employed scientifically or politically.

II

I will try to perform such a reconstruction in several steps—not least of all in order to make clear that at each step other options would lead to different results.

(1) The concept of public opinion refers to the social system of society. It does not refer to what actually occurs in the consciousness(es) of individual/many/all persons at a particular point in time.[9] Thus what is meant is not what actual persons actually think, what they perceive, what attracts their attention or what they can remember. If this is what was meant, it would amount to an indescribable chaos of simultaneous difference, if and the impossibility of any co-ordination; for no

other reason than for the simultaneity of experience. Therefore the restriction to the system-reference of society (instead of psychical systems) appears to be unavoidable if one wishes to save anything of the tradition of the concept.

Accordingly, public opinion is a matter of a communication network that does not force participation—in distinction to many other forms of private knowledge (for example, in the career area or wherever "education" *[Bildung]* makes a difference). Whether one reads, watches TV or listens to the radio or not, whatever one chooses remains at one's discretion without having this intrude on the ideas about public opinion. One need not be astonished then that the effects of public communication apparently perversely—can be observed as a loss of orientation for individuals.[10]

This only increases the problem of creating attention for anyone who wants to work in the medium of public opinion.[11] Attention is the psychical version of the "loose coupling" of public opinion. And without attention public communication cannot continue. Nevertheless, the assumptions about attracting attention follow social, not psychical, laws. Otherwise than in the court politics of the baroque state, they do not presuppose a knowledge of human nature. And as far as psychically mediated effects are concerned, they may reveal themselves as unrealistic.

(2) In distinction to psychical systems, society is a social system that is constituted by communications and only communications. Of course, communication comes about only through a continual coupling with conscious (psychical) systems.[12] But the continual reproduction of communication through communication (autopoiesis) is specified and conditioned in its own network, regardless of what occurs in the minds of the psychical systems.

(3) Therefore communication cannot be understood as a "transference" of information, reports or elements of meaning from one side to another. Early information theory's concept of information had already given up the metaphor of transference and essentially the distinction of sender and receiver when it defined information as a selection from a repertoire common to both sides.[13] Thus an indispensable component of information already had to be present on the side that was to receive information. And so communication can only be understood as the dissemination of information within a system—as a dissemination that uses information to lead to information and in this way changes information as well as the state of the medium in which the information creates forms. Communication is the creation of an emergent reality, namely of society, that, for its part, resides in the continual reproduction of communication by communication. This may be the source of binding effects on individual conscious systems[14] just as much as the source of fleeting or permanent irritations, dissociations and distrustful rejections, too. Whatever a consciousness initiates through its own communicative experiences remains its own business and leads to an indescribable multiplicity of forms. The emergence of an auto-dynamically reproduced communicative network merely offers the opportunity to have such experiences again and again. It does not determine them.

The socio-phenomenological perspective already emphasized this independence of the "social construction of reality."[15] But viewed methodologically as well as theoretically, this version still always presupposes a "subject" to which something appears as a "phenomenon." The question of which this subject is forces the postulation of the "person" (in the singular). But there is no empirical reference for this.

The result is a description of the phenomena without stating anything about their subject.[16] It is perhaps better, then, to go over to a theory of self-descriptive systems.

(4) If we start from these premises, public opinion can be understood as a *medium* in which forms are created and again dissolved through continual communication. Therefore, following Fritz Heider,[17] we will distinguish medium and form. Media reside in a loose coupling of elements that are present in overabundance, while forms reside in the selection of such elements for a strict coupling. Forms can stamp a medium. And they assert themselves because of the underdeterminacy of the relations that are possible for the medium. Even the sounds and optical signs available to oral and written linguistic usage are forms in an underlying perceptual medium. And meaningful propositions are forms in the medium of language. If we assume all this the idea of "public opinion" presupposes that conscious states are the medium that can be coupled to specific forms of meaning. This concept of medium, i.e., the medium/form distinction, is presupposed when we no longer view communication as the transfer of information but as the processing of information in a medium through which forms are created and again dissolved; through which the state of the medium is continually changed.[18]

Of course, this is and remains a fiction cloaking the real conditions. In reality, conscious systems are structurally determined systems. They are what they are and do what they do. Therefore one can only speak of loose coupling because they are coupled only loosely to one another.[19] Thus only in the case of the social system of society is there a public opinion that exists as a medium to establish strict couplings. In this case there is nothing that speaks for the possibility of attaining actual agreements. But there is a public communication that rests on this fiction and that also keeps it going. In other words, this particular kind of communication sees the opportunity of giving public opinion ever new forms. And it finds in this opportunity the law of its own autopoiesis. On the basis of the factual self-referential closure and uncoordinatability of conscious systems, it can imagine a medium that resides in this loose coupling of enormous amounts of elements. And thereupon—without any insight into the internal states of the conscious systems—it can assume that the forms that are treated as the opinions of public opinion actually bind this medium. Whatever is contained in the unity of the concept of "public opinion" is thus medium and form at the same time.

This radically changed theory design has far-reaching consequences of which only two are to be mentioned here:

(5) In relation to the tradition, this concept of public opinion renounces any implications of rationality as well as any manifestation of the specific irrationalities of "mass psychology." Adequately rigid forms factually assert themselves in their specific medium, as for example perceptible things in the medium of air and light, prices in the medium of money, calculations in the medium of quantity. This is neither rational nor irrational. It happens by dint of the difference of loose and strict coupling. This is what is responsible for the "manipulability"[20] bound to a specific capacity. Judgments of rationality, however, are always judgments of an observer. And if one wants to know what one holds for rational or irrational, one must know one's criteria, one must observe the observer.

(6) The matter stands differently with the concept of medium in relation to the usual talk of so-called "mass media." The medium is public opinion itself. The press

and broadcasting give form to this medium. They "transfer" nothing. They stamp the medium that is tailored to and arises with them. And they owe their effectiveness to a long learning process in dealing with this medium.[21] But this effectiveness cannot be measured by what people actually think. It lies solely in the capacity to couple and uncouple the medium and to use this to keep communication of a specific type going.

III

Public opinion is not presented and fixed by the press and broadcasting in just any forms whatsoever. Instead, specific forms of forming come into play. Thus the production of form itself is subject to restrictions that for their part rest on the fact that individual consciousness remains inaccessible. Forms always rest on distinctions. Therefore one must look for underlying distinctions with which themes can be created as forms of public opinion. Of course, this is always a matter of contents: of names, places and events. But notwithstanding this, one can also distinguish more general form-producing forms with which the continual coupling and uncoupling, the continual binding and renewal of public opinion works. These are distinctions of time, quantity, and in the social dimension, distinctions of positions of conflict.

It is known only too well that the press and broadcasting always have something new to report. They live off of discontinuity, off the events of the day; but also off of reports that underline the innovative value of opinions, fashions and misfortune. This contrasts them with the great deal of repetition that characterizes the lives of most persons. Participation in this innovative value is, thus, for the individual an opportunity to escape the routine of daily life with a glance through the window— even and precisely because one can always depend on the fact that the newspaper will be delivered every day at the same time and that broadcasted news will always be on the air every day at the same time. (It is no accident then that the metaphor of the window was also a popular metaphor of romanticism, of the first cultural style completely organized by writing and printing.) Thus the rhythm of life and that of reports is a matter of an organized difference that rests on the fact that an integration is impossible—which does not deny the fact that events trigger actions; that indeed like Chernobyl, they can create a downright disoriented (because extraordinary) pressure to act. Entire routines of creating reports live off of this difference. If nothing (unusual) happens on Sunday, then there is sports. The traffic accidents of the day are taped in order to be presented later. Events of central importance like elections and summit conferences are preceded and followed by analyses. In this way time becomes reflexive while the news resides in the fact that one can report that one does not yet know in what this news resides. Thus in Europe we have the cleverly chosen shibboleth of "1992." And there is the similar argument of addressing a topic too late.[22]

As a result of this temporal structure of public opinion one cannot freeze its topics in. There can be topic areas (sports, stock market reports) in which new events occur routinely and which consequently gain a fixed place in reporting.[23] But the topics themselves acquire a history and go through a career starting from their discovery, introduction, high points through a phase of familiarity finally ending in redundancy. One can see this in the case of AIDS or de-forestation. Many topics enjoy a good chance of reactualization (terror, drugs) and result from a series of spectacular events. Others, above all reform subjects, cannot hold their own on the daily agenda. From time to time one must invent new names and points of attack in order to make them a subject of discussion. On the whole this presents a jumbled picture that, nonetheless, can be reduced to a unified principle: to the necessity of discontinuity, movement, temporal rhythmization. And consequently it belongs to political savvy to know in which phase in the career of topics one takes them up, uses them to promote oneself, profits from being on their bandwagon or, better, from jumping off the bandwagon.[24]

All of this is well known. It is the subject of managerial staff planning and needs no further comment. A second form-creating form, however, works almost unbeknownst. Or in any event it has not yet attracted the same amount of attention. I mean the form of quantity. It makes a contribution to the ordering of the dimension of public communication. Like the temporal distinction of before/after, it is a form of difference, a two-sided form of more or less. And like time, quantity possesses a clarity that rests on the fact that there are only these two sides. One cannot supplement the binary form with further aspects; e.g. before/after/better or more/less/more useful. Valorizations have to be introduced in a way that cuts across these forms, i.e., they have to have their foundations outside them.

Daily life has little to do with exactly determined quantities and with how to handle them. Husserl had already expressed the suspicion that idealized Galilean-Cartesian mathematics does not correspond to the concrete needs of the "life-world."[25] But only today has research begun to investigate the abstract distance of mathematics from the needs of the life-world and to try to ascertain the relevance of dealing with quantities in daily life and which forms of calculation actually come into play.[26] In any event one result of quantification is an explosive increase in the need for action and decision. It uncovers distinctions that otherwise would not have been noticed. Prices and their use in the motivation of consumers are a spectacular example of this. Educational reform movements would not have been able to get started without quantitative comparisons. And the same is true of the feminist movement. The data that guide economic policy are aggregate quantities and, I should like to say, completely different data from those in which businesses are interested. This again is the basis for the economic sciences and justifies their mathematization as a research strategy. And precisely because one cannot determine from a mere number whether it is good or bad, favorable or unfavorable, quantitative data are suitable for application to topics and interests. In this regard they do not attract suspicion.

Differences of time and quantity can easily be combined. The most recent statistics, increases and calculations demonstrate that specific values, market rates and quotas have gone up or down. To the extent that this becomes a topic of public opinion, an occasion for comment, if not an intervening action, arises. Quantities are thereby treated like facts. But this, of course, happens only if and to the extent that they bind the medium of public opinion and thereby direct the autopoiesis of public communication in one direction or the other. The medium/form-complex of public opinion forms an independent, self-moving, differentiated reality. It uses specific forms to produce forms, and it needs structural coupling with available attention, i.e., readers, listeners, watchers to do this. But it does not need any states of these systems themselves for this. It is not carried by conscious systems, it carries itself.

We are back on more familiar territory when we clarify the preference of public opinion for presenting conflicts. There is a form-producing form not only for the temporal and material dimensions but also for the social dimension. And it too is an explicitly two-sided form. A topic is presented as a conflict if one can show who occupies the position "for" and who the position "against." And it is understood that there are also undecided and middle positions. But these depend on the form of conflict and could not appear if there was no conflict to begin with. Conflict, too, is reflected in itself as something that should be brought closer to a "solution." And this is also where the paradox of public opinion, the invisible visible, finds its proper expression: conflicts in public opinion count as undesirable—and for this reason are preferably reproduced.

If one begins from the fact that two-sided-forms fascinate and bind the medium of public opinion in this way, then this has far-reaching consequences. The most urgent question is then: how is the unity of society observed and described if it must appear in this medium—if it must appear as permanence despite change, as a metaquantitative (qualitative?) unity and as a solidarity that relativizes all conflicts? The forms of forms determine what is and what is not seen, what is said and what cannot be said. Beginning from temporal discontinuity, from a quantity that is all too abstract and from social conflicts, society appears only negatively—as what is not grasped by the most fascinating forms, as the totality of what cannot be seen, as "puissance invisible." And perhaps this explains why we who are conditioned by this state of affairs are condemned to search for meaning.

Furthermore, the proposed theory leads to a better understanding of the meaning of time. It totally rejects the belief that what is permanent is better than what is passing or seeks the rationality of opinions in their justification in permanent forms—as if these were permanent rational grounds or eternal values. Instead, it draws attention to the meaning of temporality for the difference of medium and form. If one were to abstract from time, then the assertion of the unity of loose coupling (medium) and strict coupling (form) would be a flat contradiction. The unity of public opinion and its topics would remain incomprehensible. This unity arises only in time, only out of the fact that the success of bindings has to be purchased at the cost of their dissolvability. Accordingly, forms are more successful but, also for this reason, not as permanent as the medium itself. Or in other words, the medium regenerates itself through the continual coupling and uncoupling of the forms that are possible within it. Just like language, through the constant formation of sentences that are soon forgotten or lose their informative value. Thus the unity of medium and form (the unity of this distinction) presupposes a memory that organizes the reuse of forms, i.e., that can remember and forget selectively.

IV

Far more than other function systems, the political system depends on public opinion. For politics, public opinion is one of the most important sensors whose observation takes the place of direct observation of the environment. Topics of public opinion, reports and commentaries in the press and broadcasting possess an obvious relevance for politics which at the same time conceals with its obviousness what actually is the case. It simply has to appear in the papers.

By fulfilling the function of concealing obviousness, public opinion plays the same role as tradition in earlier societies: to offer something to which one can adhere in a way that saves one from reproach. But while tradition included a semantics of a handed-down secret, the concealing function of public opinion remained unmentioned. It itself becomes "secret." This is offset by the rapid change of topics and an openness to what is new.

One can clarify this orientation with the help of the metaphor of the mirror.[27] In this case we no longer have a mirror of virtues in which the prince can recognize his better self but the possibility of observing how the observer himself *and others* are depicted by public opinion. In any event one does not see oneself in the mirror but only the countenance that one composes for the mirror and shows to it. But this is not all. In addition, by looking over one's own shoulder, one sees others who also act before the mirror: other persons, groups, political and versions of the same topic.

Whatever one sees is only a section that is determined by one's own position and movement. The effect rests completely on the intransparency of the mirror, i.e., on an uncoupling from everything that actually occurs in the minds of actual persons at the time in which one looks into the mirror. The differentiation of the medium/form complex of public opinion and the concealment of the true complexity of a great amount of conscious processes make it possible for politics to orient itself according to public opinion.

On one hand, this means that politics can only glimpse itself in the mirror of public opinion, embedded in the artificially chosen context of its own possibilities of movement. On the other, however, the mirror also reflects back to the observer less and at the same time more than merely himself. He also sees his competitors, intrigues and possibilities that are attractive only to others, not to him. Thus the mirror of public opinion, just like the system of market prices,[28] makes possible an *observation of observers*. As a social system the political system, accordingly, uses public opinion to make itself capable of *observing itself* and developing corresponding expectational structures. Public opinion does not serve to produce external contacts. It serves the self-referential closure of the political system, the return of politics upon itself. But self-referential closure is brought about with the help of an institution that permits the system to distinguish self-reference and other-reference, i.e., politics and public opinion, in the performance of its own operations and with it to construct a picture of the boundaries of its own possibilities of action.

In the context of a theory of the political system this transformation of the concept of public opinion has far-reaching significance. First of all, it forces the surely painful renunciation of expectations of rationality and hopes of a revitalization of civil republican "life."[29] On the other hand, it clearly indicates that the political system of modern society cannot be understood in terms of a central authority whose suitability (virtus) or unsuitability can be observed by the people. The place of the central authority is taken by the observation of observers, i.e., the self-referential closure of the system. To this corresponds the fact that the political code no longer rests merely on the distinction of those who have power and those who do not (government/governed) but on the side of power is coded with the help of the schema of government/opposition. This is the nucleus to which the concept of democracy must be reduced. Then one will also begin to understand that and how in the eighteenth century the idea of political opposition could separate itself from the old court factionisms and the problem of political rivalry. And why it needed a recourse to the "puissance invisible" of public opinion.

Under such conditions the freedom of the press and opinion cannot be adequately determined as a guarantee of rationality nor as a condition of a free life of the mind. Its suppression surely works repressively and burdens many domains of societal communication including daily behavior towards strangers, instruction in schools and the courage to make intellectual or artistic innovations. To retain the metaphor (of the mirror), this concerns the front of the mirror. Its specific political function resides, however, in transferring the form of self-observation of the political system into the reflexive mode of the observing of observers. For only when public opinion offers more than merely a centralized echo of political activity can a political system develop that maintains itself not only as a successfully effected identity but also attains closure at the level of the observation of observers.

NOTES

1. In Niccolò Machiavelli, e.g. *Discorsi sopra la prima deca di Tito Livio* II, cap. 24, and *Principe* cap. 20, quoted from *Opere*, 7th ed., Milan 1976, pp. 288 and 110. This has, in time, become a standard quotation.

2. See, e.g. Giovanni Botero, *Della Ragion di Stato*, 1589, quoted from the Bologna edition of 1930, pp. 78ff. (Here on p.138 there is also a kind of two-step flow theory: the prince must first win over the religious, *literati* and *virtuosi* and then with their help the remainder of the population.) Giovanni Antonio Palazzo, *Discorso del Governo e della Ragion vera di Stato*, Venice 1606, pp. 85 ff. with the requirement: to grant the freedom of speech in the republic (p. 86).

3. For the history of the concept see Lucian Hölscher, *Öffentlichkeit und Geheimnis: Eine begriffsgeschichtliche Untersuchung zur Entstehung der Öffentlichkeit in der frühen Neuzeit*, Stuttgart 1979. But the material presented here already contradicts the thesis (p. 7) that the distinction of public/secret had been replaced in the eighteenth century by that of public/private.

4. Formulations of this kind that are typical for the time, e.g., Jacques Necker, "De l'administration des finances de la France," 1784, quoted from *Oeuvres complètes*, vols. 4 and 5, Paris 1821, reprint Aalen 1970, vol. 4, pp. 49ff.

5. See Hölscher, *op, cit.*, pp. 105 ff.

6. Cf., e.g. Ernst Brandes, *Über einige bisherige Folgen der französischen Revolution in Rücksicht auf Deutschland*, Hannover 1792, p. 58 f.: "The desire to say something new is very attractive. It is much easier to excel in attacks on constitutions, standards and persons than in their defense where, in all honesty, one almost always must concede weaknesses and imperfections . . . " p. 59.

7. Strong words under the motto "speak the truth among one another!" e.g. in Carl Theodor Welcker, *Die vollkommene und ganze Preßfreiheit nach ihrer sittlichen, rechtlichen und politischen Nothwendigkeit, nach ihrer Übereinstimmung mit deutschem Fürstenwort und nach völligen Zeitgemäßheit dargestellt in ehrerbietigster Petition an die hohe deutsche Bundesversammlung*, Freiburg 1830. For the same emphasis in another context cf., Johann Paul Anselm van Feuerbach, *Betrachtungen über die Öffentlichkeit und Mündigkeit der Gerechtigkeitspflege*, Gießen 1821.

8. As in Harlan Wilson, "Complexity as a Theoretical Problem: Wider Perspectives in Political Theory," in Todd R. La Porte (ed.), *Organized Social Complexity: Challenge to Politics and Policy*, Princeton 1975, pp. 281–331.

9. Normally one presupposes the opposite as self-evident even if one has rejected the old idealizations. "'Public opinion' in this discussion may simply be taken to mean those opinions held by private persons, which governments find it prudent to heed," is how it is presented in the, at that time, influential text of V. O. Key, *Public Opinion and American Democracy*, New York 1961, p. 14.

10. See Elisabeth Noelle-Neumann/Heinz Maier-Leibnitz, *Zweifel am Verstand: Das Irrationale als die neue Moral*, Zürich 1987.

11. For such rules of attention cf., Niklas Luhmann, "Öffentliche Meinung," in Luhmann, *Politische Planung*, Opladen 1971, pp. 9–34 (16f.).

12. Cf., Niklas Luhmann, "Wie ist Bewußtsein an Kommunikation beteiligt?" in Hans Ulrich Gumbrecht/Karl Ludwig Pfeiffer (eds.), *Materialität der Kommunikation*, Frankfurt 1988, pp. 884–905.

13. Cf., Klaus Kornwachs/Walter von Lucadou, "Komplexe Systeme," in Klaus Kornwachs (ed.), *Offenheit—Zeitlichkeit—Komplexität: Zur Theorie der Offenen Systeme*, Frankfurt 1984, pp. 110–165 (116ff.).

14. This is emphasized by Terry Winograd/Fernando Flores, *Understanding Computers and Cognition: A New Foundation for Design*, Reading, Mass. 1987, pp. 58 ff., 76 f. in connection with the theory of speech acts (Searle).

15. For application to research on mass media cf., Enric Saperas, *Los efectos cognitivos de la communicación de masas: Las recientes investigaciones en torno de la communicación de masas: 1970–1986*, Barcelona 1987, pp. 142 ff.

16. A typical representative of this position is Achille Ardigò, *Crisi di Governabilià e mondi vitali*, Bologna 1980.

17. See Fritz Heider, "Ding und Medium," in *Symposion*, vol. I (1926), pp. 109–157. Cf. also, Karl. E. Weick, *The Process of Organizing*, New York 1979, passim.

18. See also (with a surely different concept of medium) Kornwachs/von Lucadou, *op, cit.*, p. 120: "The dissemination of information is to be understood on the model of Huygen's principle; i.e., a physical carrier's property of being a channel is disseminated . . . Every step is then sender and receiver simultaneously. At the same time this process of dissemination is attributed the characteristic of changing the very medium that carries it."

19. This is, it should be reminded, unavoidable simply because they are active *simultaneously* and therefore cannot be co-ordinated causally or communicatively, something which co-ordination over longer sequences would presuppose.

20. "Public opinion has become so mighty a regulator of conduct, not because it has grown wiser, but because of the greater ease of ascertaining, focusing and directing it," believes Edward A. Ross, *Sin and Society: An Analysis of Latter-Day Iniquity*, Boston 1907, p. 25, in a, for all and intents and purposes, strenuous attempt to direct this public opinion himself.

21. Moreover, a learning process that set in during the first decades after the invention of printing, i.e., already in the fifteenth century, long before the invention of the concept of public opinion. A detailed investigation of this can be found in Michael Giesecke, *Der Buchdruck in der frühen Neuzeit: Eine historische Fallstudie über die Durchsetzung neuer Informations- und Kommunikationstechnologien*, Habilitationsschrift Bielefeld 1988.

22. Cf. for this, Paula B. Johnson/David O. Sears, "Black Invisibility, the Press and the Los Angeles Riot," in *American Journal of Sociology* vol. 76 (1971), pp. 698–721.

23. It is surely no accident that these are domains in which quantification must take place so that new at all can appear as new. We will come back to this presently.

24. These are old views of mass media research. For the resulting need for conclusive decisions (demand for closure), see e.g. Gordon W. Allport/Janet M. Faden, "The Psychology of

Newspapers: Five Tentative Laws," in *Public Opinion Quarterly*, vol. 4 (1940), pp. 687–703 (702 f.).

25. Cf. Edmund Husserl, *The Crisis of European Sciences and Transcendental Phenomenology*, Edward Carr (trans.), Evanston, Ill. 1966.

26. See Terezinha Nunes Carraher, David William Carraher, Analúcia Dias Schliemann, "Mathematics in the Streets and Schools," in *British Journal of Developmental Psychology*, vol. 3 (1985), pp. 21–29; Terezinha Carraher, Analúcia D. Schliemann, David W. Carraher, "Mathematical Concepts in Everyday Life," in G. B. Saxe/M. Gearhart (eds.), *Children's Mathematics*, San Francisco 1988, pp. 71–87; Jean Lave, "The Values of Quantification," in John Law (ed.), *Power, Action and Belief: A New Sociology of Knowledge*, London 1986, pp. 88–111.

27. The same metaphor is applied to the, for the observer, opaque market by Harrison C. White, "Where Do Markets Come From?" in *American Journal of Sociology*, vol. 87 (1981), pp. 517–547.

28. See for this Dirk Baecker, *Information und Risiko in der Marktwirtschaft*, Frankfurt 1988.

29. Today this is one of the many widely discussed vain hopes. Among others cf., John G. A. Pocock, *The Machiavellian Moment: Florentine Political Thought and the Atlantic Political Tradition*, Princeton 1975; Alasdair MacIntyre, *After Virtue: A Study in Moral Theory*, London 1981.

JÜRGEN HABERMAS

EXCERPT FROM *BETWEEN FACTS AND NORMS. CONTRIBUTIONS TO A DISCOURSE THEORY OF LAW AND DEMOCRACY* (1992)

The idea of a reasoning public introduced by Jürgen Habermas in The Structural Transformation of the Public Sphere *([1962] 1989) has been elaborated on in almost all
his subsequent works. Throughout his oeuvre, a recurring theme is how to justify a normative standard for a critical social theory. Habermas suggests that such a standard can
be derived from presuppositions inherent in communicative action, which he thinks of as
linguistic mediated interaction aiming at mutual understanding. In his major work* Theory
of Communicative Action *([1981] 1984/1987), he develops a comprehensive theory of
modernity by way of an interpretation of sociological classics, such as Weber, Durkheim,
Mead, and Parsons and the Western Marxist tradition from Lukács to Horkheimer and
Adorno. On Habermas' account, modernity is an ambiguous process of rationalization,
realizing the potentials of both instrumental and communicative reason. His idea of communicative action and rationality is internally related to democracy understood as free and
equal citizens' joint attempt to regulate their commons concerns. In* Between Facts and
Norms *([1992] 1996), he tries to bridge a normative theory of deliberative democracy
with empirical and "realistic" approaches to democracy, and to work out a new paradigm of
law and politics that transcends divergences between liberals and civic republicans. He also
revises and reactualizes his earlier theory of the public sphere, making it part of a theory
of constitutional democracy where public deliberation is seen as the basis for establishing
legitimate laws and political decisions.*

The excerpt from Between Facts and Norms *selected here focuses on how the public
sphere can identify and thematize social issues and furnish them with possible solutions in a
way that influences the process of political decision-making, and discusses the various conditions under which the public sphere can fulfill its democratic functions and "communicative power" be translated into "administrative power." The public sphere and the lifeworld
resources for public communication in civil society are portrayed as enabling conditions for
the political system, both legitimating lawmaking and promoting the possibility that political decisions can foster social integration.*

8.3 Civil Society, Public Opinion, and Communicative Power

Up to now, I have generally dealt with the public sphere as a communication
structure rooted in the lifeworld through the associational network of civil society.
I have described the political public sphere as a sounding board for problems that
must be processed by the political system because they cannot be solved elsewhere.
To this extent, the public sphere is a warning system with sensors that, though
unspecialized, are sensitive throughout society. From the perspective of democratic
theory, the public sphere must, in addition, amplify the pressure of problems, that
is, not only detect and identify problems but also convincingly and *influentially*
thematize them, furnish them with possible solutions, and dramatize them in such
a way that they are taken up and dealt with by parliamentary complexes. Besides
the "signal" function, there must be an effective problematization. The capacity of
the public sphere to solve problems *on its own* is limited. But this capacity must

be utilized to oversee the further treatment of problems that takes place inside the political system. I can provide only a broad estimate of the extent to which this is possible. I start by clarifying the contested concepts of the public sphere (sec. 8.3.1) and civil society (sec. 8.3.2). This allows me in sec. 8.3.3 to sketch some barriers and power structures inside the public sphere. These barriers, however, can be overcome in critical situations by escalating movements (sec. 8.3.4). I then summarize those elements the legal system must take into consideration when it forms its picture of a complex society like ours (sec. 8.3.5).

8.3.1

The public sphere is a social phenomenon just as elementary as action, actor, association, or collectivity, but it eludes the conventional sociological concepts of "social order." The public sphere cannot be conceived as an institution and certainly not as an organization. It is not even a framework of norms with differentiated competences and roles, membership regulations, and so on. Just as little does it represent a system; although it permits one to draw internal boundaries, outwardly it is characterized by open, permeable, and shifting horizons. The public sphere can best be described as a network for communicating information and points of view (i.e., opinions expressing affirmative or negative attitudes); the streams of communication are, in the process, filtered and synthesized in such a way that they coalesce into bundles of topically specified *public* opinions. Like the lifeworld as a whole, so, too, the public sphere is reproduced through communicative action, for which mastery of a natural language suffices; it is tailored to the *general comprehensibility* of everyday communicative practice. We have become acquainted with the "lifeworld" as a reservoir for simple interactions; specialized systems of action and knowledge that are differentiated within the lifeworld remain tied to these interactions. These systems fall into one of two categories. Systems like religion, education, and the family become associated with general reproductive functions of the lifeworld (that is, with cultural reproduction, social integration, or socialization). Systems like science, morality, and art take up different validity aspects of everyday communicative action (truth, rightness, or veracity). The public sphere, however, is specialized in neither of these two ways; to the extent that it extends to politically relevant questions, it leaves their specialized treatment to the political system. Rather, the public sphere distinguishes itself through a *communication structure* that is related to a third feature of communicative action: it refers neither to the *functions* nor to the *contents* of everyday communication but to the *social space* generated in communicative action.

Unlike success-oriented actors who mutually observe each other as one observes something in the objective world, persons acting communicatively encounter each other in a *situation* they at the same time constitute with their cooperatively negotiated interpretations. The intersubjectively shared space of a speech situation is disclosed when the participants enter into interpersonal relationships by taking positions on mutual speech-act offers and assuming illocutionary obligations. Every encounter in which actors do not just observe each other but take a second-person attitude, reciprocally attributing communicative freedom to each other, unfolds in a linguistically constituted public space. This space stands open, in principle, for potential dialogue partners who are present as bystanders or could come on the scene and join those present. That is, special measures would be required to prevent a third party from entering such a linguistically constituted space. Founded in communicative action, this spatial structure of simple and episodic encounters can be expanded and rendered more permanent in an abstract form for a larger public of present persons. For the public infrastructure of such *assemblies*, performances, presentations, and so on, architectural metaphors of structured spaces recommend themselves: we speak of forums, stages, arenas, and the like. These public spheres still cling to the concrete locales where an audience is physically gathered. The more they detach themselves from the public's physical presence and extend to the virtual presence of scattered readers, listeners, or viewers linked by public media, the clearer becomes the abstraction that enters when the spatial structure of simple interactions is expanded into a public sphere.

When generalized in this way, communication structures contract to informational content and points of view that are uncoupled from the thick contexts of simple interactions, from specific persons, and from practical obligations. At the same time, context generalization, inclusion, and growing anonymity demand a higher degree of explication that must dispense with technical vocabularies and special codes. Whereas the *orientation to laypersons* implies a certain loss in differentiation, uncoupling communicated opinions from concrete practical obligations tends to have an *intellectualizing* effect. Processes of opinion-formation, especially when they have to do with political questions, certainly cannot be separated from the transformation of the participants' preferences and attitudes, but they can be separated from putting these dispositions into action. To this extent, the communication structures of the public sphere *relieve* the public *of the burden of decision making;* the postponed decisions are reserved for the institutionalized political process. In the public sphere, utterances are sorted according to issue and contribution, whereas the contributions are weighted by the affirmative versus negative responses they receive. Information and arguments are thus worked into focused opinions. What makes such "bundled" opinions into *public opinion is* both the controversial way it comes about and the amount of approval that "carries" it. Public opinion is not representative in the statistical sense. It is not an aggregate of individually gathered, privately expressed opinions held by isolated persons. Hence it must not be confused with survey results. Political opinion polls provide a certain reflection of "public opinion" only if they have been preceded by a focused public debate and a corresponding opinion-formation in a mobilized public sphere.

The diffusion of information and points of view via effective broadcasting media is not the only thing that matters in public processes of communication, nor is it the most important. True, only the broad circulation of comprehensible, attention-grabbing messages arouses a sufficiently inclusive participation. But the rules of a *shared* practice of communication are of greater significance for structuring public opinion. Agreement on issues and contributions *develops* only as the result of more or less exhaustive controversy in which proposals, information, and reasons can be more or less rationally dealt with. In general terms, the *discursive level* of opinion-formation and the "quality" of the outcome vary with this "more or less" in the "rational" processing of "exhaustive" proposals, information, and reasons. Thus the success of public communication is not intrinsically measured by the requirement of inclusion either[1] but by the formal criteria governing how a qualified public opinion comes about. The structures of a power-ridden, oppressed public sphere exclude fruitful and clarifying discussions. The "quality" of public opinion, insofar as it is measured by the procedural properties of its process of generation, is an empirical variable. From a normative perspective, this provides a basis for measuring the legitimacy of the influence that public opinion has on the political system. Of course, actual influence coincides with legitimate influence just as little as the belief in legitimacy coincides with legitimacy. But conceiving things this way at least opens a perspective from which the relation between actual influence and the procedurally grounded quality of public opinion can be empirically investigated.

Parsons introduced "influence" as a symbolically generalized form of communication that facilitates interactions in virtue of conviction or persuasion.[2] For example, persons or institutions can enjoy a reputation that allows their utterences to have an influence on others' beliefs without having to demonstrate authority or to give explanations in the situation. "Influence" feeds on the resource of mutual understanding, but it is based on advancing trust in beliefs that are not currently tested. In this sense, public opinion represents political potentials that can be used for influencing the voting behavior of citizens or the will-formation in parliamentary bodies, administrative agencies, and courts. Naturally, political *influence* supported by public opinion is converted into political power—into a potential for rendering binding decisions—only when it affects the beliefs and decisions of *authorized* members of the political system and determines the behavior of voters, legislators, officials, and so forth. Just like social power, political influence based on public opinion can be transformed into political power only through institutionalized procedures.

Influence develops in the public sphere and becomes the object of struggle there. This struggle involves not only the political influence that has already been acquired (such as that enjoyed by experienced political leaders and officeholders, established parties, and well-known groups like Greenpeace and Amnesty International). The reputation of groups of persons and experts who have acquired their influence in special public spheres also comes into play (for example, the authority of religious leaders, the public visibility of literary figures and artists, the reputation of scientists, and the popularity of sports figures and movie stars). For as soon as the public space has expanded beyond the context of simple interactions, a differentiation sets in among organizers, speakers, and hearers; arenas and galleries; stage and viewing space. The *actors' roles* that increasingly professionalize and multiply with organizational complexity and range of media are, of course, furnished with unequal opportunities for exerting influence. But the political influence that the actors gain through public communication must *ultimately* rest on the resonance and indeed the approval of a lay public whose composition is egalitarian. The public of citizens must be *convinced* by comprehensible and broadly interesting contributions to issues it finds relevant. The public audience possesses final authority, because it is *constitutive* for the internal structure and reproduction of the public sphere, the *only* place where actors can appear. There can be no public sphere without a public.

To be sure, we must distinguish the actors who, so to speak, emerge from the public and take part in the reproduction of the public sphere itself from actors who occupy an already constituted public domain in order to use it. This is true, for example, of the large and well-organized interest groups that are anchored in various social subsystems and affect the political system *through* the public sphere. They cannot make any manifest use in the public sphere of the sanctions and rewards they rely on in bargaining or in nonpublic attempts at pressure. They can capitalize on their social power and convert it into political power only insofar as they can advertise their interests in a language that can mobilize convincing reasons and shared value orientations—as, for example, when parties to wage negotiations inform the public about demands, strategies, or outcomes. The contributions of interest groups are, in any case, vulnerable to a kind of criticism to which contributions from other sources are not exposed. Public opinions that can acquire visibility only because of an undeclared infusion of money or organizational power lose their credibility as soon as these sources of social power are made public. Public opinion can be manipulated but neither publicly bought nor publicly blackmailed. This is due to the fact that a public sphere cannot be "manufactured" as one pleases. Before it can be captured by actors with strategic intent, the public sphere together with its public must have developed as a structure that stands on its own and reproduces itself *out of itself*. This lawlike regularity governing the formation of a public sphere remains latent in the constituted public sphere—and takes effect again only in moments when the public sphere is mobilized.

The political public sphere can fulfill its function of perceiving and thematizing encompassing social problems only insofar as it develops out of the communication taking place among *those who are potentially affected*. It is carried by a public recruited from the entire citizenry. But in the diverse voices of this public, one hears the echo of private experiences that are caused throughout society by the externalities (and internal disturbances) of various functional systems—and even by the very state apparatus on whose regulatory activities the complex and poorly coordinated subsystems depend. Systemic deficiencies are experienced in the context of individual life histories; such burdens accumulate in the lifeworld. The latter has the appropriate antennae, for in its horizon are intermeshed the private life histories of the "clients" of functional systems that might be failing in their delivery of services. It is only for those who are immediately affected that such services are paid in the currency of "use values." Besides religion, art, and literature, only the spheres of "private" life have an existential language at their disposal, in which such socially generated problems can be *assessed in terms of one's own life history*. Problems voiced in the public sphere first become visible when they are mirrored in personal life experiences. To the extent that these experiences find their concise expression in the languages of religion, art, and literature, the "literary" public sphere in the broader sense, which is specialized for the articulation of values and world disclosure, is intertwined with the political public sphere.[3]

As both bearers of the political public sphere and as *members of society*, citizens occupy two positions at once. As members of society, they occupy the roles of employees and consumers, insured persons and patients, taxpayers and clients of bureaucracies, as well as the roles of students, tourists, commuters, and the like; in such complementary roles, they are especially exposed to the specific requirements and failures of the corresponding service systems. Such experiences are first assimilated "privately," that is, are interpreted within the horizon of a life history intermeshed with other life histories in the contexts of shared lifeworlds. The communication channels of the public sphere are linked to private spheres—to the thick networks of interaction found in families and circles of friends as well as to the looser contacts with neighbors, work colleagues, acquaintances, and so on—and indeed they are linked in such a way that the spatial structures of simple interactions are expanded and abstracted but not destroyed. Thus the orientation to reaching understanding that is predominant in everyday practice is also preserved for a *communication among strangers* that is conducted over great distances in public spheres whose branches are quite complex. The threshold separating the private sphere from the public is not marked by a fixed set of issues or relationships but by *different conditions of communication*. Certainly these conditions lead to differences in the accessibility of the two spheres, safeguarding the intimacy of the one sphere and the publicity of the other. However, they do not seal off the private from the public but only chan- nel the flow of topics from the one sphere into the other. For the public sphere draws its impulses from the private handling of social problems that resonate in life histories. It is symptomatic of this close connection, incidentally, that a modern bourgeois public sphere developed in the European societies of the seventeenth and eighteenth centuries as the "sphere of private persons come together as a public." Viewed historically, the connection between the public and the private spheres is manifested in the clubs and organizational forms of a reading public composed of bourgeois private persons and crystallizing around newspapers and journals.[4]

8.3.2

This sphere of civil society has been rediscovered today in wholly new historical constellations. The expression "civil society" has in the meantime taken on a mean- ing different from that of the "bourgeois society" of the liberal tradition, which Hegel conceptualized as a "system of needs," that is, as a market system involv- ing social labor and commodity exchange. What is meant by "civil society" today, in contrast to its usage in the Marxist tradition, no longer includes the economy as constituted by private law and steered through markets in labor, capital, and commodities. Rather, its institutional core comprises those nongovernmental and noneconomic connections and voluntary associations that anchor the communica- tion structures of the public sphere in the society component of the lifeworld. Civil society is composed of those more or less spontaneously emergent associations, organizations, and movements that, attuned to how societal problems resonate in the private life spheres, distill and transmit such reactions in amplified form to the public sphere. The core of civil society comprises a network of associations that institutionalizes problem solving discourses on questions of general interest inside the framework of organized public spheres.[5] These "discursive designs" have an egalitarian, open form of organization that mirrors essential features of the kind of communication around which they crystallize and to which they lend continuity and permanence.[6]

Such associations certainly do not represent the most conspicuous element of a public sphere dominated by mass media and large agencies, observed by market and opinion research, and inundated by the public relations work, propaganda, and advertising of political parties and groups. All the same, they do form the organiza- tional substratum of the general public of citizens. More or less emerging from the private sphere, this public is made of citizens who seek acceptable interpretations for their social interests and experiences and who want to have an influence on institutionalized opinion- and will-formation.

One searches the literature in vain for clear definitions of civil society that would go beyond such descriptive characterizations.[7] S. N. Eisenstadt's usage reveals a certain continuity with the older theory of pluralism when he describes civil society as follows:

Civil society embraces a multiplicity of ostensibly "private" yet potentially autonomous public arenas distinct from the state. The activities of such actors are regulated by various associations existing within them, preventing the society from degenerating into a shapeless mass. In a civil society, these sectors are not embedded in closed, ascriptive or corporate settings; they are open-ended and overlapping. Each has autonomous access to the central political arena, and a certain degree of commitment to that setting.[8]

Jean Cohen and Andrew Arato, who have presented the most comprehensive study on this topic, provide a catalog of features characterizing the civil society that is demarcated from the state, the economy, and other functional systems but coupled with the core private spheres of the lifeworld:

(1) *Plurality*: families, informal groups, and voluntary associations whose plurality and autonomy allow for a variety of forms of life; (2) *Publicity*: institutions of culture and communication; (3) *Privacy*: a domain of individual self-development and moral choice; (4) *Legality*: structures of general laws and basic rights needed to demarcate plurality, privacy, and publicity from at least the state and, tendentially, the economy. Together, these structures secure the institutional existence of a modern differentiated civil society.[9]

The *constitution of this sphere through basic rights* provides some indicators for its social structure. Freedom of assembly and freedom of association, when linked with freedom of speech, define the scope for various types of associations and societies: for voluntary associations that intervene in the formation of public opinion, push topics of general interest, and act as advocates for neglected issues and underrepresented groups; for groups that are difficult to organize or that pursue cultural, religious, or humanitarian aims; and for ethical communities, religious denominations, and so on. Freedom of the press, radio, and television, as well as the right to engage in these areas, safeguards the media infrastructure of public communication; such liberties are thereby supposed to preserve an openness for competing opinions and a representative diversity of voices. The political system, which must remain sensitive to the influence of public opinion, is intertwined with the public sphere and civil society through the activity of political parties and general elections. This intermeshing is guaranteed by the right of parties to "collaborate" in the political will-formation of the people, as well as by the citizens' active and passive voting rights and other participatory rights. Finally, the network of associations can assert its autonomy and preserve its spontaneity only insofar as it can draw support from a mature pluralism of forms of life, subcultures, and worldviews. The constitutional protection of "privacy" promotes the integrity of private life spheres: rights of personality, freedom of belief and of conscience, freedom of movement, the privacy of letters, mail, and telecommunications, the inviolability of one's residence, and the protection of families circumscribe an untouchable zone of personal integrity and independent judgment.

The tight connection between an autonomous civil society and an integral private sphere stands out even more clearly when contrasted with totalitarian societies of bureaucratic socialism. Here a panoptic state not only directly controls the bureaucratically desiccated public sphere, it also undermines the private basis of this public sphere. Administrative intrusions and constant supervision corrode the communicative structure of everyday contacts in families and schools, neighborhoods and local municipalities. The destruction of solidary living conditions and the paralysis of initiative and independent engagement in overregulated yet legally uncertain sectors go hand in hand with the crushing of social groups, associations, and networks; with indoctrination and the dissolution of cultural identities; with the suffocation of spontaneous public communication. Communicative rationality is thus destroyed *simultaneously* in both public and private contexts of communication.[10] The more the bonding force of communicative action wanes in private life spheres and the members of communicative freedom die out, the easier it is for someone who monopolizes the public sphere to align the mutually estranged and isolated actors into a mass that can be directed and mobilized in a plebiscitarian manner.[11]

Basic constitutional guarantees alone, of course, cannot preserve the public sphere and civil society from deformations. The communication structures of the public sphere must rather be kept intact by an energetic civil society. That the political public sphere must in a certain sense reproduce and stabilize itself from its own resources is shown by the odd *self-referential character of the practice of communication in civil society*. Those actors who are the carriers of the public sphere put forward "texts" that always reveal the same subtext, which refers to the critical function of the public sphere in general. Whatever the manifest content of their public utterances, the performative meaning of such public discourse at the same time actualizes the function of an undistorted political public sphere as such. Thus, the institutions and legal guarantees of free and open opinion-formation rest on the unsteady ground of the political communication of actors who, in making use of them, at the same time interpret, defend, and radicalize their normative content. Actors who know they are involved in the *common* enterprise of reconstituting and maintaining structures of the public sphere as they contest opinions and strive for influence differ from actors who merely use forums that already exist. More specifically, actors who support the public sphere are distinguished by the *dual orientation* of their political engagement: with their programs, they directly influence the political system, but at the same time they are also reflexively concerned with revitalizing and enlarging civil society and the public sphere as well as with confirming their own identities and capacities to act.

Cohen and Arato see this kind of "dual politics" especially in the "new" social movements that simultaneously pursue offensive and defensive goals. "Offensively," these movements attempt to bring up issues relevant to the entire society, to define ways of approaching problems, to propose possible solutions, to supply new information, to interpret values differently, to mobilize good reasons and criticize bad ones. Such initiatives are intended to produce a broad shift in public opinion, to alter the parameters of organized political will-formation, and to exert pressure on parliaments, courts, and administrations in favor of specific policies. "Defensively," they attempt to maintain existing structures of association and public influence, to generate subcultural counterpublics and counterinstitutions, to consolidate new collective identities, and to win new terrain in the form of expanded rights and reformed institutions:

On this account, the "defensive" aspect of the movements involves preserving *and developing* the communicative infrastructure of the lifeworld. This formulation captures the dual aspect of movements discussed by Touraine as well as Habermas's insight that movements can be the carriers of the potentials of cultural modernity. This is the sine qua non for successful efforts to redefine identities, to reinterpret norms, and to develop egalitarian, democratic associational forms. The expressive, normative and communicative modes of collective action . . . [also involve] efforts to secure *institutional* changes within civil society that correspond to the new meanings, identities, and norms that are created.[12]

In the self-referential mode of reproducing the public sphere, as well as in the Janus-faced politics aimed at the political system and the self-stabilization of public sphere and civil society, the space is provided for the extension and radicalization of existing rights: "The combination of associations, publics, and rights, when supported by a political culture in which independent initiatives and movements represent an ever-renewable, legitimate, political option, represents, in our opinion, an effective set of bulwarks around civil society within whose limits much of the program of radical democracy can be reformulated."[13]

In fact, the *interplay of* a public sphere based in civil society with the opinion- and will-formation institutionalized in parliamentary bodies and courts offers a good starting point for translating the concept of deliberative politics into sociological terms. However, we must not look on civil society as a focal point where the lines of societal self-organization as a whole would converge. Cohen and Arato rightly emphasize the *limited scope for action* that civil society and the public sphere afford to noninstitutionalized political movements and forms of political expression. They speak of a structurally necessary "self-limitation" of radical-democratic practice:

First, a robust civil society can develop only in the context of a liberal political culture and the corresponding patterns of socialization, and on the basis of an integral private sphere; it can blossom only in an already rationalized lifeworld. Otherwise, populist movements arise that blindly defend the frozen traditions of a lifeworld endangered by capitalist modernization. In their forms of mobilization, these fundamentalist movements are as modern as they are antidemocratic.[14]

Second, within the boundaries of the public sphere, or at least of a liberal public sphere, actors can acquire only influence, not political power. The influence of a public opinion generated more or less discursively in open controversies is certainly an empirical variable that can make a difference. But public influence is transformed into communicative power only after it passes through the filters of the institutionalized *procedures* of democratic opinion- and will-formation and enters through parliamentary debates into legitimate lawmaking. The informal flow of public opinion issues in beliefs that have been *tested* from the standpoint of the generalizability of interests. Not influence per se, but influence transformed into communicative power legitimates political decisions. The popular sovereignty set communicatively a flow cannot make itself felt *solely* in the influence of informal public discourses—not even when these discourses arise from autonomous public spheres. To generate political power, their influence must have an effect on the democratically regulated deliberations of democratically elected assemblies and assume an authorized form in formal decisions. This also holds, mutatis mutandis, for courts that decide politically relevant cases.

Third, and finally, the instruments that politics has available in law and administrative power have a limited effectiveness in functionally differentiated societies. Politics indeed continues to be the addressee for all unmanaged integration problems. But political steering can often take only an indirect approach and must, as we have seen, leave intact the modes of operation internal to functional systems and other highly organized spheres of action. As a result, democratic movements emerging from civil society must give up holistic aspirations to a self-organizing society, aspirations that also undergirded Marxist ideas of social revolution. Civil society can directly transform only itself, and it can have at most an indirect effect on the self-transformation of the political system; generally, it has an influence only on the personnel and programming of this system. But in no way does it occupy *the position* of a macrosubject supposed to bring society as a whole under control and simultaneously act for it. Besides these limitations, one must bear in mind that the administrative power deployed for purposes of social planning and supervision is not a suitable medium for fostering emancipated forms of life. These can *develop* in the wake of democratization processes but they cannot be *brought about* through intervention.

The self-limitation of civil society should not be understood as incapacitation. The knowledge required for political supervision or steering, a knowledge that in complex societies represents a resource as scarce as it is desirable, can certainly become the source of a new systems paternalism. But because the administration does not, for the most part, itself produce the relevant knowledge but draws it from the knowledge system or other intermediaries, it does not enjoy a natural monopoly on such knowledge. In spite of asymmetrical access to expertise and limited problem-solving capacities, civil society also has the opportunity of mobilizing counterknowledge and drawing on the pertinent forms of expertise to make *its own* translations. Even though the public consists of laypersons and communicates with ordinary language, this does not necessarily imply an inability to differentiate the essential questions and reasons for decisions. This can serve as a pretext for a technocratic incapacitation of the public sphere only as long as the political initiatives of civil society fail to provide sufficient expert knowledge along with appropriate and, if necessary, multilevel translations in regard to the managerial aspects of public issues.

8.3.3

The concepts of the political public sphere and civil society introduced above are not mere normative postulates but have empirical relevance. However, additional assumptions must be introduced if we are to use these concepts to translate the discourse-theoretic reading of radical democracy into sociological terms and reformulate it in an empirically falsifiable manner. I would like to defend the claim that *under certain circumstances* civil society can acquire influence in the public sphere, have an effect on the parliamentary complex (and the courts) through its own public opinions, and compel the political system to switch over to the official circulation of power. Naturally, the sociology of mass communication conveys a skeptical impression of the power-ridden, mass-media-dominated public spheres of Western democracies. Social movements, citizen initiatives and forums, political and other associations, in short, the groupings of civil society, are indeed sensitive to problems, but the signals they send out and the impulses they give are generally too weak to initiate learning processes or redirect decision making in the political system in the short run.

In complex societies, the public sphere consists of an intermediary structure between the political system, on the one hand, and the private sectors of the lifeworld and functional systems, on the other. It represents a highly complex network that branches out into a multitude of overlapping international, national, regional, local, and subcultural arenas. Functional specifications, thematic foci, policy fields, and so forth, provide the points of reference for a substantive differentiation of public spheres that are, however, still accessible to laypersons (for example, popular science and literary publics, religious and artistic publics, feminist and "alternative" publics, publics concerned with health-care issues, social welfare, or environmental policy). Moreover, the public sphere is differentiated into levels according to the density of communication, organizational complexity, and range—from the *episodic* publics found in taverns, coffee houses, or on the streets; through the *occasional* or "arranged" publics of particular presentations and events, such as theater performances, rock concerts, party assemblies, or church congresses; up to the *abstract* public sphere of isolated readers, listeners, and viewers scattered across large geographic areas, or even around the globe, and brought together only through the mass media. Despite these manifold differentiations, however, all the partial publics constituted by ordinary language remain porous to one another. The one text of "the" public sphere, a text continually extrapolated and extending radially in all directions, is divided by internal boundaries into arbitrarily small texts for which everything else is context; yet one can always build hermeneutical bridges from one text to the next. Segmented public spheres are constituted with the help of exclusion mechanisms; however, because publics cannot harden into organizations or systems, there is no exclusion rule without a proviso for its abolishment.

In other words, boundaries inside the universal public sphere as defined by its reference to the political system remain permeable in principle. The rights to unrestricted inclusion and equality built into liberal public spheres prevent exclusion mechanisms of the Foucauldian type and ground a *potential for self-transformation*. In the course of the nineteenth and twentieth centuries, the universalist discourses of the bourgeois public sphere could no longer immunize themselves against a critique from within. The labor movement and feminism, for example, were able to join these discourses in order to shatter the structures that had initially constituted them as "the other" of a bourgeois public sphere.[15]

The more the audience is widened through mass communications, the more inclusive and the more abstract in form it becomes. Correspondingly, the *roles of the actors* appearing in the arenas are, to an increasing degree, sharply separated from the roles of the spectators in the galleries. Although the "success of the actors in the arena is ultimately decided in the galleries,"[16] the question arises of how autonomous the public is when it takes a position on an issue, whether its affirmative or negative stand reflects a process of becoming informed or in fact only a more or less concealed game of power. Despite the wealth of empirical investigations, we still do not have a well-established answer to this cardinal question. But one can at least pose the question more precisely by assuming that public processes of communication can take place with less distortion the more they are left to the internal dynamic of a civil society that emerges from the lifeworld.

One can distinguish, at least tentatively, the more loosely organized actors who "emerge from" the public, as it were, from other actors merely "appearing before" the public. The latter have organizational power, resources, and sanctions available *from the start*. Naturally, the actors who are more firmly anchored in civil society and participate in the reproduction of the public sphere also depend on the support of "sponsors" who supply the necessary resources of money, organization, knowledge, and social capital. But patrons or "like-minded" sponsors do not necessarily reduce the authenticity of the public actors they support. By contrast, the collective actors who merely enter the public sphere from, and utilize it for, a specific organization or functional system have *their own* basis of support. Among these political and social actors who do not have to obtain their resources from other spheres, I primarily include the large interest groups that enjoy social power, as well as the established parties that have largely become arms of the political system. They draw on market studies and opinion surveys and conduct their own professional public-relations campaigns.

In and of themselves, organizational complexity, resources, professionalization, and so on, are admittedly insufficient indicators for the difference between "indigenous" actors and mere users. Nor can an actor's pedigree be read directly from the interests actually represented. Other indicators are more reliable. Thus actors differ in how they can be identified. Some actors one can easily identify from their functional background; that is, they represent political parties or pressure groups; unions or professional associations; consumer-protection groups or rent-control organizations, and so on. Other actors, by contrast, must first *produce* identifying features. This is especially evident with social movements that initially go through a phase of self-identification and self-legitimation; even after that, they still pursue a self-referential "identity politics" parallel to their goal-directed politics—they must continually reassure themselves of their identity. Whether actors merely use an already constituted public sphere or whether they are involved in reproducing its structures is, moreover, evident in the above-mentioned sensitivity to threats to communication rights. It is also shown in the actors' willingness to go beyond an interest in self-defense and take a universalist stand against the open or concealed exclusion of minorities or marginal groups. The very existence of social movements, one might add, depends on whether they find organizational forms that produce solidarities and publics, forms that allow them to fully utilize and radicalize existing communication rights and structures as they pursue special goals.[17]

A third group of actors are the journalists, publicity agents, and members of the press (i.e., in the broad sense of *Publizisten)* who collect information, make decisions about the selection and presentation of "programs," and to a certain extent control the entry of topics, contributions, and authors into the mass-media-dominated public sphere. As the mass media become more complex and more expensive, the effective channels of communication become more centralized. To the degree this occurs, the mass media face an increasing pressure of selection, on both the supply side and the demand side. These selection processes become the source of a new sort of power. This *power of the media* is not sufficiently reined in by professional standards, but today, by fits and starts, the "fourth branch of government" is being subjected to constitutional regulation. In the Federal Republic, for example, it is both the legal form and the institutional structure of television networks that determine whether they depend more on the influence of political parties and public interest groups or more on private firms with large advertising outlays. In general, one can say that the image of politics presented on television is predominantly made up of issues and contributions that are professionally produced as media input and then fed in via press conferences, news agencies, public relations campaigns, and the like. These official producers of information are all the more successful the more they can rely on trained personnel, on financial and technical resources, and in general on a professional infrastructure. Collective actors operating outside the political system or outside large organizations normally have fewer opportunities to influence the content and views presented by the media. This is especially true for messages that do not fall inside the "balanced," that is, the centrist and rather narrowly defined, spectrum of "established opinions" dominating the programs of the electronic media.[18]

Moreover, before messages selected in this way are broadcast, they are subject to *information-processing strategies* within the media. These are oriented by reception conditions as perceived by media experts, program directors, and the press. Because the public's receptiveness, cognitive capacity, and attention represent unusually scarce resources for which the programs of numerous "stations" compete, the presentation of news and commentaries for the most part follows market strategies. Reporting facts as human interest stories, mixing information with entertainment, arranging material episodically, and breaking down complex relationships into smaller fragments—all of this comes together to form a syndrome that works to depoliticize public communication.[19] This is the kernel of truth in the theory of the culture industry. The research literature provides fairly reliable information on the institutional framework and structure of the media, as well as on the way they work, organize programs, and are utilized. But, even a generation after Paul Lazarsfeld, propositions concerning the *effects of the media* remain controversial. The research on effect and reception has at least done away with the image of passive consumers as "cultural dopes" who are manipulated by the programs offered to them. It directs our attention to the *strategies of interpretation* employed by viewers, who communicate with one another, and who in fact can be provoked to criticize or reject what programs offer or to synthesize it with judgments of their own.[20]

Even if we know something about the internal operation and impact of the mass media, as well as about the distribution of roles among the public and various actors, and even if we can make some reasonable conjectures about who has privileged access to the media and who has a share in media power, it is by no means clear how the mass media intervene in the diffuse circuits of communication in the political public sphere. The *normative reactions* to the relatively new phenomenon of the mass media's powerful position in the competition for public influence are clearer. Michael Gurevitch and Jay G. Blumler have summarized the tasks that the media *ought* to fulfill in democratic political systems:

1. surveillance of the sociopolitical environment, reporting developments likely to impinge, positively or negatively, on the welfare of citizens;

2. meaningful agenda-setting, identifying the key issues of the day, including the forces that have formed and may resolve them;
3. platforms for an intelligible and illuminating advocacy by politicians and spokespersons of other causes and interest groups;
4. dialogue across a diverse range of views, as well as between power-holders (actual and prospective) and mass publics;
5. mechanisms for holding officials to account for how they have exercised power;
6. incentives for citizens to learn, choose, and become involved, rather than merely to follow and kibitz over the political process;
7. a principled resistance to the efforts of forces outside the media to subvert their independence, integrity and ability to serve the audience;
8. a sense of respect for the audience member, as potentially concerned and able to make sense of his or her political environment.[21]

Such principles orient the professional code of journalism and the profession's ethical self-understanding, on the one hand, and the formal organization of a free press by laws governing mass communication, on the other.[22] In agreement with the concept of deliberative politics, these principles express a simple idea: the mass media ought to understand themselves as the mandatary of an enlightened public whose willingness to learn and capacity for criticism they at once presuppose, demand, and reinforce; like the judiciary, they ought to preserve their independence from political and social pressure; they ought to be receptive to the public's concerns and proposals, take up these issues and contributions impartially, augment criticisms, and confront the political process with articulate demands for legitimation. The power of the media should thus be neutralized and the tacit conversion of administrative or social power into political influence blocked. According to this idea, political and social actors would be allowed to "use" the public sphere only insofar as they make convincing contributions to the solution of problems that have been perceived by the public or have been put on the public agenda with the public's consent. In a similar vein, political parties would have to participate in the opinion- and will-formation from the public's own perspective, rather than patronizing the public and extracting mass loyalty from the public sphere for the purposes of maintaining their own power.[23]

The sociology of mass communication depicts the public sphere as infiltrated by administrative and social power and dominated by the mass media. If one places this image, diffuse though it might be, alongside the above normative expectations, then one will be rather cautious in estimating the chances of civil society having an influence on the political system. To be sure, this estimate pertains only to a *public sphere at rest*. In periods of mobilization, the structures that actually support the authority of a critically engaged public begin to vibrate. The balance of power between civil society and the political system then shifts.

8.3.4

With this I return to the central question of who can place issues on the agenda and determine what direction the lines of communication take. Roger Cobb, Jennie-Keith Ross, and Marc Howard Ross have constructed models that depict how new and compelling issues develop, from the first initiative up to formal proceedings in bodies that have the power to decide.[24] If one suitably modifies the proposed models—inside access model, mobilization model, outside initiative model—from the viewpoint of democratic theory, they present basic alternatives in how the public sphere and the political system influence each other. In the first case, the initiative comes from officeholders or political leaders, and the issue continues to circulate inside the political system all the way to its formal treatment, while the broader public is either excluded from the process or does not have any influence on it. In the second case, the initiative again starts inside the political system, but the proponents of the issue must mobilize the public sphere, because they need the support of certain groups, either to obtain formal consideration or to implement an adopted program successfully. Only in the third case does the initiative lie with forces at the periphery, outside the purview of the political system. With the help of the mobilized public sphere, that is, the pressure of public opinion, such forces compel formal consideration of the issue:

The outside initiative model applies to the situation in which a group outside the government structure 1) articulates a grievance, 2) tries to expand interest in the issue to enough other groups in the population to gain a place on the public agenda, in order to 3) create sufficient pressure on decision makers to force the issue onto the formal agenda for their serious consideration. This model of agenda building is likely to predominate in more egalitarian societies. Formal agenda status, however, does not necessarily mean that the final decisions of the authorities or the actual policy implementation will be what the grievance group originally sought.[25]

In the normal case, issues and proposals have a history whose course corresponds more to the first or second model than to the third. As long as the informal circulation of power dominates the political system, the initiative and power to put problems on the agenda and bring them to a decision lies more with the Government leaders and administration than with the parliamentary complex. As long as in the public sphere the mass media prefer, contrary to their normative self-understanding, to draw their material from powerful, well-organized information producers and as long as they prefer media strategies that lower rather than raise the discursive level of public communication, issues will tend to start in, and be managed from, the center, rather than follow a spontaneous course originating in the periphery. At least, the skeptical findings on problem articulation in public arenas accord with this view.[26] In the present context, of course, there can be no question of a conclusive empirical evaluation of the mutual influence that politics and public have on each other. For our purposes, it suffices to make it plausible that in a perceived crisis situation, the *actors in civil society* thus far neglected in our scenario *can* assume a surprisingly active and momentous role.[27] In spite of a lesser organizational complexity and a weaker capacity for action, and despite the structural disadvantages mentioned earlier, at the critical moments of an accelerated history, these actors get the chance to *reverse* the normal circuits of communication in the political system and the public sphere. In this way they can shift the entire system's mode of problem solving.

The communication structures of the public sphere are linked with the private life spheres in a way that gives the civil-social periphery, in contrast to the political center, the advantage of greater sensitivity in detecting and identifying new problem situations. The great issues of the last decades give evidence for this. Consider, for example, the spiraling nuclear-arms race; consider the risks involved in the peaceful use of atomic energy or in other large-scale technological projects and scientific experimentation, such as genetic engineering; consider the ecological threats involved in an overstrained natural environment (acid rain, water pollution, species extinction, etc.); consider the dramatically progressing impoverishment of the Third World and problems of the world economic order; or consider such issues as feminism, increasing immigration, and the associated problems of multiculturalism. Hardly any of these topics were *initially* brought up by exponents of the state apparatus, large organizations, or functional systems. Instead, they were broached by intellectuals, concerned citizens, radical professionals, self-proclaimed "advocates," and the like. Moving in from this outermost periphery, such issues force their way into newspapers and interested associations, clubs, professional organizations, academies, and universities. They find forums, citizen initiatives, and other platforms before they catalyze the growth of social movements and new subcultures.[28] The latter can in turn dramatize contributions, presenting them so effectively that the mass media take up the matter. Only through their controversial presentation in the media do such topics reach the larger public and subsequently gain a place on the "public agenda." Sometimes the support of sensational actions, mass protests, and incessant campaigning is required before an issue can make its way via the surprising election of marginal candidates or radical parties, expanded platforms of "established" parties, important court decisions, and so on, into the core of the political system and there receive formal consideration.

Naturally, there are other ways in which issues develop, other paths from the periphery to the center, and other patterns involving complex branchings and feedback loops. But, in general, one can say that even in more or less power-ridden public spheres, the power relations shift as soon as the perception of relevant social problems evokes a *crisis consciousness* at the periphery. If actors from civil society then join together, formulate the relevant issue, and promote it in the public sphere, their efforts can be successful, because the endogenous mobilization of the public sphere activates an otherwise latent dependency built into the internal structure of every public sphere, a dependency also present in the normative self-understanding of the mass media: the players in the arena owe their influence to the approval of those in the gallery. At the very least, one can say that insofar as a rationalized lifeworld supports the development of a liberal public sphere by furnishing it with a solid foundation in civil society, the authority of a position-taking public is strengthened in the course of escalating public controversies. Under the conditions of a *liberal* public sphere, informal public communication accomplishes two things in cases in which mobilization depends on crisis. On the one hand, it prevents the accumulation of indoctrinated masses that are seduced by populist leaders. On the other hand, it pulls together the scattered critical potentials of a public that was only abstractly held together through the public media, and it helps this public have a political influence on institutionalized opinion- and will-formation. Only in *liberal* public spheres, of course, do subinstitutional political movements—which abandon the conventional paths of interest politics in order to boost the constitutionally regulated circulation of power in the political system—take this direction. By contrast, an authoritarian, distorted public sphere that is brought into alignment merely provides a forum for plebiscitary legitimation.[29]

This sense of a reinforced demand for legitimation becomes especially clear when subinstitutional protest movements reach a high point by escalating their protests. The last means for obtaining more of a hearing and greater media influence for oppositional arguments are acts of civil disobedience. These acts of nonviolent, symbolic rule violation are meant as expressions of protest against binding decisions that, their legality notwithstanding, the actors consider illegitimate in the light of valid constitutional principles. Acts of civil disobedience are directed simultaneously to two addressees. On the one hand, they appeal to officeholders and parliamentary representatives to reopen formally concluded political deliberations so that their decisions may possibly be revised in view of the continuing public criticism. On the other hand, they appeal "to the sense of justice of the majority of the community," as Rawls puts it,[30] and thus to the critical judgment of a public of citizens that is to be mobilized with exceptional means. Independently of the current object of controversy, civil disobedience is also always an implicit appeal to connect organized political will-formation with the communicative processes of the public sphere. The message of this subtext is aimed at a political system that, as constitutionally organized, may not detach itself from civil society and make itself independent vis-à-vis the periphery. Civil disobedience thereby refers to its own origins in a civil society that in crisis situations actualizes the normative contents of constitutional democracy in the medium of public opinion and summons it against the systemic inertia of institutional politics.

This *self-referential character* is emphasized in the definition that Cohen and Arato have proposed, drawing on considerations raised by Rawls, Dworkin, and me:

Civil disobedience involves illegal acts, usually on the part of collective actors, that are public, principled, and symbolic in character, involve primarily nonviolent means of protest, and appeal to the capacity for reason and the sense of justice of the populace. The aim of civil disobedience is to persuade public opinion in civil and political society . . . that a particular law or policy is illegitimate and a change is warranted. Collective actors involved in civil disobedience invoke the utopian principles of constitutional democracies, appealing to the ideas of fundamental rights or democratic legitimacy. Civil disobedience is thus a means for reasserting the link between civil and political society, when legal attempts at exerting the influence of the former on the latter have failed and other avenues have been exhausted.[31]

This interpretation of civil disobedience manifests the self-consciousness of a civil society confident that at least in a crisis it can increase the pressure of a mobilized public on the political system to the point where the latter switches into the conflict mode and neutralizes the unofficial countercirculation of power.

Beyond this, the justification of civil disobedience[32] relies on a *dynamic understanding* of the constitution as an unfinished project. From this long-term perspective, the constitutional state does not represent a finished structure but a delicate and sensitive—above all fallible and revisable—enterprise, whose purpose is to realize the system of rights *anew* in changing circumstances, that is, to interpret the system of rights better, to institutionalize it more appropriately, and to draw out its contents more radically. This is the perspective of citizens who are actively engaged in realizing the system of rights. Aware of, and referring to, changed contexts, such citizens want to overcome in practice the tension between social facticity and validity. Although legal theory cannot adopt this participant perspective as its own, it can reconstruct the paradigmatic *understanding* of law and democracy that guides citizens whenever they form an idea of the structural constraints on the self-organization of the legal community in their society.

8.3.5

From a reconstructive standpoint, we have seen that constitutional rights and principles merely explicate the performative character of the self-constitution of a society of free and equal citizens. The organizational forms of the constitutional state make this practice permanent. Every historical example of a democratic constitution has a double temporal reference: as a historic document, it recalls the foundational act that it interprets—it marks a beginning in time. At the same time, its normative character means that the task of interpreting and elaborating the system of rights poses itself *anew* for each generation; as the project of a just society, a constitution articulates the horizon of expectation opening on an ever-present future. From this perspective, as an *ongoing* process of constitution making set up for the long haul, the democratic procedure of legitimate lawmaking acquires a privileged status. This leads to the pressing question of whether such a demanding procedure can be implemented in complex societies like our own and, if it can, how this can be done effectively, so that a constitutionally regulated circulation of power actually prevails in the political system. The answers to this question in turn inform our own paradigmatic understanding of law. I note the following four points for elucidating such a historically situated understanding of the constitution.

(a) The constitutionally organized political system is, on the one hand, specialized for generating collectively binding decisions. To this extent, it represents only one of several subsystems. On the other hand, in virtue of its internal relation to law, politics is responsible for problems that concern society as a whole. It must be possible to interpret collectively binding decisions as a realization of rights such that the structures of recognition built into communicative action are transferred, via the medium of law, from the level of simple interactions to the abstract and anonymous relationships among strangers. In pursuing what in each case are particular collective goals and in regulating specific conflicts, politics simultaneously deals with general problems of integration. Because it is constituted in a legal form, a politics whose mode of operation is functionally specified still refers to society-wide problems: it carries on the tasks of social integration at a reflexive level when other action systems are no longer up to the job.

(b) This asymmetrical position explains the fact that the political system is subject to constraints on two sides and that corresponding standards govern its achievements and decisions. As a functionally specified action system, it is limited by other functional systems that obey their own logic and, to this extent, bar direct political interventions. On this side, the political system encounters limits on the effectiveness of administrative power (including legal and fiscal instruments). On the other side, as a constitutionally regulated action system, politics is connected with the public sphere and depends on lifeworld sources of communicative power. Here the political system is not subject to the external constraints of a social environment but rather experiences its internal dependence on enabling conditions. This is because the conditions that make the production of legitimate law possible are ultimately not at the disposition of politics.

(c) The political system is vulnerable on both sides to disturbances that can reduce the *effectiveness* of its achievements and the *legitimacy* of its decisions, respectively. The regulatory competence of the political system fails if the implemented legal programs remain ineffective or if regulatory activity gives rise to disintegrating effects in the action systems that require regulation. Failure also occurs if the instruments deployed overtax the legal medium itself and strain the normative composition of the political system. As steering problems become more complex, irrelevance, misguided regulations, and self-destruction can accumulate to the point where a "regulatory trilemma" results.[33] On the other side, the political system fails as a guardian of social integration if its decisions, even though effective, can no longer be traced back to legitimate law. The constitutionally regulated circulation of power is nullified if the administrative system becomes independent of communicatively generated power, if the social power of functional systems and large organizations (including the mass media) is converted into illegitimate power, or if the lifeworld resources for spontaneous public communication no longer suffice to guarantee an uncoerced articulation of social interests. The independence of illegitimate power, together with the weakness of civil society and the public sphere, can deteriorate into a "legitimation dilemma," which in certain circumstances can combine with the steering trilemma and develop into a vicious circle. Then the political system is pulled into the whirlpool of legitimation deficits and steering deficits that reinforce one another.

(d) Such crises can at most be explained historically. They are not built into the structures of functionally differentiated societies in such a way that they would intrinsically compromise the project of self-empowerment undertaken by a society of free and equal subjects who bind themselves by law. However, they are symptomatic of the peculiar position of political systems as asymmetrically embedded in highly complex circulation processes. Actors must form an idea of this context whenever, adopting the performative attitude, they want to engage successfully as citizens, representatives, judges, or officials, in realizing the system of rights. Because these rights must be interpreted in various ways under changing social circumstances, the light they throw on this context is refracted into a spectrum of changing legal paradigms. Historical constitutions can be seen as so many ways of construing one and the *same* practice—the practice of self-determination on the part of free and equal citizens—but like every practice this, too, is situated in history. Those involved must start with their *own current* practice if they want to achieve clarity about what such a practice means *in general.*

NOTES

1. As held by J. Gerhards and F. Neidhardt, *Strukturen and Funktionen moderner Öffentlichkeit* (Berlin, 1990), p. 19.

2. T. Parsons, "On the Concept of Influence," in Parsons, *Sociological Theory and Modern Society* (New York, 1967), pp. 355–82. On the relation between "influence" and "value," and on the delimitation of these generalized forms of communication from steering media, such as money and administrative power, see J. Habermas, *The Theory of Communicative Action*, trans. T. McCarthy, 2 vols. (Boston, 1984, 1987), 2:273–82.

3. On this function of churches and religious communities, see F. S. Fiorenza, "The Church as a Community of Interpretation: Political Theology between Discourse Ethics and Hermeneutical Reconstruction," in D. S. Browning and F. S. Fiorenza, eds., *Habermas, Modernity, and Public Theology* (New York, 1992), pp. 66–91.

4. J. Habermas, *The Structural Transformation of the Public Sphere*, trans. T. Burger and F. Lawrence (Cambridge, Mass., 1989), p. 27 [trans. altered]; see Craig Calhoun's introduction to the collection edited by him: *Habermas and the Public Sphere* (Cambridge, Mass., 1992), p. 27; see also D. Goodman, "Public Sphere and Private Life: Toward a Synthesis of Current Historical Approaches to the Old Regime," *History and Theory* 31 (1992): 1–20.

5. T. Smith, *The Role of Ethics in Social Theory* (Albany, 1991), pp. 153–74.

6. On the concept of "discursive design," see J. S. Dryzek, *Discursive Democracy* (Cambridge, 1990), pp. 43ff.

7. J. Keane, *Democracy and Civil Society* (London, 1988). Antonio Gramsci introduced this concept into more recent discussion; see N. Bobbio, "Gramsci and the Concept of Civil Society," in J. Keane, ed., *Civil Society and the State* (London, 1988), pp. 73–100.

8. S. N. Eisenstadt, ed., *Democracy and Modernity* (Leiden, 1992), p. ix; in the same volume, see also L. Roniger, "Conditions for the Consolidation of Democracy in Southern Europe and Latin America," pp. 53–68.

9. J. L. Cohen and A. Arato, *Civil Society and Political Theory* (Cambridge, Mass., 1992), p. 346.

10. E. Hankiss, "The Loss of Responsibility," in J. MacLean, A. Montefiori, and P. Winch, eds., *The Political Responsibility of Intellectuals* (Cambridge, 1990), pp. 29–52.

11. See Hannah Arendt's communication-theoretic interpretation of totalitarianism in *The Origins of Totalitarianism* (New York, 1973), pp. 473–78; e.g., pp. 473–74, 475: "[Totalitarian government] presses masses of isolated men together *and* supports them in a world that has become a wilderness for them . . . , in order to set the terror-ruled movement into motion and keep it moving. . . . [It] could not exist without destroying the public realm of life, that is, without destroying, by isolating men, their political capacities. But . . . it is not content with this isolation and destroys private life as well."

12. Cohen and Arato, *Civil Society*, p. 531.

13. Cohen and Arato, *Civil Society*, p. 474.

14. The classic study on fascism by I. Bibo *(Die deutsche Hysterie* [Frankfurt am Main, 1991]) already emphasizes this double aspect. Socialism, too, was Janus-faced, looking simultaneously toward the future and the past: in the new industrial forms of trade, it wanted to rescue the old forces of social integration found in the solidary communities of a vanishing preindustrial world. See the title essay in J. Habermas, *Die nachholende Revolution* (Frankfurt am Main, 1990), pp. 179–204.

15. J. Habermas, *Strukturwandel der Öffentlichkeit* (Frankfurt am Main, 1990), pp. 15–20. For the English, see Habermas, "Further Reflections on the Public Sphere," in Calhoun, *Habermas and the Public Sphere*, pp. 425–29.

16. 64. Gerhards and Neidhardt, *Strukturen*, p. 27.

17. Cohen and Arato, *Civil Society*, pp. 492–563.

18. M. Kaase, "Massenkommunikation und politischer Prozeß," in M. Kaase and W. Schulz, eds., *Massenkommunikation, Kölner Zeitschrift fair Soziologie und Sozialpsychologie* Sonderheft 30 (1989): 97–117.

19. This is primarily true of electronic media, which are most frequently used by a broad public; it must be qualified for newspapers and other media.

20. S. Hall, "Encoding and Decoding in TV Discourse," in Hall, ed., *Culture, Media, Language* (London, 1980), pp. 128–38; D. Morley, *Family Television* (London, 1988).

21. M. Gurevitch and G. Blumler, "Political Communication Systems and Democratic Values," in J. Lichtenberg, ed., *Democracy and the Mass Media* (Cambridge, Mass., 1990), p. 270.

22. Cf. the principles for a "regulated pluralism" of the mass media in J. B. Thompson, *Ideology and Modern Culture* (Cambridge, 1990), pp. 261ff.

23. J. Keane advocates a similar "media philosophy" in *The Media and Democracy* (Cambridge, 1991).

24. R. Cobb, J. K. Ross, and M. H. Ross, "Agenda Building as a Comparative Political Process," *American Political Science Review* 70 (1976): 126–38; R. Cobb and C. Elder, "The Politics of Agenda-Building," *Journal of Politics* (1971) : 892–915.

25. Cobb, Ross, and Ross, "Agenda Building as a Comparative Political Process," p. 132.

26. S. Hilgartner, "The Rise and Fall of Social Problems," *American Journal of Sociology* 94 (1988): 53–78.

27. For a stimulating empirical analysis of social movements as "exponents of the life-world," see L. Rolke, *Protestbewegungen in der Bundesrepublik* (Opladen, 1987).

28. J. Raschke, *Soziale Bewegungen* (Frankfurt am Main, 1985).

29. C. Offe, "Challenging the Boundaries of Institutional Politics: Social Movements since the 1960s," in C. S. Maier, *Changing Boundaries of the Political* (Cambridge, 1987), pp. 63–106.

30. J. Rawls, *A Theory of Justice* (Cambridge, Mass., 1971), p. 364.

31. Cohen and Arato, *Civil Society, pp.* 587f. On "militant tolerance," see U. Rödel, G. Frankenberg, and H. Dubiel, *Die demokratische Frage* (Frankfurt am Main, 1989), chap. 6.

32. On the scholarly legal discussion, see R. Dreier, "Widerstandsrecht im Rechtsstaat?" in Dreier, *Recht-Staat-Vernunft* (Frankfurt am Main, 1991), pp. 39–72; T. Laker, *Ziviler Ungehorsam* (Baden-Baden, 1986).

33. G. Teubner, "Reflexives Recht: Entwicklungsmodelle des Rechts in vergleichender Perspektive," *Archiv für Rechts- and Sozialphilosophie* 68 (1982): 13ff.

JOHN RAWLS

THE IDEA OF PUBLIC REASON REVISITED (1997)[†]

The American philosopher John Rawls (1921–2002) is a key figure in modern moral and political philosophy. His book A Theory of Justice *(1971) has profoundly shaped contemporary discussions within these disciplines and has had a strong impact on normative theorizing within economics and political science.*

Rawls became a doctor of philosophy at Princeton University in 1950 and in the following years taught at Princeton and Cornell Universities. In 1964, Rawls was offered a professorship in philosophy at Harvard University, where he stayed for the rest of his career.

In A Theory of Justice, *Rawls uses a hypothetical social agreement to argue for principles of justice that should regulate the institutions that constitute the basic structure of society. Rawls' first principle guarantees liberties that can be limited only for the sake of maintaining other liberties of similar significance. His second principle says that social and economic inequalities have to satisfy two conditions: They are to be attached to offices and positions open to all under conditions of fair equality of opportunity and they are to be to of the greatest benefit of the least-advantaged members of society. In* Political Liberalism *(1993), Rawls rethinks his original approach with a focus on pluralism in modern liberal democracies. How is a just and stable society possible when citizens are profoundly divided by religious, philosophical and moral beliefs or what Rawls' calls "comprehensive doctrines?"*

"Public reason," which he identifies with norms of reasoning and standards of evidence that are appropriate to officials and citizens in deliberation, is a core concept in Rawls' theory of a constitutional democracy. He distinguishes between a political forum, a public political culture, and a background culture. Public reason is restricted to fora dealing with what he calls "the constitutional essentials" and "questions of basic justice." It is separated from debate within the "public political culture," which includes political associations and media. The third level, "background culture," encompasses most of civic society and private life and is thus outside the realm of politics proper.

The following text was originally published in 1997 in University of Chicago Law Review *1997 and later included in Rawls' book on international justice,* The Law of Peoples *(1999). A lengthy excursion on the family has been left out.*

Introduction

The idea of public reason, as I understand it,[1] belongs to a conception of a well ordered constitutional democratic society. The form and content of this reason—the way it is understood by citizens and how it interprets their political relationship—is part of the idea of democracy itself. This is because a basic feature of democracy is the fact of reasonable pluralism—the fact that a plurality of conflicting reasonable comprehensive doctrines,[2] religious, philosophical, and moral, is the normal result of its culture of free institutions.[3] Citizens realize that they cannot reach agreement or even approach mutual understanding on the basis of their irreconcilable comprehensive doctrines. In view of this, they need to consider what kinds of reasons they may reasonably give one another when fundamental political questions are at stake. I propose that in public reason comprehensive doctrines of truth or right be replaced by an idea of the politically reasonable addressed to citizens as citizens.[4]

Central to the idea of public reason is that it neither criticizes nor attacks any comprehensive doctrine, religious or nonreligious, except insofar as that doctrine is incompatible with the essentials of public reason and a democratic polity. The basic requirement is that a reasonable doctrine accepts a constitutional democratic regime and its companion idea of legitimate law. While democratic societies will differ in the specific doctrines that are influential and active within them—as they differ in the western democracies of Europe and the United States, Israel, and India—finding a suitable idea of public reason is a concern that faces them all.

§ 1: The Idea of Public Reason

1. The idea of public reason specifies at the deepest level the basic moral and political values that are to determine a constitutional democratic government's relation to its citizens and their relation to one another. In short, it concerns how the political relation is to be understood. Those who reject constitutional democracy with its criterion of reciprocity[5] will of course reject the very idea of public reason. For them the political relation may be that of friend or foe, to those of a particular religious or secular community or those who are not; or it may be a relentless struggle to win the world for the whole truth. Political liberalism does not engage those who think this way. The zeal to embody the whole truth in politics is incompatible with an idea of public reason that belongs with democratic citizenship.

The idea of public reason has a definite structure, and if one or more of its aspects are ignored it can seem implausible, as it does when applied to the background culture.[6] It has five different aspects: (1) the fundamental political questions to which it applies; (2) the persons to whom it applies (government officials and candidates for public office); (3) its content as given by a family of reasonable political conceptions of justice; (4) the application of these conceptions in discussions of coercive norms to be enacted in the form of legitimate law for a democratic people; and (5) citizens' checking that the principles derived from their conceptions of justice satisfy the criterion of reciprocity.

Moreover, such reason is public in three ways: as the reason of free and equal citizens, it is the reason of the public; its subject is the public good concerning questions of fundamental political justice, which questions are of two kinds, constitutional essentials and matters of basic justice;[7] and its nature and content are public, being expressed in public reasoning by a family of reasonable conceptions of political justice reasonably thought to satisfy the criterion of reciprocity.

It is imperative to realize that the idea of public reason does not apply to all political discussions of fundamental questions, but only to discussions of those questions in what I refer to as the public political forum.[8] This forum may be divided into three parts: the discourse of judges in their decisions, and especially of the judges of a supreme court; the discourse of government officials, especially chief executives and legislators; and finally, the discourse of candidates for public office and their campaign managers, especially in their public oratory, party platforms, and political statements.[9] We need this three-part division because, as I note later, the idea of public reason does not apply in the same way in these three cases and elsewhere.[10] In discussing what I call the wide view of public political culture,[11] we shall see that the idea of public reason applies more strictly to judges than to others, but that the requirements of public justification for that reason are always the same.

Distinct and separate from this three-part public political forum is what I call the background culture.[12] This is the culture of civil society. In a democracy, this culture is not, of course, guided by any one central idea or principle, whether political or religious. Its many and diverse agencies and associations with their internal life reside within a framework of law that ensures the familiar liberties of thought and speech, and the right of free association.[13] The idea of public reason does not apply to the background culture with its many forms of nonpublic reason nor to media of any kind.[14] Sometimes those who appear to reject the idea of public reason actually mean to assert the need for full and open discussion in the background culture.[15] With this political liberalism fully agrees.

Finally, distinct from the idea of public reason, as set out by the five features above, is the *ideal* of public reason. This ideal is realized, or satisfied, whenever judges, legislators, chief executives, and other government officials, as well as candidates for public office, act from and follow the idea of public reason and explain to other citizens their reasons for supporting fundamental political positions in terms of the political conception of justice they regard as the most reasonable. In this way they fulfill what I shall call their duty of civility to one another and to other citizens. Hence, whether judges, legislators, and chief executives act from and follow public reason is continually shown in their speech and conduct on a daily basis.

How though is the ideal of public reason realized by citizens who are not government officials? In a representative government citizens vote for representatives— chief executives, legislators, and the like—and not for particular laws (except at a state or local level when they may vote directly on referenda questions, which are rarely fundamental questions). To answer this question, we say that ideally citizens are to think of themselves *as if* they were legislators and ask themselves what statutes, supported by what reasons satisfying the criterion of reciprocity, they would think it most reasonable to enact.[16] When firm and widespread, the disposition of citizens to view themselves as ideal legislators, and to repudiate government officials and candidates for public office who violate public reason, is one of the political and social roots of democracy, and is vital to its enduring strength and vigor.[17] Thus citizens fulfill their duty of civility and support the idea of public reason by doing what they can to hold government officials to it. This duty, like other political rights and duties, is an intrinsically moral duty. I emphasize that it is not a legal duty, for in that case it would be incompatible with freedom of speech.

2. I now turn to a discussion of what I have labeled the third, fourth, and fifth aspects of public reason. The idea of public reason arises from a conception of democratic citizenship in a constitutional democracy. This fundamental political relation of citizenship has two special features: first, it is a relation of citizens within the basic structure of society, a structure we enter only by birth and exit only by death;[18] and second, it is a relation of free and equal citizens who exercise ultimate political power as a collective body. These two features immediately give rise to the question of how, when constitutional essentials and matters of basic justice are at stake, citizens so related can be bound to honor the structure of their constitutional democratic regime and abide by the statutes and laws enacted under it. The fact of reasonable pluralism raises this question all the more sharply, since it means that

the differences between citizens arising from their comprehensive doctrines, religious and nonreligious, may be irreconcilable. By what ideals and principles, then, are citizens who share equally in ultimate political power to exercise that power so that each can reasonably justify his or her political decisions to everyone?

To answer this question we say: Citizens are reasonable when, viewing one another as free and equal in a system of social cooperation over generations, they are prepared to offer one another fair terms of cooperation according to what they consider the most reasonable conception of political justice; and when they agree to act on those terms, even at the cost of their own interests in particular situations, provided that other citizens also accept those terms. The criterion of reciprocity requires that when those terms are proposed as the most reasonable terms of fair cooperation, those proposing them must also think it at least reasonable for others to accept them, as free and equal citizens, and not as dominated or manipulated, or under the pressure of an inferior political or social position.[19] Citizens will of course differ as to which conceptions of political justice they think the most reasonable, but they will agree that all are reasonable, even if barely so.

Thus when, on a constitutional essential or matter of basic justice, all appropriate government officials act from and follow public reason, and when all reasonable citizens think of themselves ideally as if they were legislators following public reason, the legal enactment expressing the opinion of the majority is legitimate law. It may not be thought the most reasonable, or the most appropriate, by each, but it is politically (morally) binding on him or her as a citizen and is to be accepted as such. Each thinks that all have spoken and voted at least reasonably, and therefore all have followed public reason and honored their duty of civility.

Hence the idea of political legitimacy based on the criterion of reciprocity says: Our exercise of political power is proper only when we sincerely believe that the reasons we would offer for our political actions—were we to state them as government officials—are sufficient, and we also reasonably think that other citizens might also reasonably accept those reasons. This criterion applies on two levels: one is to the constitutional structure itself, the other is to particular statutes and laws enacted in accordance with that structure. To be reasonable, political conceptions must justify only constitutions that satisfy this principle.

To make more explicit the role of the criterion of reciprocity as expressed in public reason, note that its role is to specify the nature of the political relation in a constitutional democratic regime as one of civic friendship. For this criterion, when government officers act from it in their public reasoning and other citizens support it, shapes the form of their fundamental institutions. For example—I cite an easy case—if we argue that the religious liberty of some citizens is to be denied, we must give them reasons they can not only understand—as Servetus could understand why Calvin wanted to burn him at the stake—but reasons we might reasonably expect that they, as free and equal citizens, might reasonably also accept. The criterion of reciprocity is normally violated whenever basic liberties are denied. For what reasons can both satisfy the criterion of reciprocity and justify denying to some persons religious liberty, holding others as slaves, imposing a property qualification on the right to vote, or denying the right of suffrage to women?

Since the idea of public reason specifies at the deepest level the basic political values and specifies how the political relation is to be understood, those who believe that fundamental political questions should be decided by what they regard as the best reasons according to their own idea of the whole truth—including their religious or secular comprehensive doctrine—and not by reasons that might be shared by all citizens as free and equal, will of course reject the idea of public reason. Political liberalism views this insistence on the whole truth in politics as incompatible with democratic citizenship and the idea of legitimate law.

3. Democracy has a long history, from its beginning in classical Greece down to the present day, and there are many different ideas of democracy.[20] Here I am concerned only with a well ordered constitutional democracy—a term I used at the outset—understood also as a deliberative democracy. The definitive idea for deliberative democracy is the idea of deliberation itself. When citizens deliberate, they exchange views and debate their supporting reasons concerning public political questions. They suppose that their political opinions may be revised by discussion with other citizens; and therefore these opinions are not simply a fixed outcome of their existing private or nonpolitical interests. It is at this point that public reason is crucial, for it characterizes such citizens' reasoning concerning constitutional essentials and matters of basic justice. While I cannot fully discuss the nature of deliberative democracy here, I note a few key points to indicate the wider place and role of public reason.

There are three essential elements of deliberative democracy. One is an idea of public reason,[21] although not all such ideas are the same. A second is a framework of constitutional democratic institutions that specifies the setting for deliberative legislative bodies. The third is the knowledge and desire on the part of citizens generally to follow public reason and to realize its ideal in their political conduct. Immediate implications of these essentials are the public financing of elections, and the providing for public occasions of orderly and serious discussion of fundamental questions and issues of public policy. Public deliberation must be made possible, recognized as a basic feature of democracy, and set free from the curse of money.[22] Otherwise politics is dominated by corporate and other organized interests who through large contributions to campaigns distort if not preclude public discussion and deliberation.

Deliberative democracy also recognizes that without widespread education in the basic aspects of constitutional democratic government for all citizens, and without a public informed about pressing problems, crucial political and social decisions simply cannot be made. Even should farsighted political leaders wish to make sound changes and reforms, they cannot convince a misinformed and cynical public to accept and follow them. For example, there are sensible proposals for what should be done regarding the alleged coming crisis in Social Security: slow down the growth of benefits levels, gradually raise the retirement age, impose limits on expensive terminal medical care that prolongs life for only a few weeks or days, and finally, raise taxes now, rather than face large increases later.[23] But as things are, those who follow the "great game of politics" know that none of these sensible proposals will be accepted. The same story can be told about the importance of support for international institutions (such as the United Nations), foreign aid properly spent, and concern for human rights at home and abroad. In constant pursuit of money to finance campaigns, the political system is simply unable to function. Its deliberative powers are paralyzed.

§ 2: The Content of Public Reason

1. A citizen engages in public reason, then, when he or she deliberates within a framework of what he or she sincerely regards as the most reasonable political conception of justice, a conception that expresses political values that others, as free and equal citizens might also reasonably be expected reasonably to endorse. Each of us must have principles and guidelines to which we appeal in such a way that this criterion is satisfied. I have proposed that one way to identify those political principles and guidelines is to show that they would be agreed to in what in *Political Liberalism* is called the original position.[24] Others will think that different ways to identify these principles are more reasonable.

Thus, the content of public reason is given by a family of political conceptions of justice, and not by a single one. There are many liberalisms and related views, and therefore many forms of public reason specified by a family of reasonable political conceptions. Of these, justice as fairness, whatever its merits, is but one. The limiting feature of these forms is the criterion of reciprocity, viewed as applied between free and equal citizens, themselves seen as reasonable and rational. Three main features characterize these conceptions:

First, a list of certain basic rights, liberties, and opportunities (such as those familiar from constitutional regimes);

Second, an assignment of special priority to those rights, liberties, and opportunities, especially with respect to the claims of the general good and perfectionist values; and

Third, measures ensuring for all citizens adequate all-purpose means to make effective use of their freedoms.[25]

Each of these liberalisms endorses the underlying ideas of citizens as free and equal persons and of society as a fair system of cooperation over time. Yet since these ideas can be interpreted in various ways, we get different formulations of the principles of justice and different contents of public reason. Political conceptions differ also in how they order, or balance, political principles and values even when they specify the same ones. I assume also that these liberalisms contain substantive principles of justice, and hence cover more than procedural justice. They are required to specify the religious liberties and freedoms of artistic expression of equal citizens, as well as substantive ideas of fairness involving fair opportunity and ensuring adequate all-purpose means, and much else.[26]

Political liberalism, then, does not try to fix public reason once and for all in the form of one favored political conception of justice.[27] That would not be a sensible approach. For instance, political liberalism also admits Habermas's discourse conception of legitimacy (sometimes said to be radically democratic rather than liberal),[28] as well as Catholic views of the common good and solidarity when they are expressed in terms of political values.[29] Even if relatively few conceptions come to dominate over time, and one conception even appears to have a special central place, the forms of permissible public reason are always several. Moreover, new variations may be proposed from time to time and older ones may cease to be represented. It is important that this be so; otherwise the claims of groups or interests arising from social change might be repressed and fail to gain their appropriate political voice.[30]

2. We must distinguish public reason from what is sometimes referred to as secular reason and secular values. These are not the same as public reason. For I define secular reason as reasoning in terms of comprehensive nonreligious doctrines. Such doctrines and values are much too broad to serve the purposes of public reason. Political values are not moral doctrines,[31] however available or accessible these may be to our reason and common sense reflection. Moral doctrines are on a level with religion and first philosophy. By contrast, liberal political principles and values, although intrinsically moral values, are specified by liberal political conceptions of justice and fall under the category of the political. These political conceptions have three features:

First, their principles apply to basic political and social institutions (the basic structure of society);

Second, they can be presented independently from comprehensive doctrines of any kind (although they may, of course, be supported by a reasonable overlapping consensus of such doctrines); and

Finally, they can be worked out from fundamental ideas seen as implicit in the public political culture of a constitutional regime, such as the conceptions of citizens as free and equal persons, and of society as a fair system of cooperation.

Thus, the content of public reason is given by the principles and values of the family of liberal political conceptions of justice meeting these conditions. To engage in public reason is to appeal to one of these political conceptions—to their ideals and principles, standards and values—when debating fundamental political questions. This requirement still allows us to introduce into political discussion at any time our comprehensive doctrine, religious or nonreligious, provided that, in due course, we give properly public reasons to support the principles and policies our comprehensive doctrine is said to support. I refer to this requirement as *the proviso*, and consider it in detail below.[32]

A feature of public reasoning, then, is that it proceeds entirely within a political conception of justice. Examples of political values include those mentioned in the preamble to the United States Constitution: a more perfect union, justice, domestic tranquillity, the common defense, the general welfare, and the blessings of liberty for ourselves and our posterity. These include under them other values: so, for example, under justice we also have equal basic liberties, equality of opportunity, ideals concerning the distribution of income and taxation, and much else.

The political values of public reason are distinct from other values in that they are realized in and characterize political institutions. This does not mean that analogous values cannot characterize other social forms. The values of effectiveness and efficiency may characterize the social organization of teams and clubs, as well as the political institutions of the basic structure of society. But a value is properly political only when the social form is itself political: when it is realized, say, in parts of the basic structure and its political and social institutions. It follows that many political conceptions are nonliberal, including those of aristocracy and corporate oligarchy, and of autocracy and dictatorship. All of these fall within the category of the political.[33] We, however, are concerned only with those political conceptions that are reasonable for a constitutional democratic regime, and as the preceding paragraphs make clear, these are the ideals and principles expressed by reasonable liberal political conceptions.

3. Another essential feature of public reason is that its political conceptions should be complete. This means that each conception should express principles, standards, and ideals, along with guidelines of inquiry, such that the values specified by it can be suitably ordered or otherwise united so that those values alone give a reasonable answer to all, or to nearly all, questions involving constitutional essentials and matters of basic justice. Here the ordering of values is made in the light of their structure and features within the political conception itself, and not primarily from how they occur within citizens' comprehensive doctrines. Political values are not to be ordered by viewing them separately and detached from one another or from any definite context. They are not puppets manipulated from behind the scenes by comprehensive doctrines.[34] The ordering is not distorted by those doctrines provided that public reason sees the ordering as reasonable. And public reason can indeed see an ordering of political values as reasonable (or unreasonable), since institutional structures are open to view and mistakes and gaps within the political ordering will become exposed. Thus, we may be confident that the ordering of political values is not distorted by particular reasonable comprehensive doctrines. (I emphasize that the only criterion of distortion is that the ordering of political values be itself unreasonable.)

The significance of completeness lies in the fact that unless a political conception is complete, it is not an adequate framework of thought in the light of which the discussion of fundamental political questions can be carried out.[35] What we cannot do in public reason is to proceed directly from our comprehensive doctrine, or a part thereof, to one or several political principles and values, and the particular institutions they support. Instead, we are required first to work to the basic ideas of a complete political conception and from there to elaborate its principles and ideals, and to use the arguments they provide. Otherwise public reason allows arguments that are too immediate and fragmentary.

4. I now note several examples of political principles and values to illustrate the more specific content of public reason, and particularly the various ways in which the criterion of reciprocity is both applicable and subject to violation.

(a) As a first example, consider the value of autonomy. It may take two forms: one is political autonomy, the legal independence and assured integrity of citizens and their sharing equally with others in the exercise of political power; the other is purely moral and characterizes a certain way of life and reflection, critically examining our deepest ends and ideals, as in Mill's ideal of individuality.[36] Whatever we may think of autonomy as a purely moral value, it fails to satisfy, given reasonable pluralism, the constraint of reciprocity, as many citizens, for example, those holding certain religious doctrines, may reject it. Thus moral autonomy is not a political value, whereas political autonomy is.

(b) As a second example, consider the familiar story of the Good Samaritan. Are the values appealed to properly political values and not simply religious or philosophical values? While the wide view of public political culture allows us, in making a proposal, to introduce the Gospel story, public reason requires us to justify our proposal in terms of proper political values.[37]

(c) As a third example, consider appeals to desert in discussing the fair distribution of income: people are wont to say that ideally distribution should be in accordance with desert. What sense of desert do they have in mind? Do they mean that persons in various offices should have the requisite qualifications—judges must be qualified to judge—and all should have a fair opportunity to qualify themselves for favored positions? That is indeed a political value. But distribution in accordance with moral desert, where this means the moral worth of character, all things considered, and including comprehensive doctrines, is not. It is not a feasible political and social aim.

(d) Finally, consider the state's interest in the family and human life. How should the political value invoked be specified correctly? Traditionally it has been specified very broadly. But in a democratic regime the government's legitimate interest is that public law and policy should support and regulate, in an ordered way, the institutions needed to reproduce political society over time. These include the family (in a form that is just), arrangements for rearing and educating children, and institutions of public health generally. This ordered support and regulation rests on political principles and values, since political society is regarded as existing in perpetuity and so as maintaining itself and its institutions and culture over generations. Given this interest, the government would appear to have no interest in the particular form of family life, or of relations among the sexes, except insofar as that form or those relations in some way affect the orderly reproduction of society over time. Thus, appeals to monogamy as such, or against same-sex marriages, as within the government's legitimate interest in the family, would reflect religious or comprehensive moral doctrines. Accordingly, that interest would appear improperly specified. Of course, there may be other political values in the light of which such a specification would pass muster: for example, if monogamy were necessary for the equality of women, or same-sex marriages destructive to the raising and educating of children.[38]

5. The four examples bring out a contrast to what I have above called secular reason.[39] A view often expressed is that while religious reasons and sectarian doctrines should not be invoked to justify legislation in a democratic society, sound secular arguments may be.[40] But what is a secular argument? Some think of any argument that is reflective and critical, publicly intelligible and rational, as a secular argument; and they discuss various such arguments for considering, say, homosexual relations unworthy or degrading.[41] Of course, some of these arguments may be reflective and rational secular ones (as so defined). Nevertheless, a central feature of political liberalism is that it views all such arguments the same way it views religious ones, and therefore these secular philosophical doctrines do not provide public reasons. Secular concepts and reasoning of this kind belong to first philosophy and moral doctrine, and fall outside of the domain of the political.

Thus, in considering whether to make homosexual relations between citizens criminal offenses, the question is not whether those relations are precluded by a worthy idea of full human good as characterized by a sound philosophical and nonreligious view, nor whether those of religious faith regard it as sin, but primarily whether legislative statutes forbidding those relations infringe the civil rights of free and equal democratic citizens.[42] This question calls for a reasonable political conception of justice specifying those civil rights, which are always a matter of constitutional essentials.

§ 3: Religion and Public Reason in Democracy

1. Before examining the idea of the wide view of public political culture, we ask: How is it possible for those holding religious doctrines, some based on religious authority, for example, the Church or the Bible, to hold at the same time a reasonable political conception that supports a reasonable constitutional democratic regime? Can these doctrines still be compatible for the right reasons with a liberal political conception? To attain this compatibility, it is not sufficient that these doctrines accept a democratic government merely as a *modus vivendi*. Referring to citizens holding religious doctrines as citizens of faith we ask: How is it possible for citizens of faith to be wholehearted members of a democratic society who endorse society's intrinsic political ideals and values and do not simply acquiesce in the balance of political and social forces? Expressed more sharply: How is it possible—or is it— for those of faith, as well as the nonreligious (secular), to endorse a constitutional regime even when their comprehensive doctrines may not prosper under it, and indeed may decline? This last question brings out anew the significance of the idea of legitimacy and public reason's role in determining legitimate law.

To clarify the question, consider two examples. The first is that of Catholics and Protestants in the sixteenth and seventeenth centuries when the principle of toleration was honored only as a *modus vivendi*.[43] This meant that should either party fully gain its way it would impose its own religious doctrine as the sole admissible faith. A society in which many faiths all share this attitude and assume that for the indefinite future their relative numbers will stay roughly the same might well have a constitution resembling that of the United States, fully protecting the religious liberties of sharply divided religions more or less equal in political power. The constitution is, as it were, honored as a pact to maintain civil peace.[44] In this society political issues might be discussed in terms of political ideas and values so as not to open religious conflict and arouse sectarian hostility. The role of public reason here serves merely to quiet divisiveness and encourage social stability. However, in this case we do not have stability for the right reasons, that is, as secured by a firm allegiance to a democratic society's political (moral) ideals and values.

Nor again do we have stability for the right reasons in the second example—a democratic society where citizens accept as political (moral) principles the substantive constitutional clauses that ensure religious, political, and civil liberties, when their allegiance to these constitutional principles is so limited that none is willing to see his or her religious or nonreligious doctrine losing ground in influence and numbers, and such citizens are prepared to resist or to disobey laws that they think undermine their positions. And they do this even though the full range of religious and other liberties is always maintained and the doctrine in question is completely secure. Here again democracy is accepted conditionally and not for the right reasons.

What these examples have in common is that society is divided into separate groups, each of which has its own fundamental interest distinct from and opposed to the interests of the other groups and for which it is prepared to resist or to violate legitimate democratic law. In the first example, it is the interest of a religion in establishing its hegemony, while in the second, it is the doctrine's fundamental interest in maintaining a certain degree of success and influence for its own view, either religious or nonreligious. While a constitutional regime can fully ensure rights and liberties for all permissible doctrines, and therefore protect our freedom and security, a democracy necessarily requires that, as one equal citizen among others, each of us accept the obligations of legitimate law.[45] While no one is expected to put his or her religious or nonreligious doctrine in danger, we must each give up forever the hope of changing the constitution so as to establish our religion's hegemony, or of qualifying our obligations so as to ensure its influence and success. To retain such hopes and aims would be inconsistent with the idea of equal basic liberties for all free and equal citizens.

2. To expand on what we asked earlier: How is it possible—or is it—for those of faith, as well as the nonreligious (secular), to endorse a constitutional regime even when their comprehensive doctrines may not prosper under it, and indeed may decline? Here the answer lies in the religious or nonreligious doctrine's understanding and accepting that, except by endorsing a reasonable constitutional democracy, there is no other way fairly to ensure the liberty of its adherents consistent with the equal liberties of other reasonable free and equal citizens. In endorsing a constitutional democratic regime, a religious doctrine may say that such are the limits God sets to our liberty; a nonreligious doctrine will express itself otherwise.[46] But in either case, these doctrines formulate in different ways how liberty of conscience and the principle of toleration can cohere with equal justice for all citizens in a reasonable democratic society. Thus, the principles of toleration and liberty of conscience must have an essential place in any constitutional democratic conception. They lay down the fundamental basis to be accepted by all citizens as fair and regulative of the rivalry between doctrines.

Observe here that there are two ideas of toleration. One is purely political, being expressed in terms of the rights and duties protecting religious liberty in accordance with a reasonable political conception of justice. The other is not purely political but expressed from within a religious or a nonreligious doctrine, as when, for example, it was said above that such are the limits God sets on our liberty. Saying this offers an example of what I call reasoning from conjecture.[47] In this case we reason from what we believe, or conjecture, may be other people's basic doctrines, religious or philosophical, and seek to show them that, despite what they might think, they can still endorse a reasonable political conception of justice. We are not ourselves asserting that ground of toleration but offering it as one they could assert consistent with their comprehensive doctrines.

§ 4: The Wide View of Public Political Culture

1. Now we consider what I call the wide view of public political culture and discuss two aspects of it. The first is that reasonable comprehensive doctrines, religious or nonreligious, may be introduced in public political discussion at any time, provided that in due course proper political reasons—and not reasons given solely by comprehensive doctrines—are presented that are sufficient to support whatever the comprehensive doctrines introduced are said to support. This injunction to present proper political reasons I refer to as *the proviso*, and it specifies public political culture as distinct from the background culture.[48] The second aspect I consider is that

there may be positive reasons for introducing comprehensive doctrines into public political discussion. I take up these two aspects in turn.

Obviously, many questions may be raised about how to satisfy the proviso.[49] One is: when does it need to be satisfied? On the same day or some later day? Also, on whom does the obligation to honor it fall? It is important that it be clear and established that the proviso is to be appropriately satisfied in good faith. Yet the details about how to satisfy this proviso must be worked out in practice and cannot feasibly be governed by a clear family of rules given in advance. How they work out is determined by the nature of the public political culture and calls for good sense and understanding. It is important also to observe that the introduction into public political culture of religious and secular doctrines, provided the proviso is met, does not change the nature and content of justification in public reason itself. This justification is still given in terms of a family of reasonable political conceptions of justice. However, there are no restrictions or requirements on how religious or secular doctrines are themselves to be expressed; these doctrines need not, for example, be by some standards logically correct, or open to rational appraisal, or evidentially supportable.[50] Whether they are or not is a matter to be decided by those presenting them, and how they want what they say to be taken. They will normally have practical reasons for wanting to make their views acceptable to a broader audience.

2. Citizens' mutual knowledge of one another's religious and nonreligious doctrines expressed in the wide view of public political culture[51] recognizes that the roots of democratic citizens' allegiance to their political conceptions lie in their respective comprehensive doctrines, both religious and nonreligious. In this way citizens' allegiance to the democratic ideal of public reason is strengthened for the right reasons. We may think of the reasonable comprehensive doctrines that support society's reasonable political conceptions as those conceptions' vital social basis, giving them enduring strength and vigor. When these doctrines accept the proviso and only then come into political debate, the commitment to constitutional democracy is publicly manifested.[52] Made aware of this commitment, government officials and citizens are more willing to honor the duty of civility, and their following the ideal of public reason helps foster the kind of society that ideal exemplifies. These benefits of the mutual knowledge of citizens' recognizing one another's reasonable comprehensive doctrines bring out a positive ground for introducing such doctrines, which is not merely a defensive ground, as if their intrusion into public discussion were inevitable in any case.

Consider, for example, a highly contested political issue—the issue of public support for church schools.[53] Those on different sides are likely to come to doubt one another's allegiance to basic constitutional and political values. It is wise, then, for all sides to introduce their comprehensive doctrines, whether religious or secular, so as to open the way for them to explain to one another how their views do indeed support those basic political values. Consider also the Abolitionists and those in the Civil Rights Movement.[54] The proviso was fulfilled in their cases, however much they emphasized the religious roots of their doctrines, because these doctrines supported basic constitutional values—as they themselves asserted—and so supported reasonable conceptions of political justice.

3. Public reasoning aims for public justification. We appeal to political concep-tions of justice, and to ascertainable evidence and facts open to public view, in order to reach conclusions about what we think are the most reasonable political institu-tions and policies. Public justification is not simply valid reasoning, but argument addressed to others: it proceeds correctly from premises we accept and think others could reasonably accept to conclusions we think they could also reasonably accept. This meets the duty of civility, since in due course the proviso is satisfied.

There are two other forms of discourse that may also be mentioned, though nei-ther expresses a form of public reasoning. One is declaration: here we each declare our own comprehensive doctrine, religious or nonreligious. This we do not expect others to share. Rather, each of us shows how, from our own doctrines, we can and do endorse a reasonable public political conception of justice with its principles and ideals. The aim of doing this is to declare to others who affirm different comprehen-sive doctrines that we also each endorse a reasonable political conception belonging to the family of reasonable such conceptions. On the wide view, citizens of faith who cite the Gospel parable of the Good Samaritan do not stop there, but go on to give a public justification for this parable's conclusions in terms of political values.[55] In this way citizens who hold different doctrines are reassured, and this strengthens the ties of civic friendship.[56]

The second form is conjecture, defined thus: we argue from what we believe, or conjecture, are other people's basic doctrines, religious or secular, and try to show them that, despite what they might think, they can still endorse a reasonable po-litical conception that can provide a basis for public reasons. The ideal of public reason is thereby strengthened. However, it is important that conjecture be sincere and not manipulative. We must openly explain our intentions and state that we do not assert the premises from which we argue, but that we proceed as we do to clear up what we take to be a misunderstanding on others' part, and perhaps equally on ours.[57]

[. . .]

§ 6: Questions about Public Reason

I now turn to various questions and doubts about the idea of public reason and try to allay them.

1. First, it may be objected that the idea of public reason would unreasonably limit the topics and considerations available for political argument and debate, and that we should adopt instead what we may call the open view with no constraints. I now discuss two examples to rebut this objection.

(a) One reason for thinking public reason is too restrictive is to suppose that it mistakenly tries to settle political questions in advance. To explain this objection, let's consider the question of school prayer. It might be thought that a liberal posi-tion on this question would deny its admissibility in public schools. But why so? We have to consider all the political values that can be invoked to settle this ques-tion and on which side the decisive reasons fall. The famous debate in 1784–1785 between Patrick Henry and James Madison over the establishment of the Anglican Church in Virginia and involving religion in the schools was argued almost entirely by reference to political values alone. Henry's argument for establishment was based on the view that:

Christian knowledge hath a natural tendency to correct the morals of men, restrain their vices, and preserve the peace of society, which cannot be effected without a competent provision for learned teachers. . .[58]

Henry did not seem to argue for Christian knowledge as good in itself but rather as an effective way to achieve basic political values, namely, the good and peaceable conduct of citizens. Thus, I take him to mean by "vices," at least in part, those actions contrary to the political virtues found in political liberalism,[59] and expressed by other conceptions of democracy.

Leaving aside the obvious difficulty of whether prayers can be composed that satisfy all the needed restrictions of political justice, Madison's objections to Henry's bill turned largely on whether religious establishment was necessary to support orderly civil society. He concluded it was not. Madison's objections depended also on the historical effects of establishment both on society and on the integrity of religion itself. He was acquainted with the prosperity of colonies that had no establishment, notably Pennsylvania; he cited the strength of early Christianity in opposition to the hostile Roman Empire, and the corruption of past establishments.[60] With some care, many if not all of these arguments can be expressed in terms of the political values of public reason.

Of special interest in the example of school prayer is that it brings out that the idea of public reason is not a view about specific political institutions or policies. Rather, it is a view about the kind of reasons on which citizens are to rest their political cases in making their political justifications to one another when they support laws and policies that invoke the coercive powers of government concerning fundamental political questions. Also of special interest in this example is that it serves to emphasize that the principles that support the separation of church and state should be such that they can be affirmed by all free and equal citizens, given the fact of reasonable pluralism.

The reasons for the separation of church and state are these, among others: It protects religion from the state and the state from religion; it protects citizens from their churches[61] and citizens from one another. It is a mistake to say that political liberalism is an individualist political conception, since its aim is the protection of the various interests in liberty, both associational and individual. And it is also a grave error to think that the separation of church and state is primarily for the protection of secular culture; of course it does protect that culture, but no more so than it protects all religions. The vitality and wide acceptance of religion in America is often commented upon, as if it were a sign of the peculiar virtue of the American people. Perhaps so, but it may also be connected with the fact that in this country the various religions have been protected by the First Amendment from the state, and none has been able to dominate and suppress the other religions by the capture and use of state power.[62] While some have no doubt entertained that aim since the early days of the Republic, it has not been seriously tried. Indeed, Tocqueville thought that among the main causes of the strength of democracy in this country was the separation of church and state.[63] Political liberalism agrees with many other liberal views in accepting this proposition.[64] Some citizens of faith have felt that this separation is hostile to religion and have sought to change it. In doing this I believe they fail to grasp a main cause of the strength of religion in this country and, as Tocqueville says, seem ready to jeopardize it for temporary gains in political power.

(b) Others may think that public reason is too restrictive because it may lead to a stand-off[65] and fail to bring about decisions on disputed issues. A stand-off in some sense may indeed happen, not only in moral and political reasoning but in all forms of reasoning, including science and common sense. Nevertheless, this is irrelevant. The relevant comparison is to those situations in which legislators enacting laws and judges deciding cases must make decisions. Here some political rule of action must be laid down and all must be able reasonably to endorse the process by which a decision is reached. Recall that public reason sees the office of citizen with its duty of civility as analogous to that of judge with its duty of deciding cases. Just as judges are to decide cases by legal grounds of precedent, recognized canons of statutory interpretation, and other relevant grounds, so citizens are to reason by public reason and to be guided by the criterion of reciprocity, whenever constitutional essentials and matters of basic justice are at stake.

Thus, when there seems to be a stand-off, that is, when legal arguments seem evenly balanced on both sides, judges cannot resolve the case simply by appealing to their own political views. To do that is for judges to violate their duty. The same holds with public reason: if, when stand-offs occur, citizens simply invoke grounding reasons of their comprehensive views,[66] the principle of reciprocity is violated. From the point of view of public reason, citizens must vote for the ordering of political values they sincerely think the most reasonable. Otherwise they fail to exercise political power in ways that satisfy the criterion of reciprocity.

In particular, when hotly disputed questions, such as that of abortion, arise which may lead to a stand-off between different political conceptions, citizens must vote on the question according to their complete ordering of political values.[67] Indeed, this is a normal case: unanimity of views is not to be expected. Reasonable political conceptions of justice do not always lead to the same conclusion;[68] nor do citizens holding the same conception always agree on particular issues. Yet the outcome of the vote, as I said before, is to be seen as legitimate provided all government officials, supported by other reasonable citizens, of a reasonably just constitutional regime sincerely vote in accordance with the idea of public reason. This doesn't mean the outcome is true or correct, but that it is reasonable and legitimate law, binding on citizens by the majority principle.

Some may, of course, reject a legitimate decision, as Roman Catholics may reject a decision to grant a right to abortion. They may present an argument in public reason for denying it and fail to win a majority.[69] But they need not themselves exercise the right to abortion. They can recognize the right as belonging to legitimate law enacted in accordance with legitimate political institutions and public reason, and therefore not resist it with force. Forceful resistance is unreasonable: it would mean attempting to impose by force their own comprehensive doctrine that a majority of other citizens who follow public reason, not unreasonably, do not accept. Certainly Catholics may, in line with public reason, continue to argue against the right to abortion. Reasoning is not closed once and for all in public reason any more than it is closed in any form of reasoning. Moreover, that the Catholic Church's nonpublic reason requires its members to follow its doctrine is perfectly consistent with their also honoring public reason.[70]

I do not discuss the question of abortion in itself since my concern is not with that question but rather to stress that political liberalism does not hold that the ideal of public reason should always lead to a general agreement of views, nor is it a fault that it does not. Citizens learn and profit from debate and argument, and when their arguments follow public reason, they instruct society's political culture and deepen their understanding of one another even when agreement cannot be reached.

2. Some of the considerations underlying the stand-off objection lead to a more general objection to public reason, namely, that the content of the family of reasonable political conceptions of justice on which it is based is itself much too narrow. This objection insists that we should always present what we think are true or grounding reasons for our views. That is, the objection insists, we are bound to express the true, or the right, as seen from our comprehensive doctrines.

However, as I said in the Introduction, in public reason ideas of truth or right based on comprehensive doctrines are replaced by an idea of the politically reasonable addressed to citizens as citizens. This step is necessary to establish a basis of political reasoning that all can share as free and equal citizens. Since we are seeking public justifications for political and social institutions—for the basic structure of a political and social world—we think of persons as citizens. This assigns to each person the same basic political position. In giving reasons to all citizens we don't view persons as socially situated or otherwise rooted, that is, as being in this or that social class, or in this or that property and income group, or as having this or that comprehensive doctrine. Nor are we appealing to each person's or each group's interests, though at some point we must take these interests into account. Rather, we think of persons as reasonable and rational, as free and equal citizens, with the two moral powers[71] and having, at any given moment, a determinate conception of the good, which may change over time. These features of citizens are implicit in their taking part in a fair system of social cooperation and seeking and presenting public justifications for their judgments on fundamental political questions.

I emphasize that this idea of public reason is fully compatible with the many forms of nonpublic reason.[72] These belong to the internal life of the many associations in civil society and they are not of course all the same; different nonpublic reasons of different religious associations shared by their members are not those of scientific societies. Since we seek a shareable public basis of justification for all citizens in society, giving justifications to particular persons and groups here and there until all are covered fails to do this. To speak of all persons in society is still too broad, unless we suppose that they are in their nature basically the same. In political philosophy one role of ideas about our nature has been to think of people in a standard, or canonical, fashion so that they might all accept the same kind of reasons.[73] In political liberalism, however, we try to avoid natural or psychological views of this kind, as well as theological or secular doctrines. Accounts of human nature we put aside and rely on a political conception of persons as citizens instead.

3. As I have stressed throughout, it is central to political liberalism that free and equal citizens affirm both a comprehensive doctrine and a political conception. However, the relation between a comprehensive doctrine and its accompanying political conception is easily misunderstood.

When political liberalism speaks of a reasonable overlapping consensus of comprehensive doctrines,[74] it means that all of these doctrines, both religious and nonreligious, support a political conception of justice underwriting a constitutional democratic society whose principles, ideals, and standards satisfy the criterion of reciprocity. Thus, all reasonable doctrines affirm such a society with its corresponding political institutions: equal basic rights and liberties for all citizens, including liberty of conscience and the freedom of religion.[75] On the other hand, comprehensive doctrines that cannot support such a democratic society are not reasonable. Their principles and ideals do not satisfy the criterion of reciprocity, and in various ways they fail to establish the equal basic liberties. As examples, consider the many fundamentalist religious doctrines, the doctrine of the divine right of monarchs and the various forms of aristocracy, and, not to be overlooked, the many instances of autocracy and dictatorship.

Moreover, a true judgment in a reasonable comprehensive doctrine never conflicts with a reasonable judgment in its related political conception. A reasonable judgment of the political conception must still be confirmed as true, or right, by the comprehensive doctrine. It is, of course, up to citizens themselves to affirm, revise, or change their comprehensive doctrines. Their doctrines may override or count for naught the political values of a constitutional democratic society. But then the citizens cannot claim that such doctrines are reasonable. Since the criterion of reciprocity is an essential ingredient specifying public reason and its content, political liberalism rejects as unreasonable all such doctrines.

In a reasonable comprehensive doctrine, in particular a religious one, the ranking of values may not be what we might expect. Thus, suppose we call *transcendent* such values as salvation and eternal life—the *Visio Dei*. This value, let's say, is higher, or superior to, the reasonable political values of a constitutional democratic society. These are worldly values and therefore on a different, and as it were lower, plane than those transcendent values. It doesn't follow, however, that these lower yet reasonable values are overridden by the transcendent values of the religious doctrine. In fact, a *reasonable* comprehensive doctrine is one in which they are not overridden; it is the unreasonable doctrines in which reasonable political values are overridden. This is a consequence of the idea of the politically reasonable as set out in political liberalism. Recall that it was said: In endorsing a constitutional democratic regime, a religious doctrine may say that such are the limits God sets to our liberty.[76]

A further misunderstanding alleges that an argument in public reason could not side with Lincoln against Douglas in their debates of 1858.[77] But why not? Certainly they were debating fundamental political principles about the rights and wrongs of slavery. Since the rejection of slavery is a clear case of securing the constitutional essential of the equal basic liberties, surely Lincoln's view was reasonable (even if not the most reasonable), while Douglas's was not. Therefore, Lincoln's view is supported by any reasonable comprehensive doctrine. It is no surprise, then, that his view is in line with the religious doctrines of the Abolitionists and the Civil Rights Movement. What could be a better example to illustrate the force of public reason in political life?[78]

4. A third general objection is that the idea of public reason is unnecessary and serves no purpose in a well established constitutional democracy. Its limits and constraints are useful primarily when a society is sharply divided and contains many

hostile religious associations and secular groups, each striving to become the controlling political force. In the political societies of the European democracies and the United States these worries, so the objection goes, are idle.

However, this objection is incorrect and sociologically faulty. For without citizens' allegiance to public reason and their honoring the duty of civility, divisions and hostilities between doctrines are bound in time to assert themselves, should they not already exist. Harmony and concord among doctrines and a people's affirming public reason are unhappily not a permanent condition of social life. Rather, harmony and concord depend on the vitality of the public political culture and on citizens' being devoted to and realizing the ideal of public reason. Citizens could easily fall into bitterness and resentment, once they no longer see the point of affirming an ideal of public reason and come to ignore it.

To return to where we began in this Section: I do not know how to prove that public reason is not too restrictive, or whether its forms are properly described. I suspect it cannot be done. Yet this is not a serious problem if, as I believe, the large majority of cases fit the framework of public reason, and the cases that do not fit all have special features that both enable us to understand why they should cause difficulty and show us how to cope with them as they arise. This prompts the general questions of whether there are examples of important cases of constitutional essentials and basic justice that do not fit the framework of public reason, and if so, why they cause difficulty. In this paper I do not pursue these questions.

7: Conclusion

1. Throughout, I have been concerned with a torturing question in the contemporary world, namely: Can democracy and comprehensive doctrines, religious or nonreligious, be compatible? And if so, how? At the moment a number of conflicts between religion and democracy raise this question. To answer it political liberalism makes the distinction between a self-standing political conception of justice and a comprehensive doctrine. A religious doctrine resting on the authority of the Church or the Bible is not, of course, a liberal comprehensive doctrine: its leading religious and moral values are not those, say, of Kant or Mill. Nevertheless, it may endorse a constitutional democratic society and recognize its public reason. Here it is basic that public reason is a political idea and belongs to the category of the political. Its content is given by the family of (liberal) political conceptions of justice satisfying the criterion of reciprocity. It does not trespass upon religious beliefs and injunctions insofar as these are consistent with the essential constitutional liberties, including the freedom of religion and liberty of conscience. There is, or need be, no war between religion and democracy. In this respect political liberalism is sharply different from and rejects Enlightenment Liberalism, which historically attacked orthodox Christianity.

The conflicts between democracy and reasonable religious doctrines and among reasonable religious doctrines themselves are greatly mitigated and contained within the bounds of reasonable principles of justice in a constitutional democratic society. This mitigation is due to the idea of toleration, and I have distinguished between two such ideas.[79] One is purely political, being expressed in terms of the rights and duties protecting religious liberty in accordance with a reasonable political conception of justice.[80] The other is not purely political but expressed from within a religious or a nonreligious doctrine. However, a reasonable judgment of the political conception must still be confirmed as true, or right, by a reasonable comprehensive doctrine.[81] I assume, then, that a reasonable comprehensive doctrine accepts some form of the political argument for toleration. Of course, citizens may think that the grounding reasons for toleration and for the other elements of a constitutional democratic society are not political but rather are to be found in their religious or nonreligious doctrines. And these reasons, they may well say, are the true or the right reasons; and they may see the political reasons as superficial, the grounding ones as deep. Yet there is no conflict here, but simply concordant judgments made within political conceptions of justice on the one hand, and within comprehensive doctrines on the other.

There are limits, however, to reconciliation by public reason. Three main kinds of conflicts set citizens at odds: those deriving from irreconcilable comprehensive doctrines; those deriving from differences in status, class position, or occupation, or from differences in ethnicity, gender, or race; and finally, those deriving from the burdens of judgment.[82] Political liberalism concerns primarily the first kind of conflict. It holds that even though our comprehensive doctrines are irreconcilable and cannot be compromised, nevertheless citizens who affirm reasonable doctrines may share reasons of another kind, namely, public reasons given in terms of political conceptions of justice. I also believe that such a society can resolve the second kind of conflict, which deals with conflicts between citizens' fundamental interests— political, economic, and social. For once we accept reasonable principles of justice and recognize them to be reasonable (even if not the most reasonable), and know, or reasonably believe, that our political and social institutions satisfy them, the second kind of conflict need not arise, or arise so forcefully. Political liberalism does not explicitly consider these conflicts but leaves them to be considered by justice as fairness, or by some other reasonable conception of political justice. Finally, conflicts arising from the burdens of judgment always exist and limit the extent of possible agreement.

2. Reasonable comprehensive doctrines do not reject the essentials of a constitutional democratic polity.[83] Moreover, reasonable persons are characterized in two ways: First, they stand ready to offer fair terms of social cooperation between equals, and they abide by these terms if others do also, even should it be to their advantage not to;[84] second, reasonable persons recognize and accept the consequences of the burdens of judgment, which leads to the idea of reasonable toleration in a democratic society.[85] Finally we come to the idea of legitimate law, which reasonable citizens understand to apply to the general structure of political authority.[86] They know that in political life unanimity can rarely if ever be expected, so a reasonable democratic constitution must include majority or other plurality voting procedures in order to reach decisions.[87]

The idea of the politically reasonable is sufficient unto itself for the purposes of public reason when basic political questions are at stake. Of course, fundamentalist religious doctrines and autocratic and dictatorial rulers will reject the ideas of public reason and deliberative democracy. They will say that democracy leads to a culture contrary to their religion, or denies the values that only autocratic or dictatorial rule can secure.[88] They assert that the religiously true, or the philosophically true, overrides the politically reasonable. We simply say that such a doctrine is politically unreasonable. Within political liberalism nothing more need be said.

I noted in the beginning[89] the fact that every actual society, however dominant and controlling its reasonable citizens may be, will normally contain numerous unreasonable doctrines that are not compatible with a democratic society—either certain religious doctrines, such as fundamentalist religions, or certain non-religious (secular) doctrines, such as those of autocracy and dictatorship, of which our century offers hideous examples. How far unreasonable doctrines may be active and are to be tolerated in a constitutional democratic regime does not present a new and different question, despite the fact that in this account of public reason we have focused on the idea of the reasonable and the role of reasonable citizens. There is not one account of toleration for reasonable doctrines and another for unreasonable ones. Both cases are settled by the appropriate political principles of justice and the conduct those principles permit.[90] Unreasonable doctrines are a threat to democratic institutions, since it is impossible for them to abide by a constitutional regime except as a *modus vivendi*. Their existence sets a limit to the aim of fully realizing a reasonable democratic society with its ideal of public reason and the idea of legitimate law. This fact is not a defect or failure of the idea of public reason, but rather it indicates that there are limits to what public reason can accomplish. It does not diminish the great value and importance of attempting to realize that ideal to the fullest extent possible.

3. I end by pointing out the fundamental difference between *A Theory of Justice* and *Political Liberalism*. The first explicitly attempts to develop from the idea of the social contract, represented by Locke, Rousseau, and Kant, a theory of justice that is no longer open to objections often thought fatal to it, and that proves superior to the long dominant tradition of utilitarianism. *A Theory of Justice* hopes to present the structural features of such a theory so as to make it the best approximation to our considered judgments of justice and hence to give the most appropriate moral basis for a democratic society. Furthermore, justice as fairness is presented there as a comprehensive liberal doctrine (although the term "comprehensive doctrine" is not used in the book) in which all the members of its well ordered society affirm that same doctrine. This kind of well ordered society contradicts the fact of reasonable pluralism and hence *Political Liberalism* regards that society as impossible.

Thus, *Political Liberalism* considers a different question, namely: How is it possible for those affirming a comprehensive doctrine, religious or nonreligious, and in particular doctrines based on religious authority, such as the Church or the Bible, also to hold a reasonable political conception of justice that supports a constitutional democratic society? The political conceptions are seen as both liberal and self-standing and not as comprehensive, whereas the religious doctrines may be comprehensive but not liberal. The two books are asymmetrical, though both have an idea of public reason. In the first, public reason is given by a comprehensive liberal doctrine, while in the second, public reason is a way of reasoning about political values shared by free and equal citizens that does not trespass on citizens' comprehensive doctrines so long as those doctrines are consistent with a democratic polity. Thus, the well ordered constitutional democratic society of *Political Liberalism* is one in which the dominant and controlling citizens affirm and act from irreconcilable yet reasonable comprehensive doctrines. These doctrines in turn support reasonable political conceptions—although not necessarily the most reasonable—which specify the basic rights, liberties, and opportunities of citizens in society's basic structure.

NOTES

† Emeritus Professor of Philosophy, Harvard University. This essay is a revision of a lecture given at The University of Chicago Law School in November 1993. I should like to thank Joshua Cohen, Erin Kelly, Percy Lehning, Michael Perry, Margaret Rawls, and T.M. Scanlon for their great help and advise in writing this paper. Throughout they have given me numerous suggestions, which I have gladly accepted. Above all, to Burton Dreben I am especially indebted: as so often before, he has been generous beyond measure in his efforts; in every section he has helped me reorganize and reshape the text, giving it a clarity and simplicity it would not otherwise have had. Without their constant advise and encouragement, and that of others mentioned below, I never could have completed the revisions of my original lecture.

1. See John Rawls, *Political Liberalism*, lecture VI, § 8.5 (Columbia paperback ed. 1996). References to *Political Liberalism* are given by lecture and section; page numbers are also provided unless the reference refers to an entire lecture, section, or subsection. Note that the 1996 paperback edition of *Political Liberalism* contains a new second introduction which, among other things, tries to make clearer certain aspects of political liberalism. Section 5 of this introduction, id at I-Ivii, discusses the idea of public reason and sketches several changes I now make in affirming this idea. These are all followed and elaborated in what is presented here and are important to a complete understanding of the argument. Note also that the pagination of the paperback edition is the same as the original.

2. I shall use the term *doctrine* for comprehensive views of all kinds and the term *conception* for a political conception and its component parts, such as the conception of the person as citizen. The term *idea* is used as a general term and may refer to either as the context determines.

3. Of course, every society also contains numerous unreasonable doctrines. Yet in this essay I am concerned with an ideal normative conception of democratic government, that is, with the conduct of its reasonable citizens and the principles they follow, assuming them to be dominant and controlling. How far unreasonable doctrines are active and tolerated is to be determined by the principles of justice and the kinds of actions they permit. See § 7.2.

4. See § 6.2.

5. See § 1.2.

6. See text accompanying notes 12–15.

7. These questions are described in Rawls, *Political Liberalism*, lecture VI, § 5 at 227–30 (cited in note 1). Constitutional essentials concern questions about what political rights and liberties, say, may reasonably be included in a written constitution, when assuming the constitution may be interpreted by a supreme court, or some similar body. Matters of basic justice relate to the basic structure of society and so would concern questions of basic economic and social justice and other things not covered by a constitution.

8. There is no settled meaning of this term. The one I use is not I think peculiar.

9. Here we face the question of where to draw the line between candidates and those who manage their campaigns and other politically engaged citizens generally. We settle this matter by making candidates and those who run their campaigns responsible for what is said and done on the candidates' behalf.

10. Often writers on this topic use terms that do not distinguish the parts of public discussion, for example, such terms as "the public square," "the public forum," and the like. I follow Kent Greenawalt in thinking a finer division is necessary. See Kent Greenawalt,

Religious Convictions and Political Choice 226–27 (Oxford 1988) (describing, for example, the differences between a religious leader's preaching or promoting a pro-life organization arid leading a major political movement or running for political office).

11. See § 4.

12. Rawls, *Political Liberalism,* lecture I, § 2.3 at 14 (cited in note 1).

13. The background culture includes, then, the culture of churches and associations of all kinds, and institutions of learning at all levels, especially universities and professional schools, scientific and other societies. In addition, the nonpublic political culture mediates between the public political culture and the background culture. This comprises media— properly so named—of all kinds: newspapers, reviews and magazines, TV and radio, and much else. Compare these divisions with Habermas's account of the public sphere. See Rawls, *Political Liberalism,* lecture IX, § 1.3 at 382 n 13 (cited in note 1).

14. See id, lecture VI, § 3 at 220–22.

15. See David Hollenbach, S.J., *Civil Society: Beyond the Public-Private Dichotomy,* 5; *The Responsive Community* 15 (Winter 1994/95). For example, he says:
Conversation and argument about the common good will not occur initially in the legis-lature or in the political sphere (narrowly conceived as the domain in which interests and power are adjudicated). Rather it will develop freely in those components of civil society that are the primary bearers of cultural meaning and value—universities, religious commu-nities, the world of the arts, and serious journalism. It can occur wherever thoughtful men and women bring their beliefs on the meaning of the good life into intelligent and critical encounter with understandings of this good held by other peoples with other traditions. In short, it occurs wherever education about and serious inquiry into the meaning of the good life takes place. Id at 22.

16. There is some resemblance between this criterion and Kant's principle of the original contract. See Immanuel Kant, *The Metaphysics of Morals: Metaphysical First Principles of the Doctrine of Right* §§ 47–49 at 92–95 (AK 6:315–18) (Cambridge 1996) (Mary Gregor, trans and ed); Immanuel Kant, *On the Common Saying: 'This May be True in Theory, but it does not Apply in Practice,'* Part II, in *Kant: Political Writings* 73–87 (AK 8: 289–306) (Cambridge 2d ed 1991) (Hans Reiss, ed, H.B. Nisbet, trans).

17. See also § 4.2.

18. Rawls, *Political Liberalism,* lecture I, § 2.1 at 12 (cited in note 1). For concerns about exiting only by death, see id, lecture 1V, § 1.2 at 136 n 4.

19. The idea of reciprocity has an important place in Amy Gutmann and Dennis Thomp-son, *Democracy and Disagreement* chs 1–2 and passim (Belknap 1996). However, the meaning and setting of our views are not the same. Public reason in political liberalism is purely po-litical, although political values are intrinsically moral, whereas Gutmann and Thompson's account is more general and seems to work from a comprehensive doctrine.

20. For a useful historical survey see David Held, *Models of Democracy* (Stanford 2d ed 1997). Held's numerous models cover the period from the ancient polis to the present time and he concludes by asking what democracy should mean today. In between he considers the several forms of classical republicanism and classical liberalism, as well as Schumpeter's conception of competitive elite democracy. Some figures discussed include Plato and Aristo-tle; Marsilius of Padua and Machiavelli; Hobbes and Madison; Bentham, James Mill and J. S. Mill; Marx with socialism and communism. These are paired with schematized models of the characteristic institutions and their roles.

21. Deliberative democracy limits the reasons citizens may give in supporting their po-litical opinions to reasons consistent with their seeing other citizens as equals. See Joshua Cohen, *Deliberation and Democratic Legitimacy,* in Alan Hamlin and Philip Petit, eds, *The Good Polity: Normative Analysis of the State* 17, 21, 24 (Basil Blackwell 1989); *Review Symposium on* Democracy and Its Critics, 53 J Pol 215, 223–24 (1991) (comments of Joshua Cohen);

Joshua Cohen, *Democracy and Liberty* 13–17 (manuscript on file with U Chi L Rev), in Jon Elster, ed, *Deliberative Democracy* (forthcoming 1997).

22. Ronald Dworkin, *The Curse of American Politics,* NY Rev Books 19 (Oct 17, 1996) (describing why "money is the biggest threat to the democratic process"), Dworkin also argues forcefully against the grave error of the Supreme Court in *Buckley v Valeo,* 424 US 1 (1976). Dworkin, NY Rev Books at 21–24. See also Rawls, *Political Liberalism,* lecture VIII, § 12 at 359–63 (cited in note 1) (*Buckley* is "dismaying" and raises the risk of "repeating the mistake of the Lochner era.")

23. Paul Krugman, *Demographics and Destiny,* NY Times Book Rev 12 (Oct 20, 1996), reviewing and describing proposals in Peter G. Peterson, *Will America Grow Up Before It Grows Old? How the Coming Social Security Crisis Threatens You, Your Family, and Your Country* (Random House 1996), and Charles R. Morris, *The AARP: America's Most Powerful Lobby and the Clash of Generations* (Times Books 1996).

24. Rawls, *Political Liberalism,* lecture I, § 4 at 22–28 (cited in note 1).

25. Here I follow the definition in Rawls, *Political Liberalism,* lecture I, § 1.2 at 6, lecture IV, § 5,3 at 156–57 (cited in note 1).

26. Some may think the fact of reasonable pluralism means the only forms of fair adjudication between comprehensive doctrines must be only procedural and not substantive. This view is forcefully argued by Stuart Hampshire in *Innocence and Experience* (Harvard 1989). In the text above, however, I assume the several forms of liberalism are each substantive conceptions. For a thorough treatment of these issues, see the discussion in Joshua Cohen, *Pluralism and Proceduralism,* 69 Chi Kent L Rev 589 (1994).

27. I do think that justice as fairness has a certain special place in the family of political conceptions, as I suggest in Rawls, *Political Liberalism,* lecture IV, § 7.4 (cited in note 1). But this opinion of mine is not basic to the ideas of political liberalism and public reason.

28. See Jürgen Habermas, *Between Facts and Norms: Contributions to a Discourse Theory of Law and Democracy* 107–09 (MIT 1996) (William Rehg, trans) (defining the discourse principle). Seyla Benhabib in her discussion of models of public space in *Situating the Self: Gender, Community and Postmodernism in Contemporary Ethics* (Routledge 1992), says that: "The discourse model is the only one which is compatible both with the general social trends of our societies and with the emancipatory aspirations of new social movements like the women's movement." Id at 113. She has previously considered Arendt's agonistic conception, as Benhabib calls it, and that of political liberalism. But I find it hard to distinguish her view from that of a form of political liberalism and public reason, since it turns out that she means by the public sphere what Habermas does, namely what *Political Liberalism* calls the background culture of civil society in which the ideal of public reason does not apply. Hence political liberalism is not limiting in the way she thinks. Also, Benhabib does not try to show, so far as I can see, that certain principles of right and justice belonging to the content of public reason could not be interpreted to deal with the problems raised by the women's movement. I doubt that this can be done. The same holds for Benhabib's earlier remarks in Seyla Benhabib, *Liberal Dialogue Versus a Critical Theory of Discursive Legitimation,* in Nancy L. Rosenblum, ed, *Liberalism and the Moral Life* 143, 154–56 (Harvard 1989), in which the problems of the women's movement were discussed in a similar way.

29. Deriving from Aristotle and St. Thomas, the idea of the common good is essential to much of Catholic moral and political thought. See, for example, John Finnis, *Natural Law and Natural Rights* 153–56, 160 (Clarendon 1980); Jacques Maritain, *Man and the State* 108–14 (Chicago 1951). Finnis is especially clear, while Aquinas is occasionally ambiguous.

30. Thus, Jeremy Waldron's criticism of political liberalism as not allowing new and changing conceptions of political justice is incorrect. See Jeremy Waldron, *Religious Contributions in Public Deliberation,* 30 San Diego L Rev 817, 837–38 (1993). See the reply to Waldron's criticisms in Lawrence B. Solum, *Novel Public Reasons,* 29 Loyola LA L Rev 1459,

1460 (1996) ("General acceptance of a liberal ideal of public reason would permit the robust evolution of political discourse.")

31. See note 2 for my definition of *doctrine*.

32. See § 4.

33. Here see Rawls, *Political Liberalism,* lecture IX, § 1.1 at 374–75 (cited in note 1).

34. This thought I owe to Peter de Marneffe.

35. Note here that different political conceptions of justice will represent different interpretations of the constitutional essentials and matters of basic justice. There are also different interpretations of the same conception, since its concepts and values may be taken in different ways. There is not, then, a sharp line between where a political conception ends and its interpretation begins, nor need there be. All the same, a conception greatly limits its possible interpretations, otherwise discussion and argument could not proceed. For example, a constitution declaring the freedom of religion, including the freedom to affirm no religion, along with the separation of church and state, may appear to leave open the question whether church schools may receive public funds, and if so, in what way. The difference here might be seen as how to interpret the same political conception, one interpretation allowing public funds, the other not; or alternatively, as the difference between two political conceptions. In the absence of particulars, it does not matter which we call it. The important point is that since the content of public reason is a family of political conceptions, that content admits the interpretations we may need. It is not as if we were stuck with a fixed conception, much less with one interpretation of it. This is a comment on Kent Greenawalt, *Private Consciences and Public Reasons* 113–20 (Oxford 1995), where *Political Liberalism* is said to have difficulty dealing with the problem of determining the interpretation of political conceptions.

36. John Stuart Mill, *On Liberty* ch 3 1–9 (1859), in 18 *Collected Works of John Stuart Mill* 260–75 (Toronto 1977) (John M. Robson, ed).

37. See § 4.1 on the proviso and the example of citing the Gospel story. For a detailed consideration of the wide view of public political culture, see generally § 4.

38. Of course, I don't here attempt to decide the question, since we are concerned only with the kinds of reasons and considerations that public reasoning involves.

39. See § 2.2.

40. See Robert Audi, *The Place of Religious Argument in a Free and Democratic Society,* 30 San Diego L Rev 677 (1993). Here Audi defines a secular reason as follows: "A secular reason is roughly one whose normative force does not evidentially depend on the existence of God or on theological considerations, or on the pronouncements of a person or institution qua religious authority." Id at 692. This definition is ambiguous between secular reasons in the sense of a nonreligious comprehensive doctrine and in the sense of a purely political conception within the content of public reason. Depending on which is meant, Audi's view that secular reasons must also be given along with religious reasons might have a role similar to what I call *the proviso* in § 4.1.

41. See the discussion by Michael Perry of John Finnis's argument, which denies that such relations are compatible with human good. *Religion in Politics: Constitutional and Moral Perspectives* ch 3 at 85–86 (Oxford 1997).

42. Here I follow T.M. Scanlon's view in *The Difficulty of Tolerance,* in David Heyd, ed, *Toleration: An Elusive Virtue* 226 (Princeton 1996). While the whole is instructive, § 3 at 230–33 is especially relevant here.

43. See Rawis, *Political Liberalism,* lecture IV, § 3.4 at 148 (cited in note 1).

44. See Kent Greenawalt's example of the society of Diverse Fervent Believers in Greenawalt, *Private Consciences and Public Reasons* at 16–18, 21–22 (cited in note 35).

45. See Rawls, *Political Liberalism,* lecture V, § 6 at 195–200 (cited in note 1).

46. An example of how a religion may do this is the following. Abdullahi Ahmed An-Na'im, in his book *Toward an Islamic Reformation: Civil Liberties, Human Rights, and Interna-*

tional Law 52–57 (Syracuse 1990), introduces the idea of reconsidering the traditional interpretation of Shari'a, which for Muslims is divine law. For his interpretation to be accepted
by Muslims, it must be presented as the correct and superior interpretation of Shari'a. The
basic idea of An-Na'im's interpretation, following the late Sudanese author *Ustadh* Mahmoud
Mohamed Taha, is that the traditional understanding of Shari'a has been based on the teachings of the later Medina period of Muhammad, whereas the teachings of the earlier Mecca
period of Muhammad are the eternal and fundamental message of Islam. An-Na'im claims
that the superior Mecca teachings and principles were rejected in favor of the more realistic
and practical (in a seventh-century historical context) Medina teachings because society was
not yet ready for their implementation. Now that historical conditions have changed, An-
Na'im believes that Muslims should follow the earlier Mecca period in interpreting Shari'a.
So interpreted, he says that Shari'a supports constitutional democracy. Id at 69–100. In particular, the earlier Mecca interpretation of Shari'a supports equality of men and women, and
complete freedom of choice in matters of faith and religion, both of which are in accordance
with the constitutional principle of equality before the law. An-Na'im writes: The Qur'an does
not mention constitutionalism, but human rational thinking and experience have shown
that constitutionalism is necessary for realizing the just and good society prescribed by the
Qur'an. An Islamic justification and support for constitutionalism is important and relevant
for Muslims. Non-Muslims may have their own secular or other justifications. As long as all
are agreed on the principle and specific rules of constitutionalism, including complete equality and non-discrimination on grounds of gender or religion, each may have his or her own
reasons for coming to that agreement. Id at 100. (This is a perfect example of overlapping
consensus.) I thank Akeel Bilgrami for informing me of An-Na'im's work. I also owe thanks
to Roy Mottahedeh for valuable discussion.

47. See § 4.3.

48. Rawls *Political Liberalism*, lecture I, § 2.3 at 13–14 (cited in note 1) (contrasting public
political culture with background culture).

49. I am indebted here to valuable discussion with Dennis Thompson.

50. Greenawalt discusses Franklin Gamwell and Michael Perry, who do evidently impose
such constraints on how religion is to be presented. See Greenawalt, *Private Consciences and
Public Reasons* at 85–95 (cited in note 35).

51. Again, as always, in distinction from the background culture, where I emphasize there
are no restrictions.

52. Political liberalism is sometimes criticized for not itself developing accounts of these
social roots of democracy and setting out the formation of its religious and other supports.
Yet political liberalism does recognize these social roots and stresses their importance. Obviously the political conceptions of toleration and freedom of religion would be impossible
in a society in which religious freedom were not honored and cherished. Thus, political
liberalism agrees with David Hollenbach, S.J., when he writes: Not the least important of
[the transformations brought about by Aquinas] was his insistence that the political life of a
people is not the highest realization of the good of which they are capable—an insight that
lies at the root of constitutional theories of limited government. And though the Church
resisted the liberal discovery of modern freedoms through much of the modern period,
liberalism has been transforming Catholicism once again through the last half of our own
century. The memory of these events in social and intellectual history as well as the experience of the Catholic Church since the Second Vatican Council leads me to hope that communities holding different visions of the good life can get somewhere if they are willing
to risk conversation and argument about these visions. David Hollenbach, S.J., *Contexts of
the Political Role of Religion: Civil Society and Culture*, 30 San Diego L Rev 877, 891 (1993).
While a conception of public reason must recognize the significance of these social roots
of constitutional democracy and note how they strengthen its vital institutions, it need not

itself undertake a study of these matters. For the need to consider this point I am indebted to Paul Weithman.

53. See Rawls, *Political Liberalism*, lecture VI, § 8.2 at 248–49 (cited in note 1).

54. See id, lecture VI, § 8.3 at 249–51. I do not know whether the Abolitionists and King thought of themselves as fulfilling the purpose of the proviso. But whether they did or not, they could have. And had they known and accepted the idea of public reason, they would have. I thank Paul Weithman for this point.

55. Luke 10: 29–37. It is easy to see how the Gospel story could be used to support the imperfect moral duty of mutual aid, as found, say, in Kant's fourth example in the *Grundlegung*. See Immanuel Kant, *Groundwork for the Metaphysics of Morals* AK 4:423, in Mary Gregor, trans, *Practical Philosophy* (Cambridge 1996). To formulate a suitable example in terms of political values only, consider a variant of the difference principle or of some other analogous idea. The principle could be seen as giving a special concern for the poor, as in the Catholic social doctrine. See John Rawls, *A Theory of Justice* § 13 (Belknap 1971) (defining the difference principle).

56. For the relevance of this form of discourse I am indebted to discussion with Charles Larmore.

57. I will mention another form of discourse that I call witnessing: it typically occurs in an ideal, politically well ordered, and fully just society in which all votes are the result of citizens' voting in accordance with their most reasonable conception of political justice. Nevertheless, it may happen that some citizens feel they must express their principled dissent from existing institutions, policies, or enacted legislation. I assume that Quakers accept constitutional democracy and abide by its legitimate law, yet at the same time may reasonably express the religious basis of their pacifism. (The parallel case of Catholic opposition to abortion is mentioned in § 6.1.) Yet witnessing differs from civil disobedience in that it does not appeal to principles and values of a (liberal) political conception of justice. While on the whole these citizens endorse reasonable political conceptions of justice supporting a constitutional democratic society, in this case they nevertheless feel they must not only let other citizens know the deep basis of their strong opposition but must also bear witness to their faith by doing so. At the same time, those bearing witness accept the idea of public reason. While they may think the outcome of a vote on which all reasonable citizens have conscientiously followed public reason to be incorrect or not true, they nevertheless recognize it as legitimate law and accept the obligation not to violate it. In such a society there is strictly speaking no case for civil disobedience and conscientious refusal. The latter requires what I have called a nearly just, but not fully just, society. See Rawls, *A Theory of Justice* § 55 (cited in note 55).

58. See Thomas J. Curry, *The First Freedoms: Church and State in America to the Passage of the First Amendment* 139–48 (Oxford 1986). The quoted language, which appears in Id at 140, is from the preamble to the proposed "Bill Establishing a Provision for Teachers of the Christian Religion" (1784). Note that the popular Patrick Henry also provided the most serious opposition to Jefferson's "Bill for Establishing Religious Freedom" (1779), which won out when reintroduced in the Virginia Assembly in 1786. Curry, *The First Freedoms* at 146.

59. For a discussion of these virtues, see Rawls, *Political Liberalism*, lecture V, § 5.4 at 194–95 (cited in note 1).

60. See James Madison, *Memorial and Remonstrance* (1785), in *The Mind of the Founder* 8–16 (Bobbs-Merrill 1973) (Marvin Meyers, ed). Paragraph 6 refers to the vigor of early Christianity in opposition to the empire, while paragraphs 7 and 11 refer to the mutually corrupting influence of past establishments on both state and religion. In the correspondence between Madison and William Bradford of Pennsylvania, whom he met at Princeton (College of New Jersey), the freedom and prosperity of Pennsylvania without an establishment is praised and celebrated. See 1 *The Papers of James Madison* (Chicago 1962) (William T. Hutchinson and William ME. Rachal, eds). See especially Madison's letters of 1 December

1773, id at 100–101; 24 January 1774, id at 104–6; and 1 April 1774, id at 111–13. A letter of Bradford's to Madison, 4 March 1774, refers to liberty as the genius of Pennsylvania. Id at 109. Madison's arguments were similar to those of Tocqueville I mention below. See also Curry, *The First Freedoms* at 142–48 (cited in note 71).

61. It does this by protecting the freedom to change one's faith. Heresy and apostasy are not crimes.

62. What I refer to here is the fact that from the early days of the Emperor Constantine in the fourth century Christianity punished heresy and tried to stamp out by persecution and religious wars what it regarded as false doctrine (for example, the crusade against the Albigenses led by Innocent III in the thirteenth century). To do this required the coercive powers of the state. Instituted by Pope Gregory IX, the Inquisition was active throughout the Wars of Religion in the 16th and seventeenth centuries. While most of the American Colonies had known establishments of some kind (Congregationalist in New England, Episcopalian in the South), the United States, thanks to the plurality of its religious sects and the First Amendment which they endorsed, never did. A persecuting zeal has been the great curse of the Christian religion. It was shared by Luther and Calvin and the Protestant Reformers, and it was not radically changed in the Catholic Church until Vatican II. In the Council's *Declaration on Religious Freedom—Dignitatis Humanae*—the Catholic Church committed itself to the principle of religious freedom as found in a constitutional democratic regime. It declared the ethical doctrine of religious freedom resting on the dignity of the human person; a political doctrine with respect to the limits of government in religious matters; a theological doctrine of the freedom of the Church in its relations to the political and social world. All persons, whatever their faith, have the right of religious liberty on the same terms. *Declaration on Religious Freedom (Dignitatis Humanae): On the Right of the Person and of Communities to Social and Civil Freedom in Matters Religious* (1965), in Walter Abbott, S.J., ed, *The Documents of Vatican II* 675, 692–96 (Geoffrey Chapman 1966). As John Courtney Murray, S.J., said: "A long-standing ambiguity had finally been cleared up. The Church does not deal with the secular order in terms of a double standard—freedom for the Church when Catholics are in the minority, privilege for the Church and intolerance for others when Catholics are a majority." John Courtney Murray, S.J., *Religious Freedom*, in Abbott, ed, *Documents of Vatican II* at 672, 673. See also the instructive discussion by Paul E. Sigmund, *Catholicism and Liberal Democracy*, in R. Bruce Douglas and David Hollenbach, S.J., eds, *Catholicism and Liberalism: Contributions to American Public Philosophy* (Cambridge 1994). See especially id at 233–39.

63. Alexis de Tocqueville, 1 *Democracy in America* 294–301 (Perennial Library 1988) (J.P. Mayer, ed, George Lawrence, trans). In discussing "The Main Causes That Make Religion Powerful in America," Tocqueville says the Catholic priests "all thought that the main reason for the quiet sway of religion over their country was the complete separation of church and state. I have no hesitation in stating that throughout my stay in America I met nobody, lay or cleric, who did not agree about that." Id at 295. He continues:

There have been religions intimately linked to earthly governments, dominating men's souls both by terror and by faith; but when a religion makes such an alliance, I am not afraid to say that it makes the same mistake as any man might; it sacrifices the future for the present, and by gaining a power to which it has no claim, it risks its legitimate authority. Hence religion cannot share the material strength of the rulers without being burdened with some of the animosity roused against them.

Id at 297. He remarks that these observations apply all the more to a democratic country, for in that case when religion seeks political power it will attach itself to a particular party and be burdened by hostility to it. Id at 298. Referring to the cause of the decline of religion in Europe, he concludes, "I am profoundly convinced that this accidental and particular cause is the close union of politics and religion. . . . European Christianity has allowed itself to be intimately united with the powers of this world." Id at 300–301. Political liberalism accepts

Tocqueville's view and sees it as explaining, so far as possible, the basis of peace among comprehensive doctrines both religious and secular.

64. In this it agrees with Locke, Montesquieu, and Constant; Kant, Hegel, and Mill.

65. I take the term from Philip Quinn. The idea appears in Rawls, *Political Liberalism*, lecture VI, § 7.1–2 at 240–41 (cited in note 1).

66. I use the term "grounding reasons" since many who might appeal to these reasons view them as the proper grounds, or the true basis—religious, philosophical, or moral—of the ideals and principles of public reasons and political conceptions of justice.

67. Some have quite naturally read the footnote in Rawls, *Political Liberalism*, lecture VI, § 7.2 at 243–44 (cited in note 1), as an argument for the right to abortion in the first trimester. I do not intend it to be one. (It does express my opinion, but my opinion is not an argument.) I was in error in leaving it in doubt whether the aim of the footnote was only to illustrate and confirm the following statement in the text to which the footnote is attached: "The only comprehensive doctrines that run afoul of public reason are those that cannot support a reasonable balance [or ordering] of political values [on the issue]." To try to explain what I meant, I used three political values (of course, there are more) for the troubled issue of the right to abortion to which it might seem improbable that political values could apply at all. I believe a more detailed interpretation of those values may, when properly developed in public reason, yield a reasonable argument. I don't say the most reasonable or decisive argument; I don't know what that would be, or even if it exists. (For an example of such a more detailed interpretation, see Judith Jarvis Thomson, *Abortion*, 20 Boston Rev 11 (Summer 1995), though I would want to add several addenda to it.) Suppose now, for purposes of illustration, that there is a reasonable argument in public reason for the right to abortion but there is no equally reasonable balance, or ordering, of the political values in public reason that argues for the denial of that right. Then in this kind of case, but only in this kind of case, does a comprehensive doctrine denying the right to abortion run afoul of public reason. However, if it can satisfy the proviso of the wide public reason better, or at least as well as other views, it has made its case in public reason, Of course, a comprehensive doctrine can be unreasonable on one or several issues without being simply unreasonable.

68. Rawls, *Political Liberalism*, lecture VI, § 7.1 at 240–41 (cited in note 1).

69. For such an argument, see Cardinal Joseph Bernardin, *The Consistent Ethic: What Sort of Framework?*, 16 Origins 345, 347–50 (Oct 30, 1986). The idea of public order the Cardinal presents includes these three political values: public peace, essential protections of human rights, and the commonly accepted standards of moral behavior in a community of law. Further, he grants that not all moral imperatives are to be translated into prohibitive civil statutes and thinks it essential to the political and social order to protect human life and basic human rights. The denial of the right to abortion he hopes to justify on the basis of those three values. I don't of course assess his argument here, except to say it is clearly cast in some form of public reason. Whether it is itself reasonable or not, or more reasonable than the arguments on the other side, is another matter. As with any form of reasoning in public reason, the reasoning may be fallacious or mistaken.

70. As far as I can see, this view is similar to Father John Courtney Murray's position about the stand the Church should take in regard to contraception in *We Hold These Truths: Catholic Reflections on the American Proposition* 157–58 (Sheed and Ward 1960). See also Mario Cuomo's lecture on abortion in his Notre Dame Lecture of 1984, in *More Than Words: The Speeches of Mario Cuomo* 32–51 (St Martin's 1993). I am indebted to Leslie Griffin and Paul Weithman for discussion and clarification about points involved in this and the preceding footnote and for acquainting me with Father Murray's view.

71. These two powers, the capacity for a conception of justice and the capacity for a conception of the good, are discussed in Rawls, *Political Liberalism* (cited in note 1). See

especially id, lecture I, § 3.2 at 19, lecture II, § 7.1 at 81, lecture Ill, § 3.3 at 103, lecture III, § 4.1 at 108.

72. Id, lecture VI, § 4 at 223–27.

73. Sometimes the term "normalize" is used in this connection. For example, persons have certain fundamental interests of a religious or philosophical kind; or else certain basic needs of a natural kind. Again, they may have a certain typical pattern of self-realization. A Thomist will say that we always desire above all else, even if unknown to ourselves, the *Visio Dei*; a Platonist will say we strive for a vision of the good; a Marxist *will say* we aim for self-realization as species-beings.

74. The idea of such a consensus is discussed at various places in Rawls, *Political Liberalism* (cited in note 1). See especially Id, lecture IV, and consult the index.

75. See id at xviii (paperback edition).

76. See § 3.2. It is sometimes asked why political liberalism puts such a high value on political values, as if one could only do that by assessing those values in comparison with transcendent values. But this comparison political liberalism does not make, nor does it need to make, as is observed in the text.

77. On this, see Michael J. Sandel, *Review of* Political Liberalism, 107 Harv L Rev 1765, 1778–82 (1994), and more recently Michael J. Sandel, *Democracy's Discontent: America in Search of a Public Philosophy* 21–23 (Belknap 1996).

78. Perhaps some think that a political conception is not a matter of (moral) right and wrong. If so, that is a mistake and is simply false. Political conceptions of justice are themselves intrinsically moral ideas, as I have stressed from the outset. As such they are a kind of normative value. On the other hand, some may think that the relevant political conceptions are determined by how a people actually establish their existing institutions—the political given, as it were, by politics. Viewed in this light, the prevalence of slavery in 1858 implies that Lincoln's criticisms of it were moral, a matter of right and wrong, and certainly not a matter of politics. To say that the political is determined by a people's politics may be a possible use of the term *political*. But then it ceases to be a normative idea and it is no longer part of public reason. We must hold fast to the idea of the political as a fundamental category and covering political conceptions of justice as intrinsic *moral* values.

79. See § 3.2.

80. See Rawls, *Political Liberalism*, lecture II, § 3.2–4 at 60–62 (cited in note 1). The main points can be set out in summary fashion as follows: (1) Reasonable persons do not all affirm the same comprehensive doctrine. This is said to be a consequence of the burdens of judgment. See note 95. (2) Many reasonable doctrines are affirmed, not all of which can be true or right (as judged from within a comprehensive doctrine). (3) It is not unreasonable to affirm any one of the reasonable comprehensive doctrines. (4) Others who affirm reasonable doctrines different from ours are, we grant, reasonable also, and certainly not for that reason unreasonable. (5) In going beyond recognizing the reasonableness of a doctrine and affirming our belief in it, we are not being unreasonable. (6) Reasonable persons think it unreasonable to use political power, should they possess it, to repress other doctrines that are reasonable yet different from their own.

81. See § 6.3.

82. These burdens are discussed in Rawls, *Political Liberalism*, lecture II, § 2 (cited in note 1). Roughly, they are sources or causes of reasonable disagreement between reasonable and rational persons. They involve balancing the weight of different kinds of evidence and kinds of values, and the like, and they affect both theoretical and practical judgments.

83. Id at xviii.

84. Id, lecture II, § 1.1 at 49–50.

85. Id, lecture II, § 2–3.4 at 54–62.

86. Id, lecture IV, § 1.2–3 at 135–37.

87. Id lecture IX, § 2.1 at 393.

88. Observe that neither the religious objection to democracy nor the autocratic one could be made by public reasoning.

89. See note 3.

90. See Rawis, *A Theory of Justice* § 35 (cited in note 55) (on toleration of the intolerant); Rawls, *Political Liberalism*, lecture V, § 6.2 at 197–99 (cited in note 1).

Section V

Current Challenges

INTRODUCTION

This final section deals with pertinent challenges to the idea of the public sphere as they have emerged in the late twentieth and early twenty-first century. Though interrelated, these challenges can be linked to three different concepts describing ongoing processes of change in western societies: political and economic transnationalization, the digitalization of communications, and social and cultural diversification. How can we conceive of democracy given these processes? How can we conceptualize changes to the public sphere?

While the texts in the previous sections of this book often relate directly to each other, the field of public sphere theory in the age of transnationalization, digitalization, and diversification appears more fragmented. This is partly because of the wide range of issues dealt with in these works but it also has to do with the fact that the key issues are still in the process of being identified.

The public sphere was traditionally conceived as a phenomenon inside a nation state. But economic and political developments across state borders and around the globe have long challenged such an understanding. New forms of cooperation, conflict, and communication are being established at various inter- and trans- and supranational levels. The European Union has attracted considerable attention as a supranational political entity. For public sphere theory, the EU is especially interesting because it lacks both a corresponding public, and a sphere for it to communicate in. In this section, Bernhard Peters illustrates the challenges such changes pose to theory, and discusses European mediated political debate at the turn of the millennium. His contribution lays out the key questions researchers need to tackle when trying to grasp the public sphere in a post-national constellation.

James Bohman links this theoretical concern with the growth of the internet. The digitalisation of media technologies in general, and particularly the rise of the Internet, with its promise of openness and universality, has been widely greeted as the basis for a new and inclusive public sphere. The end of mass communication has been announced repeatedly, with observers drawing attention to the increasing segmentation of the classical "mass audience" into both the target groups of marketing and ethnically or politically defined groups with their own discrete public spheres. The question is how to interpret and evaluate these developments in relation to established notions of the public, especially in a situation where, critics argue, the Internet, far from providing a shared space of deliberation across social divisions, reproduces, and cements existing separations.

During the last decades of the twentieth century, the multicultural composition of most societies became much more pronounced and visible. Many western societies experienced a resurgence of the extreme right, often coupled with a growing dissatisfaction with democratic institutions. This amounted to a formidable challenge for deliberative forms and political processes of many kinds—both in the public and in formal political contexts. Added to which, Postmodern theorists questioned the idea of a common human reason constituting a basis for political deliberation among free and equal citizens. Two contributions in this section take up this challenge, offering diverging solutions for public sphere theory. For Chantal Mouffe, part of the problem lay in dominant democratic theories. Inspired by among others Carl Schmitt, Mouffe claimed that the consensual bias of deliberative democratic theories made them incapable of grasping the social and cultural developments of diversification and she sets out to formulate an alternative—incorporating a radically different "agonistic" conception of the public sphere as a space where antagonistic positions on how society should be organised fight for advantage. Seyla Benhabib, in contrast, aimed to develop a version of deliberative democratic theory capable of accommodating entrenched ethnocultural conflicts.

The section is rounded off by a final contribution from Jürgen Habermas. It deals with one specific dimension of contemporary political life: the consequences of the resurgence of religious faith for public debate. All the contributions discussed in this book presume a secular state. Habermas' recent writing tries to tackle the challenge of whether the public sphere can accommodate religious arguments, addressing key political questions, from education to biotechnology. He seeks to move away from an overly restrictive concept of the public use of reason—one in danger of hindering political integration. Instead, he develops an argument that recognizes the value of religious language and a way to translate religious reasons into generally accessible reasons.

Together, the texts presented in this section illustrate the range of issues dealt with within public sphere theory around the turn of the millennium. But it also points forward, making evident the continued relevance of the idea of the public sphere for our understanding of democratic life.

BERNHARD PETERS

NATIONAL AND TRANSNATIONAL PUBLIC SPHERES (1999)

Bernhard Peters (1949–2005) was a German sociologist who, from the late 1980s, worked with Jürgen Habermas at the University of Frankfurt. Peters wrote his doctoral dissertation on the rationality of law. He took this interest further in a book on the integration of modern society. From 1993, he was professor at the University of Bremen, where he came to focus his work on public deliberation and public culture.

Peters' contribution to our understanding of the public sphere is partly normative and partly empirical. With his colleagues in Bremen, he undertook several large, comparative studies of mediated political communication—both in the press and broadcasting—based on an operationalized public sphere concept. The present text, however, is a short presentation of what Peters saw as the challenges to public sphere theory by the late 1990s: What happens to the public sphere of democratic nation states when it simultaneously faces processes of internal segmentation and increasing transnationalization?

Discussing the first challenge, Peters points out that differentiation of the public sphere is unavoidable in modern society. Such differentiation is only problematic when fragmentation threatens integration across segmented parts of the public sphere—hindering the circulation of ideas, arguments, and interpretation. Peters however, finds little evidence of a growing fragmentation in this sense.

The second challenge concerns the centrifugal forces on the public sphere, linked to the transnationalization of the social, economic and political domains. By the late 1990s, transnationalization emerged as a key theme for political theory, not least in light of the European Union's emergence as a supranational political entity. This development highlighted a perceived democratic deficit because a public sphere specific to the EU was left underdeveloped. Peters employs the EU as an example, discussing different dimensions of the potential transnationalization of the public sphere—including transnational mass media, the reporting of international events, the existence of international issue publics, as well as the export and import of cultural products. Stressing the pre-eminence of a national level for the publics at that time, Peters advises against expecting the emergence of a full-fledged EU public sphere. This, in turn, raises questions of how to remove the democratic deficit of such supranational political entities.

For democratic theory, the "classical" concept of *Öffentlichkeit* involves two distinct ideas: first, that of a social sphere or space; and, second, that of a collective—the public. The public sphere is thought to be part of a society organised as a national state; the public is consequently made up of the members of this society, a political public composed of (active) citizens.

There is today widespread criticism of this view. Perhaps there never was a united "national" public sphere in this strict sense. In any case, even if it had existed, today this idea has been definitively undermined by the parallel, possibly even causally related, processes of internal segmentation, as dispersed publics emerge; and external fluidity, as communication flows ever more freely across national boundaries. But what forms of internal differentiation of the public realm do we encounter, and when might this process be described as "fragmentation"? What are the tendencies of transnationalisation, and what limits do they meet?

1 The Differentiation and Fragmentation of the Public Sphere

Let us begin with the classical concept of a *national* public sphere. As a social sphere this denotes a field of communication without specific barriers to entry: no one is excluded by social norms and institutional rules (privacy, trust, secrecy), or by special competences (expertise, credentials, etc.). As a collective concept the public sphere not only involves factual participation in a sphere of public communication, but also a collective idea of belonging to a public discussing common themes and problems. The latter could involve the formation of political opinion and will within a state, or might involve more general cultural interpretations and self-understandings.

Of course, a national public is never simply a collective in which all those present take turns in adopting the roles of speaker and listener. Instead, we find that forum and arena are differentiated into quite distinct levels—informal encounters, debates within voluntary associations and, above all, communication conveyed by the mass media. Participants of these fora become differentiated into active speakers or authors who frequently make use of mediators such as organisers or editors to present them to a receptive audience, whether this be of listeners, readers or watchers (Gerhards and Neidhardt 1991).

There are, however, other important ways in which the public is differentiated. They can form "issue publics," or publics that form around political or ideological trends. There is also a marked stratification process at work here: participants differ markedly in degree of involvement and participation, in visibility and in influence.

Within such publics we find an unequal distribution of interest in and engagement with issues and topics. There is no necessary crossover between the groupings interested in social insurance, those seeking the legal regulation of abortion, those concerned with school or university reform, or those involved in the creation of a Holocaust memorial. *Issue publics* are made up of individuals who share a raised level of interest in a particular topic.

Political, ideological or other cultural affinities form a second structural level upon which the public distributes itself into *camps*, in which internal communication, however organised, is denser than that conducted with members of other camps.

At a third level we find *patterns of stratification*. Members of the public are distinguished with regard to degree of engagement, competence, prominence and influence. These are not simply individual differences; they add together to form a stratified structure. Circles or networks of communication, also the organs through which this is effected (the press and literary publishing, programmes in electronic media) can be differentiated by degree of argumentative complexity and presupposed competence. Particular circles (representatives of political or other kinds of organisation, experts, intellectuals, journalists) can win particular prestige and public influence.

These patterns obviously intersect and are overlaid one on another. Particular groupings cut across issue publics, and differing degrees of influence develop for different camps or even issue publics. This is not the only complicating factor. The patterns of stratification are complex and difficult to establish empirically. Membership in a communicative network that demands a high level of argumentative and cognitive competence is, for example, not the same thing as the possession of great public influence, or prominence. Intellectual milieus or groups of experts can exercise influence beyond their particular circles, but they can also be more or less isolated.

This brings us to the question of the relation between these forms of differentiation and the phenomena we refer to as segmentation or fragmentation. This clearly involves a lack of unity or integration that can, in principle, be remedied. But it is scarcely possible to alter many of the forms of differentiation outlined above and they do not necessarily denote a problematic form of disintegration.

The differentiation of public space is unavoidable for one thing because of the growing gap between the limited communicative resources that each individual has, and the growth in complexity of public communication. This latter involves the increase in the number of themes, but also the increased cognitive demands posed by many of the topics. Since the chances for any one person to communicate have strict limits with regard to time, attention and specialised competence, specialisation, diversified attention and the differentiation of competence becomes necessary.

How might differentiated publics be nonetheless integrated, and when would one speak of fragmentation?

Integration presupposes that the various lines of differentiation remain permeable with respect to the diffusion of topics, information and argument. Communicative groups have to leave themselves open to mutual influence, or partially overlap. Important topics have to have a chance of discussion among larger communicative groups, important ideas or arguments must remain accessible among larger publics.

This can be effected or furthered by translation mechanisms—through particular media, experts or elites. It also assumes that the public as a whole commands a sufficiently common cultural repertoire and adequate background knowledge, as well as some common interest or structure of relevance, a degree of collective identification, a communal consciousness even of the weakest kind through which individuals or groups can think themselves part of a specific public and as participants in the process of opinion formation for this public.

Fragmentation by contrast denotes fracture of the processes through which ideas, arguments and interpretation circulate, and the mutual closure of communicative groupings. This can arise from an absence of opportunities for understanding (through the lack of a shared culture, for instance), or from other kinds of communicative impediments. Segmentation can arise from all three named types of differentiation: different issue publics may lack interest or competence in the issues of other groups, or there may be a lack of higher level issues on which they can find common ground. The polarisation of political camps can lead to the reduction of external communication, or to the adoption of excluding, non-discursive forms of communication such as agitation. Particular strata can be more or less insulated from each other—there may be too little porosity, or none at all, from top to bottom or from bottom to top; experts and intellectuals might be culturally isolated and deal in structures of relevance and interpretive frames distinct from those of other parts of the public.

Can we see in this or that form any clear trend of *growing* fragmentation? Contemporary analysis in the social sciences does make some such claim. Only three variants can be mentioned here. The first concerns the mutual closure between expert cultures and a related "fragmentation of everyday consciousness" (Habermas 1981). Linked to the increasing significance of cognitive knowledge in present-day society is the diagnosis of an increasing gulf in the knowledge of laity and experts, or of a variation in how well-informed different parts of the general public are; both of these lead to a related fragmentation of public communication. Above all, given the manner in which different forms of mass media are increasingly targeted upon precise and restricted audiences—primarily the electronic media, but also print media, fears are expressed concerning the fragmentation of public communication (Katz 1996). There is, however, little in the way of empirical evidence for this, and what little empirical evidence there is remains controversial. It hardly seems plausible to claim that the public is becoming fragmented if the nation does not all sit down to watch the news at a given time of day. Television, which began with a very limited set of channels, presents an interesting case where during a particular period of its development it played an important part in unifying public communication, That *this* form is today more or less obsolete implies little about tendencies of fragmentation.

2 Forms and Limits to the Transnationalisation of Public Spheres

The internationalisation of many social processes (mainly in the area of economic co-operation and exchange and their associated externalities) has prompted a need for political regulation and other measures transcending national frontiers. This in turn creates a need for legitimation for which the transnational formation of political opinion and political will can be of importance. This is especially true for relatively advanced transnational institutions with broad competences, a so-far unique example being the European Union. For this reason many who identify a democratic or legitimacy deficit in the EU point to the underdevelopment of a public sphere specific to the EU being a key obstacle to the genuine democratisation of European politics. This hypothesis of a democratic deficit relating to the EU is often linked to other forms of cultural lag, especially the absence of the communal consciousness of a collective identity or a shared body of memory and experience: "Europe, even limited to Western Europe, is not a community of communications, barely a community of memory, and only a very limited community of experience" (Kielmannsegg 1994).

Communication technologies and the associated infrastructure represent a decisive precondition, or even a driving element, of internationalisation processes. How does that fit with the deficit-hypothesis with respect to the extension of transnational publics?

This leads us to the question of the manner, of the form, in which transnationalisation of public spheres and their publics today takes place; or how this might happen in the future; and what the possible limitations on this might be. We can consider these issues with respect to the EU.

The *reporting of international events* is an elementary and traditional form in the internationalisation of public spheres—reports, analyses, commentary regarding interstate relations and above all regarding internal developments in foreign states. Are there any clear developmental trends in this area?

It can be said that the network of international reportage has grown tighter during the twentieth century, especially during the last few decades of the century. This has been made possible by those familiar technical factors that ease the transmission of news: the development of international news agencies and the network of foreign correspondents. Technical developments such as satellite transmission have made audiovisual reporting possible from anywhere on earth, transmitting in real time events and circumstances in distant lands and rendering them (apparently) alive and immediate.

At the same time the focus of reporting has shifted. International news is no longer entirely dominated by a diplomatic perspective, by the depiction of interstate relationships and the activities of the heads of state in other countries. The spread of international economic linkages has brought about a massive extension of economic and financial reporting, although this is for the most part concentrated in the specialised publications in the international economic and financial press, or in the pages of national broadsheets devoted to the economy. But social and cultural conditions in other countries are today more strongly emphasised. This diversification away from official politics towards the reporting of significant events involving crime, accidents and catastrophes is also reflected in domestic reporting, where lifestyle and human-interest stories, together with the reporting of social and cultural phenomena, have gained ground.

Unsystematic participant observation suggests that the selection of topics and the construction of an agenda by international reporting are still strongly influenced by the given domestic structures of relevance—what are described as news values. So far there has been no systematic study of the degree to which there has been convergence between the different national publics, for instance, within the EU or the "North Atlantic World." There is a great deal that suggests that national differences persist and that selectiveness according to given historical and cultural affinities, or animosities, with regard to economic relationships and competition between nations, and the population movements associated with migration, retains its force.

Important national differences also appear to have persisted not only in respect of agenda-setting and the distribution of interest, but also in respect of the typical interpretative frames underlying international reporting. One might compare the way in which Africa is reported in the British and the French press, or the tribulations of President Clinton as reported in the American, German, French and Italian press, or the reporting of EU affairs in the British and Continental European press.

Important here is the structure through which the public is stratified, as touched on above. Within any given national public it can in general be said that the quality press is much more cosmopolitan than the popular press, and that there are significant variations across the public with regard to their interest in local or cosmopolitical matters.

The same can be said of national publics: some appear much more international in orientation than others. Here it seems that the size of the country in question plays a role, combined perhaps with the density of external economic links. And some receive more attention from the international press than others—the United States always has material for international commentary, smaller or less developed countries only sporadically, and then usually in the event of some reported catastrophe. It is more or less trivial to observe that perhaps leading economic and political states, enjoying cultural influence or even dominance, attract more international attention than other nations. This is also true for domestic affairs—there is some evidence that shared membership in the EU has no general impact upon mutual interest in domestic affairs as compared, for example, with interest shown in the American domestic scene.

But it is not really the *content* of international communication—observing foreign countries as from a national lookout point—that raises the issue of transnational public spheres. We are more concerned with the internationalisation of *networks of public communication and communication flows*. What is happening to these forms of internationalisation?

The import and export of cultural products, contributions and ideas are an elementary form of cross-border communication. These processes are quite obvious when books, periodicals, individual articles, films, or TV programmes are imported or exported, whether in the original or in translation. Original contributions by foreign authors in print or electronic form can also be seen as the export of cultural services and a form of international communication. Less obvious forms of this process involve the diffusion of ideas or other cultural elements, via the influence that authors or other cultural producers exert through interpersonal contacts or individual observation of foreign publics (by reading their periodicals or books). Official statistics (collated by UNESCO) exist that track the trade in cultural goods. However, substantial cultural influence, the diffusion of ideas, hence the *effects* wrought by the import of cultural goods and informal communicative flows, are much more difficult to pin down.

Cultural diffusion is, of course, an old phenomenon; has it changed in any respect—especially as regards those cultural domains that we describe as "public spheres" or "opinion formation" (hence excluding technical and scientific communication on the one hand, and art, literature, entertainment and popular culture on the other)? I cannot here provide an answer based on the systematic interpretation of data. Existing statistics on the trade in cultural goods fail to distinguish sufficiently clearly between genres; and the more cultural influences and indirect forms of cultural diffusion have never been systematically recorded.

But it is plausible to assume that in this area too there are asymmetries and inequalities—either with regard to the share of "foreign trade" in the totality of a country's communication, or with respect to the "balance of trade," the relation of imports to exports. Some public spheres, such as France and the USA, depend strongly upon domestic productions; others, such as Benelux, Scandinavia, Germany appear to be more strongly oriented to foreign products, Some countries, again the USA and France, have a positive trade balance and export more than they import; others have a negative balance. That is partly to do with the relative size and economic strength of these countries, partly a consequence of advantages they enjoy in the sphere of cultural and intellectual productivity and innovation. The latter is harder to evaluate and quantify than the former. It can safely be assumed, however, that cultural economies of scale play a part here; a larger domestic market for cultural goods creates cost advantages and facilitates the employment of a larger pool of talent and the use of greater material resources in public communication and cultural production. Of course the cultural and intellectual productivity of a country depends on many other factors, such that size and economic power in no way guarantee a leading intellectual role with regard to influence over other national publics. Taking the case of the EU, it can also be supposed that flows of communication between the individual member states are weaker than the relationships that these individual states enjoy with the USA—considering here imports of books, periodicals, films, TV programmes, as well as intellectual influences upon public discourse.

Transnational mass media would be another important infrastructural element for a transnational public space. Here we should distinguish different cases. International media groups control the newspapers, magazines and TV channels of many countries. But if these products are created by a national editorial team they are not international media in the strict sense. Some newspapers and periodicals have a relatively large international circulation in comparison to their total printing, although their production structure (newsrooms, editorial teams etc.) remains national, interpretation and positions being adopted with regard to a national perspective (or binational sometimes, as in the case of Britain and the USA). Examples of this are to be found above all in the financial press *(The Economist, Financial Times, Wall Street Journal)* together with political or cultural periodicals *(New York Review of Books, Times Literary Supplement, Le Monde Diplomatique)*. These cases really belong to the import and export of cultural goods discussed above. *CNN International* is a similar example in the case of television.

Mass media with a genuinely international structure of production and distribution are either rare or non-existent. Even within the EU there have been very modest developments in this direction: the binational TV programme *Arte*; the attempt to publish simultaneously an intellectual periodical in several languages *(Lettre International*, for which there are now several independent national versions); the failure to produce a European newspaper—*The European*—which transmuted into a weekly that now appears little more than a weak competitor to the financial press.

Internationalised issue publics are beginning to emerge, using their own media or other channels of communication, sharing common structures of interest or relevance and networks of intellectual production. Internationalised intellectual milieus constitute informal networks that can from time to time be mobilised for collective action, making declarations or staging events. The environmental movement is a good example of an international issue public, as are human rights movements; they are based around international associations such as Greenpeace or Amnesty International, whose main efforts are directed at creating publicity and public awareness.

What does *not* exist, even in the EU, is an international public realm comparable in any way with those in national states. This would require the presence of a common agenda, shared structures of relevance, agreed interpretative framework and a collective identity that linked its members to common action and responsibility. That said, we should not attribute such complete unity to national publics either. But what are the reasons for the persistence of national publics, and the meagre development of international forms—even in the EU, a region whose members are in close cultural proximity and which is relatively strongly integrated in law and politics?

We can, of course, point to the existence of language barriers. These are important, but not the sole factor. Even within the areas in which one language dominates (the German-speaking countries, for example) there are clearly separated national publics. The emergence of English as the second language in the EU, as elsewhere, has so far made only a modest contribution to the internationalisation of public spheres.

Quite plainly cultural differences play a very tenacious role in marking off the differences between national publics. Collective historical memory, shared cultural knowledge, differing structures of relevance and interpretative frames linked to diverging values—all of these persist. This can be demonstrated by reading one after the other a few serious newspapers from different European countries, or viewing the more serious talk shows and TV news broadcasts.

National publics are not solely marked by cultural differences of this kind, or rather, the cultural differences are not autonomous. They are instead linked to social practices and institutional structures, which in turn influence the character of the public sphere and that of cultural reproduction. Put another way: public spheres have a social and cultural foundation that does not entirely consist of media markets and media organisations. Many other structures have importance in intellectual production and reception, they have an impact upon the definition of collective interests and collective problems. Among these are institutions for education and for research, professional associations in journalism and other professions, the networks and cliques of cultural or intellectual producers, and the structures of interest articulation and aggregation represented by political parties, interest groups and social movements. The combined effect of all these elements stamps a particular character upon a national public sphere in a manner that is hard to pin down, not forgetting the internal differentiation of this public as discussed above.

3 Conclusion: Questions for the Deficit Diagnosis

Do the above remarks confirm the enduring pre-eminence of the national level for today's publics, and account for the hesitancy we observe in the internationalisation of public communication? Where does this leave the deficit thesis? Is there, in the EU for example, a cultural lag with respect to political developments; the slowness with which a genuine European public realm is appearing lagging far behind the development of transnational political institutions of wide-ranging competence, a lag that might seem to be even more marked than in other cases of international interdependencies? Do institutions like the EU consequently suffer from a democratic deficit, or a lack of legitimation? Is there any prospect that such deficiencies will gradually disappear as a transnational public realm emerges among EU member states?

Two points are agreed: political decisions in the EU are relatively weakly linked to the processes in which public opinion and will are formed. And such public opinion that forms takes place primarily in a national context, with little transfer of topic or contribution from one country to another: by the standards of democratic theory that seems to be a deficiency.

Other questions seem more problematic. Whether in fact these deficiencies, identified through the application of normative criteria, result in an *actual* loss of legitimacy for EU institutions (and perhaps also for national institutions), in a loss of acceptance expressed either as active affirmation or passive acceptance—none of this is empirically very clear. And it is just as unclear whether a more intensive campaign of public information and encouragement of public debate would really increase the level of acceptance.

Linked to that is the question of what the real causes of this deficit are, and how they might be removed. Some plausible comments might be made here: that the democratic deficit is at least in part generated by the institutional structures and practices of the EU itself. The most important decision-making bodies are arenas of negotiation between representatives of national governments; their proceedings are for the most part arcane; their members are shielded from demands for publicity and accountability; there is a general lack of transnational structures for the articulation and aggregation of interests such as patties and associations; while at the European level a clear distinction between "government" and "opposition" is lacking. It is also plausible that reforms might ameliorate this—introducing plebiscitary elements in decision-making processes; transforming the Council of Ministers into a directly elected body, or a body that was in some other way under direct democratic control; or introducing a second chamber into EU institutions. But the question also arises whether it is not only the institutional form, but also the *substance* of European politics that hinders greater public participation. Is not a great deal of this business made up of complex technical, legal and economic issues, unsuited for political mobilisation and in any case inaccessible to a lay public? Is similar business at the national level really more accessible for a national public, do they gain any greater attention, are they more eagerly debated? Is the democratic and public deficit of the EU really any different from that of its member states in regard to similar issues and matters? Do we not find at the national level a very similar process in which state administration has far-reaching independent powers, and is beyond the control of parliament and judiciary?

Finally, is it plausible to expect or promote a development of an EU public modelled on that of national publics, whether empirically or normatively? Is it likely that an EU public sphere will develop that is as internally differentiated in the same way as the national pubic spheres described above? The factors limiting transnational developments listed above make one doubtful. An EU public sphere would need a common social, institutional and cultural infrastructure comparable to that existing at the national level today. Set against the prospect of the rapid development of such an infrastructure is the knowledge that these elements take a very long time to form, and that their development at the level of the EU would encounter opposition from the national level. And finally—is it really such a problem if opinion formation in the EU takes place largely at the national level—assuming, of course, that the member states possess a certain degree of mutual understanding and acceptance?

Bibliography

Gerhards, Jürgen and Friedhelm Neidhardt, 1991. "Strukturen und Funktionen moderner Öffentlichkeit. Fragestellungen und Ansätze," in Stefan Müller-Doohm and Klaus Neumann-Braun (eds), *Öffentlichkeit. Kultur. Massenkommunikation*, pp. 31–90. Oldenburg: Bis.

Habermas, Jürgen, 1981. *Theorie des kommunikativen Handelns.* Frankfurt am Main: Suhrkamp.

Katz, Elihu, 1996. "And Deliver Us from Segmentation," *Annals of the American Academy of Political Social Science,* 546, pp. 22–23.

Kielmannsegg, Peter Graf, 1994. "Läßt sich die Europäische Gemeinschaft demokratisch verfassen?," *Europäische Rundschau,* 22 (2), pp. 23–33.

JAMES BOHMAN

EXPANDING DIALOGUE: THE INTERNET, THE PUBLIC SPHERE, AND PROSPECTS FOR TRANSNATIONAL DEMOCRACY (2004)

James Bohman is Danforth Professor of Philosophy and Professor of International Studies at Saint Louis University, USA. His primary areas of research include political philosophy and the philosophy of social science. In Public Deliberation *(1995) and* Democracy across Borders *(2007), he has explored the possibilities for realizing democratic ideals under current conditions of cultural pluralism, inequality, social complexity, and globalization.*

In the following text, he discusses how the Internet and other forms of electronic communication might contribute to a new kind of public sphere and potentially a new form of democracy. He starts by emphasizing that communication is public only if it is directed at an indefinite audience with the expectation of a response. A public sphere always requires the expansion of dialogue beyond face-to-face encounters and is therefore always dependent on some form of communication technology.

Although traditional technologies support one-to-many communication, the new technologies support many-to-many communication networks. They create a "distributive" public sphere—a "public of publics"—rather than one distinctively unified public sphere. Such publics establish conditions for democratic deliberation, but are not themselves democratic. The communication networks as well as the publics formed within them must be embedded in a larger institutional and political context if they are to be transformed into public spheres in which citizens can make claims and expect response. However, in Bohman's view, the traditional democratic institutions are insufficient for this task.

In the unified public sphere of a nation-state citizens gain influence through a complex of parliamentary or representative institutions. In the transnational "distributive" Internet public sphere, there are no comparable institutional connections and procedures. Drawing on Nancy Fraser's distinction between "weak" and "strong" publics as well as on Jürgen Habermas' discussion of the relations between civil society and the political public sphere, Bohman argues that current Internet publics are "weak" publics, which exert influence primarily through public opinion. They may, however, become "strong" publics if they are embedded in a larger framework together with institutionalized decision-making procedures, and may as such eventually extend the dialogical character of the traditional public sphere in a cosmopolitan form.

New technologies are often greeted with political optimism. The Internet was thought to herald new possibilities for political participation, if not direct democracy, even in large and complex societies, as "electronic democracy" might replace the mass media democracy of sound-bite television. The high hopes for electronic democracy seem to have faded, however, as critics such as Sunstein (2001) and Shapiro (1999) have come to argue that central features of the Internet and computer-mediated communication generally undermine the sort of public sphere and political interaction that is required for genuine democratic deliberation. Whatever the empirical merits of such criticisms, they do point to an, as yet, unclarified problem in discussions of "electronic democracy": we still lack a clear understanding of how the Internet and other forms of electronic communication might contribute to a *new* kind of public sphere and thus to a new form of democracy. Certainly, globalization and other features of contemporary societies make it at least possible to consider whether democracy is undergoing another great transformation, of the order of the invention of representative democracy and its institutions of voting and parliamentary assemblies in early modern European cities.

Both the optimistic and pessimistic positions in the debate suffer from clear conceptual problems. Optimists take for granted that the mode of communication or technological mediation itself is constitutive of new possibilities. As examples such as the Chinese discovery of gunpowder show, however, technology is embedded in social contexts that may make its various potentials unrealizable. Pessimists make the opposite error of holding institutions fixed, here the institutions of the sovereign nation state. If we ask the question of whether or not electronic communication contributes to deliberation in representative institutions and to national public spheres, the answer is that more than likely it contributes little or even undermines them. Indeed, there has been much discussion concerning whether or not the Internet undermines sovereignty, much in the way that states previously considered the telegraph's capacity to cross borders as a direct threat to its sovereignty (see Held, 1995; Poster, 2001 and *Indiana Journal of Global Legal Studies*, 1998). But when the political context is shifted and a broader array of institutional alternatives are opened up to include a possible transnational public sphere, it seems likely that electronic and computer-mediated network communication may well expand the scope of certain features of communicative interaction across space and time, solving some of the problems of scale inherent in the literary public sphere and the limitations on deliberation in the institutions of representative democracy. A proper assessment, then, will not only have to consider new possibilities: it will also have to take more fully into consideration the fact that public spheres and democratic institutions do not exist separately but only in an ongoing historical relation to each other.

Why should these technologies lead to such opposing assessments? One reaction to such debates would be to show that many of the structural features of computer-mediated communication could just as well speak against the very idea of an electronic public sphere, including its anonymity, limitation of access and thus restricted audience, its network form, and so on. Although such empirical facts need to be considered, such an approach needs first to ask prior conceptual and normative questions concerning cyberspace as a public sphere, without which it is impossible to judge whether such facts close off possibilities or open up new ones. If the public sphere and democracy exhibit historical and institutional variation that elude the attempt to construct fixed standards, some of its supposed defects in one historical setting may well prove to be virtues in another. However successful, the sovereign nation state provides no democratic baseline for such judgments.

Such an open-ended and pragmatic approach, with its emphasis on possibilities, seems inevitably to lead to more optimistic conclusions about the public sphere and democracy under conditions of computer-mediated communication, although not unreservedly so. My argument has four steps. First, I undertake the conceptual clarification of the necessary conditions for a public sphere, with the requirements of deliberative democracy in mind. This conception of democracy and of the public sphere is dialogical, where dialogue is public only if it is able to expand and transform the conditions of communicative interaction. Second, I then consider the potentials of computer-mediated communication on the Internet in light of these necessary conditions. Since it is software rather than hardware that constructs how communication occurs over the network, the Internet's capacity to support a public sphere cannot be judged in terms of intrinsic features. If this is true, then the Internet is a public sphere only if agents make it so, if agents introduce institutional "software" that constructs the context of communication. This context is transnational rather than national, distributive rather than unified in form. Here the role that the Internet could play in specific institutions is examined through the experiences of governance in the European Union. Finally, I consider whether the novel public sphere that is created in transnational politics might itself feed back upon democratic institutions and help to promote new institutional forms that address the problems of space and time inherent in considering global democracy, including issues of collective identity. Participants in transnational public spheres become citizens of the world not merely because they form a "community of fate" via complex interdependence but, also, because they may now have the means and public sphere at their disposal to make normative claims upon each other in a properly dialogical and deliberative fashion. The first step is to unhook the conception of the public sphere from its first modern realization through the print medium and the institutions of the state.

Dialogue, Technology and the Public Sphere

Two normatively significant but potentially misleading assumptions guide most concepts of the public sphere and complicate any discussion of electronic democracy. These assumptions are normatively significant precisely because they directly establish the connection between the public sphere and the democratic ideal of deliberation among free and equal citizens. They are misleading, more often than not, because the connection that is made is overly specific and leaves out an essential condition for the existence of a public sphere in large and highly differentiated modern societies: the technological mediation of public communication. In this section I argue that if we consider this technological condition of possibility for any modern public sphere, we must relax the requirements of the public sphere as a forum for face-to-face communication. There are other ways to realize the public forum and its dialogical exchange in a more indirect and mediated manner, even while preserving and rearticulating the connection to democratic self-rule.

The public sphere (or *Öffentlichkeit* in the broad sense) is for these reasons not a univocal concept, even if it does have necessary conditions. First, a public sphere that has democratic significance must be a forum, that is, a social space in which speakers may express their views to others and who in turn respond to them and raise their own opinions and concerns. The specific ideal forum is too often taken to be a town meeting or perhaps a discussion in a salon, coffee shop or union hall, in which participants are physically present to each other in face-to-face interaction. Second, a democratic public sphere must manifest commitments to freedom and equality in the communicative interaction in the forum. Such interaction takes the specific form of a conversation or dialogue, in which speakers and hearers treat each other with equal respect and freely exchange their roles in their responses to each other. What makes dialogue so crucial is that it not only proceeds as a communicative exchange, in the form of turn-taking, but also that it is guided by the mutual expectation of uptake: that is, speakers offer reasons to each other and expect that others will consider their reasons or concerns at least to the extent that their speech acts contribute to shaping the ongoing course of the interaction, without anyone exerting control over it or having special status. What is potentially misleading is the assumption that dialogue must be modelled on one-to-one communication, perhaps counterfactually to the extent that each speaker addresses any other, demands a response, and so on. Instead, the other's response can be understood in a quite expansive spatial and temporal sense, in that someone in the indefinite future could give a response, without the speaker even conceivably having intended to address that hearer.

When modelled on the ideal process of face-to-face communication, such an interpretation of these features imposes severe spatial and temporal restrictions on public and political interaction. This leads to a third necessary feature for any public sphere, one that corrects for the limits of face-to-face interaction: communication must address an indefinite audience. In this sense, any social exclusion undermines the existence of a public sphere. This indefiniteness is required even of face-to-face interaction, since a conversation is public not simply because it could be heard by others but to the extent that it could be taken to address anyone. We might call this feature the "publicness" or "publicity" of communication, the necessary feature of its being "public." Communication is "public," then, if it is directed at an indefinite audience with the expectation of a response. In this way, it constitutes a common, open space for such interactions that is realized in iterated responses through similar acts of communication. In this way, a public sphere depends upon the opening up of a social space for a particular kind of repeated and open-ended interaction and, as such, requires technologies and institutions to secure its continued existence and regularize opportunities and access to it.

If this account of the necessary features of public communicative action is correct, then the scope of the ideal model of the face-to-face interaction needs to be revised. Such a forum is a special, rather than a general and ideal case. Furthermore, if the very existence of the public sphere is thus always dependent on some form of communications technology, then actors use that technology to create a space for social interaction that mediates and extends dialogue beyond the limits of face-to-face encounters. Historically, writing first served to open up this sort of indefinite social space of possibilities with the spatial extension of the audience and the temporal extension of uptake or response. Taking the potentials of writing further, the printed word produced a new form of communication based on a one-to-many form of interaction. With the mass literacy of the national public sphere that emerged in modernity it also produced the sort of mass audience that acquires the indefinite features proper to the public sphere. Nonetheless, it is only one such mediated public sphere that is constituted by interaction mediated through the print medium. Television and radio did not essentially alter this one-to-many extension of communicative interaction, even as they reduced entry requirements for hearers and raised the costs of adopting the speaker's role to a mass audience.

Computer-mediated communication also extends the forum, by providing a new unbounded space for communicative interaction. But its innovative potential lies not just in its speed and scale but also with in new form of address or interaction:

as a many-to-many mode of communication, it has radically lowered the costs of interaction with an indefinite and potentially large audience, especially with regard to adopting the speaker role without the costs of the mass media. Moreover, such many-to-many communication with newly increased interactivity holds out the promise of capturing the features of dialogue and communication more robustly than the print medium. At the very least, computer-mediated communication offers a potentially new solution to the problem of the extension of communicative inter-actions across space and time and thus, perhaps, signals the emergence of a public sphere that is not subject to the specific linguistic, cultural and spatial limitations of the bounded national public spheres that have up to now supported representa-tive democratic institutions. This network-based extension of dialogue suggests the possibility of re-embedding the public sphere in a new and potentially larger set of institutions. At present, there is a lack of congruity between existing political insti-tutions and the wider potential for public communicative interaction. Hence, the nature of the public or publics is changing.

Before leaping from innovative possibilities to an unwarranted optimism about the Internet's contribution to global democracy, it is first necessary to look more closely at the requirements of publicity and how the Internet might fulfill them. The sheer potential of the Internet to become a public sphere is insufficient to establish democracy at this scale for two reasons. This mediated many-to-many communica-tion may increase interactivity without preserving the essential features of dialogue, such as responsive uptake. Further, the Internet may be embedded in institutions that do not help in transforming its communicative space into a public sphere. Even if it is a free and open space, the Internet could simply be a marketplace or a commons as Lessing and others have argued (Lessing, 1999: 141). Even if this were so, actors could still transform such communicative resources and embed them in institutions that seek to extend dialogue and sustain deliberation. What would make it a "public sphere"?

Consider first the normative features of communicative public interaction. Pub-licity at the level of social action is most basic, in the sense that all other forms of publicity presuppose it. Social acts are public only if they meet two basic require-ments. First, they are not only directed to an indefinite audience but also offered with some expectation of a response, especially with regard to interpretability and justifiability. The description of the second general feature of publicity is dominated by spatial metaphors: public actions constitute a common and open "space" for in-teraction with indefinite others. Or, as Habermas puts it, publicity in this broadest sense is simply "the social space generated by communicative action" (Habermas, 1996: 360). Electronic communication is similarly dominated by such metaphors, now of "virtual" "cyberspace." However, we may here speak only of a "public space" (rather than a public sphere), which can be broader or narrower in comparison with others in terms of topics, available social roles, forms of expression, requirements of equal standing, and so on.

Entering into any such social space may be more or less difficult, depending on the requirements of background knowledge or the presence or absence of egalitar-ian norms and styles of social interaction. This difficulty gives rise to debates about a "digital divide." More than mere accessibility, some argue for the need for a "pub-lic culture," which might include a wide variety of practices, from performances to demonstrations and writing, in which participation is open to those who have mastered some basic conventions.[1] In this respect, we may see spaces on the Internet as gendered or culturally specific, even if indefinite in the communicative extension of its underlying social action. This is because the "space" for publicity must also be normatively structured and these norms open to challenge and revision.

Beyond this general and elementary level of publicity as a feature of some social actions and the space generated by them, higher levels of publicity are also possible. By higher I mean not higher on some normative scale but, rather, higher in the sense of levels of reflexivity. Higher order publicity introduces talk about talk, "second-order" deliberation and dialogue, that is, dialogue about the norms of publicity and the normative contours of the social space that is opened up by communicative interaction. Such second-order publicity requires two further nested and institutionalized features: first, not just the expectation of a response but expectations about the nature of responsiveness and accountability to others; and, second, the context of a more socially structured setting and forms of interaction than is available by means of communicative action alone. With respect to responsiveness, a higher level of publicity requires more than that speakers merely presuppose that they are addressing a potentially indefinite audience. It requires a normative concern for publicity itself.

The space of mutual accountability that is thereby opened up has a more egalitarian structure than simply being addressed by a speaker: in a public sphere, these communicative exchanges suspend the sharp distinction between audience and participants, thereby allowing exchange of speaker and hearer roles across all social positions and identities. This reciprocity of roles introduces further egalitarian features to audience-oriented communication: participation in the public sphere now means that one must be responsive to others and that they may have expectations about the appropriateness of a reason in a public context: besides speaking to an indefinite audience, one is now accountable to their objections and answerable to demands to recognize their concerns.[2] The recognition of equal standing as citizens in a political community is one potentially self-transformative form that egalitarian publicity has taken.

Introducing second order levels does not necessarily narrow the public sphere, since second order questions are themselves open to challenge. Expanding and structuring such a social space for communication requires embedding it in a wider social context. A specifically egalitarian expansion of the public sphere requires a more elaborated institutional structure to support it (such as that achieved by the modern democratic state but not identical with it), as the social contexts of communication are enlarged with the number of relevant speakers and audience. When such contexts increase the scale of public interaction and include more participants, communicative action alone cannot fully constitute or control the contours of the social space that it generates. In societies characterized by social differentiation, the political space for publicity is delimited in relation to other social domains and institutions. It is with the differentiation of society that we begin to see the emergence of what is specifically "the public sphere."

Continuing the spatial metaphor that dominates thinking about publicity, the public sphere becomes a space "in-between" the formal political institutions and civil society. Thus, the very existence of a distinct public sphere requires a certain degree of social complexity, typically in the internal differentiation of social spheres such as centralized administrative institutions (the state) on the one hand, and a separate sphere of autonomous associations and economic activity (or civil society) on the other. Not all public spheres relate to the state. There may, then, be many publics and overlapping public spheres. A city's institutions may create a local public sphere, but that public overlaps with and interacts with other publics. In this sense, it is indeterminate to whom a claim is addressed or who is expected to respond, given the indefiniteness of the audience. When a public sphere interacts with a set of institutions, the set of participants is potentially extended beyond the restrictions of membership or constituency, whenever a claim or utterance is given uptake and considered relevant. By using norms as a resource, actors in higher order public spheres cannot limit to whom they are answerable.

In differentiated societies (in whatever institutional form), one role of the distinctive communication that goes on in the public sphere is to raise topics or express concerns that cut across social spheres: it not only circulates information about the state and the economy, but also establishes a forum for criticism in which the boundaries of these spheres are crossed, primarily in citizens' demands for mutual accountability. But the other side of this generalization is a requirement for communication that crosses social domains: such a generalization is necessary, precisely because the public sphere has become less socially and culturally homogeneous and more internally differentiated into diverse normative perspectives and social positions. It is certainly the case that the relative absence of state regulation in cyberspace means that censorship is no longer the primary means of inhibiting the formation of public spheres. Those powerful social institutions that may now inhibit the formation of a public sphere in electronic space are no longer states but, rather, corporations and other market actors who increasingly design and control its architecture. Publics now develop in new and politically unbounded social contexts, some of which may even be global in scope, as civil society and the supporting institutions of the public sphere become more transnational.

While the mass and electronic media form the basis for global networks for the production and distribution of information, they produce a different kind of public space and hence develop a form of publicity different from a "cosmopolitan" or global public sphere. Certainly the costs of exchanging information across space go down considerably. In comparison with the past, the epistemic requirements for participating in large scale and potentially transnational communication are lessened, to such an extent that it is widely available beyond élites in wealthy societies. By employing new technological means for lower cost distribution and by lowering epistemic entry requirements, electronic media can create a mass audience of such a size as to be conceivably global in scope. But the type of audience so created has certain characteristics: the larger an unstructured and undifferentiated audience is, the less likely it is that the public and reflexive use of reason is required to be part of it. The audience is therefore more likely to be "anonymous," both to each other and to the producers of its publicly conveyed messages. The addressees of such anonymous communication are an indefinite audience in a purely *aggregative* sense: it is not an idealized audience that is addressed, but the aggregate audience of all those who can potentially gain access to the material and interpret it as they wish. In the print public sphere, anonymous authorship had a particular purpose, especially in resisting the institutions of the state in which it was embedded (as when Locke published his *Second Treatise* anonymously). Anonymity is employed to maintain the freedom and diversity of speech, as human rights groups, who report abuses of various governments around the world, use it on the Internet. The anonymity of such political communication is a form that, even on the Internet, continues the resistance to censorship and state power in the public sphere.

It is easy to mistake the communicative function of anonymity. Anonymity does not fully strip away the identity of the speaker, for Locke could publish his treatise with the full knowledge that the author of the *Second Treatise* would be taken to have a particular political identity, even if that identity was not that of John Locke, and thus provokes responses as such. Rather than subjective or authorial, Internet anonymity is structural. Who is speaking is not in principle independently knowable by others. For this reason, participants in networks cannot have the full range of normative expectation of face-to-face publics or even print publics in which authorship may become a textual designator. In a serial public of publics, participants may address themselves to a segment of the public rather than the whole public of publics. In a network mediated by a computer interface, we do not know who is actually speaking: we also do not know whom we expect to respond, if they will respond or if the response will be sustained. Thus, while anonymity promotes freedom of expression under certain circumstances, it changes the expectation of communication by making speaker and audience not only indefinite but also indeterminate in its many-to-many form.

In this sort of public sphere, how would actors exhibit their concern for publicity or employ the self-referentiality of the public sphere to criticize others? Instead of appealing to an assumed common norm of "publicity" or a set of culturally specific practices of communication, a *transnational* public sphere is created when at least two culturally rooted public spheres begin to overlap and intersect, as when translations and conferences create a cosmopolitan public sphere in various academic disciplines. Such culturally expansive, yet socially structured rather than anarchic, public spheres emerge as political institutions and civic associations and come to include previously excluded groups. Instead of relying on the intrinsic features of the medium to expand communicative interaction, networks that are global in scope become publics only with the development and expansion of transnational civil society. The creation of such a civil society is a slow and difficult process that requires the highly reflexive forms of communication, boundary crossing and accountability typical of developed public spheres. Thus, we can expect that under proper conditions and with the support of the proper institutions, existing vibrant global publics will expand as they become open to and connected with other public spheres. On the basis of their common knowledge of violations of publicity, their members will develop the capacities of public reason to cross and negotiate boundaries and differences between persons, groups and cultures.

In such boundary-crossing publics, the speed, scale and intensity of communicative interaction provided by the Internet provides that open social space that is a positive and enabling condition for democratic and perhaps even cosmopolitan deliberation. Contrary to misleading analogies to the national public sphere, such a development hardly demands that the public sphere be "integrated with media systems of matching scale that occupy the same social space as that over which economic and political decision will have an impact" (Garnham, 1995: 265). But if the way to do this is through multiple communicative networks rather than the mass media, then the global public sphere should not be expected to mirror the cultural unity and spatial congruence of the national public sphere: as a public of publics, it permits a decentred public sphere with many different levels. This fact also distinguishes it from the idealizations of an implied universal audience typical of the print-mediated public sphere. Disaggregated networks must always be embedded in some other set of social institutions rather than in an assumed unified national public sphere. This suggests that they will be embedded in different, disaggregated political institutions, if they are to be the institutions that transform the deliberation of such public spheres in the communicative power of collective action. Once we examine the potential ways in which the Internet can expand the features of communicative interaction, the issue of whether or not the Internet can support public spheres changes in character. It depends not only on which institutions shape its framework but also on how participants contest and change these institutions and on how they interpret the Internet as a public space. It depends on the mediation of agency, not on technology.

The Internet as a Network and as a Space of Publics

The main lesson that I wanted to draw at the end of the last section is that discussions of the democratic potential of the Internet cannot be satisfied with listing its positive or intrinsic features, as for example its speed, its scale, its "anarchic" nature, its ability to facilitate resistance to centralized control as a network of networks, and so on. The same is true for its negative effects or consequences, such as its disaggregative character or its anonymity. Taken together, both these considerations tell against regarding the Internet as a variation of existing print and national public spheres. Rather, the space opened up by computer-mediated communication supports a new sort of "distributive" rather than unified public sphere with new forms of interaction. By "distributive," I mean that computer mediation in the form of the Internet "decentres" the public sphere; it is a public of publics rather than a distinctively unified and encompassing public sphere in which all communicators participate. Rather than simply entering into an existing public sphere, the Internet becomes a public sphere only through agents who engage in reflexive and democratic activity. For the Internet to create a new form of publicity beyond the mere aggregate of all its users, it must first be constituted as a public sphere by those people whose interactions exhibit the features of dialogue and are concerned with its publicity. In order to support a public sphere and technologically mediate the appropriate norms, the network form must become a viable means for the expansion of the possibilities of dialogue and of the deliberative, second order features of communicative interaction. These features may not be the same as manifested in previous political public spheres, such as the bourgeois public sphere of private persons; what it must be is, at least, a space for publics but not itself a public sphere. It can, however, enable such a public of publics to emerge, given the emergence of democratic actors and the proper supporting transnational institutionalization.

If the Internet has no intrinsic features, it is because, like writing, it holds out many different possibilities in its transformation of the public sphere. Here it is useful to

distinguish between hardware and software. As hardware, the World Wide Web is a
network of networks with technical properties that enable the conveyance of information over great distances with near simultaneity. This hardware can be used for
different purposes, as embodied in software that configures participants as "users."
Indeed, as Lessing notes, "an extraordinary amount of control can be built in the environment that people know in cyberspace," perhaps even without their knowledge
(Lessing, 1999: 217).[3] Such computer programmes depend on "software" in a much
broader sense: software includes not only the variety of programmes available but
also the ways in which people improvise and collaborate to create new possibilities
for interaction. Software in this sense includes both the modes of social organization mediated through the Net and the institutions in which the Net is embedded.
For example, the indeterminacy of the addressees of an anonymous message can be
settled by reconfiguring the Internet into an intranet, creating a private space that
excludes others and defines the audience. This is indeed how most corporations use
the Web today, creating inaccessible and commercial spaces within the networks,
by the use of firewalls and other devices for commercial and monetary interactions
among corporations and anonymous consumers. Such actions show the variety of
ways in which power and control may be manifested in the Web. Certainly, the
Web enables the power to be distributed in civil society but it also permits power
to be manifested, less in the capacity to interfere with others than in the capacity
to exclude them and alter the freedom and openness of its public space. This same
power may alter other public spaces, as when the *New York Times* offers to deliver
a "personalized" paper that is not identical with the one that other citizens in the
political public sphere are reading. In this way, the Internet can be controlled so that
it may be used for the privatization of information as a commodity.

The fact of social power reveals the importance of institutions in preserving and
maintaining public space, and the Internet is no exception. Saskia Sassen shows
how the Internet has historically reflected the institutions in which it has been embedded and configured. Its "anarchist" phase reflected the ways in which it was created in universities and for scientific purposes. While the Web still bears the marks
of this phase as possibilities of distributed power, it is arguably entering a different
phase, in which corporations increasingly privatize this common space as a kind of
terra nullia for their specific purposes, such as financial transactions. "We are at a
particular historical moment in the history of electronic space when powerful corporate actors and high performance networks are strengthening the role of private
electronic space and altering the structure of public electronic space" (Sassen, 1998:
194). At the same time, it is also clear that civil society groups, especially transnational groups, are using the web for their own political and public purposes, where
freedom and interconnectivity are what is valued.

The broader point here is not merely to show the effects of privatization and
the particular ideology of neoliberalism that supports it, but to show how the Internet develops in interaction with the larger social structures, "offline" problems
and conflicts that it internalizes and refracts. This particular conjuncture of forces
opens the potential not only for conflicting interpretations of cyberspace but also
for newly reflexive activity of civil society actors over the public character of the
Internet, much as the eighteenth-century public sphere struggled with the state
over censorship of the print medium that created a public concerned with its own

publicity. Those concerned with the publicity, freedom and openness of the Internet as a public space may see those of its features that extend dialogical interaction threatened by its annexation by large scale economic enterprises. Such a concern requires that civil society actors not only contest the alterations of public space but, also, that these actors place themselves between the corporations, software makers, access providers and other powerful institutions that often enjoy an immediate and highly asymmetrical relation to individuals as "users" who enter into public spaces as they configure them in the literal and institutional software they create for those who enter their private cyberspaces. We are now in a period of the development of the software and hardware of the Internet in which the nature of the Web is at issue, with similar processes of political decentralization and social contestation that characterize the problems, struggles and contradictions found in many areas of social life. The process of development here is hardly unprecedented or *sui generis*.

This suggests a particular analysis of threats to public space. It is now commonplace to say that the Internet rids communication of intermediaries, of those various professional communicators whose mass-mediated communication is the focus of much of public debate and discussion and political information. Dewey lauded such a division of labour to the extent to which it can improve deliberation, not merely in creating a common public sphere but also in "the subtle, delicate, vivid and responsive art of communication." This task is, at least in part, best fulfilled by professional communicators who disseminate the best available information and technologies to large audiences of citizens. Even with this dependence on such art and techniques of communication, the public need not simply be the object of techniques of persuasion. Rather than a "mass" of cultural dopes, mediated communication makes a "rational public" possible, in the sense that "the public as a whole can generally form policy preferences that reflect the best available information" (Page, 1995). If we focus upon the totality of political information available and a surprising tendency for the public to correct media biases and distortions, as stories and opinions develop and change over time, it is possible to see how mediated communication can enhance the communication presupposed in public deliberation. In a complex, large-scale and pluralistic society, mediated communication is unavoidable if there are to be channels of communication broad enough to address the highly heterogeneous audience of all of its members and to treat issues that vary with regard to the epistemic demands on speakers in diverse locales who can discuss them intelligently.

For all of these reasons, proponents of deliberation often claim there is a net normative loss in the shift to networked communication, further amplified by "the control revolution" in which various corporations and providers give individuals the capacity to control who addresses them and whom they may respond to (Shapiro, 1999: 23).[4] Or, to put this criticism in the terms that I have been using here, the mass public sphere is not replaced by any public sphere at all; rather, communicative mediation is replaced by forms of control that make dialogue and the expansion of the deliberative features of communication impossible. In the terms of economic theory, agents whose purpose it is to facilitate individual control over the communicative environment replace intermediaries. Such a relation though inevitably leads to "the reversal of agency," where the direction of control shifts from principals to the agents they delegate. It is false to say that individuals possess immediate control: they have control only through assenting to an asymmetrical relationship to various agents who structure the choices in the communicative environment of cyberspace.

There is more than a grain of truth in this pessimistic diagnosis of the control revolution. But this leaves out part of the story concerning how the public exercises some control over intermediaries, at least those concerned with publicity. As with the relation of agent and principal, the problem here is to develop democratic modes of interaction between expert communicators and their audience in the public sphere. Citizens must now resist the "mediaization of politics" on a par with its technization by experts. The challenge is twofold. First of all, the public must challenge the credibility of expert communicators, especially in their capacities to set agendas and frames for discussing issues. And, second, as in the case of cooperating with experts the public must challenge the reception of their own public communication by the media themselves, especially insofar as they must also report, represent and even define the "public opinion" of citizens who are strangers to each other. This self-referential aspect of public communication can only be fulfilled by interactions between the media and the public, who challenge both the ways in which the public is addressed and its opinion is represented.

Mass-mediated communication inhibits deliberation in cases when experts, especially in the tight communicative circle of the media and officials, define both the nature of the public and its opinions. In the American context, it is "when officials of both parties and the mainstream media take a position similar to each other and opposed to the public" (Page, 1995: 119). This tight linkage is not merely a contingent affair. It is part of the interaction between media, government and audience that is typical of mediated political communication. Media outlets are dependent on government agencies for much of their information: and officials and candidates must use the media as their main channel for communication to the widest possible audience. Such problems are exacerbated as the mediated interaction becomes predominant in modern political and public spheres, creating new forms of social interaction and political relationships that reorder in space and time and become structured in ways less and less like mutually responsive dialogue (Thompson, 1995). The same is true for computer mediation, which always includes the constructive mediation of institutions as software that shape and maintain the space for interaction and may set up this interaction asymmetrically.

Analogous considerations of agency and asymmetries of access to the norms that shape communicative interaction are relevant to the Internet. It is clear that corporations could function as the main institutional actors in developing electronic space and exert an influence that would restrict communication in ways even more impervious to corporate media and political parties. Just as all public spheres have technological mediation of features of communicative interaction, all public spheres require counter-intermediaries and counter-public spaces of some kind or another to maintain their publicness: that is, their sustainability over time depends precisely upon those members of the public concerned with the public sphere and public opinion and, thus, concerned to have a say in the construction of the public space in whatever technical means of communication is available. The Internet and its governance now lacks the means to institutionalize the public sphere, especially since there are no functional equivalents to the roles played by journalists, judges and other intermediaries who regulated and protected the publicity of political communication in the mass media.

Who are their replacements once the technology of mediation changes? The Internet has not yet achieved a settled form in which intermediaries have been established and professionalized. As in the emerging public spheres of early modernity, the potential intermediary roles must emerge from those who organize themselves in cyberspace as a public sphere. This role falls to those organizations in civil society that have become concerned with the publicity of electronic space and seek to create, institutionalize, expand and protect it. Such organizations can achieve their goals only if they act self-referentially and insist that they may exercise communicative power over the shape and appropriation of electronic public space. Thus, contrary to Shapiro and Sunstein, it is not that the Internet gets rid of intermediaries as such; rather it operates in a public space in which the particular *democratic* intermediaries have lost their influence. This is not a necessary structural consequence of its form of communication.

With the development of the Internet as a public sphere, we may expect its "re-intermediarization," that is, the emergence of new intermediaries who counter its privatization and individualization, brought about by access and content providers for commercial purposes, and who construct the user as a private person. Actors can play the role of "counterintermediaries" when they attempt to bypass these narrow social roles on the Internet: more specifically, the role of a "user" in relation to a "provider" who sets the terms of how the Internet may be employed. The first area in which this has already occurred is in Internet self-governance organizations and their interest in countering trends to annexation and privatization. Here institutions such as ICANN have attempted to institute public deliberation on the legal and technological standards that govern the Internet (Froomkin, 2003). The other is more issue-specific, as when the Internet is used deliberatively to contest the lack of information or public debate on important issues, such as the recent successful attempt to create opposition to the "multilateral agreement on investment" in the absence of any significant print media discussion. Such actors are concerned with the public sphere itself and use the Internet as the social space in which to construct counterpublics and new forms of access to deliberation and decision making. Here it is civil society that provides counterintermediaries, that is, they transform passive "users" in a social space, into democratic agents who are concerned with the quality of the Internet as a public sphere. This and other examples of a deliberative process through multiple intermediaries bears further examination.

Given that what is needed are alternatives to the current set of intermediaries rather than the absence of them, civil society organizations have distinct advantages in taking on such a responsibility for publicity in cyberspace. They have organizational identities, they are not anonymous; they also take over the responsibility for responsiveness that remains indeterminate in many-to-many communication. Most of all, they employ the Internet, but not as Users; they create their own spaces, promote interactions, conduct deliberation, make available information, and so on. For example, a variety of organization created a forum for the debate on the Agreement on Investment, an issue that hardly registered in the national press. Not only did they make the Agreement widely available, they held detailed on-line discussions of the merits of its various provisions (Smith and Smythe, 2001: 183). As a tool for various forms of activism, the Internet promotes a vibrant civil society: it extends the public sphere of civil society but does not necessarily transform it. Even in this regard, the point is not simply to create a web site or to convey information at low cost. It becomes something more when sites interact as a public space in which free, open and responsive dialogical interaction takes place. This sort of project is not uncommon and includes experiments among neighbourhood groups, non-governmental organizations, and others. Hence the organization acts as an intermediary in a different way: not as an expert communicator but, rather, as the creator and facilitator of institutional "software" that socializes the commons and makes it a public space.

This role for civil society organizations, in periods in which public spaces are contested, is not unprecedented. Nor does it require purity from economic motives or the disinterestedness of the press journalist: it was, after all, the various trade associations that sought to establish free and open public spheres in which information about distant locales could be available, through newsletters to all, with the emergence of global trade in England. This new sort of public role, however, does change how many NGOs and civil society organizations understand themselves; they would have to understand themselves as responsible for transnational structures of communication and not simply for the particular issue at hand. They can only achieve their goals if democracy is extended in the appropriate ways, and it can he extended only if electronic space becomes a public sphere, a place in which publics of various sorts can emerge and communicate with other publics.

So long as there are cosmopolitan actors who will create and maintain such transnational communication, this sort of serial and distributed public sphere is potentially global in scope. Its unity is to be found in the general conditions for the formation of publics themselves, and in the actions of those who see themselves as constituting a public against this background. Membership in these shifting publics is to be found in civil society, in formal and informal organizations that emerge to discuss and deliberate on the issues of the day. But while the creation of publics is a matter of the agency of citizens, the sustaining of general conditions that make such a process possible is a matter for formal institutionalization, just as sustaining the conditions for the national public sphere was a central concern of the democratic nation state. In the case of such shifting and potentially transnational publics, the institutions that sustain publicity and become the focus of the self-referential activity of civil society must also be innovative, if they are to have their communicative basis in dispersed and decentred forms of publicity. At the same time, these institutions must be deliberative and democratic. Because they become the location for second order reflexive political deliberation and activity, these institutions are part of the public sphere, as its higher order and self-governing form of publicity that transforms the Internet from a commons to an institutionally organized and embedded democratic space.

From Publics to Public Sphere: The Institutional Form of
Transnational Democracy

In the last section, I argued that reflexive agency of actors within cyberspace was required, to create the "software" that could transform networks into publics making use of the distributive processes of communication in order to overcome the limitations of space and time presupposed in the national public spheres and state forms. While such publics establish positive and enabling conditions for democratic deliberation, they are not themselves democratic (even if they are transnational and cosmopolitan rather than national). Transnational civil society is a further enabling condition for the transformation of networks into publics, to the extent that it is from this sphere that we can expect to find agents who will act self-referentially so as to address, create and sustain publics; but not all such actors will have explicitly democratic goals, just as in the national public sphere a vibrant civil society need not contain only democratically oriented actors as a condition of the possibility of democratic deliberation. The public must itself be embedded in an institutional context, not only if it is to secure the conditions of publicity but also in order to promote the interaction among publics that is required for deliberative democracy. Thus, both network forms of communication and the publics formed in them must be embedded in a larger institutional and political context, if they are to be transformed into public spheres in which citizens can make claims and expect a response.

There are several reasons to think that current democratic institutions are insufficient for this task. States have promoted the privatization of various media spaces for communication, including not only the Internet but also broadcast frequencies. Even if the Internet is not intrinsically anarchistic and even if states were willing to do more in the way of protecting the public character of cyberspace, it remains an open question whether this form of communication escapes the way in which state sovereignty organizes space and time, including public space and the temporality of deliberation.[5] It is precisely its potentially aterritorial character that makes it difficult to square with centralized forms of authority over a delimited territory. This sort of process, however, does not require convergence, especially since Internet use may reflect inequalities in the access to rule-making institutions as well as other older patterns of subordination at the international level. It is also true that people do not as yet identify with each other on cosmopolitan terms. Nonetheless, new possibilities that the Internet affords for deliberation and access to influence in its distributive and network forms do not require such strong preconditions to have opened up new forms of democratization.

This is only one feature of the state's constraints on the organization of space, which also includes various cultural and linguistic limitations of the unified public sphere that is formed around and is supported by the democratic state. It is not the case that states are now entirely ineffective, nor is it true that national public spheres so culturally limited that they serve no democratic purpose. Rather, what is at stake is not so much the continued existence or specificity of either democracy or the public sphere but, rather that the Internet escapes the particular connections and feedback relations between the national public sphere and the democratic state. Whatever institutions could promote and protect such a dispersed and disaggregated public sphere will represent a novel political possibility that does not "merely replicate on a larger scale the typical modern political form" (Ruggie, 1996: 195). Indeed, it must be a political form for which such a dispersed public sphere does not produce negative consequences for the capacity to transform political communication into effective political influence and authorization but, rather, develops a form of democratically organized decision-making, in which such dispersal has the positive effect of creating wider opportunities for political participation. In the absence of such a public sphere, other, often private, sources of power intervene, with or without political delegation. In this case, forms of contestation concerning economic issues may emerge in transnational social movements that do not simply appeal to states and their current unwillingness to constrain market forces.

The difficulties that the globalization of political space poses for territorial sovereignty are widely discussed, particularly with regard to the effectiveness of state regulation of the economy. Because the political institutions of democracy must be congruent with the available forms of publicity, the difficulties posed by the disunity of a global public sphere cut much deeper for the idea of deliberative democracy. As Will Kymlicka has pointed out, territoriality continues to survive by other means, particularly since "language is increasingly important in defining the boundaries of political communities and the identities of the actors" (Kymlicka, 1999: 120). For this reason, Kymlicka argues, national communities "remain the primary forum for democratic participatory democratic debates." Whereas international forums are dominated by elites, the national public sphere is more likely to be a space for egalitarian, mass participation in the vernacular language and is thus the only forum that guarantees "genuine" democratic participation and influence. Moreover, since deliberation depends on common cultural assumptions, such as shared newspapers and political parties, the scope of a deliberative community must be limited to those who share a political culture. This argument is particularly challenging to the view defended here, since it employs the same idea of a dialogical public sphere within a democracy oriented to deliberation in order to reach the opposite conclusion. Can the argument about mediated communication and the extension of dialogue go beyond a territorial, self-governing linguistic community?

As Kymlicka thinks of the public sphere, print and mass media extend properties of linguistic interaction, insofar as a national politics facilitates mass egalitarian participation around a unified set of themes and concerns. If this is the requirement for democracy, then we face a dilemma of scale. The larger the linguistic community, the more likely it will be that citizens will not have access to influence or be able to participate in an egalitarian form of decision-making in a unified public sphere. Transnational democracy will not be participatory and deliberative, perhaps not even "genuinely" democratic at all (Dahl, 1999: 19). But here the question is simply begged in favor of pessimism: the question is not whether transnational institutions are more or less democratic by the standards of a monolinguistic national community but, rather, whether they are adequately democratic under the circumstances. The criticism holds only if democratic agents in the transnational public sphere seek to approximate the assumptions of the national variant. To look only at the constraints of size in relation to a particular form of political community begs the question of whether or not there are alternative linkages between democracy and the public sphere that are not simply scaled up. Such linkages might be more decentralized and polycentric than the national community requires. The issue here is the standard of evaluation, not whether some other public sphere or form of community "is totally or completely democratic, but whether it is adequately democratic given the kind of entity we take it to be" (MacCormick, 1997: 345). For a nation state to be democratic, it requires a certain sort of public sphere sufficient to create a strong public via its connections to parliamentary debate. A transnational and thus polycentric and pluralist community, such as the European Union, requires a different sort of public sphere in order to promote sufficient democratic deliberation. Once a transnational and post-territorial polity rejects the assumption that it must be what Rawls calls "a single cooperative scheme in perpetuity," a more fluid and negotiable order might emerge, with plural authority structures along a number of different dimensions rather than a single location for public authority and power. In this case, linguistic differences do not loom as large an impediment to egalitarian interactions as Kymlicka thinks.

Without a single location of public power, a unified public sphere becomes an impediment to democracy rather than an enabling condition for mass participation in decisions at a single location of authority. The minimal criteria of adequacy would be that, even with the diffusion of authority, participants in the public sphere would have to be sufficiently empowered to create opportunities and access to influence over transnational decision-making. This access will not be attained once and for all, as in the unified public sphere of nation sates in which citizens gain influence through the complex of parliamentary or representative institutions. These distributive publics have to gain access to influence over the deliberation governmental and non-governmental actors. Currently they are "weak" publics, who exert such influence through public opinion generally. But they may become "strong" publics when they are able to exercise influence through institutionalized decision procedures with regularized opportunities for *ex ante* input.[6] Thus, transnational institutions are adequately democratic if they permit such access to influence distributively, across various domains and levels, rather than merely aggregatively in the summative public sphere of citizens as a whole. But because there is no single institution to which strong publics are connected, the contrast between weak and strong publics is much more fluid than the current usage presupposes. That is because strong publics are assumed to be connected to a particular sort of legislatively empowered collective will. In the transnational case, strong publics may be required to seek more direct forms of deliberative influence given the dispersal of authority and the variety of its institutional locations.

Rather than look for a single axis on which to judge the democratic deficit of international and transnational institutions, it will be more useful to consider a variety of possible forms, given various ways in which publicity might be institutionalized. While the full range of such cases cannot be considered fully here, the European Union provides an interesting case study for a transnational polity, precisely because it obviously lacks the unitary and linguistic features of previous public spheres. I will consider only one aspect of the debate here: proposals that are suggestive of how a polycentric form of publicity would permit a more rather than a less directly deliberative form of governance, once we abandon the assumption that there is a unified public sphere connected to a single set of state-like authority structures that seem to impose uniform policies over its entire territory. As Charles Sabel has argued, a "directly deliberative" design in many ways incorporates epistemic innovations and increased capabilities of economic organizations, in the same way as the new regulatory institutions of the New Deal followed the innovations of industrial organizations, in the centralized mass production they attempted to administer and regulate (Dorf and Sabel, 1996: 292). Roughly, such a form of organization uses nested and collaborative forms of decision-making based on highly collaborative processes of jointly defining problems and setting goals already typical in many large firms with dispersed sites of production.

Such a process requires a design that promotes a great deal of interaction within the organization and across sites and locations. Within the normative framework established by initial goals and benchmarks, the process of their application requires deliberation at various levels of scale. At all levels, citizens can introduce factors based on local knowledge and problems, even as they are informed by the diverse solutions and outcomes of other planning and design bodies. Local solutions can also be corrected, as these solutions can be tested by the problem-solving of other groups. Thus, while highly dispersed and distributed, various levels of deliberation permit testing and correction, even if they do not hierarchically override decisions at lower levels.

Such a collaborative process of setting goals and defining problems produces a shared body of knowledge and common goals, even if the solutions need not be uniform across or within various organizations and locations. Sabel calls this "learning by monitoring" and proposes ways in which administrative agencies could employ such distributive processes even while evaluating performance at lower levels by systematic comparisons across sites. Innovations are not handed down from the top, since its learning does not assume that the higher levels are epistemically superior. It cannot do so, if it is to be a non-hierarchical alternative to agent/principal relationships that emerge across levels of governance and lead to the common problem of the reversal of agency. Besides problems of scale, democracy on the model of a national community writ large leads to a proliferation of such forms of agency in dealing with external problems as issues of "foreign policy," typically the most undemocratic component of national governance.

The European Union implements such a decentralized process of regulation in its "Open Method of Coordination." Such deliberative processes provide a space for on-going reflection on agendas and problems, as well as an interest in inclusiveness and diversity of perspectives. These enabling conditions for democracy can take advantage of the intensified interaction across borders that are byproducts of processes of the thickening of the communicative infrastructure across state borders. Regulatory, but still decentralized, federalism provides for modes of accountability in this process itself, even while allowing for local variations that go beyond the assumption of the uniformity of policy over a single bounded territory typical of nation state regulation. Sabel and Cohen argue that the European Union already has features of a directly deliberative polyarchy in the implementation of the OMC in its economic, industrial and educational standards (Sabel and Cohen, 1998).[7] The advantage of such deliberative methods is that the interaction at different levels of decision making promotes robust accountability: accountability operates upwards and downwards and, in this way, cuts across the typical distinction of vertical and horizontal accountability (O'Donnell, 1994: 61). Thus, directly deliberative polyarchy describes a method of decision-making in institutions across various levels and with plural authority structures.

Unlike attempts to exert public influence upon hierarchical representative institutions, this sort of institutionalized method is directly rather than indirectly deliberative. Indirectly deliberative institutions hold out the promise of democratic legitimacy to the extent that their formal institutions are connected to the various public spheres in which all citizens participate (although not necessarily all in the same ones). Directly deliberative institutions might, at the level of fixing general goals and standards that guide such a process, require a similar sort of connection to the European public sphere at large, which in turn may be mediated through a more effective European parliament. Given various linguistic and mass media limitations, this public sphere would not be a unified one, but a public of publics in which various linguistic public spheres debate common issues and, through intermediaries, translate across linguistic and cultural boundaries the results of deliberative processes in other publics.

But what is the public at large at the level of implementation and democratic experimentation in directly deliberative processes? Sabel provides no answer to this question, asserting only that the process must be open to the public (Sabel and Cohen, 1998: 29).[8] Without a clear account of the interaction between publics and the various levels of the institutional decision-making process, it is hard to see why the process does not simply reduce to a more open form of commitology, of expert deliberation at various levels governed by various interests which attempt to influence their decisions. In this case, such deliberation may have a certain epistemic quality but its sole claim to be democratic is that committees are internally pluralistic, across national identity, and are governed by some conception of the common European good. But committees are then hardly directly deliberative, except in the sense that there is vigorous interaction among various indirectly deliberative, loosely representative bodies with different tasks and goals. Direct deliberation must be kept institutionally distinct from commitology, precisely with respect to its particular disaggregated form of publicity. What is needed here, to go beyond commitology, is not a new method but rather a Europe that is a public of publics.

The problem for institutional design of directly deliberative democracy is to create precisely the appropriate feedback relation between disaggregated publics and such a polycentric decision-making process. As my discussion of the Internet shows, there is a technology through which this form of publicity is produced and which expands and maintains the deliberative potential of dialogue.

Thus, the European Union, at least in some of its decision-making processes, could then seek the marriage of directly deliberative decision making and computer assisted, mediated and distributive forms of publicity. When compared to the nation state democracies that are members of the EU, such a proposal is based on two different forms of disaggregation: the disaggregation of both representative democracy and the national public sphere in order to promote a more deliberative form of transnationalism. At the European level, this would require an innovative form of a symmetrical federalism that would go beyond the hierarchy of territorial federalism along the model of the United States. Most of all, it would require experimentation in reconciling the dispersed form of many-to-many communication with the demands of the forum. Rather than merely seek to determine an institutional formula such direct and vigorous interaction among dispersed publics at various levels of decision making, it is more fruitful to say that in each case, such democratization requires the existence of a vibrant, transnational civil society in which organizations and groups create publics around which various sort of decisions are debated and discussed, similar to the sort of Internet counter-public sphere that emerged around the Agreement on Investment. Appropriately designed decision-making processes and the existence of a suitable form of publicity, to enable access to influence, speak at least in favour of the feasibility of such a proposal. This sort of procedure also suggests that familiar problem of scale that plague public deliberation when it does not consider alternative ways in which the dialogical features of the public sphere may be technologically and institutionally extended and democratically secured.

Conclusion

My argument here has been two sided. On the one hand, I have developed the innovative potential of electronic public space for democracy, especially when applied to a deliberative transnationalism. This potential transformation of democratic institutions shows the fruitfulness of thinking about cyberspace in political terms that are related to the sort of publicity that it generates. On the other hand, such a potential public sphere can be secured only through innovative institutions. In each case, new circumstances suggest rethinking both democracy and the public sphere outside the limits of its previous historical forms. Tied up with the nation state and its political culture, this framework misrepresents the potentials of new forms of mediated communication for democracy and public deliberation. Rethinking publicity allows us to see that some critical diagnosis of the problems of electronic democracy are short-circuited by a failure to think beyond what is politically familiar, as when it is argued that communication over the internet leads to a general phenomena of "disintermediation," when what it actually leads to new intermediaries (Shapiro, 1999: 55). The same is true of diagnoses that see the Internet as inherently democratic and dialogical. Critical analyses of the potential of the Internet and the globalization of communication are better served neither by pessimism nor by optimism, but by examining potential transformations of our understanding of both democracy and the public sphere. If my argument is correct, that the Internet preserves and extends the dialogical character of the public sphere in a potentially cosmopolitan form, then a deliberative transnational democracy can be considered a "realistic utopia" in Rawls' sense; it extends the range of political possibilities for deliberative democracy. Even as such communication does indeed threaten some of the best realizations of political ideals of democracy that have been achieved so far in the modern era, contrary to critics such as Kymlicka, it also opens up new possibilities that are recognizably democratic and directly deliberative. Deliberative publics can be strong publics distributively, capable of exerting political influence in real decision-making processes under certain institutional conditions.

While I have rejected Kymlicka's criticism of transnational democracy as lacking an egalitarian public sphere for mass participation, he is correct to press a further point that proponents of global or cosmopolitan democracy have not taken seriously: the problem that the lack of a shared identity poses for cosmopolitan political form. In a similar vein, Habermas has also argued that solidarity at this level cannot simply be based on a shared moral conceptions of human rights but only on a shared political culture; otherwise Europe may not become a public of publics in the full democratic sense (Habermas, 2001: 126). In conclusion, I would like to suggest the ways in which these innovative forms of publicity may, when institutionally secured, themselves provide a solution to the problem of cosmopolitan identity and solidarity. It does so in light of the specific qualities of the interaction that occurs in an extended but mediated dialogical public sphere.

I have argued that the Internet and other contemporary public spaces permit a form of publicity that results in a public of publics rather than a unified public sphere based in a common culture or identity. In order for it to be an adequate extension of the dialogical public sphere for democratic purposes, a public of publics must still enable communication with an indefinite (although not unitary) audience. It cannot simply remain a fragmented series of publics but must become what I have called a serial public that is potentially connected in the proper institutional context to other publics. If this is the case, participants in the political public sphere of such publics relate to each other in a particular way that preserves perhaps the most essential feature of dialogue for democratic citizenship, in which each is equally entitled to participate in defining the nature and course of such interaction: all participants may mutually make claims upon each other, in that they address and are addressed by each other in terms of claims that every speaker puts forth as something that others ought to accept. Thus, speakers and their audience stand in the essential normative relation of dialogical interaction: they address each other in the normative attitude in which all may propose and incur mutual obligations.

This relation of mutual obligation is the core of the political relationship of citizenship: persons become citizens when they participate in an institutionalized public sphere backed by institutions that make it possible for them to make claims upon each other only if they stand as equals to those who may make the same claims upon them. To have the standing to make claims and incur obligations within an institutional framework is to have a political identity. To participate in a cosmopolitan public sphere is precisely to be open to the claims of any participant in any public, to be the addressee of claims that are made to the human community as such. Similarly, it may open up a particular community and its public sphere to the claims made by other communities in their public sphere, whether that is a claim to justice made on behalf of those who have suffered past wrongs or by those who suffer real harms in the present. Once such claims are taken up and responded to in the present or in our community, we see ourselves as standing toward others whose standing is our concern and for whom we act to constitute a larger public sphere in taking up their claims upon us.

If this obligation-constituting element of dialogue is preserved and extended and finds a new form of a deliberative public sphere, then a further essential democratic element is also possible: that the public sphere is a source of social criticism, of those whose critical claims open up the public sphere and expose its limitations. Either in adopting the role of the critic or in taking up such criticism in the public sphere, speakers adopt the standpoint of the "generalized other," the relevant critical perspective that opens up a future standpoint of the whole community. Democratic self-government clearly entails that it is, in some relevant sense, the whole community that is self-governing. This is usually taken to suggest that self-government entails that the various members of the self-governing "body-politic" must adopt a common or shared perspective, if not in deliberation itself then at least in the outcome of deliberation. Certainly, Mead saw the issue of the scope of the political community as one of being responsive to others and adopting their perspectives. As he put it: "The question whether we belong to a larger community is answered in terms of whether our own actions calls out a response in this wider community, and whether its response is reflected back into our own conduct" (Mead, 1934: 271). This sort of mutual responsiveness and interdependence is the basis for a potential democratic community, and this in turn depends on the capacity to make and respond to claims available to social actors even in cases of conflict. To the question of the applicability of such norms and institutions internationally, Mead is optimistic: "Could a conversation be conducted internationally? The question is a question of social organization." (ibid.) Given the clearly pluralist basis of international society, we might expect the institutional forms of a multiperspectival polity to unlink democratic authority from the exclusive and territorial forms of democratic citizenship and authority tied to the nation states, as it begins to reflect the enriched possibilities of politically relevant perspectives. The value of such deliberation is that it permits precisely the sort of reflection necessary for the transformation of democracy within states into multiperspectival polities that incorporate a cosmopolitan public sphere into their political life. If the distributively strong public sphere that the Internet enables contributes to making dialogue with others who serve the role of the generalized other possible, then it may also enable the mediation of dialogue across borders and publics. But it does so only if there are agents who make it so and transnational institutions whose ideals seek to realize a transnational public sphere as the basis for a realistic utopia of citizenship in a complexly interconnected world.

Bibliography

Brownell, S. (1994) *Training the Body for China.* Chicago: University of Chicago Press.
Cohen, J. and Sabel, C. (2003) "Sovereignty and Solidarity: EU and US." in J. Zeitlin and D. Trubek (2003) *Governing Work and Welfare in a New Economy.* Oxford: Oxford University Press.
Dahl, R. (1999) "Can International Organizations Be Democratic? A Skeptic's View." in J. Shapiro and C. Hacker-Cardan (1999) *Democracy's Edges.* Cambridge: Cambridge University Press.
Dorf, M. and Sabel, C. (1996) "The Constitution of Democratic Experimentalism." *Columbia Law Review* 98(2), 267–473.
Fraser, N. (1989) "Rethinking the Public Sphere." In *Habermas and the Public Sphere.* ed. C. Calhoun. Cambridge: MIT Press. 109–142.
Freeman, S. (1991) "Contractualism. Moral Motivation, and Practical Reason." *Journal of Philosophy* 88, pp. 281–303.
Froomkin, M. (2003) "Habermas@discourse.net: Towards a Critical Theory of Cyberspace." *Harvard Law Review* 16, 751–873.
Garnham, S. (1995) "The Mass Media, Cultural Identity, and the Public Sphere in the Modern World." *Public Culture* 5.
Habermas, J. (1996) *Between Facts and Norms.* Cambridge: MIT Press.
Habermas, J. (2001) *The Postnational Constellation.* Cambridge: MIT Press.
Held, D. (1995) *Democracy and Global Order.* Stanford: Stanford University Press.
Kymlicka, W. (1999) "Citizenship in an Era of Globalization." in J. Shapiro and C. Hacker-Cardan (1999) *Democracy's Edges.* Cambridge: Cambridge University Press.
Lessing, L. (1999) *Code.* New York: Basic Books.
MacCormick, N. (1997) "Democracy, Subsidiarity and Citizenship." *Law and Philosophy* 16(4) 331–54.
Mead, G. H. (1934) *Mind, Self and Society.* Chicago: University of Chicago Press.
O'Donnell, G. (1994) "Delegative Democracy." *Journal of Democracy* 5.
Page, B. (1995) *Who Deliberates?* Chicago: University of Chicago Press.

Poster, M. (2001) *What's the Matter With the Internet?* Minneapolis: University of Minnesota Press.

Ruggie, G. (1996) *Constructing the World Polity.* London: Routledge.

Sabel, C. and Cohen, J. (1998) "Directly-Deliberative Polyarchy." in *Private Governance, Democratic Constitutionalism and Supranationalism.* Proceedings of the COST A 7 Seminar, Florence, 22 to 24 May 1997. Luxembourg 1998: Office for Official Publications of the European Communities.

Sassen, S. (1998) *Globalization and Its Discontents.* New York: The New Press.

Shapiro, A. (1999) *The Control Revolution.* New York: Century Foundation.

Smith, P. and Smythe, E. (2001) "Globalization, Citizenship and Technology: the Multilateral Agreement on Investment (MAI) Meets the Internet." in F. Webster (2001) *Culture and Politics in the Information Age.* London: Routledge.

Sunstein, C. (2001) *Republic.com.* Princeton: Princeton University Press.

Thompson, J. (1995) *Media and Modernity.* Stanford: Stanford University Press.

Trachtman, J. (1998) "Cyberspace, Sovereignty, Jurisdiction, and Modernism, in *Indiana Journal of Global Legal Studies* 5(2), 561–81.

NOTES

1. The term "public culture" usually denotes those aspects of cultural identity and symbols that become the subject matter for public debate and opinion: the public sphere denotes a social space that emerges out of civil society and is outside the state control. On these debates and an analysis of sports as part of public culture in China, see Brownell (1994, ch. 3). Brownell shows the odd locations for publicity even in "state saturated societies," such as in criticisms of the Party in Chinese sports journalism. Public culture can develop autonomously from the larger culture in which it is embedded.

2. Such mutual responsiveness or answerability to others is crucial to the justificatory force of public agreements. For an elaboration of this form of justification in relation to making one's actions "answerable" to others, see Freeman (1991), p. 281, 303.

3. The issue here is that private sources of power have the same effects as public power manifested in state censorship.

4. Shapiro ignores the way in which the process of deliberation is never under the control of anyone.

5. See, for example, Joel Trachtman, "Cyberspace, Sovereignty, Jurisdiction, and Modernism," in *Global Legal Studies* (1998), especially on the problems of jurisdiction and territoriality. On why the term "aterritorial" is superior to "post-territorial" in discussing electronic space: see p. 570ff. A further advantage of the term is that it does not elide the ways in which Internet usage could reflect structural inequalities in the world economy.

6. On the distinction between strong and weak publics, see Fraser (1989), 109–142. Habermas appropriates this distinction in his "two track model of democracy" in *Between Facts and Norms* (Habermas, 1996) chapter 7. The requirements of a strong public sphere for both are closely tied to access to influence over national legislation, in which the collective will is transformed into the coercive power if law.

7. Charles Sabel and Joshua Cohen, "Directly-Deliberative Polyarchy," in *Private Governance, Democratic Constitutionalism and Supranationalism* (Florence: European Commision, 1998), 3–30. For a more direct application to the EU, see Joshua Cohen and Charles Sabel, "Sovereignty and Solidarity: EU and US," in *Governing Work and Welfare in a New Economy: European and American Experiments,* eds. J. Zeitlin and D. Trubeck (Oxford: Oxford University Press, 2003).

8. Sabel and Cohen, p. 29.

CHANTAL MOUFFE

DELIBERATIVE DEMOCRACY OR
AGONISTIC PLURALISM? (1999)

Originally from Belgium, Chantal Mouffe (b. 1943) is a professor of political theory at the University of Westminster, in the UK. Together with Ernesto Laclau, she has tried to develop a post-Marxist political theory, drawing on a number of sources, including the classical Italian Marxist Antony Gramsci and the French structuralist Marxist Louis Althusser who was particularly influential in the 1970s, poststructuralist theory, and Carl Schmitt's theory of the political. Their approach was first developed in Hegemony and Socialist Strategy: Towards a Radical Democratic Politics *(1985).*

In her later works, The Democratic Paradox *(2000) and* On the Political *(2005), Mouffe argues that the individualistic, universalistic, and rationalistic framework of dominant liberal-democratic theories makes us incapable of grasping the challenges of Western democracies. She therefore sets out to formulate an alternative—incorporating a radically different conception of the public sphere.*

Mouffe insists on separating "the political" from "politics." The former refers to the dimension of antagonism inbuilt in all human societies, the latter to the practices and institutions that seek to organize human coexistence with the dimension of the political in mind. Mouffe claims that deliberative democratic theory makes the rationality of communicative action in the public sphere into the basis for political legitimacy. Instead, she argues, the public sphere should provide channels for expressing collective passions. Mouffe contests the search for a consensus, and argues instead for constructing opponents as adversaries, but not as enemies, thereby transforming antagonism into agonism. She urges theorists to envisage the making of a public sphere where political projects confront each and embrace a model of agonistic pluralism in place of theories of deliberative democracy.

The following text—a journal article—illustrates her positioning against deliberative democratic theory. Placing the functions of the public sphere at its core, the argument also lays out the key concepts of "agonistic pluralism." As such, it serves as a concise introduction to Mouffe's project.

As testified by the increasing success of the extreme right in several countries, western societies are witnessing a growing disaffection with democratic institutions. Such a disaffection may have serious consequences for the future of democracy. Unfortunately, liberal democratic societies are ill-prepared to confront the present challenge, since they are unable to grasp its nature. One of the main reasons for this inability lies in the type of political theory currently in vogue, dominated as it is by an individualistic, universalistic, and rationalistic framework. Such a framework erases the dimension of the political and impedes envisaging in an adequate manner the nature of a pluralistic democratic public sphere.

This paper examines the most recent paradigm of liberal democratic theory: "deliberative democracy," in order to bring to the fore its shortcomings. Then, I put forward some elements for the elaboration of an alternative model that I propose to call "agonistic pluralism."

To be sure, the aim of the theorists who advocate the different versions of "deliberative democracy" is commendable. Against the interest-based conception of democracy, inspired by economics and skeptical about the virtues of political participation, they want to introduce questions of morality and justice into politics. They are looking for new meanings of traditional democratic notions like autonomy, popular sovereignty, and equality. Their aim is to reformulate the classical idea of the public sphere, giving it a central place in the democratic project. However, by proposing to view reason and rational argumentation, instead of interest and aggregation of preferences as the central issue of politics, they simply move from an economic model to a moral one. Their move consists in replacing the market-inspired view of the public sphere by another conception that conceives political questions as being of a moral nature and therefore susceptible of being decided rationally. This means that they identify the democratic public sphere with the discursive redemption of normative validity claims. It is clear that what is missing, albeit in different ways, in both approaches is the dimension of the political. This is why I consider that the deliberative model is unable to offer a better understanding of the nature of democratic politics and that it cannot provide a real alternative to the aggregative view.

Deliberative Democracy

There are many different versions of "deliberative democracy," but the most theoretically sophisticated one is the Habermasian and it is that model that I will examine here. Moreover it is also the model where the concept of "public sphere" is more fully elaborated and it is therefore particularly relevant for our concerns.

In the approach elaborated by Habermas and his followers, the main purpose of deliberative democracy is to propose a reformulation in communicative terms of the classical notions of democratic theory, especially the concept of popular sovereignty. According to Seyla Benhabib for instance, one of the central issues to be addressed is how the articulation of the common good can be made compatible with the sovereignty of the people. In her view, the main challenge confronting democracy today lies in reconciling nationality with legitimacy. She puts it in the following way:

> According to the deliberative model of democracy, it is a necessary condition for attaining legitimacy and rationality with regard to collective decisions making processes in a polity, that the institutions of this polity are so arranged that what is considered in the common interest of all results from processes of collective deliberation conducted rationally and fairly among free and equal individuals (1996, p. 69).

The basis of legitimacy in democratic institutions derives in this view from the fact that the instances that claim obligatory power do so on the presumption that their decisions represent an impartial standpoint that is equally in the interest of all. In order for this presumption to be fulfilled, those decisions must be the result of appropriate public processes of deliberation that follow the procedures of the Habermasian discourse model. The fundamental idea behind this model is that for the norms and institutional arrangements to be valid they should have been agreed

by all affected by their consequences according to as process of deliberation whose
features are defined by Benhabib in the following way:

1. Participation in such deliberation is governed by the norms of equality and
   symmetry; all have the same chance to initiate speech acts, to question, inter-
   rogate, and to open debate;
2. All have the right to question the assigned topics of conversation;
3. All have the right to initiate reflexive arguments about the very rules of the
   discourse procedure and the way in which they are applied or carried out.
   There are no prima facie rules limiting the agenda or the conversation, nor
   the identity of the participants, as long as each excluded person or group can
   justifiably show that they are relevantly affected by the proposed norm under
   question (1996, p. 70).

Let's examine this model of deliberative democracy closely. In their attempt to
ground legitimacy on rationality its advocates must make a distinction that plays a
key role in their approach, the distinction between "mere agreement" and "rational
consensus." This commands the values of the procedure, which are impartiality
and equality, openness (no one and no relevant information is excluded), lack of
coercion, and unanimity. In combination, those values will guide the discussion
towards generalizable interests to the agreement of all participants and they will
produce legitimate outcomes. In other words, the process of public discussion can
be guaranteed to have reasonable outcomes only to the extent that it realizes the
conditions of ideal discourse: the more equal and impartial, the more open that
process is and the less participants are coerced and ready to be guided by the force
of the better argument, the more likely truly generalizable interests will be accepted
by all persons relevantly affected.

Habermas and his followers do not deny that there will be obstacles to the realization of the ideal discourse but these obstacles are conceived as empirical ones. They
are due to the fact that it is unlikely, given the practical and empirical limitation
of social life, that we will ever be completely able to leave aside all our particular
interests in order to coincide with our universal rational self. This is why the ideal
speech situation must be conceived as regulative idea. On the other side, Habermas
now accepts that there are issues that have to remain outside the practices of rational
public debates like existential issues that concern not questions of justice but of the
good life, or conflicts between interests groups about distributive problems that can
only be resolved by means of compromises. But he affirms that "this differentiation
within the field of issues that require political decisions negates neither the prime
importance of moral considerations nor the practicability of rational debate as the
very form of political communication" (1991, p. 448). Habermas is adamant that
political questions can be decided rationally and that the exchange of arguments
and counter-arguments as envisaged by his approach is the most suitable procedure
for reaching the rational formation of the will from which the general interest will
emerge. He considers that the superiority of his approach with respect to Rawls' one
lies in its strictly procedural character which allow him to "leave more questions
open because it entrusts more to the *process* of rational opinion and will formation"
(1995, p. 130).

Deliberative Democracy: a Critique

There are several ways in which such an approach could be criticized but I will only envisage two of them here. We can, for instance, use Wittgenstein's insights to undermine Habermas's conception of procedure and to challenge the very idea of a neutral or rational dialogue. For Wittgenstein to have agreement in opinions there must first be agreement on the language used and this, as he points out, implies agreement in forms of life. According to him, procedure only exists as a complex ensemble of practices. Those practices constitute specific forms of individuality and identity that make possible the allegiance to the procedures. It is because they are inscribed in shared forms of life and agreements in judgments that procedures can be accepted and followed. They cannot be seen as rules that are created on the basis of principles and then applied to specific cases. Rules for Wittgenstein are always abridgments of practices, they are inseparable of specific forms of life. Therefore, distinctions between "procedural" and "substantial" or between "moral" and "ethical" that are central to the Habermasian approach cannot be maintained and one must acknowledge that procedures always involve substantial ethical commitments.

Following Wittgenstein's lead also suggests a very different way of understanding communication and the creation of consensus. As he says, "Giving grounds, however, justifying the evidence, comes to an end; but the end is not certain propositions striking us immediately as true, i.e., it is not a kind of *seeing* on our part; it is our *acting* that is at the bottom of the language-game" (1969, p. 28e). For him agreement is established not on significations (Meinungen) but on a form of life (Lebensform). It is, as has been pointed out, an *Einstimmung* fusion of voices made possible by a common form of life, not *Einverstand* product of reason—like in Habermas. Such an approach requires reintroducing into the process of deliberation the whole rhetorical dimension that the Habermasian discourse perspective is precisely at pains to eliminate. It also implies that the limits of consensus are brought to the fore: "Where two principles really do meet which cannot be reconciled with one another, then each man declares the other a fool and an heretic. I said I would 'combat' the other man, but wouldn't I give him reasons? certainly; but how far do they go? At the end of reasons comes *persuasion*" (1969, p. 81e).

It is interesting to note that the Wittgensteinian critique of deliberative democracy that I am proposing resonates with Stanley Cavell's critique of Rawls, which is also inspired by Wittgenstein. Since Rawls represents the other important version of the deliberative approach, it is clear that taking Wittgenstein seriously necessarily leads to putting into question the basic assumptions of such an approach. As Cavell points out in his Carus Lectures, Rawls' account of justice omits a very important dimension of what takes place when we assess the claims made upon us in the name of justice in situations in which it is the degree of society's compliance with its ideal that is in question. He takes issue with Rawls' assertion that "Those who express resentment must be prepared to show why certain institutions are unjust or how others have injured them" (1971, p. 553). In Rawls' view, if they are unable to do so, we can consider that our conduct is above reproach and bring the conversation on justice to an end. But, asks Cavell, "What if there is a cry of justice that expresses a sense not of having lost out in an unequal yet fair struggle, but of having from the start being left out" (1990, p. xxxviii). Giving as an example the situation of Nora in Ibsen's play *A Doll's House*, he shows how deprivation of a voice in the conversation of justice can be the work of the moral consensus itself. He urges us to realize that bringing a conversation to a close is always a personal choice, a decision that cannot be simply presented as mere application of procedures and justified as the only move that we could make in those circumstances. For that reason, we should never refuse bearing our responsibility for our decisions by invoking the commands of general rules or principles.

To take this responsibility seriously requires that we give up the dream of a rational consensus as well as the fantasy that we could escape from our human form of life. In our desire for a total grasp, says Wittgenstein, "We have got on the slippery ice where there is no friction and so in a certain sense the conditions are ideal, but also, just because of that, we are unable to walk: so we need *friction*. Back to the rough ground" (1953, p 46e).

Wittgenstein, however, is not the only one to destroy the very ground of the deliberative model. Another way of revealing the inadequacy of the Habermasian approach is by problematizing the very possibility of the notion of the "ideal speech situation" conceived as the asymptotic ideal of intersubjective communication free of constraints, where the participants arrive at consensus by means of rational argumentation. This can be done, following the lead of Slavoy Žižek, through Lacan. Indeed a Lacanian approach reveals how discourse itself in its fundamental structure is authoritarian since out of the free-floating dispersion of signifiers, it is only through the intervention of a master signifier that a consistent field of meaning can merge. As Žižek shows (1992, chapter 3), for Lacan the status of the master signifier, the signifier of symbolic authority founded only on itself (in its own acts of enunciation) is strictly transcendental: the gesture that "distorts" a symbolic field, that "curves" its space by introducing a non-founded violence in *stricto sensu* correlative to its very establishment. This means that if we were to subtract from a discursive field its distortion, the field would disintegrate, "de-quilt." Lacan undermines in that way the very basis of Habermasian view, according to which the inherent pragmatic presuppositions of discourse are non-authoritarian, since they imply the idea of a communication free of constraint where only rational argumentation counts.

What those two different types of critique bring to the fore is that, far from being merely empirical, or epistemological, the obstacles to the realization of the ideal speech situation are ontological. Indeed, the impediments to the free and unconstrained public deliberation of all on matters of common concern is a conceptual impossibility because, without those so-called impediments, no communication, no deliberation could ever take place. We therefore have to conclude that the very conditions of possibility of deliberation constitute at the same time the conditions of impossibility of the ideal speech situation. There is absolutely no justification for attributing a special privilege in this respect to a so-called "moral point of view" governed by impartiality and where an impartial assessment of what is in the general interest could be reached.

An Alternative to Deliberative Democracy

I want to stress that what is really at stake in the critique of "deliberative democracy" that I am proposing here is the need to acknowledge the dimension of power and antagonism and their ineradicable character. By postulating the availability of public sphere where power and antagonism would have been eliminated and where a rational consensus would have been realized, this model of democratic politics denies the central role in politics of the conflictual dimension and its crucial role in the formation of collective identities. This is why it is unable to provide an adequate model of democratic politics.

On contrary, this question of power and antagonism is precisely at the center of the approach that I want to put forward and whose theoretical bases have been delineated in *Hegemony and Socialist Strategy* (Laclau and Mouffe, 1985). What we attempted to do in that book was draw out all the consequences for a radical conception of democracy of the ineradicability of power, of antagonism, and of the fact that there can never be total emancipation but only partial ones. This means that the democratic society cannot be conceived any more as a society that would have realized the dream of a perfect harmony or transparency. Its democratic character can only be given by the fact that no limited social actor can attribute to herself the representation of the totality and claim in that way to have the "mastery" of the foundation. The central thesis of the book is that social objectivity is constituted through acts of power. This implies that any social objectivity is ultimately political and that it has to show the traces of exclusion that governs its constitution. The point of convergence—or rather mutual collapse—between objectivity and power is precisely what we mean by "hegemony."

This way of posing the problem indicates that power should not be conceived as an external relation taking place between two pre-constituted identities, but rather as constituting the identities themselves. Political practice in a democratic society does not consist in defending the rights of preconstituted identities, but rather in constituting those identities themselves in a precarious and always vulnerable terrain.

According to such a view, democracy requires that the purely constructed nature of social relations finds its complement in the purely pragmatic grounds of the claims to power legitimacy. This implies that there is no unbridgeable gap between power and legitimacy—not obviously in the sense that all power is automatically legitimate, but in the sense that: a) if any power has been able to impose itself, it is because it has been recognized as legitimate in some quarters; and b) if legitimacy is not based in an a prioristic ground, it is because it is based in some form of successful power. This link between legitimacy and power is precisely what the deliberative model is unable to recognize, since it has to posit the possibility of a type of rational argumentation where power has been eliminated and where legitimacy is grounded on pure rationality.

The approach that I am advocating involves a displacement of the traditional relations between democracy and power. For the Habermasian vision of "deliberative democracy," the more democratic a society is, the less power would be constitutive of social relations. But if we accept that relations of power are constitutive of the social, then the main question of democratic politics is not how to eliminate power but how to constitute forms of power that are compatible with democratic values. To acknowledge the existence of relations of power and the need to transform them, while renouncing the illusion that we could free ourselves completely from power, this is what is specific to the project of "radical and plural democracy" that we are advocating.

Another distinct character of our approach concerns the question of the de-universalization of political subjects. We try to break with all forms of essentialism. Not only the essentialism that penetrates to a large extent the basic categories of modem sociology and liberal thought and according to which every social identity is perfectly defined in the historical process of the unfolding of being; but also with its diametrical opposite: a certain type of extreme post-modern fragmentation of the social that refuses to give the fragments any kind of relational identity. By putting an exclusive emphasis on heterogeneity and incommensurability, such a view impedes recognition how certain differences are constructed as relations of subordination and should therefore be challenged by radical democratic politics.

An Agonistic Model of Democracy

The consequences of the above-mentioned theses for democratic politics are far-reaching. They provide us with the theoretical terrain necessary to formulate an alternative to the model of "deliberative democracy," one that I call "agonistic pluralism."

In order to clarify the basis of this alternative view, I propose to distinguish between "the political" and "politics." By "the political," I refer to the dimension of antagonism that is inherent in all human society, antagonism that can take many different forms and can emerge in diverse social relations. "Politics," on the other hand, refers to the ensemble of practices, discourses and institutions that seek to establish a certain order and to organize human coexistence in conditions that are always potentially conflictual because they are affected by the dimension of "the political."

It is only when we acknowledge this dimension of "the political" and understand that "politics" consists in domesticating hostility, only in trying to defuse the potential antagonism that exists in human relations, that we can pose the fundamental question for democratic politics. This question, *pace* the rationalists, is not how to arrive at a rational consensus reached without exclusion, that is, indeed, an impossibility. Politics aims at the creation of unity in a context of conflict and diversity; it is always concerned with the creation of an "us" by the determination of a "them." The novelty of democratic politics is not the overcoming of this us/them distinction—which is what a consensus without exclusion pretends to achieve—but the different way in which is established. What is at stake is how to establish the us/them discrimination in a way that is compatible with pluralist democracy.

In the realm of politics, this presupposes that the "other" is no longer seen as an enemy to be destroyed, but as an "adversary," i.e., somebody with whose ideas we are going to struggle but whose right to defend those ideas we will not put into question. This category of the adversary does not eliminate antagonism, though, and it should be distinguished from the liberal notion of the competitor, with which it is sometimes identified. An adversary is a legitimate enemy, an enemy with whom we have in common a shared adhesion to the ethico-political principles of democracy. But our disagreement concerning their meaning and implementation is not one that could be resolved through deliberation and rational discussion, hence the antagonistic element in the relation. To come to accept the position of the adversary is to undergo a radical change in political identity, it has more of a quality of a conversion than of rational persuasion (in the same way as Thomas Kuhn has argued that adherence to a new scientific paradigm is a type of conversion). To be sure, compromises are possible; they are part of the process of politics. But they should be seen as temporary respites in an ongoing confrontation.

Hence, the importance of distinguishing between two types of political relations: one of *antagonism* between enemies, and one of *agonism* between adversaries. We could say that the aim of democratic politics is to transform an "antagonism" into an "agonism." This has important consequences for the way we envisage politics. Contrary to the model of "deliberative democracy," the model of "agonistic pluralism" that I am advocating asserts that the prime task of democratic politics is not to eliminate passions nor to relegate them to the private sphere in order to render rational consensus possible, but to mobilise those passions towards the promotion of democratic designs. Far from jeopardizing democracy, agonistic confrontation is in fact its very condition of existence.

To deny that there ever could be a free and unconstrained public deliberation of all matters of common concern is therefore crucial for democratic politics. When we accept that every consensus exists as a temporary result of a provisional hegemony, as a stabilization of power and that always entails some form of exclusion, we can begin to envisage the nature of a democratic public sphere in a different way. Modern democracy's specificity lies in the recognition and legitimation of conflict and the refusal to suppress it by imposing an authoritarian order. Breaking with the symbolic representation of society as an organic body—which is characteristic of the holistic mode of social organization—a democratic society makes room for the expression of conflicting interests and values. To be sure, pluralist democracy demands a certain amount of consensus, but such a consensus concerns only some ethico-political principles. Since those ethico-political principles can only exist, however, through many different and conflicting interpretations, such a consensus is bound to be a "conflictual consensus." This is why a pluralist democracy needs to make room for dissent and for the institutions through which it can be manifested. Its survival depends on collective identities forming around clearly differentiated positions, as well as on the possibility of choosing between real alternatives. To borrow a term from system theory, we could say that pluralist politics should be envisaged as a "mixed-game," i.e., in part collaborative and in part conflictual and not as a wholly co-operative game as most liberal pluralists would have it. When the agonistic dynamic of the pluralist system is hindered because of a lack of democratic identities that one could identify, there is a risk that this will multiply confrontations over essentialist identities and non-negotiable moral values.

The inherently conflictual aspect of pluralism, linked to the dimension of undecidability and the ineradicability of antagonism is precisely what the deliberative democracy model is at pains to erase. By postulating the availability of a nonexclusive public sphere of deliberation where a rational consensus could obtain, they imagine that they can close the gap between legitimacy and rationality, finally resolving the tension that exists in democracy between the collective will and the will of all. But this is to transform pluralist democracy into a self-refuting ideal, since the moment of its realization would also be the moment of its disintegration.

This is why an approach that reveals the impossibility of establishing a consensus without exclusion is of fundamental importance for democratic politics. By warning us against the illusion that a fully achieved democracy could ever be instantiated, it forces us to keep the democratic contestation alive. An "agonistic" democratic approach acknowledges the real nature of its frontiers and recognizes the forms of exclusion that they embody, instead of trying to disguise them under the veil of rationality or morality. Awareness of the fact that difference allows us to constitute unity and totality while simultaneously providing essential limits is an agonistic approach that contributes in the subversion of the ever-present temptation that exists in democratic societies to naturalize their frontiers and essentialize their identities. Such an approach would, therefore, be much more receptive than the deliberative democracy model to the multiplicity of voices that a pluralist society encompasses, and to the complexity of the power structure that this network of differences implies.

References

Benhabib, Seyla, "Toward a Deliberative Model of Democratic Legitimacy," in *Democracy and Difference*, Benhabib, Seyla, ed. (Princeton: Princeton University Press, 1996).

Cavell, Stanley, *Conditions Handsome and Unhandsome* (Chicago: Chicago University Press, 1990).

Habermas, Jürgen, "Further Reflections on the Public Sphere," in *Habermas and the Public Sphere*, Calhoun, Craig, ed. (Cambridge: The MIT Press, 1991).

Habermas, Jürgen, "Reconciliation through the Public Use of Reason. Remarks on John Rawls's Political Liberalism," *The Journal of Philosophy* (March 1995), XXCII:3.

Laclau, Ernesto and Mouffe, Chantal, *Hegemony and Socialist Strategy. Towards a Radical Democratic Politics* (London: Verso, 1985).

Rawls, John, *A Theory of Justice* (Cambridge: Harvard University Press, 1971).

Wittgenstein, Ludwig, *Philosophical Investigations* (Oxford: Basil Blackwell, 1953).

Wittgenstein, Ludwig, *On Certainty* (New York: Harper Torchbooks, 1969).

Žižek, Slavoy, *Enjoy Your Symptom* (London: Routledge, 1992).

SEYLA BENHABIB

EXCERPT FROM *THE CLAIMS OF CULTURE: EQUALITY AND DIVERSITY IN THE GLOBAL ERA* (2002)

Seyla Benhabib (b. 1950) is a Turkish-born political philosopher based at Yale University. She is the author of an important study of the normative foundations for the idea of a critical social theory (Critique, Norm and Utopia, *1986). In* Situating the Self *(1992), she tried to rethink and clarify the premises of a Habermasian discourse ethics in the light of feminist, communitarian, and postmodern critiques of universalistic principles. Later, she has focused on issues of cultural diversity, migration, and cosmopolitanism.*

Benhabib has contributed to public sphere theory through a comparative reading of Hannah Arendt, the liberal tradition and Jürgen Habermas, where she criticizes Arendt's model for being at odds with the sociological reality of modernity and points to a possible dialogue between a discourse model of the public sphere and the feminist critique of the liberal distinction between the private and the public sphere.

In Claims of Culture: Equality and Diversity in the Global Era, *she asks how democratic theory can be reconceived to accommodate deep-rooted and deadlocked ethnocultural and nationalist conflicts. Her solution lies in a deliberative model of democracy, based on the principles of universal moral respect and egalitarian reciprocity, that stands out by being geared toward permitting "maximum cultural contestation" in the public sphere. By way of particular explications and revisions, she tries to steer deliberative democratic theory in a direction that allows it to face the challenge of a multiculturalist critique.*

The present selection from Claims of Culture *follows on from a critical discussion of John Rawls' idea of public reason, and Habermas' theory of discourse ethics. Benhabib argues that Rawls represents a minimalist version of political liberalism. This position has several problematic aspects, she argues, one of which is the relegation of many politically relevant issues to the private realm. Therefore, she holds Habermas' version as the best basis for developing her position. The selection concentrates on one fundamental critique of deliberative democratic theory: Is there something wrong with the theory itself, some deeply cognitive or affective bias, threatening to exclude certain voices from the democratic process? Addressing three different charges related to the functions of the public sphere, Benhabib argues that the critics' concerns can be accommodated without giving up on a deliberative democratic model.*

Deliberative Democracy, Self Determination, and Multiculturalism

Jorge M. Valadez states succinctly the concerns of deliberative democrats committed also to the multiculturalist cause:

Differences in worldview or disagreements in needs and interests between cultural groups can be so deep that the disadvantages of cultural minorities to induce social cooperation to attain their political objectives can remain very significant. When the animosity between cultural groups is very great, when disputes over limited resources make compromises very difficult, or when the cognitive and affective differences between groups are unbridgeable, for example, not even the equalization of epistemic resources and the capabilities of their effective use, equality of motivational resources,

multicultural education, or reforms in forums of public deliberation, may suffice to create a deliberative milieu in which the proposals of ethnocultural minorities will receive
a fair hearing. This unfortunate scenario is more likely to occur with autonomist and secessionist groups than with accommodationist groups, since the latter are typically more
willing to adopt majority values and institutional practices, as well as see themselves as
belonging to a common political community. (2001, 101)

Valadez expresses a number of concerns shared by other deliberative theorists
like James Bohman (1996), Iris Young (2000), and Melissa Williams (1998). Let
me separate these concerns into two general kinds: epistemic concerns about the
cognitive and affective biases of a deliberative consensus model; and political and
institutional concerns with the limits of deliberative politics.

Cognitive and Affective Biases of Deliberative Democracy

Deliberative democracy appears attractive to many because, unlike aggregative
and interest-group models of democratic legitimacy, it restores a sense of democracy as a cooperative enterprise among citizens considered as free and equal moral
beings. "Collective decisions," writes Valadez, "do not result merely by aggregating
the preexisting desires of citizens; rather, members of the polity attempt to influence
each others' opinions by engaging in a public dialogue in which they examine and
critique, in a civil and considerate manner, each other's positions while explaining
reasons for their own views" (2001, 5). The emphasis of the deliberative democracy
model on democratic *inclusiveness* makes it particularly attractive to the concerns
of excluded minorities, whether the sources of this exclusion lie in gender, ethnic,
"racial," cultural, linguistic, religious, or sexual preference grounds. Furthermore,
deliberative democracy promises not only inclusion but *empowerment,* in that the
insistence that democratic legitimacy can be attained only through the agreement
of *all* affected assures, at the normative level at least, that norms *cannot* be adopted
and institutional arrangements advocated at the cost of the most disadvantaged and
disaffected.

These normative conditions of inclusion and empowerment, while making deliberative democracy attractive, also make it suspect. As with any normative model,
one can always point to prevailing conditions of inequality, hierarchy, exploitation
and domination, and prove that "this may be true in theory but not so in practice"
(Kant [1793] 1994). The answer to this ancient conflict between norm and reality
is simply to say that if all were as it ought to be in the world, there would be no
need to build normative models, either; the fact that a normative model does not
correspond to reality is no reason to dismiss it, for the need for normativity arises
precisely because humans measure the reality they inhabit in the light of principles
and promises that transcend this reality (see Benhabib 1986). The relevant question therefore is; Does a given normative model enable us to analyze and distill
the rational principles of existing practices and institutions in such a fashion that
we can then use these rational reconstructions as critical guidelines for measuring
really existing democracies? Some deliberative democrats want to argue that the
problem is not simply the lack of correspondence between the normative and the
empirical, but that there may be something deeply wrong with the normative model
itself. Those who make this claim usually point to some deep-seated cognitive and

affective bias, which then is supposed to silence the voices of certain kinds of participants in democratic deliberations.

The *epistemic bias* charge takes several forms: first, that the deliberative democracy model cannot really accommodate deeply divergent, perhaps even incommensurable systems of belief and worldviews; second, that the emphasis in the deliberative model upon the "public nature of reason-giving" is biased in favor of "disembodied and dispassionate norms of speech"; third, that the condition of reaching "reasoned agreement," particularly in the version given to it by Jürgen Habermas, places the bar of consensus too high, a requirement both unrealistic and exclusionary.

Incommensurability

With respect to the first set of arguments, I want to recall here the claims made in chapter 2 against strong incommensurability. I want to insist that strong incommensurability is an incoherent position, for if such incommensurability of frameworks and worldviews existed, we would not be able to know it for we would not be able to state in what it consisted. More often than not, as epistemic contemporaries, we are aware that some of our beliefs may be mutually exclusive and contradictory with those held by our fellow citizens. We also may have little doubt about the lack of cognitive validity of some of their assumptions, but in the public sphere of liberal democracies, we have to accept the equal claim to moral respect of our dialogue partners who hold such beliefs. I am thinking of contested cases like evolutionism versus creationism. This controversy strains to the utmost the established canons of scientific evidence and validation, yet as epistemic contemporaries in liberal democracies, we have to learn to live with each other and cooperate on school boards as well as on library committees, and within other associations.[1]

I have been using the phrase *epistemic contemporaries* (see chap. 2 above for a further elucidation). Let me explain what I mean: Some forms of knowledge become available to us only as a result of certain historical experiences and factual discoveries. Most of the time in democratic dialogue we share an epistemic horizon; the most difficult and intractable cases for democratic deliberation are those that involve social life-forms that coexist in the same space but do not belong within the same time horizon of experience. Such is often the case when indigenous peoples and native tribes confront their highly technological colonizers and exploiters, usurpers and imperialists. These days it is not the conquistadors, but officials of the Brazilian or Mexican governments or multinational corporations who wrench the tribes of the Amazons and the Yucatan out of their life world and catapult them a few centuries into the future within the space of a few years.

Nevertheless, most democratic debates and contentions in contemporary societies are not clashes between radical incommensurables, though there will be degrees of incompatibility, contradiction, and exclusiveness among the belief systems, even of epistemic contemporaries. The systems of belief of ordinary agents do not have the level of coherence and systematicity of scientific worldviews. Ordinary moral and political deliberators do not have Cartesian minds, and very often may not be aware of their own contradictions. For example, the beliefs of Christian Scientists about modern medicine contradict the precepts of modern science; but Christian Scientists do not altogether reject modern science and technology in that they continue to use electricity as well as cars, air conditioners as well as the modern banking system. Most democratic dialogue is not about incommensurables, but about divergent and convergent beliefs, and very often we do not know how deep these divergences are, or how great their overlap may be, until we have engaged in conversation. If, however, the intensity as well as magnitude of supposed incommensurability can itself only be established through deliberative dialogue, then what good reasons are there for dismissing such dialogue as biased and not impartial enough even before we engage in it? Even groups and individuals with deeply held divergent beliefs are motivated to engage in democratic deliberation because there is some convergence at the level of material interests and shared life-forms. Democractic deliberation between moral contemporaries whose actions and doings affect one another builds on the imperfect convergences of imperfectly held belief systems.

When multiculturalist and deliberative theorists worry about incommensurability, they assume that it is primarily social positionality or social perspectivality that causes incommensuration. Social positionality, it is said, creates a certain perspective on the world that is incompatible and asymmetrical with the viewpoint of those who have never occupied this position. When we probe further and inquire what these social positions may be, they turn out to be the usual enumeration of groups cherished by strong identity politics: gender, "race," class, ethnicity, language, sexual preference, and the like. Social positionality then falls into pure essentialism in that it is premised upon the reduction of structures of individual consciousness to delineated group identities. There seems to be little anxiety among the defenders of social positionality as to how to define these groups, and whether in fact there are such ideal-typical worldviews or a group consciousness that may be attributed to them.[2] I believe that there are no such holistic structures of consciousness and that advocates of social positionality themselves operate with the fiction of a unitary consciousness in that they reduce the contentious debates of every human group about itself and its identity to a coherent and easily delineable narrative. Ironically, cultural essentialism comes back to haunt its most vocal critics, because those who argue that human cultures are human creations also argue that individuals are imprisoned in the perspectival refractions of their social positions. Both claims—cultural essentialism as well as social perspectivism—are false.

Valadez makes an important distinction between "understanding through translation" and "understanding through familiarization." He claims that we come to understand another conceptual framework, a way of life, not through a translation of the terms of one into the terms of the other (a view he attributes to Donald Davidson as well as Richard Rorty), but through *familiarization.* "That is, we comprehend frameworks that are radically different from our own not by finding terms and claims in our framework that isomorphically correspond to the terms and claims of theirs; rather, we gradually achieve greater and greater familiarity with the ways they use these words in their language, with the range of situations in which they use them, with the kinds of claims they make, and so forth" (2001, 91). This is a useful distinction, but must not be overdrawn. Translation involves familiarization just as much as familiarization involves some translation. When we try to understand others across time and space, we begin by translating, and if we are good enough interpreters and imaginative enough historians and linguists, ethnographers, and literary critics, we end up by familiarizing ourselves with other traditions. When we are moral contemporaries, however, and our actions and interactions have consequences for the lives of those we may not even know, then the imperative to familiarize ourselves with their ways of thinking and ways of life becomes crucial. Democratic dialogue occurs within this horizon of moral and political contemporaneity, and indeed much intercultural dialogue is such a process of familiarization. I conclude that the first objection to deliberative democracy, based on a strong thesis of incommensurability, is untenable.

The Biases in the Public Nature of Reason-Giving

It is frequently argued that the focus on *publicity* and on *public forums* in models of deliberative democracy also creates a bias in that such institutional spaces and practices privilege a certain mode of disembedded and dispassionate form of speech (Young 1996; Williams 2000). This consequently excludes the speech of groups such as women; sexual, linguistic, and ethnic minorities; and Native American peoples whose modes of discourse may be more embedded and passionate, based on storytelling and forms of greeting. There are at least three problems with this position.

First, deliberative democracy need not proceed from a *unitary model of the public sphere*. The public sphere in the Habermasian deliberative democracy model, which Cohen and Arato (1992), Nancy Fraser (1992), and I (1992 and 1996) have developed further, is not a unitary but a pluralistic model that acknowledges the variety of institutions, associations, and movements in civil society. Sociologically, the public sphere is viewed as the interlocking of multiple forms of associations and organizations, through the interaction of which an anonymous public conversation results. The de-centered public sphere consists of mutually overlapping networks and associations of opinion-forming as well as decisional bodies. Within these multiple and overlapping networks of publicity, different logics of reason giving, greeting, storytelling, and embedded speech can flourish.

Second, I find the assumption that politically and culturally underprivileged and marginalized groups represent "the other of reason" to be a species of exoticism. Why are we so quick to assume that reason corresponds to domination, while the body corresponds to marginalization and promises some form of liberation? There are different traditions of narrative style and reason giving and storytelling among human groups; but we would do well not to impose metaphysical binarisms like reason versus the body, impartiality versus embodiedness, upon such differences.

Third, the strength of the objections to the public nature of reason giving in my view derives from the following consideration: Publicity entails the normative requirement that for a principle, a law, or a course of action to be deemed acceptable, it must be judged to be so from the standpoint of all affected. Participation in the public realm imposes the obligation to reverse perspectives and to be ready to think and reason from the standpoint of concerned others. This requirement of impartiality is particularly binding for legislative and deliberative bodies that decide upon coercive rules of action for all involved. In a series of articles, Melissa Williams has voiced objections to this regulative principle of publicity (1998 and 2000).

Williams begins by noting that "deliberative democrats extend the liberal notion that legitimate government is based on consent by arguing that the terms of social and political cooperation should be the outgrowth of reasoned exchange among citizens. To sustain the claim to legitimacy, however, the processes of deliberative democracy must include all relevant social and political perspectives" (2000, 125). Williams adds that she is "not persuaded that its defenders have adequately addressed the challenges of social difference—difference defined along the lines of gender, race, ethnicity, class, sexuality and so on—to a deliberative conception of legitimacy" (125). Williams gives a very careful defense of deliberative democracy against the criticisms of group-rights theorists by pointing out how the regulative goal of deliberative democracy would entail a reinterpretation of impartiality to include hitherto excluded and suppressed *issues, persons, and participants,* and would also *counteract the bias of privileging certain institutional structures, reasons, and outcomes alone* (130–31). Nevertheless, Williams is skeptical that deliberative democracy can meet the challenges of group theorists adequately, and her central argument rests on the role of reasons and reason-giving in deliberative democratic processes. She writes: "Attention to the distinctive perspectives on political issues that follow the lines of social difference raises several doubts about deliberative theory's standard of 'reasonableness' and about how participants decide what counts as a reason for purposes of political deliberation. . . . The recognition of marginalized groups' reasons *as reasons for (or acceptable to) other citizens is* a highly contingent matter" (33–34, emphasis in the original). This is an important objection, which correctly represents the epistemic logic of deliberative democracy arguments and is also phenomenologically sensitive to what must go on if deliberative processes are to succeed at all.

In response I would like to distinguish between the *syntax* and the *semantics of reasons in the public sphere.*[3] The syntax of reasons would refer to certain structural features all statements that articulate public reasons would have to possess. Reasons would count as reasons because they could be defended as being in the best interest of all considered as equal moral and political beings. To claim that A is a reason for adopting policy X or law Y could then be parsed as stating that "X or Y are in the best interests of all considered equal moral and political beings. And we can justify this claim because we have established X or Y through processes of public deliberation in which all affected by these norms and policies took part as participants in a discourse." This is the *syntactical structure of public reasons in deliberative democracy models.*

The content of X and Y as well as the nature of the arguments and reasons advanced in discourses in the process of establishing such a conclusion concern the *semantics of reasons.* There is no way to know in advance which specific group claims and perspectives may or may not count as reasons. It is conceivable that a minority can convince the majority that it should accept its oral narratives to serve as legitimate titles to their ancestral land. This happened when the Supreme Court of Canada decided to accept the oral stories of Gitxsan Indians of Kispiox, British Columbia, as evidence to their land claims in the region (De Palma 1998). Such oral stories were given the status of legitimate title, on the grounds that from the standpoint of all citizens of Canada, it was fair and just to recognize the special history and ties of the Gitxsan people to their land. What lent legitimacy to the Canadian court's decision was precisely their recognition of a specific group's claims to be in the *best* interests of *all* Canadian citizens.

Certainly, Williams is right to point that majorities are not always willing or open-minded enough to accept such grounds, let alone recognize them as reasons.

When power over resources as well as other material interests is at stake (legitimate land use, for example), there will be resistance on the part of majorities to recognize the rightful claims of minorities. Deliberative processes do not obviate the need for democratic struggle through demonstrations, sit-ins, strikes, catcalls, and blockages. Native American groups have the right to preserve the integrity of their land by blocking the destruction of ancestral forests, preventing strip mining, or prohibiting certain forms of hunting or the dumping of toxic materials. Such political struggles build coalitions by gaining the sympathy of others who come to see that the cause of the minority is just because it involves reasons that all can identify with. These would be reasons like: It is good for all to preserve the ecologically sound use of land, as the Indians have done for centuries and generations, rather than to destroy the ecobalance and life-forms of human and other living beings for the sake of profits for timber or oil companies, or fisherman and hunters. Such statements possess the semantic structure of legitimate public reasons. Indeed, as Williams observes: "When the eradication of structures of unjust inequality depends upon affirming the social meaning of a practice for marginalized groups, the justice of deliberative outcomes depends not only upon participants exhibiting the virtues of open-mindedness and mutual respect (as deliberative theory emphasizes), but also upon their possessing the virtue of empathy, and of giving marginalized-group claims the particular advantage of their empathy" (2000, 138). I have argued in other writings that Hannah Arendt's concept of the "enlarged mentality" may be a better term than "empathy" for capturing the broadening of our horizons through coming to see the perspective of others in and through political and moral struggle (see Arendt 1961, 220–21; Benhabib 1992, 89–121). I conclude that this objection, though very substantial, does not vitiate the project of deliberative democracy.

The Unattainable Goal of Consensus through Deliberation

Since its earliest formulations in works like *Legitimation Crisis* (1975), Habermas's version of deliberative democracy and his discourse theory of legitimacy have been open to the charge that the criterion for consensus among participants is far too strong. It is illusory to expect that the "force of the better argument" will always prevail and for the same reasons. Although Habermas's work has undergone considerable modifications since these early formulations (see Bohman 1996), we still encounter claims of the sort in his most recent work as well: "Whereas parties can agree to a negotiated compromise for different reasons, the consensus brought about through argument must rest on *identical reasons* that are able to convince parties in the same way" (Habermas 1996, 344).

Such statements dismay sympathetic commentators like Bohman (1996) and Valadez (2001), each of whom is more convinced of the philosophical validity of the strong incommensurability thesis than I am. They acknowledge, however, that there are also other strands of argumentation in Habermas's work that may be more compatible with a more pluralist approach to consensus-formation. Habermas contends, for example, that we cannot know in advance which reasons are to count as public and which would be nonpublic. Since public reason is not restricted, as it is in Rawls's framework, to formulating or disputing constitutional essentials alone, the democratic give-and-take of ordinary citizens broadens our understanding of what may count as public reasons. Against Bohman and Valadez, I would like to point out that even though the semantic content of these reasons may change, their syntactical structure—that they are in the best interest of all considered as free and equal moral beings—would remain. I believe that Habermas is right on insisting on this distinction, and that even if we accept the *plurality of public reasons,* we need not *compromise on the normative syntax of public justification.*

Habermas's claim "that consensus brought about through argument must rest on *identical reasons* that are able to convince the parties in the same way" (1996, 344) needs to be carefully parsed. Habermas is concerned that the validity of normative judgments should not be reduced to agent-specific or agent-relative reasons. He argues that such justifications may yield compromises but not moral agreement. This is certainly true with respect to certain kinds of claims. Not only can we plausibly argue that moral claims, as opposed to prudential and utilitarian ones, cannot be merely agent-specific (I accept this law because it is good for me and my kin), but we can also argue that certain kinds of political principles cannot be justified merely on agent-specific grounds either. For example, suppose China and the United States are trying to reach some consensus on the content of basic human rights. The United States cannot say, "We accept human rights because, from our point of view, they are the best way to spread our way of life throughout the world"; the Chinese delegation could then argue that, "We accept a minimum list of human rights because, from our point of view, they permit us to gain international credibility and access to international markets." Very often this is exactly how delegations in international negotiations think and this is precisely why they accept certain normative arrangements on *strategic grounds.* If, however, we believe that human rights constitute the moral foundation for democracies everywhere, then we must be ready to argue for their validity on the basis of reasons we think can be justified from the standpoint of all human beings. Interpreted thus, Habermas's claim that consensually attained moral norms must convince each and every one for the same reason does not seem too implausible.

Nevertheless, political discourse and moral discourse are not identical. Political discourse is a mixed mode in which universalizable justice claims, agent- and group-relative strategic reasons, and culturally circumscribed ethical considerations, which are relative to "we communities," mix and intermingle. There is always a tension in democratic discourse between these various strands of normative reasoning and argumentation. I will argue in the next chapter that the tension between universal rights claims and the sovereignty demands of concrete human communities is constitutive of the experience of the modern nation-states within which liberal democracies are housed.

Not only are there tensions in political discourse among the constituent elements of normative and strategic reasoning, but claims and arguments may change their normative status through democratic deliberation in that *ethical considerations* may become *universalizable justice* concerns. A most interesting example of such a shift is provided by the changing international consensus on women's rights. Whereas the status of women and of children until quite recently was considered the backbone of the ethical specificity of distinct human communities, and was expected to come under the legal jurisdiction of the authorities of these communities alone, emergent international discourse on women's rights has created a transnational discursive network among women's rights activists, community representatives, legislators, and international workers. The discourse on women's and children's rights has shifted its status from a "we-specific" ethical claim to a justice-oriented universalist claim (Jaggar 1999, 320ff). Shachar's proposals for interlocking jurisdictional hierarchies are similarly motivated by the recognition that women's and children's rights are universal justice claims, which must be somehow accommodated within the framework of the cultural and legal particularities of distinct human groups. While Habermas's requirement that agreement reached through consensus should convince *all* on the *same* grounds is too strong a condition for judging the outcomes of democratic deliberations, which present mostly mixed modes of moral, strategic, and ethically specific forms of reasoning, this requirement is still useful for understanding how the logic of universalizing justice claims differs from the logic of strategic as well as ethically specific claims. Discourses are moral *and* political learning processes.

Bohman suggests that we view public deliberations as entailing "moral compromises." The requirements of morality and those of compromise need not be mutually exclusive, as Habermas sometimes suggests that they are. Public deliberation, as Valadez points out in agreement with Bohman, "is first and foremost a social cooperative activity that aims at resolving concrete problematic situations" (Valadez 2001, 63). Bohman defines moral compromise as a situation in which "the parties do not modify the framework to achieve unanimity, although they may when conflicts are not so deep. Rather, they modify their conflicting interpretations of the framework so that each can recognize the other's moral values and standards as part of it" (1996, 91). Moral compromise is a form of moral learning, and I agree with Bohman and Valadez that such processes are crucial for deliberative democratic activities, which indeed are not merely about arguments but about finding mutually acceptable ways of cooperating and continuing to exist with one another. Yet while recognizing the empirical logic of democratic deliberation and will-formation processes, we need not forfeit the regulative principle that the logic of public justification requires impartiality, through which the best interests of all considered as equal moral and political beings are taken into account. I conclude then that the critique in question—that a deliberative democracy framework based on discourse ethics contains too many epistemic and affective biases to make it function fairly within intercultural and cross-cultural contexts—is overstated, and that such concerns can be accommmodated without forfeiting the essential premises of the model.

References

Arendt, Hannah. 1961. "Crisis in Culture." In *Between Past and Future: Six Exercises in Political Thought.* New York: Meridian Books.

Benhabib, Seyla. 1986. *Critique, Norm, and Utopia: A Study of the Normative Foundations of Critical Theory.* New York: Columbia University Press.

———. 1992. *Situating the Self: Gender, Community, and Postmodernism in Contemporary Ethics.* New York: Routledge; London: Polity.

———. 1996. "Deliberative Rationality and Models of Democratic Legitimacy." In *Democracy and Difference: Contesting the Boundaries of the Political.* Princeton: Princeton University Press.

———. 1999. "The Liberal Imagination and the Four Dogmas of Multiculturalism." *Yale Journal of Criticism* 12, no. 2 (1999): 401–13.

Bohman, James. 1996. *Public Deliberation: Pluralism, Complexity, and Democracy.* Cambridge: MIT Press.

Cohen Jean L., and Andrew Arato. 1992. *Civil Society and Political Theory.* Cambridge: MIT Press.

DePalma, Anthony. 1998. "Canadian Indians Win a Ruling Vindicating Their Oral History." *New York Times*, February 9, 1998.

Fraser, Nancy. 1992. "Rethinking the Public Sphere: A Contribution to Actually Existing Democracy." In *Habermas and the Public Sphere*, edited by Craig Calhoun. Cambridge: MIT Press.

Habermas, Jürgen. 1975. *Legitimation Crisis.* Translated by Thomas McCarthy. Boston: Beacon Press.

———. 1996. *Between Facts and Norms: Contributions to a Discourse Theory of Law and Democracy.* Translated by William Regh. Cambridge: MIT Press.

Jagger, Alison, 1999. "Multicultural Democracy." In *Journal of Political Philosophy* 7, no. 3: 308–29.

James, Michael Rabinder. 1999. "Tribal Sovereignty and the Intercultural Public Sphere." *Philosophy and Social Criticism* 25 (September): 57–96.

Kant, Immanuel. [1793] 1994. "On the Common Saying: 'This May Be True in Theory, but It Does Not Apply in Practice.'" In *Kant: Political Writings*, edited by Hans Reiss, translated by H. B. Nisbet. Cambridge: Cambridge University Press.

Lippmann, Walter. [1947] 1965. "Should the Majority Rule?" In *The Essential Lippmann. A Political Philosophy for Liberal Democracy*, edited by Clinton Rossiter and James Lare, 3–14. New York: Vintage Books.

Sartre, Jean-Paul. [1960] 1982. *Critique of Dialectical Reason: Theory of Practical Ensembles.* Translated by Alan Sheridan-Smith, edited by Jonathan Ree. London: Verso.

Schutz, Alfred. 1982. *The Problem of Social Reality: Collected Papers.* Vol. 1. The Hague: Martinus Nijhof Publishers.

Valadez, Jorge M. 2001. *Deliberative Democracy, Political Legitimacy, and Self-Determination in Multicultural Societies.* Boulder: Westview Press.

Williams, Melissa. 1998. *Voice, Trust, and Memory: Marginalized Groups and the Failings of Liberal Representation.* Princeton: Princeton University Press.

———. 2000. "The Uneasy Alliance of Group Representation and Deliberative Democracy." In Will Kymlicka and Wayne Norman, eds., *Citizenship in Diverse Societies*, 124–52. Oxford: Oxford University Press.

Young, Iris M. 1996. "Communication and the Other: Beyond Deliberative Democracy." In Seyla Benhabib, ed. *Democracy and Difference: Contesting the Boundaries of the Political.* Princeton: Princeton University Press.

NOTES

1. Consider Walter Lippmann's passionate attempts to distinguish democracy from "simple majority rule," and to refute the claim that democratic majorities can determine the truths of science, philosophy and ethics: When the majority exercises the force to destroy public schools, the minority may have to yield for a time to this force but there is no reason why they should accept the result. For the votes of a majority have no intrinsic bearing on the conduct of a school. They are external facts to be taken into consideration like the weather or the hazard of fire. Guidance for a school can come ultimately only from educators, and the question of what shall be taught as biology can be determined only by biologists. The votes of a majority do not settle anything here and they are entitled to no respect whatever. They may be right or they may be wrong; there is nothing in the majority principle which will make them either right or wrong (Lippmann [1947] 1965, 13–14).

2. Iris Young, for example, writes, "Each social perspective has an account not only of its own life and history but of every other position that affects its experience. Thus listeners can learn about how their own position, actions and values appear to others from the stories they tell. Narrative thus exhibits the situated knowledge available to the collective from each perspective, and the combination of narratives from different perspectives produces the collective social wisdom not available from any position" (1996, 132). Young inherits the concept of a "social perspective" from phenomenology and in particular the later Sartre of the *Critique of Dialectical Reason* ([1960] 1982). Usually phenomenological analysis moves at the level of a transcendental of quasi-transcendental explication of the conditions of our life-world, and seeks to render visible those assumptions about ourselves, others, and our worlds that we must always already have made in order for our worlds to be put together in terms we would recognize as constituting "our world." Be it in the work of Husserl, Heidegger, the later Wittgenstein, or Sartre, there is always a problem of *mediating* the level of phenomeno-logical analysis with the empirical constituencies of any given historical life-world. Phenom-enology is not empirical sociology. Wittgenstein's language games do not overlap with the empirical attributes of ethnocultural language groups any more than Heideggers's "Das Man" refers simply to the masses in industrial democracies. Iris Young's work, although it borrows from phenomenology, is free of such anxieties about how to mediate the empirical and the transcendental. She reifies "social positions" in that she translates transcendental terms of analyses into empirical social groups; furthermore, these social groups bear an uncanny resemblance to constituencies of identity politics of recent decades in Western capitalist de-mocracies, like women, "racial" and ethnic minorities, gays and lesbians, the handicapped, Jews, Gypsies, and the like. There is no compelling reason why a phenomenological life-group would overlap or be identical to social groups mobilized as social movements. On the difficulties and subtleties of constructing social groups, see Schutz 1982, 164–203. As I have argued above (chap. 1), this confusion of levels in Young's work is also characteristic of her critique of deliberative democracy and her attempt to substitute "communicative" for deliberative democracy. See Benhabib 1996 and 1999 for further exchanges with Iris Young.

3. Michael Rabinder James distinguishes between *formal* and *substantive* criteria in the justification of norms. "These, then, are the *formal* criteria for the justification of a norm: legitimate norms must be consensually justified by all affected parties through a rational, moral discourse conducted under fair conditions. However, the substantive content of norms is not specified within Habermas's theory and hence can vary according to culture. . . . The formal conditions under which a norm was created, not the specific content of the norm itself, is what Habermas's theory evaluates. And it is these conditions of fair, rational, norma-tive consensus that provide the universalistic form for culturally diverse substantive norms" (1999, 65). This is quite an apt formulation; I would also like to add that formal conditions constrain processes of norm creation in such ways that certain material norms could simply not pass the muster of rational discourses. The formal features of the process do not constrain some, though not all, aspects of the material outcome.

JÜRGEN HABERMAS

RELIGION IN THE PUBLIC SPHERE (2006)

Since the late 1990s, Jürgen Habermas has addressed the role of religion in the public sphere. In The Theory of Communicative Action *([1981] 1984/1987), he treated religion primarily from a sociological perspective, and analyzed modernization as a process of secularization. However, in his recent work, he characterizes contemporary Western societies as "postsecular societies," where religious communities continue to exist within a secularized environment.*

In the following essay, Habermas addresses a central problem raised by John Rawls concerning the public role of religion. The institutional separation of religion and politics in liberal democracies implies that legitimate political decisions have to be impartially justified by generally accessible reasons. According to Rawls, religious utterances on public matters must in due course be supported by arguments that address non-religious and religious citizens alike.

Habermas finds the Rawlsian view too restrictive because it can estrange religious citizens from public life and political engagement. According to Habermas, religious language may represent "indispensible potentials for meaning" and secular and religious forms of thought can mutually inform and learn from each other. Therefore, religious utterances should be allowed to blossom in the wider, "wild" public sphere—before being "translated" into a generally accessible language and "filtered" into the political public sphere proper.

An important background for this reasoning is what Habermas calls the "modernization of faith." Habermas sees the capacity for self-reflection and a self-critical distancing from one's own tradition as one of the greatest cultural achievements of modernity. In modern societies, we encounter a plurality of different religious doctrines as well as the scepticism of a secular, scientific mode of knowing. Religious worldviews have to accommodate themselves to this unavoidable competition. Thus, modern faith becomes reflexive and religiously anchored claims can only prove their cognitive relevance by being communicated, discussed and criticized.

1

Religious traditions and communities of faith have gained a new, hitherto unexpected political importance since the epochmaking change of 1989–90.[1] Needless to say, what initially spring to mind are the variants of religious fundamentalism that we face not only in the Middle East, but also in Africa, Southeast Asia, and in the Indian subcontinent. They often lock into national and ethnic conflicts, and today also form the seedbed for the decentralized form of terrorism that operates globally and is directed against the perceived insults and injuries caused by a superior Western civilization. There are other symptoms, too.

For example, in Iran the protest against a corrupt regime set in place and supported by the West has given rise to a veritable rule of priests that serves other movements as a model to follow. In several Muslim countries, and in Israel as well, religious family law is either an alternative or a substitute for secular civil law. And in Afghanistan (and soon in Iraq), the application of a more or less liberal constitution must be limited by its compatibility with the Sharia. Likewise, religious conflicts are squeezing their way into the international arena. The hopes associated with the political agenda of *multiple modernities* are fueled by the cultural self-confidence of those world religions that to this very day unmistakably shape the physiognomy of the major civilizations. And on the Western side of the fence, the perception of international relations has changed in light of the fears of a "clash of civilizations"— "the axis of evil" is merely one prominent example of this. Even Western intellectuals, to date self-critical in this regard, are starting to go on the offensive in their response to the image of Occidentalism that the others have of the West.[2]

Fundamentalism in other corners of the earth can be construed, among other things, in terms of the long-term impact of violent colonization and failures in decolonization. Under unfavorable circumstances, capitalist modernization penetrating these societies from the outside then triggers social uncertainty and cultural upheavals. On this reading, religious movements process the radical changes in social structure and cultural dissynchronies, which under conditions of an accelerated or failing modernization the individual may experience as a sense of being uprooted. What is more surprising is the political revitalization of religion at the heart of the United States, where the dynamism of modernization unfolds most successfully. Certainly, in Europe ever since the days of the French Revolution we have been aware of the power of a religious form of traditionalism that saw itself as counter-revolutionary. However, this evocation of religion as the power of tradition implicitly revealed the nagging doubt that the vitality of that which is already reflexively passed down *as* tradition may have been broken. By contrast, the political awakening of an ongoing strong religious consciousness in the United States has apparently not been affected by such doubts.

There is statistical evidence of a wave of secularization in almost all European countries since the end of World War II—going hand in hand with social modernization. By contrast, for the United States all data show that the comparatively large proportion of the population made up of devout and religiously active citizens has remained constant over the last six decades.[3] More importantly: the religious Right is not traditionalist. Precisely because it unleashes a spontaneous energy for revivalism, it causes paralyzing irritation among its secular opponents.

The movements for religious renewal at the heart of Western civilization are strengthening, at the *cultural* level, the *political* division of the West that was prompted by the Iraq War.[4] The divisive issues include, among others, the abolition of the death penalty; more or less liberal regulations on abortion; setting homosexual partnerships on a par with heterosexual marriages; an unconditional rejection of torture; and in general the prioritization of rights over collective goods, e.g., national security. The European states appear to keep moving forward alone on that path which, ever since the two constitutional revolutions of the late 18th century, they had trodden side by side with the United States. The significance of religions used for political ends has meanwhile grown the world over. Against this background, the split within the West is rather perceived as if Europe were isolating itself from the rest of the world. Seen in terms of world history, Max Weber's "Occidental Rationalism" now appears to be the actual deviation.

From this revisionist viewpoint, religious traditions appear to continue with undiminished strength, washing away or at least leveling the thresholds hitherto assumed to pertain between "traditional" and "modern" societies. In this way, the

Occident's own image of modernity seems, as in a psychological experiment, to undergo a switchover: the normal model for the future of all other cultures suddenly becomes a special-case scenario. Even if this suggestive Gestalt-switch does not quite bear up to sociological scrutiny and if the contrasting evidence can be brought into line with more conventional explanations of secularization,[5] there is no doubting the evidence itself and above all the symptomatic fact of divisive political moods crystallizing around it.

Two days after the last Presidential elections, an essay appeared, written by a historian, and entitled "The Day the Enlightenment Went Out." He asked the alarmist question: "Can a people that believes more fervently in the Virgin Birth than in evolution still be called an Enlightened nation? America, the first real democracy in history, was a product of the Enlightenment values . . . Though the founders differed on many things, they shared these values of what then was modernity . . . Respect for evidence seems not to pertain any more, when a poll taken just before the election showed that 75% of Mr. Bush's supporters believe Iraq either worked closely with Al Qaeda or was directly involved in the attacks of 9/11."[6]

Irrespective of how one evaluates the facts, the election analyses confirm that the cultural division of the West runs right through the American nation itself: conflicting value orientations—God, gays and guns—have manifestly covered over more tangibly contrasting interests. Be that as it may, President Bush has a coalition of primarily religiously motivated voters to thank for his victory.[7] This shift in power indicates a mental shift in civil society that also forms the background to the academic debates on the political role of religion in the state and the public sphere.

Once again, the battle is over the substance of the first sentence of the First Amendment: "Congress shall make no law respecting an establishment of religion, or prohibiting the free exercise thereof." The United States was the political pacemaker en route to establishing a freedom of religion that rested on the reciprocal respect of the religious freedom of the others.[8] The marvelous Article 16 of the Bill of Rights penned in Virginia in 1776 is the first document of freedom of religion guaranteed as a basic right that democratic citizens accord each other across the divides between the different religious communities. Unlike in France, the introduction of the freedom of religion in the United States of America did not signify the victory of laicism over an authority that had at best shown religious minorities tolerance in line with imposed standards of its own. Here, the secularization of state powers did not serve primarily the negative purpose of protecting citizens against the compulsion to adopt a faith against their own will. It was instead designed to guarantee the settlers who had turned their backs on Old Europe the positive liberty to continue to exercise their respective religion without hindrance. For this reason, in the present American debate on the political role of religion all sides have been able to claim their loyalty to the constitution. We shall see to what extent this claim is valid.

In what follows I shall address the debate that has arisen in the wake of John Rawls' political theory, in particular his concept of the "public use of reason." How does the constitutional separation of state and church influence the role which religious traditions, communities and organizations are allowed to play in civil society and the political public sphere, above all in the political opinion and will formation of citizens themselves? Where should the dividing line be in the opinion of the revisionists? Are the opponents who are currently out on the warpath against the liberal standard version of an ethics of citizenship actually only championing the pro-religious meaning of a secular state held to be neutral, versus a *narrow secularist* notion of a pluralist society? Or are they more or less inconspicuously changing the liberal agenda from the bottom up—and thus already arguing from the background of a *different* self-understanding of Modernity?

I would like first of all to bring to mind the liberal premises of the constitutional state and the consequences which John Rawls' conception of the public use of reason has on the ethics of citizenship (2). I shall then go on to treat the most important objections to this rather restrictive idea of the political role of religion (3). Through a critical discussion of revisionist proposals that do touch on the foundations of the liberal self-understanding I shall develop a conception of my own (4). However, secular and religious citizens can only fulfill the normative expectations of the liberal role of citizens if they likewise fulfill certain cognitive conditions and ascribe to the respective opposite the corresponding epistemic attitudes. I shall explain what this means by discussing the change in the form of religious consciousness which was a response to the challenges of Modernity (5). By contrast, the secular awareness that one is living in a post-secular society takes the shape of postmetaphysical thought at the philosophical level (6). In both regards, the liberal state faces the problem that religious and secular citizens can only acquire these attitudes through complementary learning processes, while it remains a moot point whether these are "learning processes" at all, and ones which the state cannot influence by its own means of law and politics anyway (7).

2

The self-understanding of the constitutional state has developed within the framework of a contractualist tradition that relies on "natural" reason, in other words solely on public arguments to which supposedly *all* persons have *equal access*. The assumption of a common human reason forms the basis of justification for a secular state that no longer depends on religious legitimation. And this in turn makes the separation of state and church possible at the institutional level in the first place. The historical backdrop against which the liberal conception emerged were the religious wars and confessional disputes in early Modern times. The constitutional state responded first by the secularization and then by the democratization of political power. This genealogy also forms the background to John Rawls' *A Theory of Justice*.[9]

The constitutional freedom of religion is the appropriate political answer to the challenges of religious pluralism. In this way, the potential for conflict at the level of citizens' social interaction can be restrained, while at the cognitive level deep-reaching conflicts may well continue to exist between the existentially relevant convictions of believers, believers of other denominations, and non-believers. Yet the secular character of the state is a necessary though not a sufficient condition for guaranteeing equal religious freedom for everybody. It is not enough to rely on the condescending benevolence of a secularized authority that comes to tolerate minorities hitherto discriminated against. The parties themselves must reach agreement on the always contested delimitations between a positive liberty to practice a religion of one's own and the negative liberty to remain spared from the religious practices of the others. If the principle of tolerance is to be above any suspicion of oppressive features, then compelling reasons must be found for the definition of what can just about be tolerated and what cannot, reasons that all sides can equally accept.[10] Fair arrangements can only be found if the parties involved learn to take the perspectives of the others. The procedure that fits this purpose best is the deliberative mode of democratic will formation. In the secular state, government has to be placed on a non-religious footing anyway. The liberal constitution must flesh out the loss of legitimation caused by a secularization that deprives the state of deriving its authority from God. From the practice of constitution-making, there emerge those basic rights that free and equal citizens must accord one another if they wish to regulate their co-existence reasonably on their own and by means of positive law.[11] The democratic procedure is able to generate legitimation by virtue of two components—first the equal political participation of all citizens, which guarantees that the addresses of the laws can also understand themselves as the authors of these laws; and second the epistemic dimension of a deliberation that grounds the presumption of rationally acceptable outcomes.[12]

These two legitimacy components explain the kind of political virtues the liberal state must expect from its citizens. It is precisely the conditions for the successful participation in the shared practice of democratic self-determination that define the ethics of citizenship: For all their ongoing dissent on questions of world views and religious doctrines, citizens are meant to respect one another as free and equal members of their political community. And on this basis of civic solidarity when it comes to contentious political issues they are expected to look for a way to reach a rationally motivated agreement—they owe one another good reasons. Rawls speaks in this context of the "duty of civility" and "the public use of reason": "The ideal of citizenship imposes a moral, not a legal, duty—the duty of civility—to be able to explain to one another on those fundamental questions how the principles and policies they advocate and vote for can be supported by the values of public reason. This duty also involves a willingness to listen to others and a fairmindedness in deciding when accommodations to their views should reasonably be made."[13]

Only with the legal frame for a self-governing association of free and equal citizens does the point of reference arise for the use of public reason which requires citizens to justify their political statements and attitudes before one another in light of a (reasonable interpretation)[14] of valid constitutional principles. Rawls refers here to "values of public reason" or elsewhere to the "premises we accept and think others could reasonably accept."[15] In a secular state only those political decisions are taken to be legitimate as can be impartially justified in the light of generally accessible reasons, in other words equally justified vis-à-vis religious and non-religious citizens, and citizens of different confessions. A rule that cannot be justified in an impartial manner is illegitimate as it reflects the fact that one party *forces* its will on another. Citizens of a democratic society are obliged to provide reasons for one another, as only thus can political power shed its repressive character. This consideration explains the controversial "proviso" for the use of non-public reasons.

The principle of separation of state and church obliges politicians and officials within political institutions to formulate and justify laws, court rulings, decrees and measures only in a language which is equally accessible to all citizens.[16] Yet the proviso to which citizens, political parties and their candidates, social organizations, churches and other religious associations are subject is not quite so strict in the political public sphere. Rawls writes: "The first is that reasonable comprehensive doctrines, religious or non-religious, may be introduced in public political discussion at any time, *provided that in due course proper political reasons—and not reasons given solely by comprehensive doctrines—are presented that are sufficient to support whatever the comprehensive doctrines are said to support.*"[17] This means that political reasons may not simply be put forward as a pretext, but must "count" irrespective of the religious context in which they are embedded.[18]

In the liberal view, the state guarantees citizens freedom of religion only on the condition that religious communities, each from the perspective of its own doctrinal tradition, accept not only the separation of church and state, but also the restrictive definition of the public use of reason. Rawls insists on this requirement even when confronted by the objection, which he himself raises: "How is it possible . . . for those of faith . . . to endorse a constitutional regime even when their comprehensive doctrines may not prosper under it, and indeed may decline?"[19]

Rawls's concept of public reason has met with resolute critics. The objections were leveled not at his liberal premises per se, but against an overly narrow, supposedly secularist definition of the political role of religion in the liberal frame. This is not to play down the fact that eventually the dissent also touches the real substance of the liberal state. What interests me (here) is what line gets drawn to claims that reach beyond a liberal constitution. Arguments for a more generously dimensioned political role for religion that are incompatible with the secular nature of the state should not be confused with justifiable objections to a secularist understanding of democracy and the rule of law.

The principle of separation of church and state demands that the institution of the state operate with strict impartiality vis-à-vis religious communities; parliaments, courts, and the administration must not violate the prescription not to privilege one side at the cost of another. But this principle is to be distinguished from the laicist demand that the state should defer from adopting any political stance which would support or constrain religion per se, even if this affects all religious communities equally. That would amount to an overly narrow interpretation of the separation of state and church.[20] At the same time, the rejection of secularism must not succumb to leaving the door wide open for revisions that would undermine the principle itself. The toleration of religious justifications within the legislative process is, as we shall see, a case in point. That said, Rawls's liberal position has tended to direct his critics' attention less to the impartiality of state institutions than to the ethics of citizenship.

3

Rawls's opponents cite historical examples of the favorable political influence that churches and religious movements have actually had on the assertion of democracy and human rights. Martin Luther King and the US Civil Rights Movement illustrate the successful struggle for a broader inclusion of minorities and marginal groups in the political process. In this context, the religious roots to the motivations of most social and socialist movements in both the United States and European countries are highly impressive.[21] There are obvious historical examples to the

contrary, namely for the authoritarian or repressive role of churches and fundamentalist movements; however, in well-established constitutional states, churches
and religious communities generally perform functions that are not unimportant
for stabilizing and advancing a liberal political culture. This is especially true of the
form of civil religion that has developed in American society.[22]

Paul J. Weithmann makes use of these sociological findings for a normative
analysis of the ethics of democratic citizenship. He describes churches and religious
communities as actors in civil society who fulfill functional imperatives for the
reproduction of American democracy. They provide arguments for public debates
on crucial morally-loaded issues and handle tasks of political socialization by informing their members and encouraging them to take part in the political process.
The churches' commitment to civil society would, however, wither away, so the
argument goes, if each time they had to distinguish between religious and political values in keeping with the yardstick set by Rawls' "proviso"—in other words if
they were obliged to find an equivalent in a universally accessible language for
every religious statement they pronounce. Therefore, if only for functional reasons,
the liberal state must refrain from obliging churches and religious communities to
comply to such standards of self-censorship. And it must then eschew all the more
imposing a similar limitation on its citizens.[23]

That is, of course, not the central objection to Rawls's theory. Irrespective of how
the interests are weighted in the relationship between the state and religious organizations, a state cannot encumber its citizens, whom it guarantees freedom of religious expression, with duties that are incompatible with pursuing a devout life—it
cannot expect something impossible of them. This objection bears closer scrutiny.

Robert Audi clothes the duty of civility postulated by Rawls in a special "principle
of secular justifications" when he writes: "One has a prima facie obligation not to
advocate or support any law or public policy . . . unless one has, and is willing to
offer, adequate secular reasons for this advocacy or support."[24] Audi adds to the
principle a requirement that goes even further, namely the demand that the secular
reasons must be strong enough to direct the citizen's own behavior, for example
when voting in elections, quite independent of simultaneous religious motivations.[25] With regard to a moral judgment on any individual citizen, the link between
the actual motivation for his actions and those reasons he gives in public may be
relevant. But a gap between reason and action is of no consequence from the perspective of what is necessary for maintaining the democratic system as a whole,
namely in terms of the contribution citizens must make to maintain a liberal political culture. At the end of the day only manifest reasons can, and only those do have
an impact on the political system as actually affect the formation of majorities and
their decisions within political bodies.

As regards the political consequences, all and only those issues, statements, and
reasons "count" that find their way into the impersonal flow of public communication and contribute to the cognitive motivation of *any* decision (backed and
implemented by state power)—be it directly in support of the decisions of voters
or indirectly in support of the decisions taken by party leaders, members of parliament or by persons holding office (such as judges, ministers or staff attached to
the administration). This is why I shall disregard Audi's additional requirement for
motivation and his distinction between publicly expressed reasons and those moti-

vating behavior in the polling booth.[26] What is of material import for the standard version of political liberalism is simply the requirement of "secular justifications": Given that in the liberal state only secular reasons count, citizens who adhere to a faith are obliged to establish a kind of "balance" between their religious and their secular convictions—in Audi's words a theo-ethical equilibrium.[27]

This demand is countered by the objection that many religious citizens would not be able to undertake such an artificial division within their own minds without jeopardizing their existence as pious persons. This objection is to be distinguished from the empirical observation that many citizens who take a stance on political issues from a religious viewpoint do not have enough knowledge or imagination to find secular justifications for them that are independent of their authentic beliefs. This fact is compelling enough given that any "ought" implies a "can." Yet we can go one step further. There is a normative resonance to the central objection, as it relates to the integral role that religion plays in the life of a person of faith, in other words to religion's "seat" in everyday life. A devout person pursues her daily rounds by *drawing* on belief. Put differently, true belief is not only a doctrine, believed content, but a source of energy that the person who has a faith taps performatively and thus nurtures his or her entire life.[28]

This totalizing trait of a mode of believing that infuses the very pores of daily life runs counter, the objection goes, to any flimsy switch-over of religiously rooted political convictions onto a *different* cognitive basis: "It belongs to the religious convictions of a good many religious people in our society that *they ought to base* their decisions concerning fundamental issues of justice *on* their religious convictions. They do not view it as an option whether or not to do it. It is their conviction that they ought to strive for wholeness, integrity, integration in their lives: that they ought to allow the Word of God, the teachings of the Torah, the command and example of Jesus, or whatever, to shape their existence as a whole, including, then, their social and political existence. Their religion is not, for them, about *something other* than their social and political existence."[29] Their religiously grounded concept of justice tells them what is politically correct or incorrect, meaning that they are incapable of discerning "any 'pull' from any secular reasons."[30]

If we accept this to my mind compelling objection, then the liberal state, which expressly protects such forms of life in terms of a basic right, cannot at the same time expect of *all* citizens that they also justify their political statements independently of their religious convictions or world views. This strict demand can only be laid at the door of politicians, who within state institutions are subject to the obligation to remain neutral in the face of competing world views; in other words it can only be made of anyone who holds a public office or is a candidate for such.[31]

The institutional precondition for guaranteeing equal freedom of religion for all is that the state remains neutral towards competing world views. The consensus on constitutional principles, which all citizens must mutually assume their fellow citizens share, pertains also to the principle of the separation of church and state. However, in light of the afore-mentioned objection it would be to over-generalize secularization if we were to extend this principle from the institutional level and apply it to statements put forward by organizations and citizens in the political public sphere. We cannot derive from the secular character of the state a direct obligation for all citizens personally to supplement their public statements of religious convictions by equivalents in a generally accessible language. And certainly the normative expectation that all religious citizens when casting their vote should *in the final instance* let themselves be guided by secular considerations is to ignore the realities of a devout life, an existence led *in light of* belief. This proposition has however been countered by pointing to the actual situation of religious citizens in the secular milieus of a modern society.[32]

The conflict between a person's own religious convictions and secularly justified policies or bills can only arise by virtue of the fact that the religious citizen should also have accepted the constitution of the secular state for good reasons. He no longer lives as a member of a religiously homogeneous population within a religiously legitimated state. And therefore certainties of faith are always already networked with fallible beliefs of a secular nature; they have long since lost—in the form of "unmoved" but not "unmovable" movers—their purported immunity to the impositions of modern reflexivity.[33] In the differentiated architecture of modern societies, the religious certainties are in fact exposed to an increasing pressure for reflection. This epistemological objection meets in turn a counterargument: By dint of their possibly even rationally defended reference to the dogmatic authority of an inviolable core of infallible revelatory truths, religiously rooted existential convictions evade that kind of *unreserved* discursive deliberation to which other ethical orientations and world views, i.e., secular "concepts of the good" expose themselves.[34]

4

The liberal state must not transform the requisite *institutional* separation of religion and politics into an undue *mental* and *psychological* burden for those of its citizens who follow a faith. It must of course expect of them that they recognize the principle that political authority is exercised with neutrality towards competing world views. Every citizen must know and accept that only secular reasons count beyond the institutional threshold that divides the informal public sphere from parliaments, courts, ministries and administrations. But all that is required here is the epistemic ability to consider one's own faith reflexively from the outside and to relate it to secular views. Religious citizens can well recognize this "institutional translation proviso" without having to split their identity into a public and a private part the moment they participate in public discourses. They should therefore be allowed to express and justify their convictions in a religious language if they cannot find secular "translations" for them.

This need by no means estrange "mono-glot" citizens from the political process, because they do take a position with political intent even if they field religious reasons. Even if the religious language is the only one they can speak in public, and if religiously justified opinions are the only ones they can or wish to put into political controversies, they nevertheless understand themselves as members of a civitas terrena, which empowers them to be the authors of laws to which as its addressees they are subject. Given that they may only express themselves in a religious idiom under the condition that they recognize the institutional translation proviso, they can, trusting that their fellow citizens will cooperate for accomplishing a translation, grasp themselves as participants in the legislative process, although only secular reasons count therein.

The permissibility of non-translated religious utterances in the political public sphere can be normatively justified not only in view of the fact that we must not *expect* Rawls's proviso to apply to those of the faithful who cannot abstain from the political use of "private" reasons without endangering their religious mode of life. For functional reasons, we should not over-hastily reduce the polyphonic complexity of public voices, either. For the liberal state has an interest in unleashing religious voices in the political public sphere, and in the political participation of religious organizations as well. It must not discourage religious persons and communities from also expressing themselves politically *as such*, for it cannot know whether secular society would not otherwise cut itself off from key resources for the creation of meaning and identity. Secular citizens or those of other religious persuasions can under certain circumstances learn something from religious contributions; this is, for example, the case if they recognize in the normative truth content of a religious utterance hidden intuitions of their own.

Religious traditions have a special power to articulate moral intuitions, especially with regard to vulnerable forms of communal life. In the event of the corresponding political debates, this potential makes religious speech a serious candidate to transporting possible truth contents, which can then be translated from the vocabulary of a particular religious community into a generally accessible language. However, the institutional thresholds between the "wild life" of the political public sphere and the formal proceedings within political bodies are also a filter that from the Babel of voices in the informal flows of public communication allows only secular contributions to pass through. In parliament, for example, the standing rules of procedure of the house must empower the house leader to have religious statements or justifications expunged from the minutes. The truth content of religious contributions can only enter into the institutionalized practice of deliberation and decision-making if the necessary translation already occurs in the pre-parliamentarian domain, i.e., in the political public sphere itself.

This requirement of translation must be conceived as a cooperative task in which the non-religious citizens must likewise participate, if their religious fellow citizens are not to be encumbered with an asymmetrical burden. Whereas citizens of faith may make public contributions in their own religious language only subject to the proviso that these get translated, the secular citizens must open their minds to the possible truth content of those presentations and enter into dialogues from which religious reasons then might well emerge in the transformed guise of generally accessible arguments.[35] Citizens of a democratic community owe one another good reasons for their political statements and attitudes. Even if the religious contributions are not subjected to self-censorship, they depend on cooperative acts of translation. For without a successful translation there is no prospect of the substantive content of religious voices being taken up in the agendas and negotiations within political bodies and in the broader political process. By contrast, Nicholas Wolterstorff and Paul Weithman wish to jettison even this proviso. In so doing, contrary to their own claim to remain in line with the premises of the liberal argument, they violate the principle that the state shall remain neutral in the face of competing world views.

In Weithman's opinion citizens have the right to justify public political statements in the context of a comprehensive world view or a religious doctrine. In the process they are supposed to meet two conditions. First, they must be convinced that their government is justified in carrying out the laws or policies they support with religious arguments. Second, they must be willing to declare why they believe this. This milder version of the proviso[36] amounts to the demand that a universalization test be undertaken from a first-person perspective. In this way, Weithman wishes to have citizens make their judgment from the viewpoint of a conception of justice even if they conceive "justice" in terms of a religion or another substantive world view. Citizens are to consider, if only from the respective perspective of their own doctrine, what would be equally good for everyone. However, the Golden Rule is not the Categorical Imperative; it does not oblige each person among all the people involved to *reciprocally* assume the perspective of everybody else.[37] For with this method each person's own perspective on the world forms the insurmountable horizon of her deliberations on justice: "The person who argues in public for a measure must be prepared to say what she thinks would justify the government in enacting it, *but the justification she is prepared to offer may depend on claims, including religious claims, which proponents of the standard approach would deem inaccessible.*"[38]

Since no institutional filter is envisaged between the state and the public domain, this version does not exclude the possibility that policies and legal programs will be implemented solely on the basis of the religious or confessional beliefs of a ruling majority. This is the conclusion explicitly drawn by Nicholas Wolterstorff, who does not wish to subject the political use of religious reasons to any restraints whatsoever. At any rate, he allows for a political legislature making use of religious arguments.[39] If one thus opens the parliaments to the battle on religious beliefs, governmental authority can evidently become the agent of a religious majority that asserts its will and thus violates the democratic procedure.

What is illegitimate is of course not the majority vote, assuming it has been correctly carried out, but the violation of the other core component of the procedure, namely the discursive nature of the deliberations preceding the vote. What is illegitimate is the violation of the neutrality principle according to which all enforceable political decisions *must be formulated* in a language that is equally accessible to all citizens, and *it must be possible to justify them* in this language as well. Majority rule turns into repression if the majority deploys religious arguments in the process of political opinion and will formation and refuses to offer those publicly accessible justifications which the losing minority, be it secular or of a different faith, is able to follow and to evaluate in the light of shared standards. The democratic procedure has the power to generate legitimacy precisely because it both includes all participants and has a deliberative character; for the justified presumption of rational outcomes in the long run can solely be based on this.

Wolterstorff pre-empts this argument by rejecting the whole idea of a reasonable background consensus on constitutional essentials. In the liberal view, political power only loses its inherent violence by virtue of a legal domestication which accords to agreed upon principles.[40] Wolterstorff raises empirical objections here to counter this conception. He ridicules the idealizing presuppositions, inscribed in the very practices of the constitutional state, as some "Quaker meeting ideal" (though the Quaker principle of unanimity is untypical of the democratic process). He maintains that the argument between different conceptions of justice grounded in competing religions or world views can never be solved by the common presupposition of an however formal background consensus. Although he wishes to retain the majority principle from the liberal consensus, Wolterstorff imagines that majority resolutions in an ideologically divided society can at best yield reluctant adaptations to a kind of *modus vivendi*. A defeated minority will feel like saying: "I do not agree, I *acquiesce*—unless I find the decision truly appalling."[41]

It is unclear why under this premise the political community should not at any time be in danger simply of disintegrating into religious struggle. Certainly, the usual empiricist reading of liberal democracy has always construed majority decisions as the temporary subjection of a minority to the actual power of a numerically prevailing party. But this utilitarian theory explains the acceptance of the voting procedure by the willingness of rational choosers to compromise; it reckons with parties who concur in their preference for the largest possible share of basic goods such as money, security or leisure time. The parties can conclude compromises because all of them aspire to the *same* categories of divisible goods. Yet precisely this condition is not met as soon as the conflicts no longer flare up over the share in the same kind of material goods, but on competing values and mutually exclusive "goods of salvation." The conflict on existential values between communities of faith cannot be solved by compromise. They can be contained, however, by losing any political edge against the background of a presupposed consensus on constitutional principles.

5

Conflicts between world views and religious doctrines that lay claim to explaining man's position in the world as a whole cannot be laid to rest at the cognitive level. As soon as these cognitive dissonances penetrate as far as the foundations for a normative integration of citizens, the political community disintegrates into irreconcilable segments so that it can only survive on the basis of an unsteady *modus vivendi*. In the absence of the uniting bond of a civic solidarity, which cannot be legally enforced, citizens do not perceive themselves as free and equal participants in the shared practices of democratic opinion and will formation wherein they *owe one another reasons* for their political statements and attitudes. This reciprocity of expectations among citizens is what distinguishes a community integrated by constitutional values from a community segmented along the dividing lines of competing world views. The latter frees religious and secular citizens in their dealings with one another from any reciprocal obligation to justify themselves in political debate *before one another*. In such a community the dissonant background beliefs and subcultural bonds out-trump the supposed constitutional consensus and the expected civic solidarity; in the case of conflicts that cut deep, citizens need not adapt to or face *one another* as second persons.

The assumption of forgoing reciprocity and of mutual indifference seems to be justified by the fact that the liberal standard version is intrinsically self-contradictory if it equally imputes to all citizens a political ethos which in fact distributes cognitive burdens unequally between secular and religious citizens. The translation requirement for religious reasons and the subsequent institutional precedence of secular reasons demand of the religious citizens an effort to learn and adapt that secular citizens are spared having to make. This would concur at any rate with the empirical observation that even within the Churches a certain resentment has persisted for so long toward the secular state. The duty to "make public use of reason" can only be discharged under certain cognitive preconditions. Yet required epistemic attitudes are the expression of a given mentality and cannot, like motives, be made the substance of normative expectations and political appeals. Every "ought" presupposes a "can." The normative expectations of an ethics of citizenship have absolutely no impact unless a required change in mentality has been forthcoming first; indeed, they then serve only to kindle resentment on the part of those who feel misunderstood and their capacities over-taxed.

However, in Western culture we do indeed observe a change in the form of religious consciousness since the Reformation and Enlightenment. The sociologists have described this "modernization of religious consciousness" as a response to the challenge religious traditions have been facing in view of the fact of pluralism, the emergence of modern science, and the spread of both positive law and profane morality. In these three respects, traditional communities of faith must process cognitive dissonances that do not arise for secular citizens, or arise for them only if they adhere to doctrines that are anchored in a similarly dogmatic way:

Religious citizens must develop an epistemic attitude toward other religions and world views that they encounter within a universe of discourse hitherto occupied only by their own religion. They succeed to the degree that they self-reflectively relate their religious beliefs to the statements of competing doctrines of salvation in such a way that they do not endanger their own exclusive claim to truth.

Moreover, religious citizens must develop an epistemic stance toward the independence of secular from sacred knowledge and the institutionalized monopoly of modern scientific experts. They can only succeed if from their religious viewpoint they conceive the relationship of dogmatic and secular beliefs in such a way that the autonomous progress in secular knowledge cannot come to contradict their faith.

Finally, religious citizens must develop an epistemic stance toward the priority that secular reasons enjoy in the political arena. This can succeed only to the extent that they convincingly connect the egalitarian individualism and universalism of modern law and morality with the premises of their comprehensive doctrines.

This arduous work of hermeneutic self-reflection must be undertaken from within religious traditions. In our culture, it has essentially been performed by theology, from the Catholic side also by a philosophy of religions that proceeds apologetically in explicating the reasonableness of a faith.[42] Yet in the final instance it is the faith and practice of the religious community that decides whether a dogmatic processing of the cognitive challenges of modernity has been "successful" or not; only then will the true believer accept it as the result of a "learning process." We may describe the new epistemic attitudes as "acquired by learning" only if they arise from a reconstruction of sacred truths that did indeed convince people of faith in the light of modern living conditions for which no alternatives any longer exist. If those attitudes were merely the contingent result of drill and forced adaptation, then the question, how those cognitive preconditions for imputing a liberal ethics of citizenship are met, has to be answered *à la* Foucault—namely in the wake of the kind of "discursive power" that asserts itself in the purported transparency of enlightened knowledge. Of course, this answer would contradict the normative self-understanding of the constitutional state. Such a response contradicts, of course, the normative self-understanding of any constitutional state.

Within this liberal framework, what interests me is the unanswered question whether the revised concept of citizenship that I have proposed in fact imposes an asymmetrical burden on religious traditions and religious communities after all. Historically speaking, religious citizens had to learn to adopt epistemic attitudes toward their secular environment, attitudes that enlightened secular citizens enjoy anyway, since they are not exposed to similar cognitive dissonances in the first place. However, secular citizens are likewise not spared a cognitive burden, because a secularist attitude does not suffice for the expected cooperation with fellow citizens who are religious. This cognitive act of adaptation needs to be distinguished from the political virtue of mere tolerance. What is at stake is not some respectful feel for the possible existential significance of religion for some other person. What we must also expect of the secular citizens is moreover a self-reflective transcending of a secularist self-understanding of Modernity.

As long as secular citizens are convinced that religious traditions and religious communities are to a certain extent archaic relics of pre-modern societies that continue to exist in the present, they will understand freedom of religion as the cultural version of the conservation of a species in danger of becoming extinct. From their viewpoint, religion no longer has any intrinsic justification to exist. And the principle of the separation of state and church can for them only have the laicist meaning of sparing indifference. In the secularist reading, we can envisage that, in the long run, religious views will inevitably melt under the sun of scientific criticism and that religious communities will not be able to withstand the pressures of some unstoppable cultural and social modernization. Citizens who adopt such an epistemic stance toward religion can obviously no longer be expected to take religious contributions to contentious political issues seriously and even to help to assess them for a substance that can possibly be expressed in a secular language and justified by secular arguments.

Under the normative premises of the constitutional state, the admission of religious statements to the political public sphere only makes sense if all citizens can be expected not to deny from the outset any possible cognitive substance to these contributions—while at the same time respecting the precedence of secular reasons and the institutional translation requirement. This is what the religious citizens assume anyway. Yet on the part of the secular citizens such an attitude presupposes a mentality that is anything but a matter of course in the secularized societies of the West. Instead, the insight by secular citizens that they live in a post-secular society that is *epistemically adjusted* to the continued existence of religious communities first requires a change in mentality that is no less cognitively exacting than the adaptation of religious awareness to the challenges of an ever more secularized environment. In line with this changed yardstick, the secular citizens must grasp their conflict with religious opinions as a *reasonably expected disagreement*.

In the absence of this cognitive precondition, a public use of reason cannot be imputed to citizens, at least not in the sense that secular citizens should be willing to enter and engage in a discussion of the content of religious contributions with the intention of translating, if there is such a content, morally convincing intuitions and reasons into a generally accessible language.[43] An epistemic mindset is presupposed here that would originate from a self-critical assessment of the limits of secular reason.[44] However, this cognitive precondition indicates that the version of an ethics of citizenship I have proposed may only be expected from all citizens equally if both, religious as well as secular citizens, already have undergone complementary learning processes.

6

The ostensibly critical overcoming of what to my mind is a narrow secularist consciousness is itself an essentially contested issue—at least to the same extent as the demythologizing response to the cognitive challenges of Modernity. While we already observe the "modernization of religious consciousness" with hindsight and consider it the subject matter of theology, the naturalist background of secularism is still the object of an ongoing and open-ended philosophical debate. The secular awareness that we live in a post-secular world is reflected philosophically in the form of post-metaphysical thought. This mode of thought is not exhausted by an emphasis on the finiteness of reason, or by the combination of fallibilist and anti-skeptical attitudes that has characterized modern science since Kant and Peirce. The secular counterpart to religious modernization is an agnostic, but non-reductionist philosophical position. It refrains on the one hand from passing judgment on religious truths while insisting (in a non-polemical fashion) on drawing a strict line between faith and knowledge. It rejects, on the other, a scientistically limited conception of reason and the exclusion of religious doctrines from the genealogy of reason.

Post-metaphysical thought admittedly refrains from passing ontological statements on the constitution of the whole of beings; but this does not mean reducing our knowledge to the sum total of statements that at each time represents the respective "state of science." Scientism often tempts one to blur the borderline between proper scientific knowledge, which gains relevance with regard to how man interprets himself and his position in nature as a whole, on the one hand, and a naturalist world view synthetically derived from this, on the other.[45] This radical form of naturalism devalues all categories of statements that cannot be reduced to controlled observations, nomological propositions or causal explanations; in other words moral, legal and evaluative judgments are no less excluded than are religious ones. As the renewed discussion on freedom and determinism shows, advances in biogenetics, brain research and robotics provide stimuli for a kind of naturalizing of the human mind that casts into question our practical self-understanding as responsibly acting persons and encourages a call for revisions to criminal law.[46] A naturalistic self-objectification of persons that penetrates everyday life is incompatible with any idea of political integration that imputes to all citizens the presupposition of a normative background consensus.

One promising route to a multi-dimensional concept of reason that is no longer exclusively fixated on its reference to the objective world but becomes self-critically aware of its boundaries is to reconstruct the history of its own genesis. In this respect post-metaphysical thought does not restrict itself to the heritage of Western metaphysics. At the same time, it also makes sure of its internal relationship to those world religions whose origins, like the origins of Classical Greek philosophy, date back to the middle of the first millennium before Christ—in other words to what Jaspers termed the "Axis Age." The religions which have their roots in this period achieved the cognitive leap from mythical narratives to a logos that differentiates between essence and appearance in a very similar way as did Greek philosophy. And in the course of the "Hellenization of Christianity," philosophy in turn took on board and assimilated many religious motifs and concepts, specifically those from the history of salvation.[47]

The complex web of inheritance cannot be understood solely along the line of a history of Being, as Heidegger claimed.[48] Greek concepts such as "autonomy" and "individuality" or Roman concepts such as "emancipation" and "solidarity" have long since been shot through with meanings of a Judeo-Christian origin.[49] Philosophy has recurrently found in its encounters with religious traditions, and they include Muslim traditions as well, that it receives innovative stimulation if it succeeds in liberating the cognitive substance from its dogmatic encapsulation in the melting pot of rational discourse. Kant and Hegel are the best examples of this. And further evidence provides the encounter of prominent philosophers of the 20th century with a religious writer such as Kierkegaard, who thinks in a post-metaphysical, but not a post-Christian vein.

Some religious traditions would appear, even if they at times take the stage as the opaque Other of reason, to have remained present in a more vital manner than has metaphysics. It would not be reasonable to reject out of hand the idea that the world religions—as the only remaining element of the distant cultures of the Old Empires—assert a place for themselves in the differentiated architecture of Modernity because their cognitive substance has not yet waned. We cannot at any rate exclude the thought that they still bear a semantic potential that unleashes an inspiring energy for *all of* society as soon as they release their profane truth content.

In short, post-metaphysical thought is prepared to learn from religion, but remains agnostic in the process. It insists on the difference between the certainties of faith, on the one hand, and validity claims that can be publicly criticized, on the other; but it refrains from the rationalist presumption that it can itself decide what part of the religious doctrines is rational and what part irrational. The contents which reason appropriates through translation must not be lost for faith. However, an apology of faith with philosophical means is not the task of philosophy proper. At best, philosophy *circles* the opaque core of religious experience when reflecting on the intrinsic meaning of faith. This core must remain so abysmally alien to discursive thought as does the core of aesthetic experience, which can likewise only be circled but not penetrated by philosophical reflection.

Post-metaphysical thought's ambivalent attitude to religion corresponds to the epistemic attitude which secular citizens must adopt, if they are to be prepared to learn something from the contributions to public debates made by their religious counterparts, something that can also be expressed in a generally accessible language. The philosophical appropriation of the genealogy of reason appears to play that role for a self-reflection of secularism as the reconstruction work of theology plays for the self-reflection of religious faith. The required work of philosophical reconstruction goes to show that the ethics of democratic citizenship assumes secular citizens exhibit a mentality that is no less demanding than the corresponding mentality of their religious counterparts. This is why the cognitive burdens that both sides have to shoulder in order to acquiring the appropriate epistemic attitudes are by no means asymmetrically distributed.

7

The fact that the "public use of reason" (in the interpretation I have given of it) depends on cognitive preconditions which require learning processes has interesting, but ambiguous consequences. It reminds us firstly that that the democratic constitutional state, such as relies on a deliberative form of politics, is an epistemically discerning form of government that is, as it were, truth-sensitive. A "post-truth democracy," such as the *New York Times* saw on the horizon during the last Presidential elections, would no longer be a democracy. Moreover, the requirement of complex mentalities draws our attention to an improbable functional imperative that the liberal state can hardly meet by employing its own means. The polarization of world views in a community that splits into fundamentalist and secular camps, shows, for example, that an insufficient number of citizens matches up to the yardstick of the public use of reason and thereby endanger political integration. Such mentalities are pre-political in origin, however. They change incrementally and unforeseeably in response to changed conditions of life. A long-term process of this kind gets at best accelerated in the medium of public discourses among the citizens themselves. Yet is this a cumulative cognitive process at all, one that we may describe as a learning process in the first place?

A third consequence is most disquieting of all. So far, we have assumed that citizens of a constitutional state can acquire the functionally requisite mentalities by embarking on "complementary learning processes." The following consideration shows that this assumption is not unproblematic: From what perspective may we claim that the fragmentation of a political community, if it is caused by a collision of fundamentalist and secularist camps, can be traced back to "learning deficits"? Let us bring to mind here the change in perspective which we have made when moving from a normative explanation of an ethics of citizenship to an epistemological investigation of the cognitive preconditions for the rational expectation that citizens are able to meet the corresponding obligations. A change in epistemic attitudes must occur for the religious consciousness to become reflective and the secularist consciousness to transcend its limitations. But it is only from the viewpoint of a specific, normatively charged self-understanding of Modernity that we can qualify these mentality changes as complementary "learning processes."

Now, this view can of course be defended in the framework of an evolutionary social theory. Quite apart from the controversial position which such theories have within their own academic discipline, from the viewpoint of normative political theory we may at no point impose on citizens our expectation that they describe themselves in terms, for example, of a theory of religious evolution, or even rate themselves as cognitively "backward." Only the participants and their religious organizations can resolve the question of whether a "modernized" faith is still the "true" faith. And whether or not, on the other side, a scientistically justified form of secularism will not in the end win out against a more comprehensive concept of reason conceived in terms of some post-metaphysical thought is, for the time being, a moot point even among philosophers themselves. However, if political theory must leave it unanswered whether the functionally requisite mentalities can at all be acquired through learning process, then political theorists must accept that a normatively justified concept such as "the public use of reason" may for good reasons remain "essentially contested" among citizens themselves. For the liberal state is allowed to confront its citizens only with duties which the latter can perceive as reasonable expectations; this will be the case only if the necessary epistemic attitudes are in turn acquired from insight, i.e., through "learning."

We must not be misled into drawing the wrong conclusions from this self-limitation of political theory. As philosophers and as citizens, we can well be convinced that a strong reading of the liberal and republican foundations of the constitutional state should *and can* be successfully defended both intra muros and in the political arena. However, this discourse on whether a liberal constitution and an ethics of democratic citizenship is correct and we have the right understanding of it inevitably leads us into a terrain where the normative arguments no longer suffice. The controversy also extends to the epistemological question of the relationship between faith and knowledge, which itself touches on key elements of Modernity's background understanding of itself. Interestingly enough both the philosophical and the theological efforts to define the relationship between faith and knowledge generate far-reaching questions as to the genealogy of Modernity.

Let us return to Rawls's question: "How is it possible for those of faith, as well as the non-religious, to endorse a secular regime even when their comprehensive doctrines may not prosper under it, and indeed may decline?"[50] In the final analysis, the question cannot be answered just by reference to the normative explanations of political theory. Let us take the example of "radical orthodoxy,"[51] an approach that takes up the intentions and fundamental ideas of the political theology of a Carl Schmitt and develops them with the tools of deconstruction. If theologians of this ilk deny Modernity any intrinsic right[52] with the intention to once again give a nominalistically uprooted Modern world ontological anchors in the "reality of God," then the debate has to be conducted on the respective opponent's playing field. In other words, theological propositions can only be countered by theological arguments, and historical or epistemological propositions by historical and epistemological arguments.[53]

The same applies to the opposite side. Rawls's question is leveled equally at both the religious and the secular sides. A differentiated debate on fundamental philosophical issues is most certainly necessary if a naturalist world view overdraws the account of scientific knowledge in the proper sense. There can be no deriving the public demand that religious communities must now at long last cast aside the traditional statements on the existence of God and or an eternal after-life from recent neurological insights into the dependence of all mental operations on brain processes, not that is until we have clarified, from the philosophical point of view, the pragmatic meaning such Biblical statements assume in the context of the doctrine and practice of religious communities.[54] The question as to how from this angle science relates to religious doctrine again touches on the genealogy of Modernity's self-understanding. Is modern science a practice that is completely understandable in its own terms, establishing the measure of all truths and falsehoods? Or should modern science rather be construed as resulting from a history of reason that includes the world religions?

Rawls developed his "Theory of Justice" into "Political Liberalism" because he increasingly recognized the immeasurable relevance of the "fact of pluralism." He did posterity a great service in thinking at an early date about the political role of religion. Yet precisely these phenomena should have made a supposedly "freestanding" political theory aware of the limits of normative arguments. After all, whether the liberal response to religious pluralism can be accepted by the citizens themselves as the single right answer depends not least on whether secular and religious citizens, each from their own respective angle, are prepared to embark on an interpretation of the relationship of faith and knowledge that first enables them to behave in a self-reflexive manner toward each other in the political public sphere.[55]

References

Arens, E. (1982), *Kommunikative Handlungen*. Düsseldorf: Patmos Verlag.

Audi, R. and Wolterstorff, N. (1997), *Religion in the Public Sphere*. New York: Rowman and Littlefield.

Audi, R. (2005), "Moral Foundations of Liberal Democracy, Secular Reasons, and Liberal Neutrality Toward the Good," *Notre Dame Journal of Law, Ethics, & Public Policy*, 19: 197–218.

Bellah, R., Madsen, R., Sullivan, W. M., Swidler, A. and Tipton, S. M. (1985). *Habits of the Heart*. Berkeley. First published in English as chapter 5 of *Between Naturalism and Religion* (Cambridge: Polity Press, 2006). Originally published in *Zwischen Naturalismus and Religion* (Frankfurt: Suhrkamp Verlag, 2005): University of California Press.

Berger, P. L. (ed.) (1999), *The Desecularization of the World*. Washington, DC: Ethics and Public Policy Center.

Birnbaum, N. (2002), *After Progress*. Oxford: Oxford University Press.

Blumenberg, H. (1985), *Legitimacy of the Modern Age*, tr. Wallace R. M. Cambridge, MA: MIT Press.

Brunkhorst, H. (2002), *Solidarität*. Frankfurt/Main: Suhrkamp.

Bultmann, R. (1984). *Theologische Enzyklopädie*, Annex 3: *Wahrheit und Gewissheit*. Tübingen: Mohr Siebeck.

Buruma, I. and Margalit, A. (2004), *Occidentalism. The West in the Eyes of its Enemies*. Harmondsworth: Penguin.

Detel, W. (2004), "Forschungen über Hirn and Geist," *Deutsche Zeitschrift für Philosophie*, 6: 891–920.

Forst, R. (1994), *Kontexte der Gerechtigkeit*. Frankfurt/Main: Suhrkamp.

——. (2003), *Toleranz im Konflikt*. Frankfurt/Main: Suhrkamp.

Gaus, G. F. (1966), *Justificatory Liberalism*. New York: Oxford University Press.

Geyer, C. (ed.) (2004), *Hirnforschung und Willensfreiheit*. Frankfurt/Main: Suhrkamp.

Goodstein, L. and Yardley, W. (2004). "President Bush Benefits from Efforts to Build a Coalition of Religious Voters," *New York Times*, Nov. 5, 2004, A 19.

Habermas, J. (1996), *Between Facts and Norms*, tr. Rehg William. Cambridge, MA: MIT.

——. (1991), "Vom pragmatischen, ethischen und moralischen Gebrauch der praktischen Vernunft, Abschnitt IV," in his *Erläuterungen zur Diskursethik*. Frankfurt/Main: Suhrkamp, 112–5.

——. (2003), "Glauben und Wissen," in his *Zeitdiagnosen*. Frankfurt/Main: Suhrkamp, 249–263.

——. (2004), *Der gespaltene Westen*. Frankfurt/Main: Suhrkamp.

Heidegger, M. (1989), *Beiträge zur Philosophie (Vom Ereignis)*. Frankfurt/Main: Klostermann.

Lutz-Bachmann, M. (1992), "Hellenisierung des Christentums?," in C. Colpe, L. Honnefelder and M. Lutz-Bachmann (eds.), *Spätantike and Christentum*. Berlin: Wiley, pp. 77–98.

——. (2002), "Religion-Philosophie-Religionsphilosophie," in M. Jung, M. Moxter and T. M. Schmit (eds.), *Religionsphilosophie*. Würzburg: Echter, 19–26.

Madson, R., Sullivan, W. M., Swindler, A. and Tipton, S. M. (eds.) (2003), *Meaning and Modernity: Religion, Polity, and Self*. Berkeley, Calif.: University of California Press.

Milbank, J. (1990), *Theology and Social Theory: Beyond Secular Reason*. Oxford: Oxford University Press.

Milbank, J., Pickstock, C., and Ward, G. (eds.) (1999), *Radical Orthodoxy*. London and New York: Routledge.

Norris, P. and Inglehart, R. (2004), *Sacred and Secular, Religion and Politics Worldwide*. Cambridge: Cambridge University Press.

Pauen, M. (2004), *Illusion Freiheit?* Frankfurt/Main: Fischer Verlag.

Rawls, J. (1971), *A Theory of Justice*. Cambridge, Mass: Harvard University Press.

———. (1993), *Political Liberalism*. New York: Columbia University Press.

———. (1997), "The Idea of Public Reason Revisited," *The University of Chicago Law Review*, 64: 765–807.

Schleiermacher, F. (1830–1). *Der christliche Glaube*; reprinted Berlin: De Gruyter, 1999.

Schmidt, T. M. (2001), "Glaubensüberzeugungen und säkulare Grunde," Zeitschrift für *Evangelische Ethik*, 4: 248–61.

———. (2005), "Postsäkulare Theologie des Rechts. Eine Kritik der radikalen Orthodoxie," in M. Frühauf and W. Löser (eds.), *Biblische Aufklärung—die Entdeckung einer Tradition*. Frankfurt/Main: Knecht, 91–108.

Weithman, P. J. (2002), *Religion and the Obligations of Citizenship*. Cambridge: Cambridge University Press.

Wills, G. (2004). "The Day the Enlightenment Went Out," *New York Times*, Nov. 4/2004, A 31.

NOTES

1. Cf. Berger (ed.) 1999.
2. Cf. Buruma and Margalit 2004.
3. Cf. Norris and Inglehart 2004: Ch. 4.
4. Cf. Habermas 2004.
5. Norris and Inglehart 2004: Ch. 10 defend the classical hypothesis that secularization wins out to the extent that along with improved economic and social conditions for life it also spreads the feeling of "existential security." Alongside the demographic assumption that fertility rates in developed societies are falling, this hypothesis initially explains why secularization today has all in all only seized root in the "West." The United States forms an exception, mainly because of two facts. First of all a rather blunt kind of capitalism has effects which are less cushioned by a welfare state and thus exposes the population on average to a higher degree of existential uncertainty. And second the comparatively high rate of immigration from traditional societies where the fertility rates are correspondingly high explains the stability of the relatively large proportion of religious citizens.
6. Wills 2004.
7. Goodstein and Yardley 2004. Bush was voted for by 60% of the Spanish-speaking voters, by 67% of the white Protestants, and by 78% of the Evangelical or Born-Again Christians. Even among the Catholics, who previously tended to vote Democrat, Bush turned the traditional majorities around. The fact that the Catholic bishops took sides is astonishing, for all the concurrence on the question of abortion, if we bear in mind that unlike the Church the administration defends the death penalty and put the lives of tens of thousands of US soldiers and Iraqi civilians at risk for a war of aggression that violated international law for which it could only cite dubious reasons.
8. On this "concept of respect" see the wide-ranging historical and yet systematically convincing study in Forst 2003.

9. Rawls 1971: §§ 33f.

10. On the concept of tolerance as reciprocal respect, see Forst 2003.

11. See Habermas 1996: Ch. 3.

12. See Rawls 1997: 769: "Ideally citizens are to think of themselves as if they were legislators and ask themselves what statutes, supported by what reasons satisfying the principle of reciprocity, they would think it most reasonable to enact."

13. Rawls 1993: 217.

14. Rawls speaks of a "family of liberal conceptions of justice" to which the use of public reason can refer when interpreting constitutional principles; see Rawls 1997: 773f.

15. Rawls 1997: 786.

16. For a specification of the demand for reasons in a "generally accessible" language see Forst 1994: 199–209.

17. Rawls 1997: 783f. (my italics). This amounts to a revision of the more narrowly formulated principle in Rawls 1994: p. 224f. Rawls confines the proviso to key issues relating to "constitutional essentials"; I consider this reservation unrealistic with regard to modern legal systems in which basic rights in both, legislation and adjudication apply immediately to specific statutes so that almost all controversial legal issues can be redefined such as to become issues of principle.

18. Rawls 1997: 777: "They are not puppets manipulated from behind the scenes by comprehensive doctrines."

19. Rawls 1997: 781. I shall return to this objection later.

20. See the debate between Robert Audi and Nicholas Wolterstorff in Audi and Wolterstorff 1997: 3f., 76f. and 167f.

21. Cf. Birnbaum 2002.

22. See the influential study by Bellah, Madsen, Sullivan, Swidler and Tipton 1985. On Bellah's decisive publications in this field see the festschrift: Madson, Sullivan, Swindler and Tipton (eds.) 2003.

23. On this empirical argument see Weithman 2002: 91: "I argued that churches contribute to democracy in the United States by fostering realized democratic citizenship. They encourage their members to accept democratic values as the basis for important political decisions and to accept democratic institutions as legitimate. The means by which they make their contributions, including their own interventions in civic argument and public political debate, affect the political arguments their members may be inclined to use, the basis on which they vote, and the specification of their citizenship with which they identify. They may encourage their members to think of themselves as bound by antecedently given moral norms with which political outcomes must be consistent. The realization of citizenship by those who are legally entitled to take part in political decision-making is an enormous achievement for a liberal democracy, one in which the institutions of civil society play a crucial role."

24. Audi and Wolterstorff 1997: 25.

25. Audi and Wolterstorff 1997: 29.

26. This distinction also prompts Paul Weithman to differentiate the argument in line with his modified proviso; see Weithman 2002: 3.

27. Meanwhile, Robert Audi has introduced a counterpart to the principle of secular justification: "In liberal democracies, religious citizens have a prima facie obligation not to advocate or support any law or public policy that restricts human conduct, unless they have, and are willing to offer, adequately religiously acceptable reasons for this advocacy or support" (Audi 2005: 217). This principle of religious justification is evidently meant to impose an act of critical self-scrutiny on citizens who are informed in their thinking by religious reasons.

28. On the Augustinian distinction of *fides quae creditur* and *fides qua creditur* see R. Bultmann 1984: 185 ff.

29. Wolterstorff in Audi and Wolterstorff 1997: 105.

30. Weithmann 2002: 157.

31. This brings us to the interesting question of the extent to which during an election campaign candidates may confess or indicate that they are religious persons. The principle of separation of church and state certainly extends to the platform, the manifesto, or the "line," which political parties and their candidates promise to realize. Seen normatively, electoral decisions that boil down to a question of personality instead of programmatic issues are problematic anyway. And it is all the more problematic if the voters take their cue from candidates' religious self-presentations. See on this point the ideas elaborated by Weithman 2002: 117–20: "It would be good to have principles saying what role religion can play when candidates are assessed for what we might call their "expressive value"—their fittingness to express the values of their constituencies . . . What is most important to remember about these cases, however, is that elections should not be decided nor votes cast entirely or primarily on the basis of various candidates' expressive value."

32. Schmidt 2001.

33. Schmidt bases his objection on Gaus 1966.

34. Incidentally, this special status prohibits an assimilation of religious convictions to ethical conceptions, as proposed by Forst (1994: 152–61) who, from the perspective of normative political theory, gives the difference between religious and secular reasons a backseat to the precedence of procedural over substantive criteria of justification. Only from competing religious beliefs do we know a fortiori that a justified consensus cannot be reached. In his latest book Forst (2003: 644–47) recognizes the special status of this category of beliefs.

35. Habermas 2003: 256ff.

36. Weithman 2002: 3: "Citizens of a liberal democracy may offer arguments in public political debate which depend on reasons drawn from their comprehensive moral views, including their religious views, without making them good by appeal to other arguments—provided they believe that their government would be justified in adopting the measures they favor and are prepared to indicate what they think would justify the adoption of the measures."

37. Habermas 1991.

38. Weithman 2002: 121 (my italics).

39. Audi and Wolterstorff 1997: 117f.

40. Rawls 1993: 137: "Our exercise of political power is fully proper only when it is exercised in accordance with a constitution the essentials of which all citizens as free and equal may reasonably be expected to endorse in the light of principles and ideals acceptable to their common human reason."

41. Audi and Wolterstorff 1997: 160.

42. I have my correspondence with Thomas M. Schmidt to thank for the characterization of a philosophy of religion that is not pursued from the agnostic side: it aims at religion's self-enlightenment, but does not speak, like theology, "in the name of" religious revelation, nor just as "its observer." See also Lutz-Bachmann 2002. On the Protestant side, Friedrich Schleiermacher played an exemplary role. He carefully distinguished between the role of the theologian and that of the apologetic philosopher of religion (who did not rely on the Aquinian tradition but instead on Kant's transcendental idealism) and combined both in his own person. See the introduction to his explication of the Christian doctrine in Schleiermacher 1830–1: §§ 1–10.

43. In this sense, Forst (1994: 158) likewise speaks of "translation" when he demands that "a person must be able to make a (gradual) *translation* [his emphasis] of his/her arguments into reasons that are acceptable on the basis of the values and principles of public reason." However, he considers translation not as a joint venture in the search for truth, in which secular citizens should take part even if the other side restricts itself to religious statements. Forst formulates the demand the way Rawls and Audi do, as a civic duty for the religious

person, too. Incidentally, the purely procedural definition of the act of translation with a view to a "unrestricted reciprocal justification" does not do justice to the semantic problem of transposing the contents of religious speech into a post-religious and post-metaphysical form of representation. As a result, the difference between ethical and religious discourse gets lost. See, for example, Arens 1982, who interprets Biblical metaphors as innovative speech acts.

44. In his masterful study of the history of the notion of tolerance, Rainer Forst termed Pierre Bayle the "greatest thinker on tolerance" because Bayle provides in exemplary fashion such a reflexive self-limitation of reason in relation to religion. On Bayle see Forst 2003: § 18 as well as §§ 29 and 33 on the systematic argument.

45. Wolterstorff draws our attention to an all too often blurred distinction between secular reasons, that are meant to count, and secular world views, that like all comprehensive doctrines are not meant to count. See Audi and Wolterstorff 1997: 105: "Much if not most of the time we will be able to spot religious reasons from a mile away . . . Typically, however, comprehensive secular perspectives will go undetected."

46. Geyer (ed.) 2004; Pauen 2004.

47. Lutz-Bachmann 1992.

48. See the sketches to a history of Being in Heidegger 1989.

49. See the interesting discussions in Brunkhorst 2002: 40–78.

50. See footnote 19.

51. Milbank 1990; Milbank, Pickstock, and Ward (eds.) 1999.

52. On the opposite position see the early work of Hans Blumenberg 1985.

53. Schmidt 2005.

54. See the final comment by W. Detel in his marvelously informed article Detel 2004.

55. My thanks go to Rainer Forst and Thomas M. Schmidt for their insightful comments, both of whom have already published several instructive works on this theme. I am also grateful to Melissa Yates for useful references and stimulating discussions.

Further Readings

Introduction and Overview

Splichal, Slavko, *Public Opinion: Developments and Controversies in the Twentieth Century*. Lanham, Md.: Rowman & Littlefield, 1999.

The Public Sphere Vol. I–IV. Edited by Jostein Gripsrud, Hallvard Moe, Anders Molander and Graham Murdock. London: Sage Publications, 2010.

Kant

The Cambridge Companion to Kant. Edited by Paul Gruyer. Cambridge: Cambridge University Press, 1992. Chapters by Onora O'Neill, J. B. Schneewind and Wolfgang Kersting.

Habermas, Jürgen, *The Structural Transformation of the Public Sphere: An Inquiry into a Category of Bourgeois Society*. Cambridge, Mass.: Polity Press, [1962] 1989. Ch. 4, "The Basic Blueprint."

O'Neill, Onora, *Constructions of Reason. Explorations of Kant's Practical Philosophy*. Cambridge: Cambridge University Press, 1989. Ch. 2, "The public use of reason."

Rosen, Allen D., *Kant's Theory of Justice*. Itacha and London: Cornell University Press, 1993.

Hegel

The Cambridge Companion to Hegel. Edited by Frederick C. Beiser. Cambridge: Cambridge University Press, 1993. Ch. 8 by Kenneth Westphal, "The Basic Context and Structure of Hegel's *Philosophy of Right*."

Habermas, Jürgen, *The Structural Transformation of the Public Sphere: An Inquiry into a Category of Bourgeois Society*. Cambridge, Mass.: Polity Press, [1962] 1989. Ch. 4, "The Basic Blueprint."

Avineri, Shlomo, *Hegel's Theory of the Modern State*. Cambridge: Cambridge University Press, 1972.

Mill

The Cambridge Companion to Mill. Edited by John Skorupski. Cambridge: Cambridge University Press, 1998. Ch. 14 by Alan Ryan, "Mill in a Liberal Landscape."

314 *Further Readings*

Habermas, Jürgen, *The Structural Transformation of the Public Sphere: An Inquiry into a Category of Bourgeois Society*. Cambridge, Mass.: Polity Press, [1962] 1989. Ch. 4, "The Basic Blueprint."

Ten, Chin Liew, "Mill's Defence of Liberty," in *J. S. Mill—On Liberty in Focus*. Edited by John Gray and G. W. Smith. London: Routledge, 1991.

Urbinati, Nadia, *Mill on Democracy: From the Athenian Polis to Representative Government*. Chicago: University of Chicago Press, 2002.

Lippmann

Steel, Ronald, *Walter Lippmann and the American Century*. New Brunswick: Transaction Publishers, 1999, new edition 2004.

Dewey

Bohman, James, "Democracy as Inquiry, Inquiry as Democratic: Pragmatism, Social Science and the Democratic Division of Labour," *American Journal of Political Science* 43(2): 590–607, 1999.

Festenstein, Matthew, *Pragmatism and Political Theory: From Dewey to Rorty*. Chicago: Chicago University Press, 1997.

Honneth, Axel, "Democracy as Reflexive Cooperation: John Dewey and the Theory of Democracy Today," *Political Theory*, 26(6): 763–83, 1998.

Schmitt

Cohen, Jean L. and Arato, Andrew, *Civil Society and Political Theory*. Cambridge, Mass.: MIT Press, 1992. Ch. 5, "The Historicist Critique: Carl Schmitt, Reinart Koselleck, and Jürgen Habermas."

Law as Politics: Carl Schmitt's Critique of Liberalism. Edited by David Dyzenhaus. Durham, N.C.: Duke University Press, 1998.

Scheuermann, William E., "Carl Schmitt's Critique of Liberal Constitutionalism," *The Review of Politics* 58(2): 299–322, 1996.

Slagstad, Rune, "Liberal Constitutionalism and Its Critics: Carl Schmitt and Max Weber," in *Constitutionalism and Democracy*. Edited by Jon Elster and Rune Slagstad. Cambridge: Cambridge University Press, 1988.

Schumpeter

Elster, Jon, *Explaining Technical Change*. Cambridge: Cambridge University Press, 1983. Ch. 5, "Schumpeter's Theory."

Mackie, Gerry, "Schumpeter's Leadership Democracy," *Political Theory* 37(1): 128–53, 2009.

Medearis, John, *Joseph Schumpeter's Two Theories of Democracy*. Cambridge, Mass.: Harvard University Press, 2001.

Arendt

Benhabib, Seyla, *The Reluctant Modernism of Hannah Arendt*. Thousand Oaks: Sage Publications, 1996.

Benhabib, Seyla, "Models of Public Space: Hannah Arendt, the Liberal Tradition, and Jürgen Habermas," in *Habermas and the Public Sphere*, edited by Craig Calhoun. Cambridge, Mass.: MIT Press, 1991.

The Cambridge Companion to Hannah Arendt. Edited by Dana Villa. Cambridge: Cambridge University Press, 2000.

Cohen, Jean L. and Arato, Andrew, *Civil Society and Political Theory*. Cambridge, Mass.: MIT Press, 1992. Ch. 4, "The Normative Critique: Hannah Arendt."

Habermas, Jürgen, "Hannah Arendt's Communications Concept of Power," in *Power*, edited by Steven Lukes. New York: New York University Press, 1986.

Habermas I

Cohen, Jean L. and Arato, Andrew, *Civil Society and Political Theory*. Cambridge, Mass.: MIT Press, 1992. Ch. 5, "The Historicist Critique: Carl Schmitt, Reinart Koselleck, and Jürgen Habermas."

Habermas, Jürgen, *The Structural Transformation of the Public Sphere: An Inquiry into a Category of Bourgeois Society*. Cambridge, Mass.: Polity Press, [1962] 1989.

Habermas and the Public Sphere. Edited by Craig Calhoun. Cambridge, Mass.: MIT Press, 1991.

Hohendahl, Peter U., *The Institution of Criticism*. Ithaca, NY/London: Cornell University Press, 1979. Chapter "Critical Theory, Public Sphere, and Culture: Jürgen Habermas and His Critics."

McCarthy, Thomas, *The Critical Theory of Jürgen Habermas*. Cambridge, Mass: MIT Press, 1978.

Negt and Kluge

Hansen, Miriam, "Unstable Mixtures, Dilated Spheres: Negt and Kluge's The Public Sphere and Experience, Twenty Years Later." *Public Culture* 10 (1993): 179–212.

Fraser

Fraser, Nancy, *Unruly Practices: Power, Discourse and Gender in Contemporary Social Theory*. Minneapolis: University of Minnesota Press and Polity Press, 1989.

Fraser, Nancy, *Redistribution or Recognition? A Political-Philosophical Exchange*. (co-authored with Axel Honneth). London: Verso, 2003.

Fraser, Nancy, *Scales of Justice: Reimagining Political Space in a Globalizing World*. Cambridge: Polity Press, 2008.

Elster

Elster, Jon, "Introduction" and "Deliberation and Constitution Making," in *Deliberative Democracy*, edited by Jon Elster. Cambridge: Cambridge University Press, 1998.

Elster, Jon, *Explaining Social Behavior*. Cambridge: Cambridge University Press, 2007, Ch. 24, "Collective Decision Making."

Luhmann

Cohen, Jean L. and Arato, Andrew, *Civil Society and Political Theory*. Cambridge, Mass.: MIT Press, 1992. Ch. 7, "The System-Theoretic Critique: Niklas Luhmann."

King, Michael and Thornhill, Chris, *Niklas Luhmann's Theory of Politics and Law*. Basingstoke: Palgrave Macmillan, 2003.
Luhmann, Niklas, *The Reality of Massmedia*. Cambridge: Polity Press, [1996] 2000.

Habermas II

The Cambridge Companion to Habermas. Edited by Stephen K. White. Cambridge: Cambridge University Press, 1995.
Habermas, Jürgen, *Between Facts and Norms: Contributions to a Discourse Theory of Law and Democracy*. Cambridge, Mass.: The MIT Press, [1992] 1996.
Cohen, Jean L. and Arato, Andrew, *Civil Society and Political Theory*. Cambridge, Mass.: MIT Press, 1992. Ch. 8, "Discourse Ethics and Civil Society."
Rosenfield, Michael and Arato, Andrew, *Habermas on Law and Democracy: Critical Exchanges*. Berkeley, Calif.: University of California Press, 1998.

Rawls

The Cambridge Companion to Rawls. Edited by Samuel Freedman. Cambridge: Cambridge University, 2002.
Freeman, Samuel R., *Rawls*. London: Routledge, 2007.
Rawls, John, *Political Liberalism*. New York: Columbia University Press, 1993.

Peters

Public Deliberation and Public Culture—The Writings of Bernhard Peters, 1993–2005. Edited by Hartmut Wessler. Basingstoke: Palgrave, Macmillan, 2008.

Bohman

Bohman, James, *Public Deliberation. Pluralism, Complexity and Democracy*. Cambridge, Mass.: MIT Press, 1996.
Bohman, James, *Democracy Across Borders: From Dêmos to Dêmoi*. Cambridge, Mass.: MIT Press, 2007.
Dahlberg, Lincoln, "The Internet and Discursive Exclusion: From Deliberative to Agonistic Public Sphere Theory," in *Radical Democracy and the Internet. Interrogating Theory and Practice*, edited by Lincoln Dahlberg and Eugenia Siapera. Basingstoke: Palgrave, 2007.

Mouffe

Brady, John S., "No Contest? Assessing the Agonistic Critiques of Jürgen Habermas's Theory of the Public Sphere," *Philosophy & Social Criticism* 30(3): 331–54, 2004.
Mouffe, Chantal, *The Democratic Paradox*. New York, London: Verso, 2000.
Mouffe, Chantal, *On the Political*. Abingdon: Routledge, 2005.

Benhabib

Benhabib, Seyla, *Situating the Self. Gender, Community and Postmodernism in Contemporary Ethics*. Cambridge: Polity Press, 1992.

Benhabib, Seyla, "Deliberative Rationality and Models of Democratic Legitimacy," in *Democracy and Difference: Contesting the Boundaries of the Political*, edited by Seyla Benhabib. Princeton: Princeton University Press, 1996.

Benhabib, Seyla, *Another Cosmopolitanism. Hospitality, Sovereignty and Democratic Iterations*. Oxford: Oxford University Press, 2006.

Habermas III

Philosophy & Social Criticism, 35(1–2), Special issue: Religion and the Public Sphere. Edited by Jonathan Harmon and James W. Boettcher, 2009.

Breinigsville, PA USA
12 October 2010
247140BV00004B/1/P